A Reopening of the Muslim Mind

The Reconstruction of Islamic Theology in a Qur'anic Perspective

Abdul Hafeez Fāzli

Aasanian Foundation Pakistan

Published by 'Aasaniyan Foundation Pakistan'

Title:

A Reopening of the Muslim Mind: The Reconstruction   of Islamic Theology in a ur'anic Perspective

Author: Abdul Hafeez Fāzli
Lahore, Pakistan.

hafeez.phil@pu.edu.pk
hafeez.fazli@gmail.com
hafeez.aasaniyan@gmail.com

First Edition: March 2023

ISBN:
Price:

BISAC: Islam / Islamic Theology / Epistemic Fallacy/ the Qur'anic Ontology/ the Qur'anic Cosmology/ Constructivist Epistemology and Ontology/ Islam, Science and Philosophy Relationship

Minds become closed when dogma, tradition, rituals, superstitions and speculations are given the status of faith, rationalisation is given preference over reasoning, and principles of the interpretation of the Qur'an given by the Qur'an itself are disregarded. It is necessary that the Muslims reopen their minds and reconstruct their theology based on Qur'anic principles for translation and commentary of the Qur'an.

The Qur'an is the source of *sharī'ah* (divine law) and is ultimate, absolute and universal. The implementation of *sharī'ah* cannot be a source of *sharī'ah* itself. *Ḥadīth* is the precedent of the implementation of a divine law, set by the Prophet (pbuh) in particular circumstances when it was being revealed. Ijtehād of the rightly-guided caliphs, the honourable companions of the Prophet (pbuh) and the jurists of earlier centuries, too, have the status of being the precedent. To associate absoluteness and universality with them is to close the Muslim minds and to close the doors of ijtehād.

The Ash'arites contrived their atomism (*nazriya-i-jawahir*— known in the west as Ash'arite occasionalism) as an explanation to the creation and then administration of the universe. Its presuppositions clearly contradict with the Qur'anic tenets. This theory has hampered the development of empirical sciences and empirical attitude in Islamic civilization for centuries, resulting in the closing of Muslim mind, intellectual decline and downfall of Islamic civilization. It clearly instances, how much harm such a theory could mete out to the community if it enters in Islamic theology, turns into creed, and assumes sanctity.

Books already published by the author:

i)   The Qur'anic Theology, Philosophy and Spirituality (2016)

ii)   Muslim Fiker ki Qur'ani Jihāt (Urdu) (2018)

iii)   Ittehād bain al-Muslimīn, (Urdu Booklet)

The manuscript of 'The Basic Tenets of The Islamic Theology' is near completion.

Work on the classification of the Qur'anic verses into Muḥkamāt and Mutashābihāt is in progress.

Published books are available for free download at the following links:

https://www.researchgate.net/.../Abdul-Hafeez-Fazli/research

https://punjablahorepakistan.academia.edu/HafeezFazli

https://www.quranwithscience.com/essays-articles.html

For purchasing printed copies, please contact at Link:...

https://kdp.amazon.com/en_US/bookshelf

The Bank Account of the author is given below for those who would like to participate, as a token of gratitude, in the furtherance of research work like the present one.

PK25HABB0001820021846601

PK10MEZN0002640102962790

CONTENTS

CONTENTS

PREFACE

Allah's Word is *Al-Ḥaqq*. (Q. 6:73, 2:42 etc.) *Al-Ḥaqq* means 'the standard of truth'. Whenever Allah reveals *Al-Ḥaqq*, it comes to humankind as the certain truth. (Q. 32:2-3; 34:6 etc.) And, *al-bāṭil* (falsehood, untruth), *aḍ-ḍalāl* (error) or *ẓann* (conjecture or opinion) have no reality of their own. *Al-bāṭil* is but the attempted rejection of *Al-Ḥaqq*. To say anything in violation to *Al-Ḥaqq* is without justification and wrongful (*bi ghayr 'l ḥaqq*). (Q. 02:61; 03:21 etc.) To interpret a *mutashābih* verse of the Qur'an without ensuring its accordance with the *muhkamāt* is to prove oneself diseased at heart and a mischief monger. (Q. 3:07)

To prefer suspicions, conjectures or opinions in the face of *Al-Ḥaqq* is to follow *ẓann*. Whatever the Qur'an upholds is truth (ḥaqq), whatever it disapproves is untruth (bāṭil). To express views without reference to *Al-Ḥaqq* is to express opinion or conjecture and "Assuredly conjecture can by no means take the place of truth." (Q.10:36)

Aḍ-ḍalāl (error) is nothing except deviation from The Truth. (Q.10:32) It results in the generation of erroneous ideas and ideological systems. It is the outcome of giving equal importance as *Al-Ḥaqq* to speculations, man made ideologies, suppositions, human experiments, theories, opinions, suggestions, insights, imaginations, arbitrary interpretation of visions (*ro'yā*), unveiling (*kashf*), direct witnessing (*shahūd*) and heresy and confounding them to *Al-Ḥaqq* (the Word of Allah). It is the Way of Allah that "He wipes out the falsehood and establishes the truth with His Words."(Q. 08:7-8)

Allah commands the believers "not to utter aught concerning Allah save the truth" (4:171). For saying anything about Allah, not supported by the Qur'an, is iftirā (concoction). (Q. 3:94) To mould the truth according to one's desires is *fisq* (transgression) and it is the *fasiqoon* whom Allah misleads. (Q. 02:42, 109, 144, 146, 213; Q. 07:118; Q. 18:56, Q. 40:78; and Q. 10:32, 36; Q. 53:28, Q. 13:17 and Q. 17:81 etc.)

Al-Ḥaqq is the epithet used for Allah's Word revealed to His Messengers (Peace be upon them!). (Q.4:46; 5:13, 41; etc.) Allah is the One whose Word (*Kalamullah*) revealed to His Prophets has the status of *Al-Ḥaqq* (The Truth/ Authority). Allah is the Descender of *Al-Ḥaqq*. (cf. Q. 5:83, 84; 11:120, etc.) The Qur'an verifies that the People of the Book have tampered *Al-Ḥaqq* revealed in the past (cf. Q. 4:46; 5:13, 41 etc.). The Qur'an is Allah's revealed truth for the whole humankind. The Qur'an verifies that Allah has taken upon Himself to protect the Qur'an against any such attempt. (cf. Q. 15:9) Therefore, the epithet *Al-Ḥaqq* (*The Truth*) rightfully applies to the Qur'an alone as Allah says in Surah Muhammad: '…what has been sent down upon Muḥammad [pbuh]- it is the truth' [*huw l Ḥaqq*] from their Lord'…'(Q. 47:2) At present the status of authority lies with it only. It is the Qur'an, which is The Truth (*Al-Ḥaqq*). Allah is the Descender of The Truth (*Al-Ḥaqq*). Whenever '*Al-Ḥaqq*' will be used to denote Allah, it will necessarily mean 'The Descender of The Truth'. To use the title '*Al-Ḥaqq*' for the Qur'an as well as for Allah in identical sense (i.e., as The

      THE RECONSTRUCTION OF ISLAMIC THEOLOGY

Truth) is contrary to the teachings of the Qur'an and results in inserting confusion and contradiction in the translation and commentary of the Qur'an and in theology.

Islamic theology is a discipline that emerged in the early centuries for the formulation of Islamic beliefs in rational terms. To believe something as religious doctrine and as part of faith without knowing its accordance with the *muḥkamāt*, and having no clear idea of its religious implications, is dogma. Belief of the born Muslims, mostly, is of this nature. A dogma can be a right religious belief, or it cannot be a right religious belief. Formulation of the dogma in rational terms, converts it into a theological doctrine. When a doctrine gets currency in the religious community, it becomes a creed (*'aqīda*). Instances of dogma misperceived as right beliefs, converted into religious doctrines, abound in Islamic theology(gies). Through the translations and commentaries of the Qur'an such misperceived doctrines seep into the theological system, and affect the generations. This study argues that such un-Qur'anic premises have entered into Islamic theology and there is an impending need to identify these un-Qur'anic assumptions, purge the foundations of Islamic theology from them and reconstruct Islamic theology on purely Qur'anic grounds. This is the basic message and conclusion of this treatise.

Let us see what are un-Qur'anic assumptions identified in this book and what suggestions have been given to reconstruct theology on Qur'anic grounds.

Ideas thrive upon terms and travel in history riding on their back. Terms are never neutral; they always follow a certain metaphysics or ontology. When a term coined in certain metaphysics is employed in a discourse that differs from it in metaphysics, it is bound to give rise to doubt, inconsistency and misperception. The confusion, inconsistency and misperception thus caused do not remain confined to a specific area of that thought-system alone. It translates into all other dimensions of that very ideology and in the manifestations of culture and civilizations based on it, and travels in history for centuries until such a time, the root cause of these contradictions is identified, reconstructed, and rectified.

This is exactly what has happened to Muslim thought and civilization. The misperceptions that arose in traditional Muslim theology, because of unintentionally accepting un-Qur'anic ontology from Greeks or Christians and terms coined in it, transmitted into all areas of Muslim thought and civilization including translation and commentary of the Qur'an, status of *Ḥadīth* with reference to *Sharī'ah* (حدیث کی تشریعی حیثیت), the jurisprudence, epistemology, axiology, philosophy, spirituality and statecraft etc.

Study in this book does not consist of historical academic research on any specific problem related to any dimension of Muslim thought. It is a philosophical study, confined to the identification of un-Qur'anic ontology (metaphysics) that lies in the foundation of various Islamic theology(ies). It is an analytical study of important alien terms, couched in this un-Qur'anic metaphysics, unconsciously accepted by Muslim theologians from Greeks. It is a critical study of the equally un-Qur'anic cosmology, based on this un-Qur'anic ontology and alien terms directly or indirectly accepted from Greeks. In short, this study is a philosophical investigation of the principles, approaches and factors responsible for causing confusion, inconsistency and misperception in traditional Muslim theology, Muslim philosophy and commentary of the Qur'an; and of causing disorientation to Muslim civilization giving rise to sectarianism, religious dissension and intellectual decline. Points selected for examination in this study consist of the following:

i) **The Epistemic Fallacy**: Overlooking of the fact by the Qur'an scholars that the Qur'an has been descended in the style of Speech and Address (*Taqrīr* / Khitab) and not in the style of Writing, and employing rules for its interpretation meant for a text delivered in the style of Writing (*Teḥrīr*).

ii) Being revealed in the Clear Arabic language (*Arabi-yim-mubeen*), rules of grammar and syntax are basic and necessary for determining the meaning of the verses of the Qur'an. Keeping in view the unique character of the Qur'anic revelation (delivered piecemeal in the style of speech and address, extending over a period of about twenty-three years), the significance of the rules of Arabic grammar and syntax become secondary, and the significance of the Qur'anic principles for its own interpretation, and comprehension of the objective (*maqsid*) intended by the Descender of this revealed Speech, become primary and necessary. The theologians and the Qur'an scholars have never recognized this factor throughout Islamic history till today. The author has selected a few of these most important Qur'anic principles for discussion in this book.

iii) Categorising everything including God as 'eternal' or as 'created' (contingent), is an ontology that is contrary to Qur'anic teachings. However, it is prevalent as the foundation of Islamic theology since twelfth century A. D. and is religiously followed by the exegetes and the translators of the Qur'an as creed. The Qur'an conceives Allah as The Absolute Originator of everything. The Qur'an categorises everything originated from God by His Will and Decree (کُنْ Be!), as Allah's *Khalq* (Creation) or as Allah's *Amr* (Command). The Qur'an holds that neither of these is eternal, nor participates in Allah's Divinity. As absolute Originator, as singularly Unique, and supremely Transcendent from any likeness to the originated beings, Allah does not include in any ontological category Himself. The un-Qur'anic ontology unintentionally borrowed from Greeks by classical Muslim theologians and handed over to succeeding generations, that has acquired the status of creed and is prevalent till today, is one of the most important points discussed in this book as source of doubt and inconsistency in Muslim thought.

iv) Acceptance of certain un-Qur'anic, philosophical terms, for instance 'divine attributes', and taking un-Qur'anic stance on the ontological status of divine attributes (*ṣiffah*) as compared to the Comely Names of Allah (*al-Asmā' al-Ḥusnā*), and the problems of createdness vs. eternity of the Qur'an, Divine omniscience and human freewill, conflict between Islam and science relationship etc. have also been discussed in detail to show untoward implications of this un-Qur'anic ontology for Muslim beliefs.

v) Giving no importance to the Qur'anic principles for the interpretation of the Qur'an and, instead, giving preference to devising arbitrary paradigms for it. Especially to be noted is their absolutely ignoring the principle given in verse 7 of surah Āl-e-

Imran 3 which categorises verses of the Qur'an into *muḥkamāt* (explicitly imperatival) and *mutashābihāt* (non-imperatival ones); and characterises *muḥkamāt* as *Umm-ul-Kitab* (the cornerstone, pivotal, or the foundation of the Book). It is usually held that verses which are imperatival, decisive, precise, unambiguous and definite in meaning, are *muḥkamāt* and which are otherwise i.e. ambiguous and liable to more than one interpretation, are *mutashābihāt*. However, this is not correct. A *muḥkam* verse must consist of an explicit divine imperative; it is the Divine imperative that comprises the divine law (*Sharī'ah*). This is the only essential characteristic of a *muḥkam* verse. Verse 07 of Surah Āl-e-Imran (3) itself is a *muḥkam* verse. It explicitly contains the divine imperative to keep the interpretation of a *mutashābih* verse subservient to the *muḥkamāt*. The absence of a divine imperative is the essential characteristic of a *mutashābih* verse. Of course, *muḥkamat* are decisive, precise, unambiguous and definite in meaning, but these features alone do not comprise the defining characteristics of being a *muḥkam* verse. These are necessary but only as accompanying characteristics of a *muḥkam* verse. There are many *mutashābih* (non-imperatival) verses, which are clear in statement, definite in meaning and are not liable to more than one interpretation. The Qur'an labels verses other than *muḥkamāt* (i.e., *Umm-ul-Kitāb*) as *mutashābihāt*. *Mutashābihāt,* though, include all non-imperatival verses yet these occur in the Qur'an in various ways as narratival, metaphorical, allegorical, metaphysical, or eschatological verses. Symbolic and abstract verses consisting of 'separate letters' also come in the same category. Verses containing Allah's promise, pledge, a glad tiding or a threat, admonish or advice, too, are instances of *mutashābihāt.* Verses that Allah recommends or approves for the sake of making prayer before Him or for entreating or beseeching to Him, are also *mutashābih* verses.[1] The Qur'an marks those who leap towards the interpretation of *mutashābihāt* (i.e., overlooking accordance of their interpretation with the *muḥkamāt*) as the diseased at heart and the mischief-mongers. As per this Qur'anic categorisation of verses, one must firmly believe that classification of verses into *muḥkamāt* and *mutashābihāt* is definitely feasible. There definitely are verses in the Qur'an that are so clearly *muḥkamāt* (for example verses which consist of divine laws or imperatives), and there are certain others which are so clearly *mutashābihāt* (the Light verse, the Chair verse, the Throne verse, verses consisting of Separate Letters etc). Other verses can be sorted out, based upon them. It is not necessary as per any Qur'anic imperative, that while translating a verse one determines whether it is a Makki or a Madinite. Keeping in view the universal nature of Qur'anic message, it is necessary that while making translation or exposition of a verse, the Qur'an scholar must distinguish a verse as a *muḥkam* or a *mutashābih* verse, before he proceeds further. If he distinguishes the verse in question as a *muḥkam* verse, he must be sure that no *muḥkam* verse (one of the cornerstone verses) can ever conflict with any other *muḥkam* verse, or abrogate or cancel it. If the Qur'an scholar is certain that the verse in question is a *mutashābih* verse, he must make sure that its interpretation necessarily accords with the verses already identified by him as *muḥkamāt*. It is very disappointing that the theologians and the Qur'an scholars have made no effort to classify verses of the Qur'an in accordance with this Qur'anic categorisation, and have not followed this principle in their translation and commentary of the Qur'an.

vi) The ontological status of the Qur'an is that it belongs to the category of Allah's *amr* (command). As Allah's *amr,* the Qur'an is Allah's *Ḥukam* (Ordinance, Command, Book of Divine imperatives). The ontological status of *Ḥadīth* is that it reports the elaboration or implementation of Allah's *Ḥukam* in the holy hands of the Prophet (pbuh). Overlooking the fact by the Qur'an scholars that Allah's *Ḥukam* (ordinance) is universal and final, and the implementation of Allah's ordinance is bound to accord with the time, place, quantity and capacity, is the outcome of not rightly identifying the ontological status of *Ḥadīth*. It has been argued in the relevant chapter, that *Ḥadīth*, as reporting the implementation of Allah's injunctions, is the precedent of the implementation of a divine law. So, it cannot be the source of divine law itself. Moreover, it is as necessary for the interpretation of a *Ḥadīth* to accord with the *muḥkamāt* (imperatival verses) of the *Aḥsan-al-Ḥadīth Kitāb,* as is necessary for the interpretation of the *mutashābihāt* of the Qur'an to accord with them. Arbitrary and un-Qur'anic view on the ontological status of *Ḥadīth* by Muslim scholars, is another key factor that has given rise to doubt and inconsistency in the exposition of the Qur'an and dissension in the Ummah.

vii) The Ash'arite cosmology, (the Ash'arite atomism; or occasionalism as known in the west) based on their un-Qur'anic ontology, which denies any enduring nature (*fiṭrah*) to things, also denies the existence of laws of nature regulating the phenomena. Denying the principle of universal causation and the objective reality of objects of nature, it presents an extreme form of Divine interventionism. No empirical science could ever be constructed on such cosmology. The chapter on "The Dilemma of an Interventionist Deity" is an attempt to reconstruct a cosmology based on the Qur'anic ontology, developed in the relevant chapter in the first section. This cosmology provides the basis to the development of an empirical science on Qur'anic lines.

viii) The last chapter "Evolving a Qur'anic Paradigm of Science and Philosophy" examining the attempts of Ibn Sina, Sir Syed Ahmad Khan, Dr. Muhammad Iqbal, and various renowned contemporary schools and scholars on Islam, science and philosophy relationship, reformulates the problem and develops a paradigm in the Qur'anic perspective, for relating empirical and rational knowledge with the revealed Qur'anic knowledge.

Well-researched chapters on various aspects of theology included in the following latest books published by Cambridge, Oxford, Routledge, and the article published by Brill

The Cambridge Companion to Classical Islamic Theology, edited by Tim Winter published by Cambridge University Press in 2008

The Oxford Handbook of Islamic Theology edited by Sabine Schmidtke, published by Oxford University Press UK in 2016

The Oxford Handbook of ISLAMIC PHILOSOPHY Edited by KHALED EL-ROUAYHEB and SABINE SCHMIDTKE, Published in 2017 by OXFORD UNIVERSITY PRESS USA.

Routledge Handbook of Islamic Law, Edited by Khaled Abou El Fadl, Ahmad Atif Ahmad, and Said Fares Hassan, Routledge London and New York: Taylor & Francis Group, 2019 [26 Chapters by 24 Contributors besides separate 'Introductions' by the editors]

The Oxford Handbook of Qur'anic Studies edited by Mustafa Shah and Muhammad Abdel Haleem, published by Oxford University Press UK, in 2020

Leah Kinberg, "*Muḥkamāt* and Mutashābihāt (The Qur'an 3/7): Implication of a Qur'anic Pair of Terms in Mediaeval Exegesis", in Arabica, T. 35, Fasc. 2 (Jul., 1988), 143-172, Published by: BRILL

can be presented as authority that none of of the scholars belonging to any of the schools or strands of Islamic/ Muslim theology(ies) has ever realised that the ontology, on which the foundation of these Muslim/Islamic theologies has been laid down, was contrary to the teachings of the Qur'an. Article by Leah Kinberg can be presented as authority to support the contention that Muslims have never accomplished classification of verses into *muḥkamāt* and *mutashābihāt* and have never used it as a principle of interpretation of the Qur'an. Chapters in the same books can be presented as authority to support the contention of the author on other points discussed above.

This book consists of 5 Sections comprising 9 chapters including the summary of main issues. Literature review and glossary of selected terms, have also been added as chapter 10 and 11. First eight chapters are unpublished. These chapters examine epistemic fallacies committed by Muslim theologians in the formulation of theological doctrines, in misperceiving ontology borrowed from Greeks as the Qur'anic in origin, bluntly ignoring principles of hermeneutics given by the Qur'an itself and devising arbitrary paradigms for the interpretation of the Qur'an. Chapter Four "Some Unfortunate Implications of un-Qur'anic Ontology" traces the origin of some basic Muslim beliefs in philosophical doctrines of the Greek philosophers.

The study propounds that the alien philosophical terms, and the ontology riding on their back, as unconsciously borrowed by early Muslim theologians and the Qur'an commentators, were contrary to Qur'anic teachings. Examining the theological foundations of the Qur'anic hermeneutics, study in the first section holds un-Qur'anic terms and, most of all, the ontology borrowed from Greeks, mainly responsible for causing confusion, inconsistency, misperception in Muslim thought, disorientation in Muslim civilization and intellectual decline in the Ummah, and reconstructs the Qur'anic ontology in accordance with the Qur'anic teachings.

The traditional Muslim ontology borrowed from Greeks conceives whatever there is including God either as eternal or as created (contingent). It conceives God and His *Khalq* (creation) as the ultimate ontological principles. Whereas the Qur'anic ontology propounded in this book conceives God as Singularly Unique, Absolutely Transcendent and the Sole Originator of everything. It conceives everything originated by God, either as Allah's *Khalq* (creation) or as Allah's *Amr* (command). *Khalq* is created and contingent. *Amr* is uncreated but not eternal. The Qur'anic ontology propounded in this book also conceives terms like eternity, immutability and timelessness held by traditional Muslim theologians as Divine attributes, as contrary to the *muḥkamāt* of the Qur'an.

Committing fallacies regarding the ontological status of *Ḥadīth* is another main source, which let doubt and inconsistency to enter into theology and the interpretation of the Qur'an, contributed in causing confusion and dissension among Muslim Ummah. This problem relates to the questions: Whether the '*Aḥsan-al-Ḥadīth Kitāb*' (The Qur'an) holds primacy over *Ḥadīth*, or is it *Ḥadīth*, which hold *authority* over the '*Aḥsan-al-Ḥadīth Kitāb*'? Is *Ḥadīth*, too, source of divine law as the Qur'an, or is it irrelevant to the interpretation of the Qur'an? Second section, working out the implications of this misconception, reconstructs the ontological status of *Ḥadīth*, and argues that *Ḥadīth* is neither authority over the Qur'an not is irrelevant to it; the Qur'an is Allah's Imperative (*Ḥukam*) and *Ḥadīth* reports its implementation by the Prophet (pbuh). The Imperative (*Ḥukam*) is universal whereas its implementation is must to accord with the requirements of time, place, quantity and capacity. Therefore, the status of *Ḥadīth* is that it is precedent of divine law.

Cosmology is always based on a specific ontology. If the ontology presumed in Islamic theology is contrary to the Qur'anic teachings, the resultant cosmology will be intrinsically flawed as well. Examining the Ash'arite atomism (known in the west as occasionalism), and the traditional Islamic cosmology as it is perceived at present, attempt has been made to evolve a Qur'anic cosmology based on the Qur'anic ontology developed in the First Chapter.

Ontology, the philosophical study of being in general, investigates the ultimate principles of reality. This is why the general definition of metaphysics is 'doing ontology'. As per contemporary scientific ontology, the universe is materialistic and running in accordance with the laws of nature (laws of quantum mechanics being the latest discovery). This cosmology conceives empirical knowledge as the only source of knowledge dependable in science. Cosmology deals with nature and structure of the universe and God-universe relationship etc. Islam does not deny the significance of empirical knowledge, but gives ultimate primacy to revelation as source of knowledge, and basic principles of Islamic ontology and cosmology are given in the Qur'an.

Dr. Pervez Amirali Hoodbhoy (b.1369/1950), in his book *Islam and Science: Religious Orthodoxy and the Battle for Rationality* identifies a very genuine problem that lies beneath the failure of all Muslim attempts at bringing about reconciliation between Islam and science. Hoodbhoy formulates this problem as *'The Dilemma of an Interventionist Deity'*. Highlighting the fundamental dichotomy between traditional Muslim cosmology and modern scientific cosmology Dr. Hoodbhoy argues that until the problem identified in the dilemma is satisfactorily addressed, no attempt at the reconciliation between Islam, science and philosophy, or for that matter, developing an Islamic Science, Islamization of Science or

Islamization of Knowledge etc. is destined to succeed. Hoodbhoy highly deserves appreciation for this thought-provoking contribution. Section four 'Qur'anic Cosmology' consists of only one chapter. Examining the dilemma in this chapter, an attempt has been made to meet the challenge by developing cosmology based on ontology constructed in Qur'anic perspective, in the first section.

The significance of defining the nature of relationship between a revealed religion, and rational and empirical sciences of their times, has been identified by religious scholars in all periods of history. Realising this fact, Muslim scholars too, have made efforts in various periods of Muslim history at the formulation of an appropriate theology, suited to this purpose. Examining the merits and demerits of the efforts of Ibn Sina, Sir Syed Ahmad Khan, Dr. Muhammad Iqbal and some contemporary scholars including Dr. Israr Ahmed, Dr. Zafar Ishaq Ansari, Maurice Buccaile, Ziauddin Sardar, Seyyed Hossein Nasr and IIIT affiliates, the author in the last chapter "Evolving a Qur'anic Paradigm for Relating Sciences and Philosophy with Islam" argues, that all above attempts suffer from serious flaws in terms of their ontology and cosmology. Chapter 8 included in this section presents a humble attempt of the writer for evolving a Qur'anic Paradigm in this regard in line with the principles given in the Qur'an. This is the abridged and updated version of an extended article included in the writer's already published book *The Qur'anic Theology, Philosophy and Spirituality*, because of its intimate relevance with the theme of the present book.

The writer has already published two books on various aspects of Muslim thought. *The Qur'anic Theology, Philosophy and Spirituality,* is published in 2016 and Urdu book *Muslim Fiker ki Qur'āni Jihāt* [Qur'anic Approach to Various Dimensions of Muslim Thought] is published in 2018 by the Punjab University Press Lahore Pakistan. Both are available at Amazon.

The writer is working on a new book that will include among other things an elaborate account of the Qur'anic principles for the interpretation of the Qur'an. It may also include a critical review of Robert R. Reilly's ideas presented in his book *Closing of the Muslim Mind*. However, a brief account of criticism on Robert Reilly here will be quite timely and relevant.

There is no doubt that Ash'arite theology prevalent in the Muslim world for centuries has many flaws in it; but the reason identified by Robert Reilly, is incorrect. He identifies dehellenization of theology by the Ash'arites as their basic fault, which is not correct. Idealising the Greek philosophical way of thinking, the Mu'tazilites acknowledged the primacy of reason over revelation. The Ash'arites did the opposite, which deserves appreciation. However, the epistemic fallacy, which unconsciously got committed by the Ash'arites, was that while borrowing philosophical terms from speculative theologians in the formulation of their theological doctrines, they failed to realise that they were at the same time allowing un-Qur'anic ontology (rooted in Greek philosophy) enter into their theological system. This fault marred their theology with contradictions.

The second fault the Ash'arites committed was that they gave equal importance to dogmas handed over to them by tradition, which they should have given to the beliefs derived from the Qur'an alone. For instance a term '*the non-recital revelation*' (*waḥi-i-ghair matlu* وحی غیر مَتلو) devised by traditional theologians for *Ḥadīth*, put *Ḥadīth* over and above the *muḥkamāt* of the *Aḥsan-al-Ḥadīth Kitāb* and paved the way for insertion of any kind of unauthentic dogmas, *traditions* (*rawayāt*) and baseless Israelite stories in translation and commentary of the Qur'an and in theology. Though apparently they did not give philosophical speculations primacy over revelation, they gave generally accepted unauthentic dogmatic beliefs primacy over the revelation. Another fault they committed was that they accepted un-Qur'anic terms like eternity, timelessness, absolute perfection (implying immutability) coined in Greek ontology, as attributes of Allah to employ in the formulation of their doctrine of the Oneness of Allah and other theological doctrines, and used them in the translation and commentary of the Qur'an. The solution suggested by Robert Reilly and by Dr. Fazalur Rahman that the Muslims should turn towards philosophy if they want to come out of intellectual decline, is quite misleading. The minds get closed when dogma, tradition, rituals, superstitions and speculations are given the status of faith, rationalisation is given preference over reasoning, and principles of the interpretation of the Qur'an given by the Qur'an itself are disregarded. It is necessary that the Muslims reopen their minds and reconstruct their theology based on the Qur'anic terms and Qur'anic ontology and focus on the Qur'anic principles for the translation and commentary of the Qur'an.

I am grateful to Haḍrat Muhammad (pbuh) and the prophets and messengers of Allah sent before him, and their true followers. (Peace be upon them all!) Haḍrat Muhammad (pbuh), the Last of the prophets, sent towards the whole humankind, is the ultimate source of all love, mercy, light and illumination that shines the hearts of the believers, whose holy heart was enlightened by the Grace of Almighty Allah to deliver His light and message to humankind, and on whose holy heart *Al-Ḥaqq* (the Qur'an/ The Truth) has been revealed by the Descender of *Al-Ḥaqq*. I am also grateful to my grand master Haḍrat Ali (a.s.) who, as per my experience, has very important role in the dispensation and distribution of this Divine love, mercy, light and illumination. I am also grateful to my beloved son Shakir Boo Ali for his valuable suggestions. I pay my humble salutations to all holy Grand Masters (*shahidīn*) and their followers in good faith. I am grateful to my mentor Late Haḍrat Muhammad Ashraf Fāzli (d. Dec. 2016) for enlightening my heart with the light of the Qur'anic wisdom, and I am grateful to my mentor at present Haḍrat Malik Shamasuddin Qadri Fāzli (b. 1960), for elevating this knowledge, light and illumination to ever-rising heights, and for attesting the contents of this book.

I am also grateful to my family members: to my wife, daughters and daughter-in-law for their love, cooperation and appreciation. I am especially grateful to Shahnam Shakir, the grandson, for the delight he has added to my heart and the family's life.

Abdul Hafeez Qadri Fāzli   Dated: January 18, 2023
Secretary publications 'Aasaniyan Foundation Pakistan'
(Ex-Chairman Philosophy Department,
University of the Punjab, Lahore Pakistan.)

HOW DOUBT AND INCONSISTENCY ENTER INTO THE QUR'ANIC COMMENTARY AND THEOLOGY!

CHAPTER 1

UNCOVERING EPISTEMIC FALLACIES

To believe the Qur'an to be the Fairest of Texts Book (*Ahsan-al-Hadīth Kitāb*), free of doubt and fully consistent in itself, the Standard of Truth (*Al-Haqq*), the Criterion (*Furqān*) and the Balance (*Meezan*), is absolutely necessary before a believer sets about to its translation, writing exegesis, or formulation of a theological doctrine. It is not only a requirement of faith (Q. 2:02, Q. 39:23) but also one of the main Qur'anic principles for its interpretation. If, it is not observed, it will give rise to thought-contradiction.[2] Allah's Word holds the status of 'authority', as Allah says: What remains there after The Truth [The Qur'an], save error (ad-dalāl)! (Q. 10:32) (TF)[3] The principle that derives from this Qur'anic statement is that "coherence with The Truth is necessary and what is coherent with 'The Truth' (*Al-Haqq*) is true (*Haqq*). It further implies that disregard for coherence with The Truth, giving preference to one's opinion, conjecture and speculation results in error, and thought-contradiction in one's ideas. (Q. 50:5)

Wherever one comes across a contradiction during translation or exposition of the Qur'an that he fails to resolve, he must realise that since the Qur'an (The Truth) is absolutely free of doubt, inconsistency and self-contradiction, fault definitely lies somewhere in his approach; that somewhere 'the Truth' must have been compromised by him, or accordance with the *muhkamāt* has been overlooked. In order to save believers from committing mistakes in translation, exposition or exegesis, Allah has given principles of interpretation of the Qur'an in the Qur'an itself. Not giving due importance to the Qur'anic principles, the translators and the exegetes have given preference to their own arbitrarily devised paradigms. Let us see an instance of thought-contradiction arising from not giving due regard to the Qur'anic principles.

To be '*Al-Haqq*' (The Truth) is the title and status of the Qur'an as Allah says in Surah Ar-Ra'd:

> "*And whatever is revealed on you [O Prophet-pbuh] by your Lord is The Truth (Al-Haqq) ...*" (Q. 13:1). (TF)[4]

In verse 2 of Surah Muhammad 47 Allah says:

> "*...that which is revealed unto Muhammad - and it is The Truth (Al-Haqq) from their Lord...*" (Pickthall)[5]

Verse 2 and 3 of Surah As-Sajdah 32 say:

> "*The revelation of the Scripture whereof there is no doubt is from the Lord of the Worlds. Or say they: He hath invented it? Nay, but it is the Truth [Al-Haqq] from thy Lord, ...*" (Pickthall)[6]

What follows from these verses is that Allah Almighty is 'The Descender of *Al-Haqq*'(The Truth), the Revealer of *Al-Haqq*, the One whose Word descended to Hadrat Muhammad (pbuh) is '*Al-Haqq*' (The Truth). It is must to keep in view that whenever the epithet '*Al-Haqq*' is used to refer to Allah, it must not be taken to mean, "Allah is The Truth." Rather it must be taken to mean, "Allah is the Descender of 'The Truth' or Allah is the One, whose Word descended upon Haḍrat Muhammad—pbuh is 'The Truth'." To ascribe '*Al-Ḥaqq*' as Title in the sense of 'The Truth' to Allah, and include it in His Comely Names is to insert contradiction in Muslim thought. The Ash'arite theological school, and *waḥdat al-wujud* school — an offshoot of Ash'arism in mystical direction, are mainly responsible for promoting this contradiction. Hazrat Abu al-Ḥassan al-Ash'ari, the founder of Ash'arite school, converted this un-Qur'anic dogma into a doctrine.[7] Centuries have passed since this contradiction entered in Islamic discourse. This falsehood, contradiction and confusion has tarnished many other ideas through the formulation of theological doctrines and through translation and exegesis of the Qur'an.

The Qur'an is revealed by Allah in the style of an Address/Speech (*Khatāb*) and not in the style of Writing (*Teḥrīr*).[8] It makes a huge difference if the rules meant for making out the meaning of a *Kalam* delivered as Writing are applied to a *Kalam* delivered piecemeal as Speech extended over about 23 years, and compiled as a Book under Divine guidance. None of the translators and exegetes deny the fact that the Qur'an is descended as Speech, but confining its interpretation to lexicon and rules of grammar and syntax meant for making out 'the meaning' of a text delivered in the style of Writing (*Thrīr*), in conjunction with *asbāb-i-nazool* (presumed contextual background of revelation[9]), Israelite traditions and historical references, they have, by all means, converted Divine Address into a piece of 'Writing'. None of the above-mentioned implements is free of doubt, dispute, and contradiction. Whereas the Qur'an, which is explained based on these standards, is absolutely free of doubt, fully consistent in itself, and is the Fairest of Texts Book. The most important factor that distinguishes a text edited in the style of 'Speech' from a text edited in the style of 'Writing' is 'the objective' (*maqṣid*) of the Speaker. What the Speaker wants, approves, ordains, requires or wishes from the addressees is the basic and pivotal in Address. The 'meaning' of a word as per lexicon, import (*mafhoom*) of a sentence according to the rules of grammar and syntax keeping in view the contextual perspective, becomes required in the elaboration of a text delivered in the style of 'Writing'. In Speech (edited as Book) the listener or the reader visualising himself as the addressee, exerts himself to capture what the Speech-Giver wants from him to do. Taking the Qur'anic text as a piece of 'Writing' either the reader takes it as a thing to be recited for *thawāb* (heavenly reward) or makes out its meaning according to above-mentioned implements. This difference becomes even more important if the text of Speech is a universal Divine revelation meant for the whole humankind. In a Divine message revealed as Speech, the purpose is to drive the addressees towards a specific goal i.e., a specific mode of action.

To make the distinction clear between the objective, intent and purpose of a Speech, and meaning and import of a sentence in style of Writing, let us present verse 28 of Surah al-Kahf (18) as an example. In this verse, Allah commands a believer never to lend allegiance to him, in whom he finds the following three evils:

whose heart Allah has made neglectful of His remembrance;

who follows his desires;

who has no respect for Allah's prescribed limits.

One who will concentrate on the objective of this revelation, whenever he finds himself in a situation where he is compelled to lend allegiance to one, who, as to his conviction, has all the three evils stated in this verse, keeping Allah's injunction in mind, he will keep himself on his guard. He, who takes it as a piece of Writing, will consider it meant for recitation or for making scholarly analysis, carrying no obligation for him at present. The purpose and objective of Allah's Kalām does not reveal on the reciter until he understands that it is addressed to him at present.

If the reference to cultural conditions, circumstances and *asbāb-e-nazool,* in conjunction with rules of grammar and syntax, is necessary to make out the meaning of a part of Divine Address, two things are necessary to be kept in view:

i)   No reference to a particular event will be allowed to confine the universality and purpose of Divine Speech (which is universal and ultimate in nature) to that event alone;

ii) Narration of the event, occasion, circumstance, or interpretation of the tradition or *hadīth* presumed as shān-*e-nazool* must not contradict with the *muḥkamāt*. Otherwise, the tradition shall be rejected or will be reconstructed and interpreted to accord with the *muḥkamāt*. Two instances, one from Bani Israel, and the second, ascribed as contextual background to the preliminary verses of Surah 'Abasa, have been given below to make the point clear.

When Ḥazrat Musā (pbuh) went to Holy Ṭūr leaving behind his brother Ḥazrat Aaron (pbuh) as his vicegerent, a group of Bani Israel took to worshipping of calf in his absence. On his return from Ṭūr, making his brother accountable for not preventing them from calf-worship, Ḥaḍrat Musā (pbuh) harshly asks:

"When you realised they had gone astray, what prevented you, Aaron, from coming after me? How could you disobey my orders?" (Q. 20: 92-93) (Abdel Haleem) [10]

Ḥazrat Aaron (pbuh) replies:

"… I feared, you would say, "You have caused division among the children of Israel and have not heeded to what I said." (Q. 20: 94) (Abdel Haleem) [11]

Had the Qur'an scholars realised and observed difference in taking the Qur'an as Speech rather than Writing and focused their attention on the purpose of the Address-Giver, they had extracted out of these verses, that 'dividing believers into sects and factions is a sin much bigger than even carving a representation of Allah and of worshipping it. They had stressed on the point that Allah, the Descender of these verses, demands, rather commands and ordains, not to label fellow Muslims, who differ with them in the comprehension of certain beliefs and the way of acting upon them, as disbeliever, atheist, polytheist, apostate, hypocrite and liable to be slain.[12] Had the contemporary Qur'an scholars realised this fact, they had rejected the registration of mosques, religious madrassas and centres of religious learning in the name of sectarian identities in favour of unity among Muslims.

None of the translators or the exegetes, to the knowledge of this writer, has given attention to the purpose of revelation implied in Ḥaḍrat Aaron's reply. Division among a religious community cannot be other than sectarian in nature. Most of them, including

Tafseer Ibn-e-Kathīr, Al-Dur al-Manthur, Tafseer Zia ul Qur'an, Tadabbur-ul-Qur'an, Tafheem ul-Quran, have written expansively in narrating doubtful, baseless, fictitious traditions, fabricated stories and self-contradictory speculations in elaboration of verse under discussion without any real relevance, lesson or guidance for the believers. None except Maulana Maududi has touched this point, and he too draws the conclusion categorically contrary to the objective intended by Allah in the revelation of this verse. Instead of making it manifest that dividing the Ummah into sects and factions is bigger a crime than any other form of going astray (even if it is as big a sin as assuming something as representation for Allah and worshipping it) Maulana Maududi says:

> *"To take this part of the verse to mean that safeguarding the unity of the community and keeping the ummah undivided is more important as objective near Allah than becoming united at giving leniency to a section of community on committing shirk [associating partners/equals with Allah], is to draw a false corollary."*[13]

Actually Maulana's comment is based on his un-Qur'anic understanding of *shirk.* There are many imperatival and non-imperatival but decisive verses in the Qur'an, that substantiate the fact emphasised in this study, as implied in Haḍrat Aaron's reply. For instance:

> *Allah did not make Prophet Musā (pbuh) call those who took to the worshipping of calf, idolaters or polytheists (mushrikīn). Allah made His Prophet Musā (pbuh) call them 'who went astray'. (Q. 42:13) But Allah very much calls those, who divide the community of believers into factions and do not keep back from sectarianism, the polytheists (mushrikīn) and 'the rebellion among themselves (baghyan baynahum)' at Q. 42:14.*[14]

> *The same Judgement is passed on such people at Q. 30: 31-32.*[15] *The same content is repeated at Q. 23:51-54.*[16] *Splitting up believers into sects and factions is such a big sin that Allah says to His Prophet (pbuh) that 'he (pbuh) has no concern with those who have divided their Deen (religion) and broken up into factions.' (Q. 6:159)*[17]

It is not the case that those who divide believers into factions and promote sectarianism, are ignorant of Allah's command, and do it unknowingly. Allah says, 'They do it out of transgression, after knowledge has come to them." (Q. 42:14)[18]

> *'Allah commands the believers not to split up into factions and be united as one community by holding fast, all together, to Allah's rope, which He stretches out for them.' (cf. Q. 3:103)*

> Allah also ordains the believers 'not to be like those who split into factions and fall into conflicts after they had been given Clear Revelation, and to whom a terrible punishment awaits.' (cf. Q. 3:105)

> *Allah asserts the splitting up of the believers' community into discordant factions, and broken into warring sects, as a kind of Allah's torment on the people at Q. 6:65.*[19]

Institutions to bring about schism among Muslims are, at times, established on the pretext of doing good to them. Allah commands the Muslims not to have any concern with them. One such institution was established in the lifetime of the Prophet (pbuh) in the form of a mosque termed by the Qur'an as *aḍ-ḍirār* (the harmful one) and was demolished at the behest of the Prophet (pbuh). (Q. 9:107-110) In contemporary times, many such institutions work at a global scale on the pretext of promoting research in Islamic studies, in Qur'anic sciences, in disciplines of *Ḥadīth*, or establishing publishing houses, issuing research journals and holding international conferences on various aspects of Islam.

The role of the translator or the exegete of the Qur'an is to dig out and enlighten the goal intended by Allah, the Address-Giver; make explicit what Allah ordains, demands, approves, advises expects or wishes from the addressees, the recipients, beneficiaries and the believers; and guide the addressees to meet that goal. But what they have been actually doing instead, in the exposition of cases like that of calf-worship, is that they are narrating mythical, fake and fabricated stories having no relevance with the purpose of revelation of these verses.   Thus, promoting doubt, dispute and dissension among the addressees deviating them from the real purpose. In order to enlighten other aspects of the same event in verse 150 of Surah Al-A'rāf 7 Ḥaḍrat Aaron has been made to say:

> *"…O son of my mother! Indeed the people judged me weak ('Inna Al-Qawma Astaḍ`afūnī) and were about to kill me (Wa Kādū Yaqtulūnanī), …" (Q. 7:150) (Moḥsin Khan)* [20]

The translators of all the seven parallel English translations of the Qur'an including i) Sahih International, ii) Pickthall, iii) Yusuf Ali, iv) Shakir, v) Muḥammad Sarwar, vi) Moḥsin Khan, vii) Arberry, available at website titled *Qur'anic Arabic Corpus: Language Research Group University of Leeds,* plus the 8th translation by M. A. S. Abdel Haleem (WordPress.com) and the 9th *The Meaning of the Quran* (First English translation of *Tafheem ul-Qur'an*) by Maulana Abu al-A'lā Maududi (at english*Tafseer*.com) have translated the statement *Wa Kādū Yaqtulūnanī* in the sense of *"They were about to kill me."* Does this translation not contradict with these translators' rendering of the statement *''Innī Khashītu 'An Taqūla Farraqta Bayna Banī 'Isrā'īla Wa Lam Tarqub Qawlī'* (I feared lest you say, 'you have split Bani Israel, and did not keep in view my advice.) at Q. 20:94? This contradiction arises if the Qur'an is taken as 'Writing'. If taken as Address, it simply means that at one occasion the Descender of Speech tells that the 'people' who had gone astray were so resolute on their transgression, that they were ready to fight with Ḥaḍrat Aaron (pbuh), had he decided to take some strict action to prevent them. At verse 94 of Surah Ṭā Hā 20 the Speech-Giver makes it clear that Ḥaḍrat Aaron did not refrain from preventing the calf-worshippers because he feared lest they would fight with him (or kill him).   Rather, he refrained from preventing them 'lest the Bani Israel get divided into sects and the direction given by Ḥaḍrat Mūsā (pbuh) gets overlooked and violated.'

This part of the verse '*Wa Kādū Yaqtulūnanī*' does not necessarily mean '*they were about to kill me.*' Actually this means '*They were resolute to fight with me.*' There are no less than nine places in the Qur'an where derivatives of the root *qāf-tā-lām* do not refer to 'killing' or 'slaying'. At these places they occur in the sense of 'to fight unjustly and unlawfully'.[21] The same hermeneutic fallacy is being committed by most of the translators and commentators of the Qur'an in the case of verse 61 of Surah al-Baqara 2 where it is said:

> *"…And they were covered with humiliation and poverty and returned with anger from Allah [upon them]. That was because they [repeatedly] disbelieved in the signs of Allah and killed the prophets without right. (Wa Yaqtulūna An-Nabīyīna Bighayri Al-Ḥaqqi). That was because they disobeyed and were [habitually] transgressing." (Q. 2:61)* [22] *(Sahih International)*

The Qur'an nowhere states that any of the Prophets (*an-Nabīyīn*) was ever killed by their people. Even the belief of the crucifixion of Prophet Īsā (pbuh), on which the foundation of one of the world's largest religions is laid down, has been categorically denied by the Qur'an. (Q. 4:157) And, in presence of the fact that no less than nine places in the Qur'an confirm that the derivatives of the root *qāf-tā-lām* has been used in the sense of *'fighting without just cause'*, yet giving preference to Israelite traditions very renowned translators and commentators have been translating *'Wa Yaqtulūna An-Nabīyīna Bighayri Al-Ḥaqqi'* (Q. 2:61) as *'and killed the prophets (An-Nabiūn) unlawfully.'* Let us see one more instance of how the doubt, inconsistency and contradiction enter in the translation and commentary of the Qur'an and in theology because of taking the Qur'an as Writing instead of Address, or giving primacy to *tradition* over the Qur'an.

It is said in verses 22-24 of Surah An-Nūr 24, that those who falsely accuse chaste women, are cursed in this world. And, in verse 25, it is said that on the Day of Judgement Allah will pay them what they really deserve, and they will come to know that Allah is the Perfect in Justice as the Manifester of truth (*Al-Ḥaqq al-Mubīn*) by giving the evil-doers their just due. The next verse reads as follows:

الْخَبِيثَاتُ لِلْخَبِيثِينَ وَالْخَبِيثُونَ لِلْخَبِيثَاتِ وَالطَّيِّبَاتُ لِلطَّيِّبِينَ وَالطَّيِّبُونَ لِلطَّيِّبَاتِ أُوْلَائِكَ مُبَرَّءُونَ مِمَّا يَقُولُونَ لَهُمْ مَغْفِرَةٌ وَرِزْقٌ كَرِيمٌ

Al-Khabīhātu Lilkhabīhīna Wa Al-Khabīhūna Lilkhabīhāti Wa Aṭ-Ṭayyibātu Lilṭṭayyibīna Wa Aṭ-Ṭayyibūna Lilṭṭayyibāti 'Ūlā'ika Mubarra'ūna Mimmā Yaqūlūna Lahum Maghfiratun Wa Rizqun Karīmun. (Q. 24:26)

Most of the translators and commentators since centuries have been translating this verse like this

"Corrupt women are for corrupt men, and corrupt men are for corrupt women; good women are for good men and good men are for good women. The good are innocent of what has been said against them; they will have forgiveness and a generous provision." (Q. 24:26) (Abdel Haleem) [23]

Eight out of the nine translators mentioned above translate it in the sense given above. This translation explicitly contradicts with verses 10 and 11 of Surah At-Teḥrīm 66 which confirm that wives of Haḍrat Noah and Haḍrat Lūt (the two prophets of Allah) were impure and corrupt; and the wife of Pharaoh was a pure and righteous woman whereas Pharaoh has been confirmed as corrupt and transgressor. This translation is wrong on another count too. It implies the corruptness of one of the spouses from the corruptness of the other spouse, and chastity of one of the spouses, if the chastity of the other is confirmed.

This is contrary to the basic teachings of the Qur'an as well as the content of verse 10 and 11 of Surah At-Teḥrīm. Verse 26 of Surah An-Nūr is a *mutashābih* verse and since it is not interpreted keeping in view its accordance with the *muḥkamāt,* it has been inserting contradiction in the translation and commentary of the Qur'an since centuries, with the translators finding no way out.

Tafseer-e-Fāzli translates this verse as the following:

"Vile discourse relates to the vile people, and vile people are for vile discourse; chaste discourse relates to the chaste people, and the chaste people are for the chaste discourse. These [the chaste

people] are free of bad things they [the vile people] express [about them]. For them is forgiveness and provision honourable." (Q. 24:26) [24]

If an exegete or a commentator translates verse Q. 24:25, Q. 24:26 or any other verse in such a way which ensures the full consistency of the Qur'an, should we defend a deficient interpretation by referring to the lexicon or rules of grammar. Should we defend a deficient interpretation by referring to the eleven centuries tradition of its translation? Is consensus sufficient as an argument for truth, even if it inserts contradiction in the Qur'an? Should we not prefer deriving rules from within the Qur'an itself, if it guarantees consistency! Let us see, which translation of this verse the Qur'an substantiates:

The words 'Khabīth (خبيث unchaste and bad) and Ṭayyib (طيّب chaste and good), together or separate, occur in the Qur'an for things, soil, dwellings, towns, trees, sustenance, life and the progeny at Q. 2:172, 267; Q. 4:64; Q. 5:100; Q. 8:37; Q. 16:32. These adjectives occur for statements or discourse at Q. 14:24, 14:26 and Q. 22:26. So if Tafseer-e-Fazli translates words Khabīth and Ṭayyib as the quality of statements or discourse, is it without evidence from the Qur'an? Moreover, does it contradict in any way with the umm-ul-kitab verses (muḥkamāt) of the Qur'an? If the explicit contradiction contained in the traditional translation of verse Q. 24:26 is eliminated by relating this statement to the Hereafter with reference to verse 7 of Surah At-Takwīr 81(as done by Mr. Javed Ahmed Ghamdi), it too does not work. Those who try to translate these words as 'good or bad things' that too does not fit in contextual perspective nor makes any sense.[25]

CHAPTER 2

ADDRESS IN SECOND PERSON SINGULAR OR IN THIRD PERSON SINGULAR

Though immediate addressees of 'the Qur'an were Arabs of the Prophet's (pbuh) era but from the very first day it is meant for the whole humankind and for all the times to come. The Qur'an is universal. No part of its teachings, no matter how particular it may seem to be, is bereft of universal content. It is never necessary that the Speech while addressed in second person singular (*you*), is particularly addressed to the Prophet (pbuh) as has been mistakenly understood by Pickthall (and many others) in the translation of following verses:

"It is the Truth from thy Lord (O Muhammad), so be not thou of those who waver." (Q. 2:147) and

"(This is) the truth from thy Lord (O Muhammad), so be not thou of those who waver."(Q. 3:60)

It is a specific feature of the Qur'anic Speech that at times addressed in 'second person singular', it addresses each and every individual, present as well as not-present, including those who are yet to come till the Last Day. The same part of the Address requires differently from the individual, the community or humankind as to their status, authority and the capacity. Instances of all these features of Speech are present in the Qur'an, some of which have been presented in the text of this book as well as in the endnotes.[26]

There is at least one specific place in the Qur'an where Allah, referring to someone as '*he*', addresses in 'third person singular'. Allah narrates an event about a companion (r.a.) of the Prophet (pbuh) in the preliminary verses (1-10) of Surah 'Abasa 80. This event relates to some weakness in the worthy companion's way of preaching. To safeguard the dignity of the worthy companion (r.a.) of the Prophet (pbuh), and to ensure the universality of Divine Advice, 'Allah, the Concealer of Flaws (*As-Sattār al-'oyūb*) keeps the identity of the person undisclosed. (Cf. Q. 49:12) However, those who took the Qur'an as a piece of text in the style of Writing, in their habit to make out stories, instead of emphasising the purpose of this specific revelation, wisdom behind it, and the lesson implied in it, fabricated a story and put someone's name there. Is it not defiance of the Qur'anic teaching *'to veil the flaws of fellow believers'* at Q. 49:12, and defiance of Allah's injunction forbidding believers from stepping ahead of Allah and His Messenger (pbuh) at Q. 49:1? How demeaning it is that, depending upon a hateful tradition the exegetes ascribed the blemish mentioned in these verses, to be directed towards the most beloved, the most respected servant of Allah (pbuh), who is the absolute role model of servitude to Allah for the whole humankind! (Q. 33:21) Does ascribing such an act to the Prophet (pbuh), not tantamount to hurting Allah and His Messenger (pbuh) and clear defiance of what Allah says in Surah al-Aḥzāb:

"Those who hurt Allah and His Messenger – to them God has cursed in the present world and the world to come, and has prepared for them a humbling chastisement." (Q. 33:57) (Arberry)[27]

How disdainful it is that the translators and commentators, instead of enlightening and elaborating the rule of protecting alleged person's dignity, while imparting correction to anyone's behaviour, and teaching lesson to others, as purpose of descending this revelation, have been narrating this disrespectful and disdainful tradition since centuries? This exposition inserts contradiction in the Qur'an at all those places where the dignity of the Prophet (pbuh) as *role model of excellent character* (Q. 68:4), and *an excellent pattern of life for humankind* (Q. 33:21), has been stated. It inserts contradiction in the exposition of the Qur'an where *obedience of the Prophet (pbuh) has been declared as Allah's obedience and a guarantee for having granted guidance* (Q. 3:32, Q. 24:54). Or, where *the dignity of the Prophet* (pbuh) *as granter of the knowledge of the Book and wisdom (ḥikma)* and *the granter of the purification (tazkia),* or *the granter of Allah's Mercy to humankind* (Q. 21:107) has been stated and *keeping in view the respect and reverence of the Prophet (pbuh)* has been ordained as a basic requirement of faith. (Q. 49:2)

CHAPTER 3

ACCEPTANCE OF AN UN-QUR'ANIC ONTOLOGY

Another very important thing not realised by the translators, the Qur'an commentators, the Qur'an scholars, and experts of Islamic sciences until today, relates to the Qur'anic ontology. This point holds central importance in this treatise. Ontology is a philosophical discipline that studies ultimate categories of *being* and their relationship to each other. The Qur'anic ontology, as propounded in this study, conceives Being in two ultimate but originated categories of *Khalq* (Creation) and *Amr* (Command), with God (Allah) as the absolute Originator of these categories. On the other hand, the classical and traditional Muslim theology conceives Islamic ontology as consisting of God (Allah), who is eternal (*Qadīm*), and *Khalq* (creation) which is contingent (*ḥādith*). Traditional Muslim theologians, the Mu'tazilites and the Ash'arites both, (all others too) committing an epistemic fallacy accepted this ontology under the impress of Greeks through Christianity and assimilated it into their theology(ies) conceiving it congruent with their Scriptural teachings.

Eternity (أزلِيَّت, *qidm*) and contingence (حدوث, *ḥadūth*), as conceived in traditional Muslim ontology, are polar concepts. Whatever is eternal, it must be uncreated; and whatever is created (contingent), it cannot be eternal. So, to be uncreated necessarily implies being eternal. According to the Qur'anic ontology as propounded in this book, whatever there is belongs either to the category of 'creation' (*khalq*) or to the category of Allah's command (*amr*). If anything is 'creation' (*khalq*), then it is contingent; and if anything is not creation (*khalq*), then it is command (*amr*); so uncreated but not eternal. Allah as the Absolute Originator of *khalq* and *amr* is Supremely Unique and Absolutely Transcendent of *khalq* and *amr* both. As to the relation of these ultimate ontological categories with each other, '*khalq*' has a beginning and a conceivable end too. *Amr* as reality that is issued, fused, blown, descended or revealed into *khalq*, has a beginning too, as Allah ordained the angels that

> '*When I have fashioned him [Adam] and breathed rūḥ [from the category of My command] into him, bow down before him,*' (Q. 15:29) [28]

Rūḥ belongs to the category of Allah's *amr* (command). Neither *khalq* nor *amr* participate in the divinity of Allah in any way, nor do any of these have any likeness with Allah.

Not realising this fundamental ontological difference, the Qur'an translators, the exegetes, the theologians, scholars of *Ḥadīth*, the jurists, the sufis and scholars of other Islamic sciences from early period of Muslim history till today, have been using mismatched terms coined in Greek ontology. Let us see a few implications of committing this epistemic fallacy for the translation, exegesis, theology and Muslim thought in general.

'Whether the Attributes of God are real in their own right and superadded to the Being/Essence of God; or, are the Essence and Attribute of God identical with each other and He does not possess any attributes apart from and in addition to His essence'? is known in Muslim theology as the problem of the ontological status of Divine attributes. The Ash'arites held the former, whereas the Mu'tazilites held the later view. This problem arose in Muslim theology because of the acceptance of un-Qur'anic terms of 'essence' and 'attributes' by Muslim theologians, unaware that these were coined in Aristotelian metaphysics. It made Muslim theologians to conceive the Being of God, Who is singularly Unique and absolutely transcends any analogy, likeness or comparison with anything or anyone, consisting of Essence and Attributes. Aristotelian logic uses the terminology of 'subject' and 'predicate' (corresponding to the terms 'essence' and 'attributes' of Aristotelian metaphysics) in its propositions to affirm or deny the relation of a certain predicate to a certain subject. The Mu'tazilites and the Ash'arites both accepted this logic too.[29]

The problem of 'eternity vs. createdness of the Qur'an' arose in Muslim theology as an offshoot from the above problem. The Mu'tazilites, having denied the independent reality of Divine attributes as a prerequisite of Allah's unity, asserted the Qur'an to be created and contingent (*ḥādith*). The Ash'arites, having affirmed the independent reality of eternal Divine attributes as superadded to the Being of God, held the Qur'an to be uncreated and eternal (*qadīm*).[30] Both groups followed Greek ontology in the formulation of their doctrines. The Mu'tazilites considered the Ash'arites' insistence on the uncreatedness of the Qur'an, another infringement on God's unity, like affirmation of eternal Divine attributes by them. The Ash'arites feared the Mu'tazilites' insistence on the createdness of the Qur'an, to be an infringement on the universality and finality of the Qur'an. Both held their views with religious zeal and fervour without realising that the ontology presupposed in the very question was un-Qur'anic, and very principle inferred from Greek ontology "what is uncreated is eternal' has no basis in the Qur'an.

It is no doubt that referring to verse Q. 30:25 and Q. 07:54 Al-Ash'ari distinguishes Allah's command (*amr*) from His creation (*khalq*) and argues that Allah's command (*amr*) is something which makes His creation stand firm as Allah says:

"Among His signs, too, is the fact that the heavens and the earth stand firm by His command." (Q. 30:25) (Abdel Haleem)

Referring to verse 7 of surah 54 *"...all creation and command belong to Him."* [31] Al-Ash'ari argues that command of Allah is His Word and Speech, and in these verses

> **"He [Allah] speaks of the *command* [*amr*] as something other than all *creation* [*khalq*], and so, our account of this matter is a proof that *command* of God is uncreated and all His *creation* stands firm by His *Command*."[32]**

But what he failed to realise was that in these verses and especially in verse Q. 54:7 Allah has given them the Qur'anic concept of ontology. Had he realised it, they could hold the Qur'an to be belonging to the category of Allah's *amr*, so uncreated; and the Mu'tazilites, if they still insisted that the Qur'an was created, could hold that it belonged to the category of Allah's *khalq*. Remaining within the orbit of Qur'anic categories, both could argue in favour of their respective positions.

Al-Ash'ari could not visualise that the ontology that asserted 'what is uncreated is eternal' was un-Qur'anic, and thus comprised a false premise. It is here that he commits an epistemic fallacy and goes out of the way to argue that the Qur'an is a predicate of God's attributes of Knowledge and Will; therefore, uncreated and eternal. As Knowledge and Will are eternally with God's Being as His attributes, so is the Qur'an eternally with God as unarticulated speech immanent in these attributes.'[33]

"The Mu'tazilites believed that the Holy Qur'an is 'created' and 'contingent'. Some believed, that the Holy Qur'an was initially created on the preserved tablet (*lohim-maḥfūẓ*) in non-verbal form, which after its revelation took the form in which it is recited; some of them believed that it was created during its revelation. They argued that the belief in an uncreated and eternal Qur'an was opposed to the belief in the Oneness of God. They did not deny the Qur'an to be the 'Word of Allah'; however, they denied its uncreatedness and eternity."[34]

Al-Ash'ari, as we have seen, argues that the 'Word of Allah' (Q. 9:06) could not be created (and contingent), and that 'Creation' and 'Command' were two different categories. He further argues that Allah's Speech (*Kalam Ullah*) must belong to the category of His Command (*amr*); therefore the Qur'an too belongs to the category of His 'Command'. Al-Ash'ari further argues: it is necessary that the 'command' precedes 'creation'; for if some other 'command' is perceived to precede the 'command', it will again be a 'command'; and infinite regress makes everything unintelligible. Thus, Al-Ash'ari argues that as inherent in Allah's Attribute of *Kalām*,[35] Allah's Word (The Qur'an) was with God from ever as unarticulated speech (*kalam-i nafsi*). So the Qur'an is uncreated and eternal (*qadīm*) in its essence. At the beginning of the creation, it was placed on the Preserved Tablet as 'Pre-existent Qur'an'; it remained there until its revelation in articulated form (*kalam-i lafzi*). [36]

If the Qur'an is conceived to be subsistent in Allah, as immanent in His knowledge and Will from ever, as Abu al-Hassan al-Ash'ari has formulated his doctrine, then everything stated in the Qur'an — particulars (like the condemnation of Abu Lahab and his wife, drowning of Pharaoh and his troops or the rejection of Iblīs, destinies of individuals etc.) or universals (like moral values, disvalues, rules of behaviour, genres, species and members belonging to them etc.) will become subsistent in God's 'Knowledge' and 'Will' from ever in implicit form. It will give rise to such a concept of omniscience in which everything, belonging to *khalq* and *amr* both, as possibility, potentiality or in unarticulated and immanent form, will become with God from ever like His Knowledge, Will and other attributes. It will make everything predestined, in principle, leaving no scope for freedom of man as well as of God. Allah will, no more remain the Creator or Originator of the archetypes of His Knowledge, and will become like Plato's philosopher god, who is not creator of eternal ideas in Plato's 'world of ideas'.[37] Wolfson seems right in tracing the origin of the problem of the createdness vs. eternity of the Qur'an in the intradeical interpretation of Platonic ideas.[38]

Identification of *Al-Ḥaqq* with Allah

Identification of *Al-Ḥaqq* with Allah is one of the two basic presuppositions of the doctrine of *waḥdat al-wujūd*. It even holds primacy over the other presupposition (which says that God is 'Absolute Existence having two aspects: the transcendence and the immanence.') Presupposition under-discussion is so important that if this is withdrawn, the doctrine of *waḥdat al-wujūd* caves in on its own foundations.[39] Whatever translation or the Qur'anic commentary one takes, it is replete with the confusion, inconsistency and contradiction arising from holding the Qur'an (*Al-Ḥaqq*) as well as The Descender of the Qur'an as *Al-Ḥaqq* in the same sense (i.e., in the sense of 'The Truth').

With this doctrine, the idea that '*Al-Ḥaqq*' is one of *al-Asmā' al-Ḥusnā*, entered Muslim theology and became an established creed.[40] Doctrine of abrogation, doctrines of freewill vs. predestination, Divine omniscience and human freedom, confusion between Allah's Will (*mashiyat*) and Allah's Pleasure (*raḍa*), doctrine of *waḥdat-al-wujūd*, taking *rūḥ* (soul/spirit) either as something having close affinity with Allah, or taking *rūḥ* as Allah's creation, and the Ash'arite occasionalism[41] are some of the many doctrines, theories or perennial problems, which arose in Muslim theology because of denying Allah's *Amr* (Command) as an ontological category, and taking '*Al-Ḥaqq*' as one of *al-Asmā al-Ḥusnā* following al-Ash'ari's speculations about eternal subsistence of the Qur'an in Allah's Being.

When a theology is constructed on incorrect foundations, it cannot remain without creating contradictions in its doctrines. Here the doctrine of abrogation enters in theology to rescue. The doctrine of abrogation provided the theologians, especially to the Ash'arites, with a safe and easy way to cancel, alter or frustrate the objective of a *muḥkam* verse of the Qur'an, as suited to anyone's desire or sectarian agenda, without denying the Qur'an to be eternal and uncreated. This Ash'arite doctrine meted out more harm to the Qur'an by directly hitting at the *muḥkamat*, the universal and obligatory teachings of the Qur'an, which the Qur'an calls *Umm-al-Kitāb* ('The Cornerstone of the Book).' It gave free hand to people like Hibat Allah Ibn Salāma (d. 410/1020) to hold as many as 500 verses to be abrogated, which he did not find in accordance with his desires, speculations or agenda.[42] Even a scholar of the status of al-Ghazali, known as Hujjatul Islam (The Proof of Islam), (c. 1058 – December 1111) could not find reasons to refute such baseless doctrine. Sadly yet, scholars like Imam Jalaluddin Al-Suyuti (1445-1505 A.D.) and Ḥaḍrat Shah Waliullah Dehlavi (1703-1762 A.D.) in their attempt to reduce the number of abrogated verses to twenty and to five respectively, granted authentication to this doctrine instead of rejecting it altogether.[43]

The Ash'arite Atomism (occasionalism)

The modern empirical scientific cosmology sees the universe running from the very beginning according to the immutable laws of nature. The law of universal causation, the basis of modern science, denies supernatural intervention in nature in any form. The traditional orthodox Muslim cosmology, though constrained by the grand progress of modern empirical science has been compelled to perceive the role of immutable laws of nature in the universe, it still conceives God as a capricious and 'interventionist deity' who has to intervene in nature to keep it running smoothly. The Muslim scholars are making attempts since centuries to construct a science, which could reconcile these two drastically opposite cosmological doctrines.[44]

The Ash'arites, in the very early centuries of Muslim thought, grappling with the problem of the creation of the world have contrived a very ingenious cosmological theory known as 'The Ash'arite Atomism' known in the west as occasionalism.[45] The Ash'arite occasionalism is a very original attempt to formulate a worldview based on the idea of a Divinely Administered Universe. They explained everything i.e., time, space, causality, laws of nature etc. based on this theory. The Ash'arites gave a view that the universe is restless and is continuously developing; nothing in the universe would stay two instants in a stationary state. Occasionalism, as predecessor of modern Muslim cosmology, is the most extreme form of interventionism which neither admits the existence of enduring nature (*fitrah*) of things nor any immutable laws of nature nor any real existence of the physical universe.

Altaie states five basic theological principles as given below, on which this 'theology of nature' (or *Daqīq al-Kalām* as they called it) is based:

Temporality

This stipulates that the world is temporal, finite and limited and that the creation took place *ex nihilo*.

Discreteness

This stipulates that the structure of space, time, energy and matter and every associated property is discrete.

Continual creation

This stipulates that the world is re-created every moment anew.

Indeterminism

This stipulates that the laws of nature that we recognize are contingent and undetermined. (Altaie sees this notion resonating in the Copenhagen interpretation of quantum theory.)

Space-time integrity

This stipulates that space has no meaning of its own and would exist only if a body existed, and that time has no meaning of its own without an event taking place in space.' [46]

These principles, as believed in by them, are based on the insight derived from the teachings of the Qur'an. This is why al-Baqillani and other fellow theologians transformed the doctrinal status of their 'theory of nature' (i.e. the Ash'arite atomism), from being a mere premise in support of specific religious beliefs, to an essential part of the Ash'arite creed.

The Ash'arite cosmology, being based on un-Qur'anic ontology, could not produce results except severely deterring the development of empirical and rational sciences in line with the Qur'anic teachings; and it is the same till today.

The Qur'anic cosmology, as argued in this study, conceives the universe as an originated reality, divinely administered with Allah's *amr* (command) subsisting in everything (of Allah's *khalq*) in the whole universe, as enduring nature (*fitrah*) and as guiding principle giving rise to laws of nature. Divine interventionism becomes irrelevant in such a universe.

It is because of the above-mentioned flaw in their ontology (and the cosmology) that all classical, modern and contemporary Muslim attempts, at reconciliation between Islam and science (the Ptolemaic, the Newtonian or the Einsteinian),[47] or for the construction of an empirical science in accordance with Qur'anic teachings, from Ash'arite occasionalism to Ibn Sina's (circa 980-1037) emanationism, Sir Syed Ahmad Khan's (d. 1898) reconstruction of Qur'anic naturalism in line with Newtonian mechanics, Dr. Muḥammad Iqbal's (d. 1938) construction of a scientific form of religious knowledge in the perspective of Einsteinian theory of relativity, Islamization of knowledge and Islamization of sciences project of Isma'īl al-Rājī Al-Farūqi (1921-1986) and scholars associated with IIIT (from 1981 A.D.), Bucailleism starting from Maurice Bucaille (d. 1998) based on distinction between 'scientific theories' and 'established scientific facts', and Seyyed Hossein Nasr's (b. 1933) reconstruction of a 'Sacred Science', Ijmali school of thought Viewing Science as a Cultural Activity,[48] Dr. Israr Ahmad's (d. 2010) attempt at blending creation and evolution together, Dr. Hoodbhoy's (b.1950) formulation of the dilemma of an interventionist deity, Dr. Muhammed Basil Altaie's (b.1952)[49] reconciliation of science and religion based on the insights of classical Islamic theology, activities of the forums like Kalām Research & Media etc.—— in spite of most sincere efforts and superb intellectual capabilities of scholars related to these schools and forums, have not been able to succeed. Until and unless the confusion and flaw arising from un-Qur'anic ontology and cosmology is addressed, and the orthodox and the traditional Ash'arite theology is thoroughly revised and reconstructed accordingly, it is argued in this study that Islam and science relationship in line with the teachings of the Qur'an cannot be worked out and formulated.

Qur'anic Ontology and Status of the Qur'an as 'Al-Ḥaqq'

Let us turn towards Qur'anic ontology and status of the Qur'an as 'Al-Ḥaqq'

1. Al-Ḥaqq (The Truth) is the epithet used in the Qur'an for the Qur'an itself, descended by Allah to Ḥaḍrat Muḥammad (pbuh). Let us see some verses:

"And those who believe and do righteous deeds and believe in what has been sent down upon Muḥammad [pbuh]- and 'it is the truth' [huw l Ḥaqq] from their Lord - He will remove from them their misdeeds and amend their condition." (Q. 47:2) (TF vol. 7)

Surah Muḥammad 47 verse 2 above, clearly specifies and all the nine translators (mentioned above) conjoined with *Tafseer*-e-Fazli testify the fact that

"Which has been descended to Ḥaḍrat Muḥammad (pbuh) from their Lord is The Truth (Al-Ḥaqq)".[50]

Verse 1 of Surah Ar-Ra'd 13 confirms the same fact when it says:

"Alif Lam Mim Ra. These are the signs [verses] of the Scripture. What your Lord has sent down to you [Prophet] is The Truth, yet most people do not believe." (Q. 13:1) (Abdel Haleem)[51]

Verses 1, 2 and 3 of Surah As-Sajdah 32 besides corroborating the above fact very clearly assert the Qur'an to be free of doubt:

"Alif Lam Mim. The Scripture which is free from all doubts [Al-Kitābi Lā Rayba Fīhi] has been descended from the Lord of the Worlds. Or they say, he has fabricated it! It [the Scripture] 'is The Truth (huw l Ḥaqqu) from your Lord', for you to warn a people to whom no warner has come before you, so that they may be guided." (Q. 32:1-2-3) (TF vol.5)[52]

Surah Al-An'am says

"But your people (O Muḥammad SAW) have denied it (the Quran) though it is The Truth. Say: "I am not responsible for your affairs." (Q. 6:66) (Moḥsin Khan)

All the nine celebrated translators of the Qur'an mentioned above conjoined with *Tafseer-e-Fazli* as the tenth, agree that:

The clause "Huw l Ḥaqq" ("It is The Truth.") and the epithet "*Al-Ḥaqq* (The Truth)" included in verse 2 of Surah Muḥammad 47, verses 6 and 62 of Surah Al-Hajj 22, verse 6 of Surah As-Saba 34, and verse 66 of Surah al-An'am 6, verse 3 of Surah As-Sajdahh 32, refer to the Qur'an as 'The Truth' descended by Allah to Ḥaḍrat Muḥammad (pbuh).[53]

All of the nine translators mentioned above agree that verse 3 of Surah Muḥammad 47

"This is because the disbelievers follow falsehood [al-Bātil], while the believers follow The Truth [Al-Ḥaqq] from their Lord. In this way God shows people their true type." (Q. 47:3) (Abdel Haleem) [54]

perceives *al-Bātil* (Falsehood) as religion, ideology or teaching which is opposite to *Al-Ḥaqq* (The Truth) revealed by Allah to Ḥaḍrat Muḥammad (pbuh). This verse does not perceive *al-Bātil* as anything opposite to Allah, but what is opposite to the Qur'an (*Al-Ḥaqq*).

All the above-mentioned verses, though not *muḥkamāt* (imperatival), being clear, precise, definite in meaning, not liable to more than one interpretation, are decisive in their content. Nothing in these verses contradicts with the *muḥkamat* of the Scripture. All these decisive verses (including many more given at the endnote)[55] confirm that:

'*Al-Ḥaqq* (*The Truth*)' wherever it occurs as epithet in the Qur'an, refers to the Qur'an descended by Allah to Ḥaḍrat Muḥammad (pbuh).

> Therefore, 'Allah is The Descender of *Al-Ḥaqq* (The Truth)' and Allah is the One whose Word descended to His Prophet (pbuh) is The Truth.
>
> And 'Al-Bāṭil (Falsehood) wherever it occurs in the Qur'an as epithet, refers to the teaching, precept, principle, practice, ideology and religion the disbelievers follow as opposed to 'the Qur'an / *Al-Ḥaqq*.'
>
> Therefore, to translate Al-Bāṭil (Falsehood) anywhere in the Qur'an as opposite to Allah (The Descender of *Al-Ḥaqq*) shall be a wrong rendering and will insert contradiction in its interpretation as it does not accord with the *muḥkamāt* of the Qur'an.[56]

To translate "*Al-Ḥaqq* (*The Truth*)" occurring as epithet in simple form as '*Al-Ḥaqq*' or in compound form as '*Huw l Ḥaqq*' (Q. 22:6, Q. 22:62) or *Mawlāhumu Al-Ḥaqq* (Q. 6:62), *Rabbukum Al-Ḥaqqi* (Q. 10:32), *Al-Walāyatu Lillāhi Al-Ḥaqqi* (Q. 18:44), *Al-Maliku Al-Ḥaqqu* (Q. 23:116), or '*Anna Allāha Huwa Al-Ḥaqqu Al-Mubīnu* (Q. 24:25) to denote to Allah as "The Truth" is to insert contradiction at all these places.[57]

2. All the above-mentioned nine translators (and all others too) confirm that the epithet '*Aḥsan-al-Ḥadīth Kitāb*' used by Allah in verse 23 of Surah Az-Zumar 39 pronounces that the Qur'an is:

The Fairest of Texts Book.

Fully consistent in itself; is free of self-contradiction.

Free of doubt.

In it the teachings repeat in various ways, yet parts of the Qur'an resemble/reconcile each other and do not conflict or contradict each other.

3. Having categorically affirmed that *Al-Ḥaqq* (The Truth) refers to the Qur'an as shown in section 1, and having authenticated the Qur'an to be 'the Fairest of Texts Book, free of doubt and fully consistent with itself, let us see the following translation of verses Q. 22:6, Q. 22:62 and Q. 31:30 given below

"That is because God is The Truth [howa 'l- Ḥaqq]. Lo! He brings the dead back to life, He has power over things;" (Q. 22:6), (Abdel Haleem)

"So it will be, because it is God alone who is The Truth [howa 'l- Ḥaqq], and whatever else they invoke is sheer falsehood [howa 'l -Bāṭil]; it is God who is the Most High, the Most Great." (Q. 22:62), (Abdel Haleem)

"This is because God is The Truth [howa 'l- Ḥaqq], and what they invoke beside Him is False [al-Bāṭil]. He is the Most High, the Most Great." (Q. 31:30) (Abdel Haleem)

Does it need any proficiency in logic to perceive that to translate *Al-Ḥaqq* (*The Truth*) anywhere in the Qur'an to denote Allah, and to translate '*al-Bāṭil* (*The Falsehood*)' to denote anything opposite to 'Allah' is to insert sheer contradiction in the Qur'an as is evident in the translation of three verses given above? Whereas the Qur'an says:

"Were it from someone other than God, they would have found many contradictions therein." (Q4:82)

Eight, out of the nine above-mentioned worthy translators and renowned Qur'an scholars, translate the clause '*Howa 'l- Ḥaqq*' in above three verses as "God is *The Truth*". Abdullah Yousaf Ali alone translates this clause as "Allah is the (only) *Reality*". But it is no better a translation than the above-mentioned ones. If Allah is the only *Reality* then whatever else is to be held 'the absolute unreality'. Thus Abdullah Yousaf Ali's translation contradicts the whole of the Qur'an by implying the creation (*khalq*), the command (*amr*), the angels, the paradise, the hell, heavens and the earth and whatever therein is, the life, the world and the hereafter as unreal, meaningless and without purpose.[58]

The view that 'Al-Ḥaqq' denotes to Allah (in the sense of 'The Truth') and is one of al-Asmā' al-Ḥusnā cannot be held without contradicting the Qur'an at all places where the derivatives from the root Hā-Qāf-Qāf occur in clear and definite sense, in verses which pronounce that "what has been descended to Ḥaḍrat Muḥammad (pbuh) by Allah is 'Al-Ḥaqq' (The Truth)." Derivatives of the root hā-qāf-qāf occur at 227 places in the Qur'an implying 'reality' or 'truth' of things and events in one way or the other. The Qur'an states that Allah's creation is real, Allah's command is real, the world is real, the Hereafter is real, the Day of Judgement is real, requital is real, heaven is real, hell is real; that promises, threats etc. and eschatological events stated by Allah are reality. For example: Allah created the heavens and the earth for a true purpose, to reward each soul according to its deeds; and they will not be wronged. (Q. 45:22) Also see Q. 06:73; 10:05; 14:19; 15:85; 16:03; 29:44; 30:08; 39:05; 44:39; 46:03; 64:03.

According to the Qur'anic ontology, the created order of being is Reality and Allah is the Originator of Reality; similarly the Qur'an is The Truth and Allah is The Descender of The Truth.[59] The Qur'an is Allah's *Amr* (*Ḥukman Arabiyyan*, Q. 13:37)[60] and Allah is the Originator of the ontological category of *Amr* (Command). Using '*Al-Ḥaqq*' as epithet for

Allah and for the 'Word of Allah' in identical sense mars categorial distinction and amounts to disregarding Allah's Command *'Alā Lahu al-Khalqu wa al-'Amru...(all creation and command belong to Him)* (Q. 07:54) and amounts to committing logical contradiction.

Is there any way to translate verses Q. 22:6, Q. 22:62 and Q. 31:30 (*mutashābih* verses) such that they do not contradict with the clear, definite in meaning and decisive verses Q. 47:2, Q. 47:3 and Q. 13:01?

Here is a translation of these verses which does not contradict with any of the *muḥkamāt* of the Qur'an along with clear, definite in meaning verses from among the *mutashābihāt,* and elaborate the real meaning and objective of the Qur'an. This translation follows Qur'anic principles of its interpretation:

1. *"That is because Allah, He is the Real God [Howa 'l-Ḥaqq]. Lo! He quickens the dead, and He is Able to do all things." (Q. 22:6) (Tafseer-e-Fazli)* [61]

2. *"This is because, Allah is the Real God [Howa 'l-Ḥaqq], and their calling upon anything instead of Him is falsehood [i.e., is al-bāṭil]; and verily Allah, He is The Sublime, The Great." (Q. 22:62) (Tafseer-e-Fazli)*

3. *"That is because servitude of Allah is the truth [Howa 'l-Ḥaqq] and what they invoke other than Him is falsehood. He is the Most High, the Most Great." (Q. 31:30) (Tafseer-e-Fazli)* [62]

5. *"On that day Allah will pay them their just due in full; and they will realise that Allah is the Rightful Manifester [of truth]."('Anna Allāha Huwa Al-Ḥaqqu Al-Mubīnu). (Q. 24:25) (TF)*

In contextual perspective, verse Q. 24:25 relates to the realisation of the accusers of chaste women, concerning the Dignity of the absolute Awarder of justice, *that He is the Rightful Manifester of the truth and the Perfect in Justice (Al-Ḥaqqu Al-Mubīn/).*[63]

The terms *Ḥādith* (حادث contingent) and *Qadīm* (قديم eternal) in the above discussion also need to be examined.

Everything which begins in time is *ḥādith* (حادث, contingent). Whereas '*qadīm*' is equivalent in meaning to the term 'eternal' (i.e., something/someone whose beginning is inconceivable) and '*qidm*' denotes 'eternity'. The term *abad* (ابد) denotes everlastingness. What is eternal is everlasting too. A being whose beginning and end is inconceivable is *qadīm* (eternal).[64] It should be noted that eternity in both aspects presupposes existence in time. In Christian theology '*qidm*' (eternity) has been conceived in two senses: i) infiniteness with reference to past and future; ii) Timelessness—transcendence from time.[65] Eternity in the first sense does not befit Allah for it conceives God as a being who exists in time. Conceiving Allah as uncaused first cause, primordial cause, or conceiving Being and attributes of Allah eternal, or conceiving Divine attributes infinite as compared to finitude of human attributes are the outcome of conceiving Allah eternal in this sense. It is tantamount to conceiving Allah, as a temporal being. The same concept of eternity is presupposed in the problem of the eternity vs. createdness of the Qur'an.

Timelessness has its own implications. Being transcendent from time means being outside from time. On the analogy of a man sitting on the top of a hill, who sees in front of him as vividly as he sees behind him, being outside time God sees the future from ever, as vividly as the past. It makes the future as predetermined in God's knowledge from ever, as the past.

Eternity (*qidm*) is a term that the Christians assimilated from Greek philosophers as a divine attribute, from where it entered Muslim theology.[66] It makes the time infinite, uncreated and a permanent feature in God's Being.[67] Eternity, infinity, timelessness, perfection and immutability are the terms coined in Greek ontology and visualised as divine attributes. Timelessness implies determinism, perfection implies denial of 'Will (*Irādah*) and immutability for God,[68] immutability implies absolute inaction and denial of the knowledge of particulars for God. If knowledge of particulars for God is affirmed based on these attributes, it invites the objection of conceiving knowledge of God incremental.[69]

The doctrine of 'timelessness' was formulated by Christian theologians for providing backing to the doctrine of divine immutability.[70] Concepts of perfection, eternity, immutability and timelessness maintain omniscience in a sense that makes human freewill incompatible with God's Knowledge. These not only created problems in Christian theology, but also besides creating a perennial problem in Muslim theology, these have been creating confusion and inconsistency in translation and commentary of the Qur'an since centuries.[71] The Mu'tazilites and the Ash'arites, accepting these terms from Christianity, introduced them in Islamic theology as attributes of Qur'anic God. No Good-Name of God in the Qur'an amounts to the concepts of 'eternity', 'timelessness' or absolute perfection (implying 'immutability') as they are presupposed by Muslim theologians, the Qur'an translators and exegetes in a discourse relating to 'divine knowledge and human freewill'. *Qadīm* (قديم) occurs thrice in the Qur'an but nowhere does it denote to God.[72] Many problems in Muslim theology and *Tafseer* have arisen because of considering these un-Qur'anic terms as divine attributes. Allah, the Qur'anic God, is 'Supremely Singular, Absolutely Unique' and 'Beyond all Determinations'. He absolutely transcends from all likeness to anything either *khalq* or *amr*. Perfection as defined by Aristotle and immutability inferred from it, and ineffability as attributed by Plotinus to god does not match Allah's Holy Being as divine attributes.[73]

The Qur'an bars the believers to talk about God without authority of the Qur'an and calls it concoction (*iftirā*). (Q. 11:18) While talking about God we must keep in mind that our assertion must be based on authority from the Qur'an. The Qur'an says:

"The Most Excellent Names belong to God: use them to call on Him, and keep away from those who abuse them—they will be requited for what they do." (07:180) (Abdel Haleem)

CHAPTER 4

SOME UNFORTUNATE IMPLICATIONS OF UN-QUR'ANIC ONTOLOGY

Problem of Predestination and Freewill

The problem of the ontological status of Divine attributes arose in Muslim theology as a result of the acceptance of un-Qur'anic terms 'essence' (*dhāt*) and 'attributes' (*ṣifāt*) from Aristotelian metaphysics which conceives everything as composed of *essence* and *attributes,* and application of Aristotelian metaphysics and logic on the Qur'anic God. The problem of the eternity vs. createdness of the Qur'an, as discussed in the previous chapter arose as an offshoot from this problem. Propositions of Aristotelian logic use terminology of *subject* and *predicate* to affirm or deny a certain predicate (attribute) for a certain subject. Aristotle argued that 'pure form' and 'pure matter' are two ultimate principles, which lie parallel to each other from eternity (i.e. having no beginning). Pure matter, according to him, is only a logical substratum, a capacity of receiving 'form' and being moulded into things. Form refers to the set of essential characteristics of a thing.

Aristotle holds 'reason' to be the ultimate source of knowledge. He affirms another principle too, that "what is rationally intelligible is real."[74] Pure Form and Pure Matter are absolutely real but do not exist, for to exist means to exist in space and time. 'Pure form' is absolutely matterless and absolute perfection; 'pure matter' is absolutely formless and absolute imperfection. Aristotelian metaphysics conceives 'pure form' and 'pure matter' as two ultimate ontological principles of all becoming. Aristotle conceives 'pure form' as god too. Thus in Aristotelian metaphysics, god and primordial matter are coeternal to each other.

Aristotle argued, if god were not eternal, it would also not be perfect. It must be in need of presupposing something for its own coming into being which was perfect and eternal. To exist means to exist as an individual contingent thing, with a beginning in time. Contingent things cannot come into being from an absolutely perfect eternal god (pure form) unless there is an absolutely formless primordial matter.

Absolute perfection of god (pure form) attracts pure matter (absolute imperfection), this is how movement necessary for all becoming, generates. Thus, pure formless matter begins to acquire forms, and things begin to originate. In Aristotle all becoming consists of acquiring form by formless matter, or acquiring higher forms by species of lower forms, which already have come into being. 'Pure form' because of its absolute perfection, is the absolute ideal for everything. All becoming is directed towards this ideal. This ideal, though unachievable, is the cause of all change and evolution in nature. Aristotelian god does not start the process of becoming by its Will (*Iradah*). In Aristotle, becoming (*takween*) and evolution are autonomous. Since no conceivable beginning can be ascribed to god (absolute perfection) and the primordial matter (absolute imperfection), the process of becoming must start from eternity. Universe as such is eternal, but each and everything in it is contingent.

Since god in Aristotelian metaphysics is eternal (*qadīm*), this is how 'eternity', later on, entered Jewish, Christian and Muslim religious thought as an attribute of God. We have examined the concept of eternity above as infinity with respect to beginning, everlastingness and timelessness; We have seen that it does not befit to the Majesty of the Qur'anic God, and is not equivalent to any of the Comely Names of Allah derivable from the Qur'an.

Aristotle defines 'will' or 'volition' (*iradah*) as a capacity to attain something which one lacks or to remove deficiency which one suffers. A perfect being can neither lack in anything which it should will to acquire nor have any defect which it should will to remove. So he argues:

> "Volition implies change;
>
> Change implies imperfection;
>
> Therefore, the attribute of will/volition (irādah) cannot be ascribed to god.

Aristotle admits 'absolute perfection' as the attribute of god. In Aristotle 'absolute perfection' of god implies 'immutability' (absolute inaction, عدم تغیّر). Thus, according to Aristotle, change, activity or *shān* (glory) as a 'willing agent' is not worthy of god.

This is how 'absolute perfection' (*kamāl-e-muṭliq*) implying absolute immutability of god, enters into Jewish, Christian and Muslim religious thought as Divine attribute. There is no Good Name of Allah in the Qur'an which could be translated into absolute perfection conceived as immutability. The glory of Allah as stated in the Qur'an is: "كُلَّ يَوْمٍ هُوَ فِي شَأْنٍ ..." everyday He is active in a novel Glory" or "...everyday His Glory (Shān) appears with a novel splendure." (Q. 55:29)

Aristotelian god is not a willing agent, for having 'will' conflicts with its 'absolute perfection'. Whereas 'Will' or 'Volition' (*Iradah*) has been very much stated in the Qur'an as the Dignity and Majesty of the Qur'anic God. He not only creates the universe at His Will, but also by His Command (*KUN!* which means BE!). A universe created at Divine Will and Command must have a beginning. It must be *ex nihilo* too.[75] It cannot be eternal and absolutely autonomous. It cannot come into being as a process of emanation, too. Such a universe will be running as a divinely administered universe under laws instilled in its nature as Allah's command. It must presuppose its Creator as Setter of its laws and Giver of direction and Descender of command (*amr*). Such a universe as a whole, as well as nothing particular or general in it, cannot be without a well-defined purpose, because it is beyond the dignity of God that He creates anything just for play. (Q. 21:16) Everything in the universe has been created as a pair as Allah says: "And We created pairs of all things so that you [people] might take note."(Q. 51:49). Such a universe cannot be discrete because pairs always correlate and complement each other. Each and everything in such a universe must be interlinked according to the command (*amr*) instilled in it by the same God. Nor can it be a continual creation in the sense of being recreated every instant anew. Laws of nature in a created universe will, of course, be contingent as part of a contingent universe, but as manifestation of Allah's command (*amr*), and subservient to it; they are neither un-interlinked (discrete) and absolutely determined, nor autonomous. These must be having parameters, these must be interlinked with similar laws regulating other realms of existence, layers of reality and domains of experience. To encompass Allah's *amr* in its unfathomable depths, is not possible for man. Theories about laws of nature are bound to change with the discoveries of more aspects and conditions about them. This is like what Professor Muhammad Basil Altaie differentiates between laws of nature and laws of physics, biology or chemistry etc. [76]

As mentioned above, philosophers admit reason as the basic source of knowledge. Even if they are sceptical about its capacity to take them to ultimate reality, yet they will establish this conclusion based on reason. Aristotle reaches his concept of god through logical reasoning. What the reason identifies or reaches at, as Aristotle maintains, cannot be other than rational in its essence. 'Thought' is the characteristic manifestation of reason. Having denied volition (*iradah*) as an attribute for his absolutely matterless, perfect and immutable god, Aristotle conceives his god as 'pure thought'. Knowledge is the outcome of thought. Aristotle conceives 'knowledge' rather than 'volition' as the attribute of his philosophical god. Muslims did not remain unaffected by this concept too. Knowledge cannot be conceived of without *known* (i.e., the object of knowledge). Aristotelian god is eternal; its knowledge must also be eternal. If knowledge of god is eternal, the object of god's knowledge must also be eternal. Aristotelian god is absolute perfection. There cannot be anything except god itself to be the object of its knowledge. Therefore, the Aristotelian god itself is the object of its eternal knowledge. Aristotle conceives god as 'Self-Thinking Thought'.

Knowledge of the absolutely perfect, immutable and inactive Aristotelian god must also be absolutely perfect. Nothing is to be added in it, or modified, or deleted from it ever. So, knowledge of an immutable god must also be absolutely unchanging and immutable. In other words, the knowledge of an absolutely perfect god cannot be incremental. Then what does the knowledge of god consist of? Knowledge of Aristotelian god must consist of infinite possibilities of the composition of form and matter (in accordance with immutable laws of deductive logic) which can ever come into being from eternity to everlastingness.

Since 'thought' expresses itself according to certain laws, known as laws of logic, and in perfect expression of thought, conclusion infers from its premises with certainty. In it, the conclusion actually unfolds what is already implicit in the premises. Thus, the movement of becoming, eternally generated by the attraction of the absolute perfection of the Aristotelian god to the primordial matter, follows laws of deductive logic at each step of its generation, corruption or evolution. No event in any realm of existence or layer of reality or domain of experience, in the whole Aristotelian universe can ever defy laws of logic. Thus, logical determinism prevails in the whole Aristotelian universe which renders infinite future as absolutely predetermined in god's knowledge, as infinite past. Christian formulation of the notion of Timelessness as an attribute of God, which necessitates that God sees the future as vividly as the past, as a man sitting on the top of a hill sees in front of him as vividly as he sees behind him, is another implication of this view. Chriastians formulated this doctrine to provide backing to their doctrine of the immutability of God's knowledge. Concepts of perfection, eternity, immutability and timelessness maintained God's omniscience in a sense that was incompatible with human freedom, and from here stems the problem of omniscience vs. human freewill as implication.[77] Absolute infallibility of god's eternal, immutable knowledge of everything from eternity to everlasting future arises as another implication of this view. Acceptance of above view provides basis to the problem of predestination vis-à-vis human freewill amongst Muslims as it has already provided for Christians. Exactly this Aristotelian view of god's absolute knowledge is central to the Ash'arite understanding of the problem of destiny (*taqdīr*) in all its dimensions i.e., as presupposed in their doctrines on the problem of omniscience and human freewill, omnipotence and freewill, inexorability of the appointed term and freewill, preordained sustenance and freewill; and the same has entered into the translation, exposition, and exegeses of the Qur'an. Compilations of *Ḥadīth* too, could not remain secure from it.[78]

Though the Ash'arites did not accept the concept of the eternity of the universe, they seem to have assimilated the Aristotelian concept of god's eternal knowledge of everything into their theological system. If everything from eternity (*azal* ازل) to everlasting future (*abad* ابد) is eternally known to god, and if god's knowledge is un-incremental and absolutely infallible, how can man be free in his moral choice and decisions? This view of God's knowledge makes everything, including free human choices, decisions and actions predestined in God's knowledge from ever. This is how the problem of reconciliation between All-Knowingness of Allah (omniscience) and human freedom enters into Muslim thought. The Ash'arites are known as predestinarians. They try to reconcile belief in God's infinite, eternal, and infallible knowledge of everything to an everlasting future, with human freewill, in various ways. The Mu'tazilites are known as libertarians. They do not believe in the predestination of human moral actions. As is evident this debate enters into Muslim theology because of assimilating various concepts from Aristotelian philosophical theology.

Another problem, which arises in this perspective, relates to God's knowledge of particulars (علم جزئيات). If everything is known to God from all eternity then denial of God's knowledge of events happening at present becomes necessary; for if everything is already known to God from eternity then there remains nothing to be known by God at present. God knows every particular thing or event, from eternity, along with His Own predestined response. It makes prayers, supplications and invoking God's help at any occasion meaningless.

To admit knowledge of particulars for God, will render God's knowledge incremental, and go against the belief in absolute perfection of God taken in the Aristotelian sense.

Muslim philosophers, al-Farabi and Ibn Sina, too accepted this Aristotelian concept of god with all its implications except replacing Aristotelian concept of becoming by Plotinus' concept of emanation in their philosophy. They even accepted the Aristotelian concept of 'will' (*Irādah*), and his argument for denial of Divine 'will' in their philosophical reconstruction of Islamic theological doctrines. This is how they asserted the identity of 'God's Will' with 'God's Knowledge' and replaced 'divine will' with 'divine knowledge' in their philosophical system.[79] Knowledge implies thinking. As to what is the object of Divine Thought, the Muslim philosophers replied that the Being of God Himself is the object of His Thought! Since nothing except Him is from ever with Him therefore the object of Allah's Thought cannot be anything other than His Own Being. He is a Self-Thinking Thought, an eternally Self-Contemplating Being.[80] If 'Thought' in the Qur'anic God is equivalent to 'Will (*Irādah*), then what is equivalent to His Command (*Amr*)? Having denied 'Will' for Allah, and having no place for Allah's Command (*amr*) in their system, Muslim philosophers, compelled as they were, conceived becoming of the universe as an eternal process of emanation initiating from God's self-contemplation. A universe coming into being as a process of emanation, cannot be other than being eternal as against the Qur'anic universe which is necessarily created and contingent. Thus, Muslim philosophers had to translate the Qur'anic belief in the creation (at will and command) of a contingent, non-deterministic, divinely administered universe into an eternal, emanationistic, autonomous and logically deterministic universe.

Though they conceive emanation as a graded process through ten stages (as against Plotinus who conceives emanation as direct process from god), yet they conceive becoming of each and every universal and the particular at any step as logically necessary unfolding of ultimate and eternal divine knowledge. So, logical determinism prevails everywhere in the Avecennian universe from the highest to the lowest, from eternity to everlasting infinity. Not to talk of human beings, even God does not remain free in His activity in such a universe. Each particular in this universe is contingent, but the universe conceived as a whole becomes coeternal with God. God in the Avicennian universe is only logically prior and the universe is only logically posterior, temporally God and the universe both become simultaneous. This is how they are forced to conceive God as the Uncaused First Cause or the Primordial Cause of everything and this is how the un-Qur'anic concept of God, the Uncaused First Cause of the universe, enters into Muslim theology, and philosophy. Sir Syed Ahmad Khan, too, conceives God as an Uncaused First Cause, in the formulation of his theology of modernity.

Everything of the universe belongs either to the category of Allah's *creation* or to the category of His *command*. Allah is the Absolute Originator of both *creation* and *command*. Allah created heavens and the earth and everything in between them, in six days. It is He Who regulates every affair (*yudabbir-ul-Amr*). (Q. 32:4-5). He is the Regulator of Affairs (*Mudabbir-ul-amoor*). His command descends between heavens and the earth. He administers all affairs by His Command(*amr*). (Q. 65:12) He is the Granter of resources to be made use of in Allah's cause. (Q. 18:84; 34:11-12; 38:36) Only in this sense, He can be said to be the Granter of resources (*musabab-ul-asbāb*). To hold Him as First Cause, is to conceive Him as a temporal being, as a polar concept opposite to the efficient cause, and is contrary to the Qur'anic teachings because of being based on the un-Qur'anic Greek ontology. The Muslim Philosophers, Al-Farabi and Ibn Sina, were so influenced by Plato and Aristotle's philosophy that they held their philosophy as 'rational version of truth' and held the Qur'an to be 'revealed version of truth'. Pronouncing their self-made principle 'truth cannot contradict truth', they set on the reconstruction of a rational model of Islam in terms of Aristotelian, and neoplatonic philosophy.

It is usually considered that it were the Muslim philosophers, al-Farabi and Ibn Sina, who in their attempt to mould the Qur'anic teachings to accord with philosophy, deformed Islamic doctrines; and had not al-Ghazali refuted their arguments and philosophical doctrines in his *Tahafa tul Falasifa* [Refutation of the Philosophers] they would have meted out a great harm to Islam. It is, no doubt true, that al-Ghazali, very proficiently refuted Muslim philosophers' reconstruction of Islamic universe as an emanationistic-deterministic philosophical cosmology. It is also true that, had the Ash'arites not refuted the Mu'tazilites' reconstruction of rationalistic theology, they too would have meted out a great harm to Islam. However, it is equally true that Ash'arite theology itself has not meted out less harm to Islam, by having assimilated almost all un-Qur'anic implications of Plato's and Aristotle's thought into their theological doctrines. With Ash'arite theology acquiring the status of creed in the twelfth century amongst a great majority of the Sunnite Muslims, these deformed theological doctrines are still prevalent in the Ummah as the official interpretation of Islamic beliefs.

The Mu'tazilites and the Ash'arites both accepted philosophical terminology and logic without realising that these were coined in an un-Qur'anic dualistic Aristotelian metaphysics. Accepting un-Qur'anic terminology in the problem of 'the ontological status of divine attributes' while formulating the doctrine of the Oneness of Allah, and in the problem of 'the eternity vs. createdness of the Qur'an', and applying Aristotelian logic in these matters made un-Qur'anic philosophical ontology enter into Muslim theology.[81]

Sources of *Waḥdat al-Wujud* in Greek and Christian Ontology

Disciple of Socrates and teacher of Aristotle, great Greek philosopher Plato (428 – 348 BC), while philosophising over coming into being of the universe, reached the conclusion that the material world as it seems to us is not the real world, but only a shadow of the real world; and that a non-spacio non-temporal world of ideas, a creator god, a primordial matter, space & time, a world-soul having dual nature and some other such eternal entities were necessary for the explanation of the universe. Regarding the world of ideas, he thought it should comprise timeless, immutable, non-existent but real, incorporeal but intelligible perfect archetypes or patterns corresponding to all worldly things, relations, qualites, quantities, structures, states, feelings, impressions etc.

Thus the Platonic 'theory of ideas' (also known as 'theory of forms') maintains that two distinct levels of reality exist: the visible world of becoming that we inhabit, and the intelligible 'world of ideas or forms' that stands above the visible world and endows it being. It is argued that the material world as it seems to us, is not the real world, but only a shadow of the real, non-spacio non-temporal world of eternal ideas'.

The theory of 'the world of ideas' is the core of Plato's philosophy. He explains everything with reference to this theory. One thing which Plato somehow left unexplained was the nature of relationship between 'ideas' comprising 'world of ideas' and the demiurge (Plato's philosophical god).' The interpreters of Platonic Philosophy, got divided into two schools on this issue. Interpretations offered by these groups are known as 'intradeical interpretation of Platonic ideas' and 'extradeical interpretation of Platonic ideas'. The former theory argues that the ideas comprising the 'world of ideas' actually are the eternal ideas of god's mind. They are eternally in god's mind as uncreated ideas. While creating the universe, god first created these eternal ideas in an intelligible form apart from it (i.e. god's mind), and then created this intelligible world in physical form.[82] 'Extradeical interpretation' sees 'the world of ideas' eternally lying apart and outside god's mind as parallel and uncreated reality.

'The intradeical interpretation of Plato's ideas has impressed religious people belonging to all religious traditions. It has also exerted an immense influence on various dimensions of Muslim thought especially the *wahdat al-wujudi* sufism!"[83] There is perhaps no area where Muslim thought has remained unaffected by Plato and his disciple Aristotle. Here it is enough to say that '*wahdat al-wujud*' represents a typical blend of 'intradeical interpretation of Platonic ideas' with mystic experience based on unveiling and direct-witnessing claimed by *wahdat al-wujud* sufies. This is how Plato's concept of 'eternal ideas' as archetypes of knowledge lying in his philosophical god's mind (translated in Arabic diction as '*āyan-e-thabitah*' اعیانِ ثابتہ) entered Muslim '*wahdat al-wujud*' discourse as interpretation of their religious experience. The doctrine known as '*Haqiqat-e-Muhammadiyah*' is one of the products of this blend of philosophy and '*wahdat al-wujud* sufism.

As explained in the last chapter, Philo (20 BCE – c. 50 CE), a Jewish scholar, was the first to strive for a reconstruction of Jewish religious thought in terms of Platonic philosophy. The origin of Philo's philosophy is traceable to the intradeical interpretation of Platonic ideas. According to Philo's reconstruction of this theory, while creating the universe on his own good will, "god, at first, out of the ideas which had been in his mind from eternity, constructed an '*intelligible world*', and this *intelligible world* he placed in the *logos* (reason/mind), which had likewise existed from eternity in god's mind. Then in the likeness of this *intelligible world* of ideas, he created this "*visible world*" of ours."[84] This is here Philo introduces *logos* as an entity which has dual-nature. While in god's mind *logos* is *intradeical* and with god from all eternity, having created apart from him in intelligible form and then in visible form it becomes extradeical and created entity. This is how Philo accomplishes reconciliation between two different interpretations of Plato's eternal ideas in the rational reconstruction of Jewish religion. Impressed by Philo, the Christians, too, followed him. They replaced *logos* of Philo by Christ in the philosophical reconstruction of Christian theology. So Christ, in Christian theology appears as an entity having dual nature. In Aristotle's philosophy the Christians found a principle which stated that 'everything gives birth to its own kind'.[85] This provided them philosophical footing to call Christ, the son-god. There had also been a concept of holy spirit in Christianity. Though at early stage it was not clear whether the Christ and the holy spirit were one and the same entity or they were separate from each other. However, Christianity finally came to decide that holy spirit, as distinguished from the Christ, was another entity eternally with god. According to our research the origin of the doctrine of trinity is ultimately traceable to intradeical interpretation of Plato's 'theory of ideas' through Philo.

Whether Muslim *wahdat al-wujudi* sufis, theologians or philosophers admit it or not, this intradeical interpretation of Plato's 'theory of the world of ideas' has deep influence on their various doctirnes especially on the doctrine titled '*haqiqat-e-Muhammadiyah*'.

Even people like Shah Wali Ullah Dehlvi and Dr. Israr Ahmed, as will be evident, are no exception to it. Is it not true that through creation apart from god in *intelligible form* at the first stage, and in *visible form* in the second stage, the eternal, uncreated, incorporeal ideas of the 'mind of god' placed in a dual-natured entity called *logos* by Philo, conceived as *Christ* by Christianity, makes everything essentially the manifestation of god? Christian theologians by theological arguments and mystics in their mystic experience asserted verification of their above mentioned doctrine.

The doctrine of 'Ḥaqiqat-e-Muhammadiyah'

When Muslims came to know of these views through translations of Greek and Christian philosophical treatises or through discussions with them, they too, got highly impressed by their theo-philosophical speculations.[86] 'Haqiqat-e-Muhammadiyah', to our mind, is one of the main doctrines that came into being under this influence and is ultimately traceable to *intradeical* interpretation of Plato's 'theory of the world of ideas' by Philo. Muslims replaced *logos* of Jewish and Christ of Christian theology by the honourable name of the Prophet Muhammad (pbuh) conceiving *'haqiqat-e-Muhammadiyah'* as that dual-natured reality, making it essentially eternal and divine and the *locus of a'yan-e-thabita* as world soul (*rūh-e-kāināt*) created in intelligible form at the first stage and in *visible form* at the next stage. Muslim *waḥdat al-wujudi* sufi affirmed the reality of *a'yan-e-thabita* (ideas) and *'ālim-e-imthāl* (world-of-ideas) and other entities corresponding to other concepts of Plato's philosophy, in what they claimed a special type of inner experience, a higher source of knowledge i.e., in their unveiling and direct-witnessing (*kashaf-o-shahood*).

Muslim philosophers, al-Farabi and Avicenna, conceiving Allah as the Absolute Intellect, replaced the doctrine of *'haqiqat-e-Muhammadiyah'* by their 'doctrine of intellects'. They coined the term *a'ql-e-awwal* (the first intellect) for what the mystics had called *'haqiqat-e-Muhammadiyah'* and argued that the first determination that took place from Allah (The Absolute Intellect) must be *'an intellect'* in nature. In their philosophy, this first intellect, is the source of all other determinations and becoming. They further argued that this coming into being of determinations was from all eternity. So Allah and the first intellect (*haqiqat-e-Muhammadiyah*) both are co-eternal, but Allah, being the logical cause, is logically prior and the first intellect logically dependent on God, is logically posterior but temporally they are simultaneous.

Aristotle, the most renowned disciple of Plato, had argued that the concept of god is the concept of a perfect being. He had further argued that volition (*irādah*) was contrary to the absolute perfection of god. Accepting this argument, Plotinus (204-270 AD), an interpreter of Platonic philosophy, a mystic-philosopher by temperament, propounded the doctrine of emanation in place of the religious doctrine of creation at will from god, as an explanation of the coming into being of everything from god through the first intellect. Muslim philosophers' doctrine of the intellects as a philosophical explanation of the coming into being of the universe from God by way of emanation was under the impress of Plato, Aristotle, Philo, Plotinus and Christian theo-philosophical thought. However, in order to make it coherent with the Ptolemaic model of the universe (scientific model of that era) they promulgated a concept of graded-emantion.[87] Aristotle, disciple of Plato, and a most renowned independent Greek philosopher, had renounced Plato's theory of ideas on his maturity of thought, saying that "Plato is dear to me but the truth is dearer." but the Muslim philosophers and especially the *waḥdat al-wujudi* mystics had been talking in terms of *'a'yan-e-thabita'* till the near past.[88]

The philosophical problem in response to which the '*doctrine of waḥdat al-wujud*' has been propounded

A philosophical theory is presented as a solution to some philosophical problem. The philosophical problem against which the '*doctrine of waḥdat al-wujud*' has been presented is known as 'the problem of the relationship of temporality with eternality' (*rabṭ al-hādith bil-qadīm*). '*Al-qadīm*' (the eternal), here refers to Allah, and *al-hādith* refers to 'what is other than Allah'. It has been discovered by modern philosophers, that a kind of intellectual problems that looked very genuine and had engaged the intellectuals for centuries, were actually not genuine. They were pseudo problems. They were formulated on incorrect terms. Presuppositions, in their foundations, were inappropriate.

The problem of '*rabṭ al-hādith bil-qadīm*' (the relationship of 'temporality with eternality'), in Muslim thought is one of such problems.[89] Apparently it looks very genuine, which it never is. The worth of the doctrine of *waḥdat al-wujud,* which has been offered as a solution to this pseudo problem can be determined from the fact that both the problem and the solution are constituted in such terms and based on such presuppositions which are absolutely inappropriate for this discourse. How are the terms inappropriate and incorrect? Scholars working in the field of religion must keep in mind that the terms are never neutral. Metaphysical ideas ride on the back of terms and travel in history. If they are contrary to the metaphysics of the discourse in which they are being used, they are bound to lead to false formulation of the problems and to false conclusions. Let us analyse the problem under discussion in this perspective.

The Qur'an, nowhere uses the epithet '*al-qadīm*' (قديم, eternal) to refer to Allah. *Azal* (ازل, eternal with respect to beginning) and *abad* (ابد, everlasting), *dāim* (دائم, for ever, universal) are Arabic words of similar meaning used in the Qur'an. But none of these have been used by Allah with reference to His Own Person. He is absolutely High above that these epithets are ascribed to Him.

Philosophers accept reason as source of knowledge in their search of truth and what conclusions they reach by logical reasoning, they hold it as real following Aristotlian principle "What is rational, is real". Sufis hold 'intuition' as a source of knowledge higher than reason, and embark upon their journey in search of truth. What conclusion they reach in their journey through their intuitive experience (*kashaf-o-shahood*), they assert it as truth and reality. However, intuitive experience can neither attain the status of knowledge nor can become communicable, until it is rationally expressed and interpreted.

One way for the rational interpretation of intuitive experience is to borrow terms from Plato, Aristotle and other philosophers. In the shape of Philo, Plotinus and Christian mystics and religious philosophers, precedents of this way of interpretation were abound. The other way is to borrow terms from the Qur'anic diction, and interpret one's intuitive experience keeping in view its accordance with the *muḥkamāt* of the Qur'an.

As said earlier, terms are never neutral; it is impossible that one borrows terms from philosophy, and interpret his intuitive experience in a Qur'anic perspective. This is what has occurred to Muslim *waḥdat al-wujudi* sufis, theologians and philosophers belonging to Shi'a, Sunni and other Islamic traditions. Taking the terms '*qadīm*' (eternal) for Allah, *waḥdat al-*

wujud for their doctrine, first intellect or *'ta'ayyin-e-awwal* (first determination for what they held as first emanation from Allah), and six descentions (*tanazzlat-e-sitta*), seven stages (*maratab-e-saba'*), *hadrat-e-khamsa*, *a'yān-e-thabita* etc. (Platonic archetypes of knowledge) from philosophers, they had tried to read them in the Qur'an by arbitrary interpretations.

Ash-Shaikh Muhayyuddin Ibn al-'Arabi (r.a.), the founder of the *wahdat al-wujud* school makes the doctrine of 'six descensions' (*tanazzalāt-e-sitta*) basis for interpreting his mystic experience concerning 'manifestation of the eternal in contingent' (*zahoor al-hādith bil-qadīm*) and 'on the relation of the contingent with the eternal' (*rabat al-hādith bil-qadīm*). This doctrine is known as *wahdat al-wujud*. In mystics the word 'descension' (*tanazzal*) is used to mean 'manifestation' (*zahoor*). Some other sufis have presented the same ideas as '*maratab-e-saba*' (seven stages or levels) or '*hazrāt-e-khamsa*' (five decensions).

Abu al-Hassan al-Alvi presents a very good comparative study of Dr. Israr Ahmed's views on *wahdat al-wujud* with Hadrat Ibn al-'Arabi in his Urdu article "*Nazriya-e-wahdat al-wujud and Dr. Israr Ahmed*". The points discussed here have been taken from that article.[90]

As per Abu al-Hassan Alvi's article, according to Ibn Arabi the first descension that took place from the Absolute Being is '*Haqiqat-e-Muhammadiyah*' and this descension took place in His Attribute of Knowledge."

The second descension takes place from '*Haqiqat-e-Muhammadiyah*' to '*a'yān-e-thabita*'. The third descension that takes place is from '*a'yān-e-thabita*' to '*the spirit*' (*ruh*); and the fourth one from '*the spirit*' (*ruh*) to *mithāl* (*incorporeality*); the fifth from *mithāl* to *physicality* (*jism/body*); and the sixed descension took place from *Jism* to *Insān* (human being).

According to Ibn al-'Arabi, when Allah Almighty on His Good Pleasure decided to bring about creation, he made an *ijmāli* (implicit/abstract) idea of it. This *implicit idea* in *wahdat al-wujudi* school is known as '*Haqiqat-e-Muhammadiyah*'. Among *wahdat al-wujudi* sufi scholars, this idea of '*Haqiqat-e-Muhammadiyah*' is also articulated as '*martaba-e-wahdat*' or '*mawjud-e-ijmāli*' or '*haqiqat al-haqāiq*' or 'first intellect' or '*ālim-e-sifāt*' (the world of attributes), or 'the first manifestation' or 'the world of covert realities' (*ālim-e-ramuz*), and '*umm al-faiz*' etc. As per Shaikh Ibn al-'Arabi, after this implicit idea (*ijmāli tasawwur*) Allah Almighty made an explicit idea (*tafsīli tasawwur*) of what were to be the creature. Shaikh Ibn al-'Arabi articulates this stage as '*ayān-e-thabita*'. In sufi literature' this is also stated as '*martaba-e-wahidiyat*' (stage of Oneness), *qābliyat-e-zahoor* (potential manifestation), *wajud-e-Fāiz* and *zill-im-mamdood*.

'*Ayān-e-thābita*' as visualised by Hadrat Ibn al-'Arabi, are the images of all creatures which lay in Allah's attribute of Knowledge.

These three stages i.e., *Dhāt-e-Ilāhiya* (Being of God), '*Haqiqat-e-Muhammadiyah*' (*tasawwur-e-ijmāli*) and '*Ayān-e-thābita*'(*tasawwur-e-tafsīli*), in Ibn al-'Arabi's *wahdat al-wujud,* are called *maratab-e-Ilahiya* (levels of manifestation of God-hood). These are *maratab-e-Ilahiya*, because it either as Allah's implicit Knowledge (*Ijmāli 'Ilm*), in case of the first descension, or as Allah's explicit Knowledge (*Tafsīli 'Ilm*), in case of the second descension, is Allah's Attribute; and Allah's Attributes are identical with His Being. So all these three levels are the stages related to His own Being (*maratab-e-Ilahiya*).

A very important view of Shaikh Ibn al-Arabi is that *'a'yān-e-thābita'* have not even smelled the existence of external things. What does this mean? Because *'A'yān-e-thābita'* are eternal images and ideas in Allah's Knowledge, of absolute perfections of all things whatsoever to be created by Allah, so they can never exist as particular things. The things which come into being as existents in the world at third, fourth, fifth and sixth stage of descensions from Allah as *rûh, mithāl, jism,* and finally as *insān* are only shadows and reflections of these *'a'yān-e-thābita'*. It means that the external existents at third to sixth stage are only relatively-real or half realities. The third, fourth and fifth descensions in Ibn al-Arabi's thought are known as *'maratab-e-koniya'* or *'maratab-e-imkāniya'* (possible existents) because they have no existence in the external world. As Abu al-Hassan 'Alvi in his article puts it, according to Shaikh Ibn al-'Arabi the universe and whatever therein is, are actually reflections of the ideas of Allah's Knowledge. It has no real existence. In reality nothing besides the Being of Allah exists. This is what sufis call *waḥdat al-wujud.*[91]

Abu al-Hassan Alvi writes that in Shaikh Ibn al-'Arabi, the descensions (*tanazzalāt*) have occurred in Allah's Attribute of Knowledge. Shaikh Ibn al-'Arabi believes in the identity of Divine Attributes with Allah's Being. As the Attribute of Knowledge is no different than His Being, so descension actually has taken place in the Being of Allah Himself in the form of determinations in His Knowledge. It means that in Shaikh Ibn al-'Arabi's system of thought, Allah's attribute of Knowledge is the basis of coming into being of the universe.[92]

Let us examine this view in the light of the Qur'an (Allah's revealed 'The Truth').

Nowhere in the Qur'an Allah Almighty uses the word 'ṣifah' (صفات *attributes*) to talk about Himself. Rather the Qur'an ordains the believers to call on Allah by His Goodly Names (*al-Asmā' al-Ḥusnā*) and leave those who blaspheme against His Comely Names:

"And the Most beautiful Names belong to Allah; so invoke Him by them, and keep away from those who blaspheme His Names. They will be requited for what they used to do." (Surah al-A'raf, 7:180)

The Personal Name of the Creator of all, the true Master, and the Sustainer of the worlds is Allah. All other Excellent Names are His attributive Names. His *al-Asmā' al-Husnā* are either mentioned in the Holy Qurān or derivable from it in line with the *muhkamāt.* To invoke any of His Names for the satisfaction of base desires or to fulfil an evil purpose, to accomplish an evil design, or to make arbitrary addition or deletion in His Names, are various ways to blaspheme His Names. It is strictly forbidden and Allah ordains to leave those who blaspheme against His Comely Names.

All the above discourse about Ibn al-'Arabi, defies this command and contradicts with the *muḥkamāt.* It talks about Allah in terms of His attributes.

Holding Allah eternal, His attributes, too, become eternal. Holding His attributes eternal, all the six descensions from His Attribute of Knowledge become eternal.

One of the basic assumption of the doctrine of *wahdat al-wujud,* as stated above (to call Allah as 'Al-Ḥaqq' in the sense of 'The Truth') is also blasphemous.

According to un-Qur'anic Greek ontology on which this doctrine is falsely based, all celestial entities (*maratab-e-Ilahiya*) not only become eternal (*qadīm*) but also become part of the Being of Allah.

How strange it is that all this is presented in the name of intuitive experience, unveiling and direct-witnessing as a higher source of knowledge. It is presented from those who claim to be *gnostics* (*ārifeen*). If one compares the details of the doctrines of 'the manifestation of the eternal in contingent' or 'descension (*zahoor*) of the contingent from the eternal' (*zahoor al-hādith bil-qadīm*)' and 'the relation of the contingent with the eternal' (*rabat al-hādith bil-qadīm*), the sub-doctrines of *wahdat al-wujud,* there is hardly any essential difference in Plato's views and of Ibn al-'Arabi school.

Those who prefer their own liking to truth "assert His servants to be part of Him." The Qur'an confirms them as manifest ingrates." (cf. Surah az-Zukhruf, 43:15)

Haḍrat Muhammad (pbuh) is the servant of Allah (عبدہ *'Abdū*). To assert Allah's servants, or His creation, part of Him, may it be as shadows and reflections, is absolutely contrary to the Qur'an (The Truth) descended upon Haḍrat Muhammad (pbuh). Allah is the Originator of everything. The creation (*khalq*) or the command (*amr*) cannot be the part of Allah. Allah is Almighty.

On the problem of 'the relation of the contingent (*al-hādith*) with the eternal (*al-qadīm*)' differing with Shaikh Ibn al Arabi, Dr. Israr Ahmed argues that the descensions took place in Allah's attribute of Speech (*Kalām*). According to Him when Allah, Wills (intends) to bring about creation, and issues the command "*KUN*"(Be!), the first time, no creation ensues from it. Rather, the command '*KUN*' transforms into an indeterminate kind of absolute light (*Noor*) as if it was the first determination ensuing from Allah's attribute of Kalām, from which come out other *descensions* (*tanazzalāt*).

Abu al-Hassan Alvi considers the ensuing of descensions from Allah's attribute of *Kalām* (Speech) in Dr. Israr Ahmed as compared to ensuing of descensions from the attribute of Knowledge (*'ilm*) in Shaikh Ibn al-'Arabi, as the essential difference between the two versions of *wahdat al-wujud.*

This study sees no essential difference between the two because both of them hold one or the other Divine Attribute as the origin of ensuing of *descensions*. The same criticism as hurled on Ibn al-'Arabi above equally applies to Dr. Israr Ahmed. Dr. Israr Ahmed does not stop for a while to ponder that where from the Muslim sufis and philosophers have accepted the term '*qadīm*' (eternal) for Allah, what are the various senses in which it is used, and that can it be applied to Allah remaining true to the Qur'an! He also does not stop for a while, to think over the un-Qur'anic ontology lying in the foundations of *wahdat al-wujud,* and its implications too. He fails to perceive that the problems of '*rabat al-hādith bil-qadīm*' and of '*zahoor al-hādith bil-qadīm*' are formulated on un-Qur'anic concept of God; therefore they are pseudo problems, and so is the doctrine of *wahdat al-wujud* which is offered as a solution to these problems.

Let us see the concept of '*Ḥaqiqat-e-Muhammadiyah*' in the light of the teachings of the Qur'an. The Qur'an says:

Allah has not created the heavens and the earth and all in between them just as a play. Rather Allah has created them with truth. (Q. 44:38-39)

The wise people who remember Allah standing, sitting and lying down on their sides, when they reflect on the creation of the heavens and the earth, they could not help professing "O Lord! You have not created anything in vain." (cf. Q. 3:191)

Creation of the heavens, the creation of the earth, the creation of all that is in between them is such a big job that it cannot be accomplished with any less than Divine Knowledge nor can it be understood without it. Creation of anything without a purpose is a logical impossibility for it is contrary to the Dignity of Allah that He creates anything for play.

Allah is absolutely free of desire, need, deficiency, flaw, weakness etc. He is neither eternal nor temporal. He is neither timeless nor everlasting. He is neither al-Dahr (Time) nor Pure Duration. The concepts *qidm/azliyat* (ازليت), *abdiyat* (ابديت), *dwām* (دوام), *infinity* are related to the created beings. None of these concepts is worthy of Allah's Being. He is beyond all determinations of space, time, understanding, intuitive experience or whatever. Nothing whatsoever can encompass Him. He is Singularly Unique and Supremely Transcendent of having any likeness to anything. There was no Will to create the universe or not to create it from ever. Creation of the universe had not added to His Dignity and Honour, which He would lack had He not created it. Both these possibilities were absolutely alike for Him. In His absolute freedom of Will and absolute transcendence from need, desire, deficiency or inner compulsion He willed to create it; so He created it. He has created everything by His Will and then by His Command (*amr*). Whatever has originated from the Absolute Originator, belongs either to the category of His creation (*khalq*) or to the category of His command (*amr*). Even *amr* does not issue from Him because of any inner compulsion. No descensions (*tanazzalāt*) could ever ensue from Him without His Will (*Iradah*) and Command(*Amr*). His Goodly Names (and not the Attributes) are the channel of the origination of *khalq* or *amr* from Him. So nothing in any way participates in His Divinity or is part of Him. To conceive Allah as '*wujud-e-mutliq*' (absolute existence), because of having no *authority* from the Qur'an at its back, is sheer concoction. Nothing has come into being from Him because of any inner compulsion, by way of anything like emanation. He has created everything with Knowledge and on His Will and Command. He alone sustains everything. He sustains everything. He sustains everything with Knowledge. His Knowledge encompasses everything. Even a leaf does not fall, but it is in His Knowledge. His Power encompasses everything; He has absolute control over everything. All consequences flow from His Will(*mashiyat*). His Will (*mashiyat*) is from His Knowledge. Volition is a Dignity for Him. To be Immutable is against His Dignity. He has sent His Messengers from among the human beings, and has revealed His Scriptures. His Scriptures are The Truth (*Al-Ḥaqq*). Scriptures descended in the past, verify the scripture descended at present, and the scripture descended at present verifies the scriptures descended in the past. The authenticity of the scriptures descended in the past has been compromised. What Allah has descended as Scripture on Haḍrat Muhammad (pbuh) is *Al-Ḥaqq* (The Truth) at present.

The system of the world is *dār-al-'amal* (to see how we behave) and there is *dār-al-Jaza* (the day of requital) too. When He Wills a thing to be, the command is issued; it sets the caption (*unwān*) of its coming into being. *KUN* (Be!) is a command which determines the *caption*. It does not mean that things will necessarily come into being instantaneously. Factors begin to accumulate as per Allah's Knowledge, Will and Wisdom. He has not created anything for His own sake. He absolutely needs nothing for His own sake. Allah has created the servants (humankind), for Himself, and everything of the world for His servants. It means that it is the servants which are the reason for creation and coming into being of the universe. Haḍrat Muhammad (pbuh) is the most reverend servant of Allah (*'abdihi'*, *'abduhu'*) and is the highest in cader to everything originated from Allah. The prophets, the messengers (pbut), *shuhadā'* (plural of *'shahid'*) and the righteous ones are all *in togetherness* (*ma'iyat*) with Him and reason for the creation of the universe. But neither Haḍrat Muhammad (pbuh) nor anyone else among the messengers (Peace be upon them all!) or angels participate in Allah's Divinity. There is no concept of a dual-natured being in Islam like Philo's logos, Christ and holy ghost of the Christians, Ibn al-'Arabi's '*ḥaqiqat Muhammadiyah*', and Evicenna's first intellect.

The *ḥaqiqat* (reality or nature) of Haḍrat Muhammad (pbuh) is that he is the nearest to Allah than anyone else in the whole creation (*khalq*) and command (*amr*). He (pbuh) as servant of Allah (*'Abdihi*) is also *noor* (light). Being the best and the highest in creation, he (pbuh) is the role model and ideal for the whole humankind. The reality (*ḥaqiqat*) of the ideal is *light*. In darkness, one loses his orientation. Presence of light, enlightens in man the consciousness of 'what he is at present' and 'what is the destiny.' This is true of all prophets, messengers, the *shahideen* and the righteous men and women all. (Peace be upon them all.) They are all *noor* (light).

Haḍrat Muhammad (pbuh) is the distributor of Allah's Mercy for the whole humankind. If Allah, who is supremely Unique and Absolutely Singular, and Free of any want, need, deficiency or weakness, can honour His servant Haḍrat Muhammad (pbuh) with the authority to distribute His Mercy among humankind, why can't Haḍrat Muhammad (pbuh) bless any of his beloved followers with the honour to 'distribute Allah's mercy' to his fellow human beings! All the prophets and the messengers (pbut) were the distributors of Allah's blessings to their people. Haḍrat Muhammad (pbuh) has been honoured by this status for the whole humankind, and for all times. The blessings are given by Allah for distribution, they are being distributed at present, and will keep on till the Last Day. 'Immanence' (*suryaniat*), ingivinness (*halool*) and union-with-God (*ittehād*), promulgated *by waḥdat al-wujud* school on man-God relationship, are un-Qur'anic concepts based upon un-Qur'anic interpretation of their mystic experiences.[93] It is contrary to the Qur'anic teachings and inconsistent with the *muḥkmāt* of the Qur'an. The Qur'an gives the concept of *m'aiyyat* i.e., togetherness with, with-ness to Allah. Being the best and the highest as servant of Allah, Haḍrat Muhammad (pbuh) is in perfect togetherness with Allah. All the prophets, messengers, *shuhadā* (plural of *shāhid*—true followers of the prophets and the messengers)' and the righteous servants (Peace be upon them all.) are in Allah's togetherness (*m'aiyyat*) but not in union-with-Allah, and none can ever be in union-with-Allah.

MISCONCEPTIONS OF THE QUR'ANIC HERMENEUTICS

CHAPTER 5

CLASSIFICATION OF VERSES INTO *MUḤKAMĀT* AND *MUTASHĀBIHĀT*

The Qur'an divides all verses comprising the Qur'anic text, into two kinds as it says:

"It is He who has sent this Scripture down to you [Prophet]. Some of its verses are definite in meaning [muḥkamāt]–these are the cornerstone of the Scripture [Umm-al-Kitāb]–and others are ambiguous [mutashābihāt]. The perverse at heart eagerly pursue the ambiguities [mutashābihāt] in their attempt to make trouble and to pin down a specific meaning of their own: only God knows the true meaning. Those firmly grounded in knowledge [ar-rāsikhūna fil-IIm] say, 'We believe in it: it is all from our Lord'–only those with real perception will take heed." (Q. 3:7) (Abdel Haleem)

Some verses of the Qur'an as per above verse 7 of surah Āl-e-Imrān (3), are *muḥkamāt* while the verses other than these are *mutashābihāt.* It is usually held by scholars, Muslims as well as the orientalists, that the verses, which are decisive, definite in meaning, precise in reference and are not liable to more than one interpretation, are *muḥkamāt.* It implies that *mutashābihāt*, by definition, are the verses which are not definite in meaning or are ambiguous. All the nine translators, exegetes and the Qur'an scholars referred to at endnote no.2 i.e.

(i) Sahih International, The Qur'ān (English Meanings) Abul-Qasim Publishing House, 1997 Al-Muntada Al-Islami, 2004;

ii) Pickthall; iii) Yusuf Ali; iv) Shakir; v) Muḥammad Sarwar; vi) Muḥsin Khan; and vii) Arberry.

And

viii) Eng. tr. of Maulana Abu 'al A'la Maududi's Tafhīm–ul-Qur'an, at englishtafsir.com ix) M. A. S. Abdel Haleem, The Qur'an: A new translation

and almost all others I have come across during my studies and research, distinguish *muḥkamāt* and *mutashābihāt* in the above manner. However, this definition is not correct. Of course, *muḥkamat* are necessarily decisive, precise in reference, unambiguous and definite in meaning, but the presence of these characteristics alone does not qualify a verse to include in the category of *muḥkamāt.* A *muḥkam* verse must consist of an explicit divine imperative, command or ordinance; or an explicit divine imperative is derivable from it. This is the only essential characteristic of a *muḥkam* verse. There are many verses, which are clear in statement, precise and definite in meaning having no ambiguity in their statement, yet do not include in the category of *muḥkamāt* because they do not consist of a divine imperative. It is the absence of an explicit divine imperative that makes a verse to include in the category of *mutashābihāt.* Verse 07 of Surah Āl-e-Imran 3 itself is a *muḥkam* verse. It explicitly contains a divine imperative to distinguish *mutashābihāt* from *muḥkamāt* and keep the interpretation of a *mutashābih* verse accord with the *muḥkamāt*; if the Qur'an scholar does not want to prove himself diseased at heart and a mischief-monger. Though *mutashābihāt* do not consist of any divine imperative, yet they are not meant for recitation alone. Allah has not revealed verse under discussion solely for adding information to the believers on the categorisation of verses, and on the ontological status of *muḥkamāt* as cornerstone of the Qur'anic Scripture. The *mutashābihāt* are not meant only that the believers keep them reciting for heavenly reward. As a necessary part of Allah's Word they definitely contain divine guidance, insight and teachings and it is obligatory for the believers to act upon the insight, guidance, teachings discerned from them. The Qur'an gives *muhkamāt* the status of *Umm-ul-Kitāb* (Foundation of the Book, Cornerstone of the Scripture, the Pivotal verses). *Mutashābihāt* are usually translated as ambiguous, unspecific, allegorical, metaphorical or symbolic. Of course *mutashābihāt* also consist of such verses too. However, according to the author, the right rendering of a *mutashābih* verse is that it is non-imperatival because the categories are mutually exclusive. Verses belonging to the category of *mutashābihat* occur in different forms: stating a story or a narrative, making a comparison or asserting an analogy; or are allegorical, metaphorical, metaphysical, eschatological, moral, and symbolical and abstract (as consisting of 'separate letters'). They also occur as prayers to invoke for Allah's forgiveness, mercy, and help and guidance in troubles and turmoil, or express one's gratefulness and servitude on His blessings in situations of comfort and joys as taught by Allah Himself in the Qur'an. Verses containing Allah's promise, pledge, a glad-tiding or a threat, admonish or advice too are instances of *mutashābihāt*. Verses addressing in second person singular and third person singular, too, are *mutashābihāt*. Surah an-Noor (24) consists of 64 verses and it is stated in the very first verse that imperatives explicitly stated in its verses, or 'does' and 'don'ts' derivable from them as consequences, are obligatory. Yet it does not mean that all of its verses are necessarily considered to be *muḥkamāt*. This surah also consists of *mutashābih* verses.

The imperatival verses (*muḥkamāt*) by virtue of their status as *Umm-ul-Kitāb*, are the criterion pertaining to the interpretation of all types of non-imperatival (*mtashabihāt*) verses. Whatever conclusion is drawn from the *mtashabihat*, shall have to accord with the *muḥkamāt*. The interpretation of a *mutashābih* verse, which does not accord with the *muḥkamāt,* will present an incorrect rendering; and if the interpreter insists upon it, it will prove him diseased at heart and a mischief-monger. Those who are perverse at heart, do not accept Allah Almighty's command and try to determine the meanings of that kind of non-imperatival verses (*mutashābihāt*) which are liable to more than one interpretation in arbitrary manner according to what suits their desire or agenda. Allah compares this offence with '*fitna*'—creating trouble and evil mongering. Allah declares *fitna* worse than killing at Q. 2.191.

The right rendering of verse 7 of surah 3, keeping in view the above discussion on the definition of *muḥamāt* and *mutashābihāt* should be as follows:

هُوَ الَّذِي أَنْزَلَ عَلَيْكَ الْكِتَابَ مِنْهُ آيَاتٌ مُحْكَمَاتٌ هُنَّ أُمُّ الْكِتَابِ وَأُخَرُ مُتَشَابِهَاتٌ فَأَمَّا الَّذِينَ فِي قُلُوبِهِمْ زَيْغٌ فَيَتَّبِعُونَ مَا تَشَابَهَ مِنْهُ إِلَّا اللَّهُ وَالرَّاسِخُونَ فِي الْعِلْمِ يَقُولُونَ آمَنَّا بِهِ كُلٌّ مِنْ عِنْدِ رَبِّنَا وَمَا يَذَّكَّرُ إِلَّا أُولُوا ابْتِغَاءَ الْفِتْنَةِ وَابْتِغَاءَ تَأْوِيلِهِ وَمَا يَعْلَمُ تَأْوِيلَهُ الْأَلْبَابِ

"It is He who has sent this Scripture down to you [Prophet]. Some of its verses are imperatival [muḥkamāt]—these are the cornerstone of the Scripture [Umm-al-Kitāb]—and others are non-imperatival [mutashābihāt]. The perverse at heart eagerly pursue the non-imperatival

[mutashābihat] in their attempt to make trouble and to pin down a specific meaning of their own: only God knows the true meaning. Those firmly grounded in knowledge [ar-rāsikhūna fil-Ilm] say, 'We believe in it: it is all from our Lord'–only those with real perception will take heed." (Q. 3:7)

The right way, enunciated in this verse for translators and the exegetes by Allah, is that at first they shall classify a verse, and if they classify it as non-imperatival (*mutashābih*), then doing their best in keeping the interpretation of these verses congruent with the *muḥkamāt* (*Umm-ul-Kitāb*), they must not claim finality for their interpretation, and with the admission that '*none except Allah knows their true meaning*' they should pronounce that: '*They have faith in the Book. The whole of it [the muḥkamat and the mutashābihāt both] is from Allah.*' The Qur'an calls them '*blessed with deep knowledge (ar-rāsikhūna fil-'ilm)*'. Irrespective of how congruent with the *muḥkamāt* the interpretation of a *mutashābih* verse may become, the verse in question will ever remain in the class of *mutashābihāt*.

Allah is Almighty and The Wise. (Q. 3:6)

The Book has good counsel, cure, guidance, and mercy for the believers. (Q. 10:57)

Those who do not accept Allah's good counsel, in order to insert their own suggestion, opinion, conjecture, speculation, philosophy, desire, bias or sectarian agenda in the Qur'an, on one pretext or the other overlook God-given principle and run for arbitrary interpretation of the *mutashābihāt*. These ones insert doubt and inconsistency in the Qur'anic translation, commentary and theology and promote factionalism and sectarianism in Muslim community. Those who do not follow the advice of The Wise (i.e., Allah), as per Word of Allah, they are not wise.

Verse 23 of Surah az-Zumer (39) says:

اللَّهُ نَزَّلَ أَحْسَنَ الْحَدِيثِ كِتَابًا مُتَشَابِهًا مَثَانِيَ تَقْشَعِرُّ مِنْهُ جُلُودُ الَّذِينَ يَخْشَوْنَ رَبَّهُمْ ثُمَّ تَلِينُ جُلُودُهُمْ وَقُلُوبُهُمْ إِلَى ذِكْرِ اللَّهِ ذَلِكَ هُدَى اللَّهِ يَهْدِي بِهِ مَنْ يَشَاءُ وَمَنْ يُضْلِلِ اللَّهُ فَمَا لَهُ مِنْ هَادٍ ﴿۞﴾

"Allah has descended 'the Fairest of Texts Book' (Aḥsan-al-Ḥadīth Kitāb) consistent with itself, and yet repeating its teachings in various ways…" (Q. 39:23)

It is necessary for 'the Fairest of Texts Book' that it be self-consistent and free of contradiction. The teachings have been so repeated in it, that add to the coherence of its verses and the efficacy of its teachings. If there is a claim at one place, some other place attests it as evidence. The verses of '*Aḥsan-al-Ḥadīth Kitāb*' support each other; they cannot contradict or conflict with each other. They must resemble each other in style, message and content.

If a non-imperatival (*mutashābihāt*) verse is elaborated and interpreted based on the imperatival ones (*muḥkamāt*), at least another place from within the Qur'an must be brought forth to testify the contention that the verses support each other'. Such translation or exegesis will prove our faith in the Qur'an as 'The Fairest of Texts Book' true. The *muḥkamāt* will always remain *muḥkamāt*. In no case, a *muḥkam* verse can conflict with any of the *muḥkamāt,* and the status to be the *Umm-ul-Kitāb* will always remain with them alone.

Let us see the interpretation of verse 35 of Surah Al-Nūr 24 as a typical instance of a *mutashābih* verse. Abdel Haleem translates it as the following:

"God is the Light of the heavens and earth. His Light is like this: There is a niche, and in it is a lamp. The lamp is inside a glass. Glass is like a glittering star, fuelled from a blessed olive tree that is from neither east nor west. Its oil almost gives light even when no fire touches it – light upon light – Allah guides whomever He will to His Light; He draws such comparisons for people; God has full knowledge of everything."

All the nine translators mentioned above translate the verse in almost the same sense, especially the first part, as '*God is the Light of the heavens and earth.*' The Qur'anic ontology that conceives everything either as Allah's *khalq* or as Allah's *amr* will not allow any translation of this verse as "*Allah is the Light of the heavens and earth.*" or development of the metaphor *"His Light is like this..."* in a manner which could lend itself to pantheism, immanence, unicity (*itehād*) or in-givenness (*ḥalūl*) etc.[94] However, there are a few others too, for example Maulana Amin Aḥsan Iṣlaḥi, and the authors of *Tafseer-e-Fazli* etc. who would translate the part "...اللَّهُ نُورُ السَّمَاوَاتِ وَالْأَرْضِ" like this: *"The heavens and the earth are luminous with the light of Allah's guidance..."* Let us see how the metaphor expressed in this verse can be developed and interpreted which accords with the *muḥkamāt*, with the Qur'anic ontology and other the Qur'anic principles.

Allāhu Nūru As-Samāwāti Wa Al-'Arḍi	By Allah is the light of the heavens and the earth.
Mathalu Nūrihi Kamishkāatin	Similitude of His light is that of a niche;
Fīhā Miṣbāḥun	In it is a lamp.
Al-Miṣbāḥu Fī Zujājatin	The lamp is inside a glass.
Az-Zujājatu Ka'annahā Kawkabun Durrīyun	The glass is like a glittering star.
Yūqadu Min Shajaratin Mubārakatin Zaytūniatin Lā Sharqīyatin Wa Lā Gharbīyatin	It is fuelled by the oil of a blessed tree–the olive–which is neither to the east nor to the west.
Yakādu Zaytuhā Yuḍī'u Wa Law Lam Tamsas/hu Nārun Nūrun `Alá Nūrin	The oil may likely kindle though fire has hardly touched it –light upon light–
Yahdī Allāhu Linūrihi Man Yashā'u Wa Yaḍribu Allāhu Al-'Amthāla Lilnnāsi	Allah guides to His light [gnosis] whoever He Wills, and Allah states examples for the people,
Wa Allāhu Bikulli Shay'in `Alīmun	and Allah has Knowledge of everything. (*Tafseer-e-Fazli*)

The reality of light is guidance.[95]

The heavens and earth, i.e., the universe is Allah's creation (*khalq*) which is active and functional with Allah's command (*amr*).

Allah, being Singularly Unique, transcends all analogies. *"Nothing, certainly is, like unto Him" (Q. 42:11)* The analogy referred to in this part of the verse denotes the light of guidance of Allah placed in the heavens and earth.

Al-Nūr (The Light) is the Good-Name of Allah and Allah has placed the light of guidance in the heavens and the earth.[96] The heavens and the earth and whatever therein is, is lit and luminous with the light of Allah's guidance as filled with His signs. It is in this sense that Allah is the light of the heavens and the earth. (3:116; 3:190; 10:6)

The heart of man is like a niche in which the lamp is placed. The lamp is encased in a glassy globe. The globe is so clean that it glitters like a star. Imagine how much illumination the globe can add to the light of the lamp when it is lit, and how beautifully it will distribute this light!

The lamp in the heart of man is filled with blessed oil, the Reason (*'aql*). Heart is the seat of Reason. (Q. 22:46)[97] This blessed oil is pure like the oil extracted from the fruit of an olive tree which is neither in the east nor in the west but in the centre of the garden where the sun shines over it from morning till it sets. The oil of such a tree is so pure that it is just to be lighted up as soon as a spark approaches it. Now imagine when this lamp is lighted, how luminous it would be! Light upon light!

The role of Reason is to free man from contradictions.

Those who do not use reason ('aql) are worse than animals. (Q. 25:44)

Reason (*'aql*) is the ability to identify contradiction in one's thought (*qaul*), and in one's action (*'aml*), and in one's knowledge (*'ilm*) and to purge oneself from it.

Only those human beings who use reason ('aql), accept Allah's Advice. (Q. 3:7)

The Qur'an is The Truth. To follow The Truth is to follow Reason. What contradicts The Truth is contrary to Reason. Going astray is to deviate from *Al-Ḥaqq* = Reason.)

Reason, when pure, has the greatest capacity to catch light from the light of guidance of Allah by which the heavens and the earth are lit and luminous. But when man follows his desires, reason loses its purity.[98] The heavens and the earth are lit with the light of Allah's guidance. If there is a heart whose oil has not lost its purity and whose globe has not lost its shine, Allah guides him to the way of His light, to the way of His gnosis (*irfān-i-ḥaqq*).[99] This is the heart of the believer. When it is lit with gnosis, it becomes light upon light. Allah is the Knower of everything, He knows with absolute knowledge whom to bless with this favour. Allah sets parables for the guidance of humankind.

Let us see another *mutashābih* verse, usually presented out of context, and interpreted without regard to the Qur'anic principles. It is verse 3 of Surah al-Ḥadīd 57 which says:

هُوَ الأَوَّلُ وَالآخِرُ وَالظَّاهِرُ وَالْبَاطِنُ وَهُوَ بِكُلِّ شَيْءٍ عَلِيمٌ ⟪

(*Huwa Al-'Awwalu Wa Al-'Ākhiru Wa Až-Žāhiru Wa Al-Bāṭinu Wa Huwa Bikulli Shay'in `Alīmun*) "He is the First and the Last; the Evident and the Hidden; He has knowledge of all things." (Q, 57:3) (TF)

Abdel Haleem translates it as the following:

"He is the First and the Last; the Outer and the Inner; He has knowledge of all things." (Abdel Haleem)

This translation by Abdel Haleem clearly lends itself to all-inclusiveness, immanence, in-givenness, *waḥdat al-wujud* and emanation and defies Allah's Transcendence, Absolute Uniqueness and Supreme Singularity from His creation and command. This is one of the typical *mutashābih* verses which the theologians, sufis, philosophers and exegetes of *waḥdat al-wujud* school present, out of context, to support their position. Six verses, two of which occur before this particular verse (no.3 in sequence), and four which occur after this verse determine its context. *Tafseer*-e-Fazli translates it as the following:

1. Whatever there is in the heavens and the earth, Glorifies His Majesty. He is the Almighty, the Wise.

2. The Kingdom of the heavens and the earth belongs to Him alone, Who gives life, Who gives death, and Who is All-Powerful over everything.

3. So He is the First, the Last, the Manifest and the Hidden. And He is the Knower of everything. [هُوَ الأَوَّلُ وَالآخِرُ وَالظَّاهِرُ وَالْبَاطِنُ وَهُوَ بِكُلِّ شَيْءٍ عَلِيمٌ ⟪]

4. He, it is Who created the heavens and the earth in six days, and established He on the throne. He knows everything that enters into the earth and knows whatever comes out of it; and knows whatever descends from the heavens and whatever ascends to it. He is with you, wherever you are. And He sees your actions.

5. Kingdom of the heavens and the earth belongs to Him. And all affairs turn towards Him.

6. He merges the night into the day, and the day into the night; and knows what is hidden in the chests.

7. So affirm faith in Allah and His Messenger, and spend out of what He has given in your control. He who comes to believe and spend (as desired by Allah) will have a great reward. (Q. 57:1-7)[100]

Reciting signs of His Glory, Majesty and Grandeur in the first six verses of this Surah, in the 7th verse Allah Almighty invites the people to affirm faith in Allah and His Messenger (pbuh) and commands the believers to spend in His way, out of which He has bestowed to them. Then He gives them the glad-tidings that he who affirms faith and spends in the way of Allah will be blessed with a great reward. (cf. Q. 57:7) Nothing like immanence (*suryaniat*), unicity (*Ittehād*), emanation (*ṣadūr, faizān*), in-givenness (*ḥalūl*), all-inclusiveness or *waḥdat al-wujūd* can be drawn from verse 3 of Surah al-Ḥadīd 57.

Having seen it in contextual perspective, let us see it in ontological perspective:

The heavens and earth (and whatever lies therein) either belong to the category of Allah's *khalq* (creation) or to the category of His *amr* (command). Allah is the absolute Originator of *khalq* and *amr* both. So as absolute Originator, Allah is Prior (*Al-Awwal*) to everything. As the creation (*khalq*) and the command (*amr*) have beginning, conceiving an end for them does not make us confront any logical contradiction. So after their end Allah is Posterior to them all (*Al-Ākhir*). The Dignity and Grandeur of Allah, the Absolute Originator, is so evident in His creation and command that the statement of His Dignity and Grandeur will never end even if all the trees on the earth were the writing instrument, and the ocean, with seven more oceans behind it, were ink. (Q. 31:27) So Allah is The Evident (*Aẓ-Ẓāhir*) in the heavens and the earth through His signs. Nothing in the heavens and earth is conceivable without having purpose. As the Conferrer of 'purposiveness' to everything, none is more Hidden (*Al-Bāṭin*) than He is in the heavens and earth.

It is very disappointing that the theologians and the Qur'an scholars have made no effort to classify verses of the Qur'an into *muḥkamāt* and *mutashābihāt* in accordance with this Qur'anic categorisation, and have not followed this principle in their translation and commentary of the Qur'an.

It is necessary that the Muslim scholars classify verses of the Qur'an into *muḥkamāt* and *mutashābihāt* in order to make this principle of the Qur'anic interpretation functional. This is a long pending work in Islamic theology, which should have been accomplished centuries ago. The study argues that all scholars will definitely agree on a certain number of verses to be *muḥkamāt* and a certain number of verses to be *mutashābihāt*; let other verses be classified in comparison with them.

———————————————

THE ONTOLOGICAL STATUS OF HADĪTH

CHAPTER 6

REVISITING THE ONTOLOGICAL STATUS OF HADĪTH

Another very important principle of the interpretation of the Qur'an relates to the relationship of *Hadīth* with the Qur'an. The Qur'an calls itself '*Ahsan-al-Hadīth Kitāb*' (The Fairest of Texts Book) (Q. 39:23) When it is necessary for the very non-imperatival verses (*mutashābihāt*) of the Qur'an itself to accord with its 'imperatival verses' (*muhkamāt*) for their interpretation, why the same rule is not necessary and applicable for the text and interpretation of *Hadīth*? It is the *muhkamāt* of the Qur'an which as *Umm-ul-Kitāb* (The Cornerstone verses of the Book) are authority (*qāzi*) in all matters of *Dīn*. To make *Hadīth* authority (*qāzi*) over the *muhkamāt* is to turn everything upside down.

The epistemological status of the Qur'an is that as *Al-Haqq* it is the The Truth (i.e., The Standard of Truth) in matters pertaining to *Dīn* Islam and it is absolutely free of doubt, inconsistency and crookedness. This is never true about the epistemological status of *Hadīth*. Any view, idea, belief, philosophical or scientific theory, ideology, ontology, cosmology, eschatology, axiology, interpretation, principle of interpretation of the Qur'an or of *Hadīth*, or principle of Jurisprudence, a wise saying, unveiling and direct-witnessing (*kashaf-o-shahood*), or interpretation of intuition or of mystical experience that does not accord with the Qur'an, is not true. To accord with the Qur'an means, to accord with the *muhkamāt* (imperatival verses) of the Qur'an.

Any *hadīth* whose interpretation does not accord with the *muhkamāt* of the *Ahsan-al-Hadīth Kitāb*, does not qualify to be ascribed to the Prophet (pbuh) no matter in whatever compilation of *hadīth* it may appear or whatever process of scrutiny it may have passed through or to whosoever name its narration is ascribed. An arbitrary interpretation of a *hadīth* which does not accord with the *muhkamāt* of the *Ahsan-al-Hadīth Kitāb* is as false as the arbitrary interpretation of a *mutashābih* verse of the Qur'an.

Some Unfortunate Implications of Un-Qur'anic Ontological Status of *Hadīth*

Hadīth, if rightly ascribed, is must to be coherent with Allah's revealed Scripture (Q. 75:16-19) as the Qur'an says:

"And when you do not recite a verse to them, they say: Why did you not make it yourself! Say: I follow only that which is revealed to me by my Lord. This is nothing but Light from your Lord, and Guidance and Mercy for people who believe." (Q. 7:203) (TF)

Who can give a better introduction of His Prophet than Allah when He says:

"Say, 'I am nothing new among Allah's Messengers. I do not know what will be done with me or with you. I only follow what is revealed to me. And I am but a plain warner.'" (Q. 46:9) (TF)

Similarly the Qur'an says:

"Those who do not judge by what Allah has revealed, are disbelievers (humu al-kāfirūna)." (Q. 5:44) (TF)

"Those who do not judge according to what is revealed by Allah, are indeed wrong-doers (humu al-ẓālimūna)." (Q. 5:45) (TF)

"Those who do not judge by that which has been sent by Allah, are transgressors (humu al-fāsiqūna)." (Q. 5:47) (TF)

A Comparative View of the Relationship of the Qur'an and *Ḥadīth*—An Instance from *Ḥadīth-i-Qudsi*

Let us have a comparative view of the relationship of the Qur'an and *Ḥadīth*.

The Holy Qur'an is the 'Word of Allah'. *Ḥadīth* is not called 'Word of Allah' even if it is a *Ḥadīth-i-Qudsi*.[101]

It is said that the text of a *ḥadīth-i-qudsi* (divine tradition as compared to the prophetic tradition) consists of Allah's Words like the text of the Qur'an except that it is not to be recited in ritual prayers. Therefore, as they claim, it is the most authentic category of *ḥadīth* as to their text. Some go too far to call it extra-Qur'anic-revelation (وحئ غير متلو *wahi-i-ghair matlu*). These are the people, as this study argues, finding them unable to tamper with the Qur'anic text to their desires, want to anyhow make its authority (as The Truth) doubtful. Let us examine one such *ḥadīth-e-qudsi*:

"La tasubu addahr, fa innallaha howa addahr." (Do not vilify time for Allah is time.) is classified as *ḥadīth-e-qudsi*.

This tradition is narrated in five versions by Haḍrat Abu-Huraira (r.a.) and included by Imam Ahmad Hanbal in his Musnad, V, 299 and 311. It also occurs at, Bukhari, *Tafseer*, 45; Tawhid: 35; Ādāb:101; and Muslim, Alfāz2-4.[102]

The version under-discussion is the last of the five. It absolutely contradicts with the *muḥkamāt* of the Qur'an, if taken in its literal meaning. Therefore, cannot be a saying of the Prophet (pbuh). First and the fourth versions are clearly compatible with the *muḥkamāt* of the Qur'an. The 2nd and the 3rd versions are ambiguous, liable to be interpreted both ways. The word *'ad-dahr'* (الدهر, the time) occurs only at two places in the Qur'an at Surah al-Jāthiya (Q. 45:24) and Surah *al-Dahr* (also known as Surah al-Insān) (Q. 76:1). Nowhere in the Qur'an Allah identifies Himself with *Time (al-dahr)*. There is absolutely no sense in drawing the identification of Allah with *al-Dahr* or taking *al-Dahr* as a Good-Name of Allah based on these verses. It can be said on the authority of the Qur'an that the Prophet (pbuh) could never have meant identification of Allah with *al-Dahr*, or the vice versa, nor did he (pbuh) ever take it as the Good Name of Allah.

Narration of this Divine tradition in five versions (by Haḍrat abu Huraira alone) which contradict each other, authenticates that even the text of *hadith-i-qudsi*, which is mistakenly held as authentic by some as the Qur'an, is never free of flaw and deficiency. This particular instance beyond any doubt shows that even a *ḥadīth-i-qudsi* is must to be interpreted in accordance with the *muḥkmat*. No *ḥadīth-i-qudsi* should be taken over and above the *muḥkmat*. If, instead of ensuring accordance of this *ḥadīth-i-qudsi* with the *muḥkamāt*, *hadith-i-qudsi* under-discussion is given primacy over the Qur'an and the Qur'an is interpreted in accordance with it, it will ruin the translation, exegesis and theology with contradictions and devastate its Divine intent. Iqbal, an eminent Muslim philosopher of the sub-continent and no doubt a great scholar, unfortunately commits this epistemic fallacy, and conceives 'time' as an essential element in God's Being and offers the above mentioned Divine tradition as proof.[103] 'Iqbal's philosophy of ego' is rooted in this invalid identification. The Qur'an does not endorse the view that "Allah is Time".[104]

Text of the Qur'an is revelation. Text of *hadīth* is not revelation. It is a narration ascribed to a chain of narrators about the elaboration of a verse, a report about the implementation of an Allah's revealed injunction, or about a saying, action or response of the holy Prophet (pbuh). Compilation of verses and arrangement of surahs by the Prophet (pbuh) is as directed by Allah as Allah has revealed the Qur'anic text on him. It is not a work of human acumen to the least.[105] Order of compilation of *hadīth* is not revealed; it is work of human acumen. Allah has taken on Him to protect the Qur'an from any type of forgery, tampering or human error.[106] The text of the Holy Qur'an, order of verses and arrangement of suras is attested by the Prophet (pbuh) then attested by the successors witnessed by him (*shāhidīn*).[107] The text of the Qur'an is fixed, final and ultimate. Text of *hadīth* is not fixed, final and ultimate. Scrutinization, categorisation, chapterization and compilation of *hadīth* is a handiwork of believers on their own intellect. The Qur'an is absolutely free of any flaw, tampering, contradiction, crookedness, and error (Q. 6:38; Q. 6:59; Q. 18:01) and it is a part of faith to believe it as such for Allah certifies the Qur'an to be a consistent Book par excellence when He says: *"Praise be to Allah Who hath revealed the Scripture unto His slave, and hath not placed therein any crookedness." (Q. 18:01)* The worthy compilers of *hadīth* (r.a.) themselves admit that *hadīth* is 'not free of any flaw, tampering, contradiction, crookedness, and error' when they classify *hadīth* with respect to its authenticity admitting fake tradition (حديث وضعى *waḍ'ī ḥadīth*) as a category.

The Epistemological Status of *Ḥadīth*

The Qur'an is Qaul (قول) i.e., teaching, precept, principle, guidance, commandment and much more. In case of imperatival verses, *hadīth* reports their implementation at the hands of the Prophet (pbuh); in case of non-imperatival verses *hadīth* reports their elaboration ascribed to the Prophet (pbuh).

The Qur'an is Al-Kitāb (The Scripture). Compilations of *hadīth* are not Al-Kitāb (The Scripture). The title Siḥaḥ-i-Sitta (صحاح ستّه Six Authentic Compilations) has no revealed authentication at its back. Allah categorises the verses of the Qur'an into '*muhkamāt*' and '*mutashābihāt*'. Allah declares the '*muhkamāt*' to be '*Umm-ul-Kitāb*' i.e., and legislates that the interpretation of the '*mutashābihāt*' must conform to the former ones, otherwise it will prove the interpreter diseased at heart and a transgressor. (Q. 3:7) This Divine rule is equally applicable to the elucidation of *hadīth* as per verses Q. 7:203, and Q. 5:44-45, 47 of the Qur'an mentioned earlier.

Can *Ḥadīth* abrogate Umm-ul-Kitāb Verses of the Qur'an?

As we have seen above, Allah's revelation *i.e.,* the Qur'an is the absolute standard to be followed while passing judgement on anything. To hold that *ḥadīth* can ever insert any addition, deletion or alteration in the Qur'an is to challenge the status of the Qur'an as The Truth (*Al-Ḥaqq*) and as *Aḥsan-al-Ḥadīth Kitāb'* and to challenge the status of *muhkamāt* as *Umm al-Kitāb* ('The Foundation of the Book').

No verse of the Qur'an is ever abrogated or annulled (*mansūkh*). Since the Qur'an has been revealed as an address/speech (خطاب *khitab*) extending over a period of about 22 years, in the case of some *muhkamat* an earlier revealed verse acquires its detailed explanation, completeness and ultimate qualification in some other *muhkam* verse or verses revealed later. Every Command of Allah is perfect at its time. However, after ultimate completion of revelation, they are supposed to be read in conjunction with each other in the perspective of the completed Qur'an. Allah says:

> *Today I have perfected your religion for you, completed My blessing upon you, and chosen Islam as your religion:... (Q. 5:3) (Abdel Haleem)*

It does not mean that before this Islam was imperfect! It simply means that 'this day' it has got its ultimate completeness and perfection. Similarly, no Qur'anic revelation was ever incomplete or imperfect; however, it got its ultimate detail and completeness on the revelation of a certain later verse; and all the commandments got their ultimate perfection at the completeness of the Qur'anic revelation, as the Qur'an says:

> *"... And hasten not (O Muhammad) with the Qur'an ere its revelation hath been perfected unto thee, and say: My Lord! Increase me in knowledge." (Q. 20:114) (Pickthall)*

To take immediately available component/s of a complete command, is to make haste, and it is forbidden. (cf. Q. 20:114)

The Qur'an says:

> *"Alif, Lam, Ra. [This is] a Book whose verses are perfected and then presented in detail from [One who is] Wise and Acquainted." (Q. 11.1) (Sahih International)*

> *"...its parts resembling each other in goodness and truth, oft-repeated..." (Q. 39:23) (Moḥsin Khan)*

> *"Thus do We detail (nufaṣṣilu) Our verses for the people who have knowledge." (Q. 7:32) (Pickthall)*

> *"Certainly, We have brought to them a Book (the Qur'an) which We have explained in detail (faṣṣalnāhu) with Knowledge,.." (Q. 7:52) (Moḥsin Khan)*

> *"...We have detailed (faṣṣalnā) Our Revelations for a people who take heed..." (Q. 6:127) (Pickthall)*

> *"...We have explained everything in detail (faṣṣalnāhu)." (Q. 17:12) (Abdel Haleem)*

Parts of the Qur'anic Address detail each other in various ways. Because of short-sightedness people begin to think that at some places, the verses revealed later have abrogated the injunction (or a component) contained in the verse revealed earlier; whereas the Qur'an employs the derivatives of the infinitive '*to detail*' while using the words like '*fuṣṣilat/ nufassilu/ faṣṣalnāhu/ faṣṣalnā*' for it as shown above.

Verses on which the Doctrine of Abrogation is based

"Any revelation that We cancel or cause to be forgotten, is replaced by Us with a better one or a similar. Don't you know that Allah has power over all things?" (Q. 2:106), (TF) and

"When We substitute (<u>baddalnā</u>) one revelation for another – and God knows best what He reveals—they say, 'You are just making it up,' but most of them have no knowledge." (Q. 16:101) (TF)

The above two verses which are made the basis of the doctrine of abrogation, are themselves *mutashābih* verses. No imperative is contained in them. Interpretation of the *mutashābih* verses themselves is bound to be subservient to the *muḥkamāt*. How can a *muḥkam* verse (imperatival, cornerstone of the Qur'an) be held abrogated, cancelled or replaced on the authority of *mutashābih* (non-imperatival) verses or amended and altered based on them? Can it be conceived that *muḥkamāt* (*Umm-ul-Kitāb*) conflict, contradict, cancel or abrogate each other? Then what would calling the Qur'an *'fully consistent in itself'* and that *'parts of it resemble in colour'* (Q. 39:23) and *'free of flaw and crookedness'* (Q. 18:1) mean? Allah's injunction in one *muḥkam* verse may get detailed, qualified and fully explained when read in conjunction with such other *muḥkam* verse, but it is absolutely inconceivable that *muḥkamāt*, which comprise *umm-al-kitāb* can contradict, conflict, cancel or abrogate each other.[108]

Injunctions are provisional as well as permanent. The verses Q. 2:106 and Q. 16:101 both relate to revelations descended to previous Prophets (May peace be upon them all!). In spite of their being perfect for the people and the time they were revealed, they contained provisional commandments too, not meant for the whole humankind and for all times to come. When the objective intended by provisional commandments is fulfilled, they are substituted and lasting and permanent commandments take their place. None of the commandments contained in *muḥkamāt* is provisional in nature. All the imperatives stated in the Qur'an are permanent, and lasting. Verses consisting of permanent, lasting and universal commandments cannot be abrogated.

As has been shown above, the Qur'anic rule that the interpretation of *mutashābihāt* must accord with the *muḥkamāt*, equally applies to *ḥadīth* too. Interpretation of a *ḥadīth* must be subservient to the *muḥkamāt* of the *Aḥsan-al-Hadīth Kitāb* and not the vice versa. To make *ḥadīth* authority (*qāzi*) over the *Aḥsan-al-Ḥadīth* verses, as is claimed in some cases of abrogation, is to upturn the order. In these cases, it is *the ḥadīth* that is taken as authority to classify some of the *muḥkamāt* (imperatival and the cornerstone verses) as abrogating and some others as abrogated. It makes the verses, which have been declared foundation of the *Aḥsan-al-Ḥadīth Kitāb* subservient to *ḥadīth*, which is tantamount to inserting a severe contradiction in the Qur'an.

The Qur'an alone is the ultimate source of *sharī'ah* and the *muḥkamāt* are Foundation of the Scripture. So, in fact it is the *muḥkamāt* which are the source of *sharī'ah* (divine law). *Muḥkamāt* consist of divine laws (*aḥkām*) in definite, explicit or implied manner. A *muḥkam* verse may require differently with respect to acting upon it as to the capacity and status, from an individual, the society, the nation or humankind as a whole[109] but the injunction (*hukm*) stated in it is ultimate and universal and in no way to be cancelled, abrogated, altered, superseded or suspended. Since the way of implementation of one and the same Divine imperative by the Prophet (pbuh), as reported in *hadīth*, may vary at occasions to accord with the requirements of time, place, quantity (i.e., individual, group, community, nation, humankind) and capacity,[110] it is misjudged as abrogation of the Qur'anic imperative by *sunnah* of the Prophet (pbuh). *Hadīth* reporting it, is misjudged as source of law in itself. As to draw anything from *mutashābihāt* in the name of *sharī'ah* without ensuring their accordance with the *muhkamāt*, is to go astray from Allah's revealed guidance, to draw anything from *hadīth* without ensuring their accordance with the *muhkamāt* of the *Ahsan al-Hadīth* tantamount to going astray, too.

As Allah's *Amr* the Holy Qur'an has the status of 'Judgement, Authority or Commandment (*hukm*) and is in Arabic language. (Q. 13:37) As such it is the source of divine law, and *hadīth* reports its implementation reached to us through a chain of narrators. Law, and its implementation, cannot both be considered the ultimate source of law, for no two ultimates can ever exist at par with each other in the same capacity. It is necessary that one of them holds primacy. Let us see which of them should hold primacy:

Allah authenticates that it [the Qur'an] is free of doubt and contradiction. (Q. 2:2, Q. 32:2)

Allah authenticates that *He has taken upon Him the protection of its [the Qur'anic] text.* (Q. 15:9)

Allah authenticates that *its verses (muhkam and mutashābih both) resemble in colour i.e., fully consistent with each other, and repeat themselves in various ways to corroborate each other.* (Q. 39:23)

Allah authenticates that *untruth/disbelief cannot enter into it [i.e. the Qur'an], neither from the front nor from behind.* (Q. 41:42)

Allah authenticates that *'the Qur'an, whose verses are in Arabic, has been detailed for the knowledgeable ones.'* (Q. 41:3)

Allah authenticates that *'This Book has been made comprehensible and detailed with Knowledge.'* (Q. 7:52)

Allah verifies that *'It consists of verses, perfected and full of wisdom, which appropriately qualify each other.'* (Q. 11:1)

Allah certifies that *'Appropriate explanation of verses in the Qur'an has been given.'* (Q. 6:126)

Allah authenticates that 'He has left no deficiency in it.' (Q. 6:38, Q. 6:59; 18:1)

Hadīth and its compilations bear none of these divine authentications. How can the Qur'an be made subservient to *hadīth* and its anthologies? It is impossible that the doubt, conjecture, uncertainty, scepticism, dissension and sectarianism do not enter into the discourse, translation, exposition, commentary of the Qur'an, theology or jurisprudence where *hadīth* is made the basis, or the authority over the Qur'an.

The paradigms developed for interpreting the Qur'an have serious flaws in them because of not being based on the Qur'anic principles. They need serious revision and improvement. We need a paradigm that does not allow doubt, uncertainty, conjecture, opinion, speculation, contradiction or un-Qur'anic ontology, cosmology or terminology to enter into translation or exegesis of the Qur'an. Flaws in paradigms of translation and *tafseer* give rise to schism, dissension, conflict and sectarianism in theology. It is necessary that the faulty paradigms of the interpretation of the Qur'an and *hadīth*[111] are considered for replacement by such a paradigm which gives primary importance to making the objective (*maqṣad*) of the Address-Giver clear taking the Qur'an as Speech.

The Qur'an was revealed to the Prophet (pbuh). The Prophet (pbuh) was given the knowledge of the Book. He was given the knowledge of granting purification (*tazkiyah*).[112] He was given *hikmah*. Allah granted whatever knowledge He pleased, to His servant Haḍrat Muhammad (pbuh); yet no knowledge given to the Prophet (pbuh) was ever superadded to the Qur'an as parallel to *sharī'ah* or supposed to supersede the Qur'an. *Sharī'aht* is teaching (*qaul*), *tariqat* is action (*ámal*), *haqiqat* is knowledge (*'ilm*) and *ma'rifat* (gnosis) is a blessed reward. *Sharī'aht* is the beginning of the journey and *ma'rifat* is the ultimate end of *sharī'ah*. No knowledge is ever superadded to *sharī'ah.* Any kind of knowledge demonstrated by the Prophet (pbuh) was entirely rooted in the Qur'an. The Prophet (pbuh) had been given no personal knowledge that was not rooted in the Qur'an. Parallels never meet, even if drawn up to infinity. The Qur'an and the *hadīth* are never parallel. Nothing said, or done by way of elaboration or implementation by the Prophet (pbuh) or acted upon by him in his holy life was ever over and above the *muhkamāt* of the Qur'anic revelation. None can encompass or define the limits of knowledge granted to *the Rahma-tulill-'Ālamīm'* (pbuh) by *Rabb-ul-'Ālamīm*. One can say about it only what can be said on the authority of the *muhkamāt* of the Qur'an.

Hadīth as Precedent of the Implementation of a Divine Law

The implementation of the imperatives of '*Ahsan-al-Hadīth Kitāb*' as reported in *hadīth* was not based on the desire of the Prophet (pbuh). The Qur'an says:

> *The Prophet (pbuh) does not say anything of his own desire. He only says what is revealed to him (pbuh). (Q. 53:3-4)*

It was done by him (pbuh) with God-given knowledge and wisdom (*hikmah*). Since no implementation of a Qur'anic commandment (*hukm*), better than the one executed by the Prophet (pbuh) in a particular situation, could be thought of, so the implementation, if rightly reported in a *hadīth*, will be ultimate and final (*hatmi*) in that particular situation. However, it will not be universal (*dāimi*). *Hadīth* is precedent of the implementation of a divine law set by the Prophet (pbuh). Ascription of addition, deletion or modification in sharī'ah to *hadīth* only shows one's inability to understand the universal nature of divine law and particular nature of its implementation. Revelation is truth; and components of truth cannot ever contradict each other. The Qur'an as *Al-Haqq* is the Standard of Truth.

Variant Readings of the Qur'an

Another Attack, based on *Ḥadīth,* on the Absolute Authenticity of the Qur'an

The Muslims claim absolute authenticity of the Qur'anic text. They believe that once the revelation of the Qur'an was completed and collected in its final form in the last days of the lifetime of the Prophet (pbuh) and memorised by many of his companions (May God be pleased with them!). It was transmitted to the next generations both orally and in script form such that the verbal transmission superseded the written one, under the custodianship of the illustrious companions (rta) declared 'foremost of the race' (*as-sabiqūn al-awwalūn*) by the Qur'an. The Prophet (pbuh) witnessed some of these *'as-sabiqūn al-awwalūn'* in his holy life as 'the dwellers of paradise'. It is the oral transmission in the custodianship of these 'witnessed companions' (rta) that has actually safeguarded the Qur'anic text, which otherwise could have been read variously. The 'witnessed companions' (rta), after the Prophet (pbuh), became the centre of love and submission for those who wanted to liberate their lives from doubt and contradiction in their submission to Allah and the Prophet (pbuh). The 'Witnessed Companions-turned *shāhidīn*', in turn, witnessed from among their beloved followers whom they found in their footspteps and perfect in submission with love and sincerity. The chain of 'witnessed followers turned *shāhidīn*' continues and will keep on till the Last Day.

'Ashra-i-Mubashira were the ten of those illustrious companions (rta) who were witnessed at a single occasion. The first four caliphs (rta) of Islamic empire were from among these ten illustrious Companions (rta). To ascribe anything to these illustrious companions (rta) on the collection and compilation of the Qur'an, based on dubious historical reports found in *hadīth* anthologies, or to interpret archived data having questionable reliability to draw conclusions that conflict with the account given in the Qur'an itself, is to cast doubt on these illustrious Companions (rta) whose integrity and clearheaded-ness has been witnessed by the Prophet (pbuh) himself.

All written texts of the Qur'an during centuries of Islamic history are actually compiled and written based on the oral transmission witnessed by these *shahideen*. The oral tradition of transmission is the real mode of transmission of the Qur'anic text. It is this oral transmission, which was used later on by the Ummah to write the vowel sounds on the Qur'anic text for the benefit of non-'Arab readers.

Another unfortunate implication of giving primacy to *hadīth* over verses of the *Aḥsan al-Hadīth* Kitāb has made Muslim scholars helpless in believing the view of relative authenticity of the Qur'an, which is being promoted based on some vague and dubious historical reports found in some compilations of *hadīth*. By getting *Mushif* of the Qur'an printed in Variant Readings (Qalon, Warsh, Douri, Shuba, Jamahiriya, Roh and several others) and published by various Muslim countries under orientalists' influence, the Muslims are being made to believe that

"The Qur'an is an authentic text to the extent that it largely retains the material initially delivered by Muhammad [pbuh]. No evidence of any addition to the text exists and, in respect of the vast number of variant readings and missing passages that have been recorded, there does not appear to be anything actually affecting or contradicting the basic content of the book. In this respect, one can freely assume a relative authenticity of the text in the sense that it adequately retains the gist and content of what was originally there. On the contrary, there is no basis in history, facts or the evidences for the development of the text, to support the cherished hypothesis that the Qur'an has been preserved absolutely intact to the last dot and letter." [113]

The doctrine of the relative authenticity of the Qur'an, another attack on the absolute authenticity and completeness of the Qur'an, no less harmful or lethal than the doctrine of abrogation, is based on another *hadīth* that says:

"This Qur'an has been revealed in seven *ahruf*. You can read it in any way you find easy from among them".

(Narrated by al-Bukhaari, 2287; Muslim, 818)
https://hadeethenc.com/en/browse/hadith/10834
https://islamqa.info/en/answers/5142/the-revelation-of-the-quraan-in-seven-styles-ahruf-sing-harf

The attack on the absolute authenticity and completeness of the Qur'an has been launched, in the form of promoting 'the doctrine of the Variant Readings of the Qur'an.' The very meanings of the word '*ahruf*' are so baffling that "no one has ever been able to present a convincing interpretation of it. Imam Jalaluddin Al-Suyuti has cited no less than thirty-five different interpretations of this word, in his treatise *Al-Itqan fi 'Ulumil-Qur'an"*.[114] There is no authority in the Qur'an to endorse that Almighty Himself descended the Qur'an (Al-Kitāb) in various readings. The narratives and historical reports, to this effect, absolutely do not accord with the *muḥkamāt* of the Qur'an. The Qur'an is The Truth. What does not harmonise with it, is untrue (*bāṭil*). Untruth (*bāṭil*) inheres contradiction in it. What requires is, to dig it out with acumen based on the strength of faith. The verses of Surah Al-Qiyāmah:

إِنَّ عَلَيْنَا جَمْعَهُ وَقُرْآنَهُ ۚ فَإِذَا قَرَأْنَاهُ فَاتَّبِعْ قُرْآنَهُ

"Verily, upon Us is its collection and recital. So when We have recited it, follow this recital [of Ours]." (75:17-18)

explicitly contend that the whole of the Qur'an was recited on One Reading alone and the Almighty recited the Qur'an in a single reading. Verse 58 of Surah Ad-Dukhān 44

" فَإِنَّمَا يَسَّرْنَاهُ بِلِسَانِكَ لَعَلَّهُمْ يَتَذَكَّرُونَ *And indeed, We have eased the Qur'an in your tongue that they might be reminded."*

witnesses that the Qur'an was revealed in the language the Prophet (pbuh) used to speak.

As to the nature of difference among these variant readings, Mufti Taqi Usmani, in the Introduction of *Ma'arif ul Qur'an* classifies the difference in Variant Readings of the Qur'an as compared to the Qirā'at ul 'Aamma/The Universal Reading (popularly known as Qira't-i-Ḥafṣ) into following seven types:

1. **"The difference in nouns:** This includes the difference concerning singular, dual, plural, as well as, masculine and feminine...[115]

2. **The difference in verbs:** That there be past in one reading, the present in another and the imperative in yet another....

3. **The difference in the placement of diacritical marks:** That which shows variance in *I'rāb,* which reflects variance in grammatical mode of a word and is demonstrated through desinential inflections, such as *asara, fataḥa, ḍammah...*

4. **The difference caused by addition and deletion of words:** That there be some words missing in one reading, while it has been added on in another;…

5. **The difference of precedence and succession:** That there is a word which precedes in one reading, while it succeeds in the other…

6. **The difference caused by transposition:** This happens when a word found in one reading is replaced by another word in another reading…

7. **The difference caused by manners of reading:** It includes variations in *tafkīm* (velarisation, making sound heavy), *tarqīq* (making a letter sound soft), *imālah* (inclination, bending the sound of a short vowel), *madd* (prolongation), *qasr* (to shorten), *hamz: hamzatation* (providing a letter with *hamzah*), *izhār* (clear pronunciation) and *idgām* (assimilation). It means that, by doing these, the actual word does not change…

Anyhow, many readings were revealed [???][116] incorporating these seven types of different renderings. This difference between them really made no difference in meaning. The latitude so given, was aimed at making recitation easy."[117]

Dr Shehzad Saleem, is a renowned Islamic scholar, He is a Research Fellow of Al-Mawrid. He holds a PhD on the History of the Qur'an from the University of Wales, UK. Al-Mawrid has published his PhD research by the title 'History of the Quran: A Critical Study', in 2019. It is a highly valuable research on this subject, the outcome of eighteen years of a dedicated effort to dig out the truth on the matter. It examines, with great acumen, all the traditional narratives of the collection and compilation history of the Qur'an that challenge the absolute authenticity of the Qur'anic text. Dr. Shehzad Saleem, tells us why in his opinion none of these variant readings can be accepted in any way. He says:

"The whole of the Muslim Ummah today, except for a few North African countries, is united in reading the Qur'an in just one way. .. These areas of the African continent did not even fall into the mainstream of the Muslim Ummah, conquered by the Companions of the Prophet (sws) during the time of the Rightly Guided Caliphate. The only complete reading of the Qur'an which is in vogue in all the mainstream areas from the time of the Prophet (sws) is the Qirā'at al-'Aammah (the Universal Reading) – the very reading read out to the Prophet (sws) once the revelation of the Qur'an had been completed. It was this very reading which existed among the companions of the Prophet (sws).

The reading of Abu Bakr, 'Umar, 'Uthman and Zayd Ibn Thabit and that of all the Muhajirun and the Ansar was one. They would read the Qur'an according to the Qirā'at al-'Aammah. This is the same reading which was read out to the Prophet (sws) in the year of his death by Gabriel. Zayd Ibn Thabit was also present in this reading [called] the *'Ardah-i-Akhirah'*. It was in this very reading that he [pbuh] taught the Qur'an to people till his death. (Zarkashi, Burhan, 2nd ed., vol. 1, [Beirut: Daru'l-Fikr, 1980] p. 237) This reading is generally known today as the Reading of Hafs (Qirā'at-i-Hafs). However, its correct name is the Qirā'at al-'Aammah.

If the variant readings, which actually change the meaning of a verse, are incorporated in the text and reflected upon in light of the coherence of the Divine Book and its sublime language, it

becomes evident that the text of the Qur'an totally rejects them on grounds contained within the text."
(http://www.al-mawrid.org/index.php/articles/view/collection-and-transmission-of-the-quran-part-1-3, placed by Dr. Shehzad Saleem on February 01, 2020. Accessed: March 17, 2020.)

Earlier Dr. Shehzad Saleem sums up his deliberations about the whole Qur'anic scheme of its own collection and compilation in the following words:

"1. The Qur'an was given piecemeal to the Prophet (sws) according to the circumstances which arose and which required divine guidance.

2. [I] Its chronological revelation is of no significance. [II] It was arranged in a new sequence by the Almighty. [III] Once its initial revelation was over, the Almighty through Archangel Gabriel read it out to the Prophet (sws) a second time. [IV] In this second recital, temporary [provisional] directives were revised or deleted permanently.[118]

3. This final arrangement and recital was done once the Qur'an had been collected and compiled in the form of a book. It was read out to the Prophet (sws) in a manner that it was rendered absolutely secure from any loss or doubt.

4. After this final recital, the Prophet (sws) was bound by the Almighty to follow this recital only. He was not allowed to read it according to the previous recital.

5. In this final recital, if any directive needed further explanation, it was furnished by the Almighty Himself at this time of compilation."
(http://www.al-mawrid.org/index.php/articles/view/collection-and-transmission-of-the-quran-part-1-3, placed by Dr. Shehzad Saleem on February 01, 2020. Accessed: March 17, 2020.)

We have seen above that according to Mufti Taqi Usmani and his honourable father (Late) Maulana Mufti Muhammad Shafi', these variant readings differ from the Universal Reading of the Qur'an (known as *Qirā'at-i-Hafṣ*) in seven ways. How strange it is that they say:

"This difference between them really made no difference in meaning."

They further say:

"The latitude so given, was aimed at making recitation easy."

Whereas Allah says in the Qur'an that

"فَإِنَّمَا يَسَّرْنَاهُ بِلِسَانِكَ لَعَلَّهُمْ يَتَذَكَّرُونَ ﴿ *And indeed, We have eased the Qur'an in your tongue that they might be reminded." (Q. 44:58)*

A table contrasting the text in Variant Readings——of *Warsh, Douri, Qalon, and Shuba, Roḥ* and *Jamahiriya* ——at around two hundred fifty places with the Qur'anic Text as given in The Universal Reading (Qirā'at al-'Aammah) has been given below.[119] (There are several other versions of the variant readings of the Qur'an published from various Muslim countries or under preparation in these countries.)[120] These places represent just a small number of variations made in the Qur'anic Text. If all places in all the variant readings published so far, which differ with the Qirā'at al-'Aammah, are accumulated, they will make it several times more than this. These instances confirm that these variant readings incorporate all the seven types of distortions (*teḥrīf*) i.e., a singular noun instead of a dual or a plural noun or the vice versa; difference in gender i.e., feminine in place of the masculine or the vice versa; change in the form of the verb i.e., a verb in past tense changed in to present or the imperative form; distortion with reference to *i'rāb* and grammatical mode of a word; difference in the placement of diacritical marks; addition or deletion of a word in the Revealed Holy Qur'anic Text; changes, which affect the imperatives of *sharī'ah* contained in the *mūḥkamāt*, and such other distortions as stated above.

Institutions working on the unholy agenda of making the most authentic, revealed Islamic document controversial, are persistently working on the project to prepare as many such versions as possible.

Is this not a very unfortunate implication of the un-Qur'anic view of the status of *Ḥadīth* that the absolute authenticity of the Qur'anic Text, the most authentic document of Islam, has been put at stake?

Let us see the table given below:

Sr. No.	UNIVERSAL NARRATION Qirā'at al-'Aammah Known as Qirā'at-i-Hafṣ VARIANT READINGS Qirā'at-i-Warsh, Douri, Qalon, Shuba, Roḥ, Jamahiriya
1.	صِرَاطَ ٱلَّذِينَ أَنْعَمْتَ عَلَيْهِمْ غَيْرِ ٱلْمَغْضُوبِ عَلَيْهِمْ وَلَا ٱلضَّالِّينَ (الفاتحہ1 : 7) *Al-Qur'an (Qirā'at al-'Aammah)* صِرَاطَ الَّذِينَ أَنْعَمْتَ عَلَيْهُمْ غَيْرِ الْمَغْضُوبِ عَلَيْهُمْ وَلاَ الضَّالِّينَ *(Roḥ)*
2.	مَالِكِ يَوْمِ الدِّينِ *Al-Qur'an (Qirā'at al-'Aammah)*، (الفاتحہ1 : 03) مَلِكِ يَوْمِ الدِّينِ *(Warsh)*، *(Douri)*، *(Qalon)*،
3.	إِنَّ الَّذِينَ كَفَرُوا سَوَاءٌ عَلَيْهِمْ أَ أَنْذَرْتَهُمْ (البقرہ2: 6) *Al-Qur'an (Qirā'at al-'Aammah)* إِنَّ الَّذِينَ كَفَرُوا سَوَاءٌ عَلَيْهُمْ أَ أَنْذَرْتَهُمْ --- *(Roḥ)*
4.	يُخَادِعُونَ اللَّهَ وَالَّذِينَ آمَنُوا وَمَا يَخْدَعُونَ إِلاَّ أَنفُسَهُمْ وَمَا يَشْعُرُونَ *Al-Qur'an (Qirā'at al-'Aammah)*، (البقرہ2: 09)

	يُخَادِعُونَ اللَّهَ وَالَّذِينَ آمَنُوا **وَمَايُخْدِعُونَ** إِلاَّ أَنْفُسَهُمْ --- (Douri)، (Qalon) (Jamahiriya)
5.	فِى قُلُوبِهِم مَّرَضٌ فَزَادَهُمُ اللَّهُ مَرَضًا ۖ وَلَهُمْ عَذَابٌ أَلِيمٌ بِمَا كَانُوا۟ **يَكْذِبُونَ** ﴿ (البقره2: 10) *Al-Qur'an (Qirā'at al-'Aammah)* --- وَلَهُمْ عَذَابٌ أَلِيمٌ بِمَا كَانُوا **يُكَذِّبُونَ** ﴿ *(Roḥ)، (Jamahiriya)، (Douri)، (Warsh)، (Qalon)*
6.	أَلَآ إِنَّهُمْ هُمُ الْمُفْسِدُونَ وَلَكِن لاَّ **يَشْعُرُونَ** ﴿ (البقره2: 12) *Al-Qur'an (Qirā'at al-'Aammah)* أَلَا إِنَّهُمْ هُمُ الْمُفْسِدُونَ وَلَكِنْ لاَ **يَشْعُرُونَ** ﴿ *(Qalon)، (Roḥ)، (Jamahiriya)*
7.	---وَإِذَا أَظْلَمَ **عَلَيْهِمْ**--- ﴿ (البقره2: 20) *Al-Qur'an (Qirā'at al-'Aammah)* ---وَإِذَا أَظْلَمَ **عَلَيْهُمْ**--- ﴿ *(Roḥ)*
8.	ثُمَّ يُحْيِيكُمْ ثُمَّ إِلَيْهِ **تُرْجَعُونَ** ﴿ (البقره2: 28) *Al-Qur'an (Qirā'at al-'Aammah)* ثُمَّ يُحْيِيكُمْ ثُمَّ إِلَيْهِ **تَرْجِعُونَ** ﴿ *(Roḥ)*
9.	فَمَنْ تَبِعَ هُدَايَ **فَلاَ خَوْفٌ عَلَيْهِمْ**--- ﴿ (البقره2: 38) *Al-Qur'an (Qirā'at al-'Aammah)* فَمَنْ تَبِعَ هُدَايَ **فَلاَ خَوْفَ عَلَيْهُمْ**--- ﴿ *(Roḥ)*
10.	--- وَلاَ تَشْتَرُوا بِآيَاتِي ثَمَنًا قَلِيلًا وَإِيَّايَ **فَاتَّقُونِ** ﴿ (البقره2: 40) *Al-Qur'an (Qirā'at al-'Aammah)* --- وَلاَ تَشْتَرُوا بِآيَاتِي ثَمَنًا قَلِيلًا وَإِيَّايَ **فَاتَّقُونِ** ے *(Roḥ)*
11.	--- وَلاَ **يُقْبَلُ** مِنْهَا شَفَاعَةٌ---(البقره2: 48) *Al-Qur'an (Qirā'at al-'Aammah)* --- وَلاَ **تُقْبَلُ** مِنْهَا شَفَاعَة--- (Douri)، *(Roḥ)*
12.	وَإِذْ **وَاعَدْنَا** مُوسَى أَرْبَعِينَ لَيْلَة--- ﴿ (البقره2: 48)

	Al-Qur'an (Qirā'at al-'Aammah) وَإِذْ وَاعَدْنَا مُوسَى أَرْبَعِينَ لَيْلَة--- (Douri) ، (Roḥ)
13.	--- وَقُولُوا حِطَّةٌ نَغْفِرْ لَكُمْ خَطَايَاكُمْ --- (البقره2: 58) *Al-Qur'an (Qirā'at al-'Aammah)* --- وَقُولُوا حِطَّةٌ يُغْفَرْ لَكُمْ خَطَايَاكُمْ --- (Warsh) ، (Qalon) ، (Jamahiriya)
14.	--- سَأَلْتُمْ وَضُرِبَتْ عَلَيْهِمُ الذِّلَّةُ وَالْمَسْكَنَةُ وَبَاءُوا بِغَضَبٍ مِنَ اللَّهِ--- (البقره2: 61) *Al-Qur'an (Qirā'at al-'Aammah)* --- سَأَلْتُمْ وَضُرِبَتْ عَلَيْهِمُ الذِّلَّةُ وَالْمَسْكَنَةُ وَبَاءُوا بِغَضَبٍ مِنَ اللَّهِ--- (Roḥ)
15.	--- وَلاَ خَوْفٌ عَلَيْهِمْ وَلاَ هُمْ يَحْزَنُونَ (البقره2: 62) *Al-Qur'an (Qirā'at al-'Aammah)* --- وَلاَ خَوْفٌ عَلَيْهُمْ وَلاَ هُمْ يَحْزَنُونَ (Roḥ)
16.	--- وَقُولُوا لِلنَّاسِ حُسْنًا --- (البقره2: 83) *Al-Qur'an (Qirā'at al-'Aammah)* --- وَقُولُوا لِلنَّاسِ حَسْنًا --- (Roḥ)
17.	--- تَقْتُلُونَ أَنفُسَكُمْ وَتُخْرِجُونَ فَرِيقًا مِنكُمْ مِنْ دِيَارِهِمْ تَظَاهَرُونَ عَلَيْهِمْ بِالْإِثْمِ وَالْعُدْوَانِ--- وَمَا اللَّهُ بِغَافِلٍ عَمَّا تَعْمَلُونَ (البقره2: 85) *Al-Qur'an (Qirā'at al-'Aammah)* --- تَقْتُلُونَ أَنفُسَكُمْ وَتُخْرِجُونَ فَرِيقًا مِّنكُمْ مِنْ دِيَارِهِمْ تَظَاهَرُونَ عَلَيْهِمْ بِالْإِثْمِ وَالْعُدْوَانِ--- وَمَا اللَّهُ بِغَافِلٍ عَمَّا يَعْمَلُونَ (Roḥ) (Warsh) (Shuba) --- تَظَاهَرُونَ عَلَيْهِمْ --- وَمَا اللَّهُ بِغَافِلٍ عَمَّا يَعْمَلُونَ (Qalon) ، (Jamahiriya) تَظَاهَرُونَ عَلَيْهِمْ --- وَمَا اللَّهُ بِغَافِلٍ عَمَّا تَعْمَلُونَ (Douri)
18.	--- أَنفُسَهُمْ أَنْ يَكْفُرُوا بِمَا أَنزَلَ اللَّهُ بَغْيًا أَنْ يُنَزِّلَ اللَّهُ مِنْ فَضْلِهِ عَلَى مَنْ يَشَاءُ مِنْ عِبَادِهِ--- (البقره2: 90) *Al-Qur'an (Qirā'at al-'Aammah)* --- أَنفُسَهُمْ أَنْ يَكْفُرُوا بِمَا أَنزَلَ اللَّهُ بَغْيًا أَنْ يُنَزِّلَ اللَّهُ مِنْ فَضْلِهِ عَلَى مَنْ يَشَاءُ مِنْ عِبَادِهِ --- (Douri) ، (Shuba) ، (Warsh) ، (Roḥ) ، (Qalon)

19.	--- ثُمَّ اﹾ تَّخَذْتُمُ الْعِجْلَ مِنْ بَعْدِهِ---﴾ (البقرة2: 92) *Al-Qur'an (Qirā'at al-'Aammah)* --- ثُمَّ اﹾ تَّخَذْتُمُ الْعِجْلَ مِنْ بَعْدِهِ---﴾ (Roḥ)، (Jamahiriya)
20.	--- وَأُشْرِبُوا فِي قُلُوبِهِمُ الْعِجْلَ بِكُفْرِهِمْ---﴾ *Al-Qur'an (Qirā'at al-'Aammah)* (93 :2) --- وَأُشْرِبُوا فِي قُلُوبِهِمِ الْعِجْلَ بِكُفْرِهِمْ---﴾ (Douri)، (Roḥ)
21.	وَلَنْ يَتَمَنَّوْهُ أَبَدًا بِمَا قَدَّ مَتْ أَيْدِيهِمْ وَاللَّهُ عَلِيمٌ بِالظَّالِمِينَ﴾ *Al-Qur'an (Qirā'at al-'Aammah)* (95 :2) وَلَنْ يَتَمَنَّوْهُ أَبَدًا بِمَا قَدَّ مَتْ أَيْدِيهُمْ وَاللَّهُ عَلِيمٌ بِالظَّالِمِينَ﴾ (Roḥ)،
22.	--- وَاللَّهُ بَصِيرٌ بِمَا يَعْمَلُونَ﴾ (البقرة2: 96) *Al-Qur'an (Qirā'at al-'Aammah)* --- وَاللَّهُ بَصِيرٌ بِمَا تَعْمَلُونَ﴾ (Roḥ)
23.	--- أَنْ يُنَزَّلَ عَلَيْكُمْ مِنْ خَيْرٍ مِنْ رَبِّكُمْ---﴾ (البقرة2: 105) *Al-Qur'an (Qirā'at al-'Aammah)* --- أَنْ يُنَزِّلَ عَلَيْكُمْ مِنْ خَيْرٍ مِنْ رَبِّكُمْ---﴾ (Douri)، (Roḥ)،
24.	--- فَلَهُ وَ أَجْرُهُ و عِنْدَ رَبِّهِ وَلَا خَوْفٌ عَلَيْهِمْ وَلَا هُمْ يَحْزَنُونَ﴾ *Al-Qur'an (Qirā'at al-'Aammah)* (112 :2) --- فَلَهُ وَ أَجْرُهُ و عِنْدَ رَبِّهِ وَلَا خَوْفَ عَلَيْهُمْ وَلَا هُمْ يَحْزَنُونَ﴾ (Roḥ)،
25.	إِنَّا أَرْسَلْنَاكَ بِالْحَقِّ بَشِيرًا وَنَذِيرًا وَلَا تُسْئَلُ عَنْ أَصْحَابِ الْجَحِيمِ﴾ *Al-Qur'an (Qirā'at al-'Aammah)* (119 :2) إِنَّآ أَرْسَلْنَاكَ بِالْحَقِّ بَشِيرًا وَنَذِيرًا وَلَا تُسْئَلُ عَنْ أَصْحَابِ ٱلْجَحِيمِ﴾ (Mushaf Madina) *Referensi: https://www.bayan.id/quran/2-119/* إِنَّا أَرْسَلْنَاكَ بِالْحَقِّ بَشِيرًا وَنَذِيرًا وَلَا تَسْئَلْ عَنْ أَصْحَابِ الْجَحِيمِ﴾ (Warsh)، (Qalon) (Roḥ)، (Jamahiriya)
26.	--- قَالَ وَمِنْ ذُرِّيَّتِي قَالَ لَا يَنَالُ عَهْدِى الظَّالِمِينَ﴾ (البقرة2: 124) *Al-Qur'an (Qirā'at al-'Aammah)* --- قَالَ وَمِنْ ذُرِّيَّتِي قَالَ لَا يَنَالُ عَهْدِى الظَّالِمِينَ﴾ (Douri)، (Qalon)،

	(Jamahiriya) ، (Shuba) ، (Warsh) ، (Roḥ)
27.	‏أَن طَهِّرَا بَيْتِيَ لِلطَّائِفِينَ وَالْعَاكِفِينَ وَالرُّكَّعِ السُّجُودِ‏ (البقره2: 125) --- Al-Qur’an (Qirā’at al-’Aammah) ‏أَن طَهِّرَا بَيْتِيَ لِلطَّائِفِينَ وَالْعَاكِفِينَ وَالرُّكَّعِ السُّجُودِ‏ --- (Douri) ، (Shuba) ، (Roḥ)
28.	‏رَبَّنَا وَاجْعَلْنَا مُسْلِمَيْنِ لَكَ وَمِن ذُرِّيَّتِنَا أُمَّةً مُسْلِمَةً لَكَ وَأَرِنَا مَنَاسِكَنَا وَتُبْ عَلَيْنَا إِنَّكَ أَنتَ التَّوَّابُ الرَّحِيمُ‏ (البقره2: 128) Al-Qur’an (Qirā’at al-’Aammah) ‏رَبَّنَا وَاجْعَلْنَا مُسْلِمَيْنِ لَكَ وَمِن ذُرِّيَّتِنَا أُمَّةً مُسْلِمَةً لَكَ وَأَرِنَا مَنَاسِكَنَا وَتُبْ عَلَيْنَا إِنَّكَ أَنتَ التَّوَّابُ الرَّحِيمُ‏ (Roḥ)
29.	‏رَبَّنَا وَابْعَثْ فِيهِمْ رَسُولًا مِنْهُمْ يَتْلُو عَلَيْهِمْ آيَاتِكَ وَيُعَلِّمُهُمُ الْكِتَابَ وَالْحِكْمَةَ وَيُزَكِّيهِمْ إِنَّكَ أَنتَ الْعَزِيزُ الْحَكِيمُ‏ (البقره 2: 129) Al-Qur’an (Qirā’at al-’Aammah) ‏رَبَّنَا وَابْعَثْ فِيهُمْ رَسُولًا مِنْهُمْ يَتْلُو عَلَيْهِمْ آيَاتِكَ وَيُعَلِّمُهُمُ الْكِتَابَ وَالْحِكْمَةَ وَيُزَكِّيهِمْ إِنَّكَ أَنتَ الْعَزِيزُ الْحَكِيمُ‏ (Roḥ)
30.	‏أَمْ تَقُولُونَ إِنَّ إِبْرَاهِيمَ وَإِسْمَاعِيلَ وَإِسْحَاقَ وَيَعْقُوبَ وَالْأَسْبَاطَ كَانُوا هُوداً أَوْ نَصَارَى ---‏ (البقره2: 140)، Al-Qur’an (Qirā’at al-’Aammah) ‏أَمْ يَقُولُونَ إِنَّ إِبْرَاهِيمَ وَ إِسْمَاعِيلَ وَ إِسْحَاقَ وَيَعْقُوبَ ---‏ (Jamahiriya) ، (Roḥ) ، (Shuba) ، (Qalon) ، (Warsh) ، (Douri)
31.	‏سَيَقُولُ السُّفَهَاءُ مِنَ النَّاسِ مَا وَلَّاهُمْ عَنْ قِبْلَتِهِمُ الَّتِي كَانُوا عَلَيْهَا - -‏ (البقره2: 142)، Al-Qur’an (Qirā’at al-’Aammah) ‏سَيَقُولُ السُّفَهَاءُ مِنَ النَّاسِ مَا وَلَّاهُمْ عَنْ قِبْلَتِهِمُ الَّتِي كَانُوا عَلَيْهَا‏ - (Douri)، (Roḥ)
32.	‏--- وَإِنَّ الَّذِينَ أُوتُوا الْكِتَابَ لَيَعْلَمُونَ أَنَّهُ الْحَقُّ مِن رَّبِّهِمْ وَمَا اللَّهُ بِغَافِلٍ عَمَّا يَعْمَلُونَ‏ (البقره2: 144) Al-Qur’an (Qirā’at al-’Aammah) ‏--- وَإِنَّ الَّذِينَ أُوتُوا الْكِتَابَ لَيَعْلَمُونَ أَنَّهُ الْحَقُّ مِن رَّبِّهِمْ وَمَا اللَّهُ بِغَافِلٍ عَمَّا تَعْمَلُونَ‏ (Roḥ)
33.	‏أُولَٰئِكَ عَلَيْهِمْ صَلَوَاتٌ مِّن رَّبِّهِمْ وَرَحْمَةٌ وَأُولَٰئِكَ هُمُ الْمُهْتَدُونَ‏ (البقره2: 157) Al-Qur’an (Qirā’at al-’Aammah)

	أُولَٰئِكَ عَلَيْهِمْ صَلَوَٰتٌ مِنْ رَبِّهِمْ وَ رَحْمَةٌ وَ أُولَٰئِكَ هُمُ الْمُهْتَدُونَ 🡑 (*Roḥ*)
34.	--- وَمَنْ تَطَوَّعَ خَيْرًا فَإِنَّ اللَّهَ شَاكِرٌ عَلِيمٌ 🡑 (البقره2: 158) *Al-Qur'an (Qirā'at al-'Aammah)* --- وَمَنْ يَطَّوَّعْ خَيْرًا فَإِنَّ اللَّهَ شَاكِرٌ عَلِيمٌ 🡑 (*Roḥ*)
35.	--- فَأُولَٰئِكَ أَتُوبُ عَلَيْهِمْ وَأَنَا التَّوَّابُ الرَّحِيمُ🡑 (البقره2: 160) *Al-Qur'an (Qirā'at al-'Aammah)* --- فَأُولَٰئِكَ أَتُوبُ عَلَيْهُمْ وَأَنَا التَّوَّابُ الرَّحِيمُ🡑 (*Roḥ*)
36.	ـوَلَوْ يَرَى الَّذِينَ ظَلَمُوا إِذْ يَرَوْنَ الْعَذَابَ أَنَّ الْقُوَّةَ لِلَّهِ جَمِيعًا وَ أَنَّ اللَّهَ شَدِيدُ الْعَذَابِ 🡑 (البقره 2: 165) *Al-Qur'an (Qirā'at al-'Aammah)* ـوَلَوْ تَرَى الَّذِينَ ظَلَمُوا إِذْ يَرَوْنَ الْعَذَابَ أَنَّ الْقُوَّةَ لِلَّهِ جَمِيعًا وَ أَنَّ اللَّهَ شَدِيدُ الْعَذَابِ 🡑 (*Roḥ*)، (*Qalon*)، (*Warsh*)
37.	--- وَرَأَوُا الْعَذَابَ وَتَقَطَّعَتْ بِهِمُ الْأَسْبَابُ🡑 (البقره 2: 166) *Al-Qur'an (Qirā'at al-'Aammah)* --- وَرَأَوُا الْعَذَابَ وَتَقَطَّعَتْ بِهِمِ الْأَسْبَابُ🡑 (*Douri*)، (*Roḥ*)
38.	--- كَذَٰلِكَ يُرِيهِمُ اللَّهُ أَعْمَالَهُمْ حَسَرَاتٍ عَلَيْهِمْصلى وَمَا هُم بِخَارِجِينَ مِنَ النَّارِ🡑 (البقره 2: 167) *Al-Qur'an (Qirā'at al-'Aammah)* --- كَذَٰلِكَ يُرِيهُمُ اللَّهُ أَعْمَالَهُمْ حَسَرَاتٍ عَلَيْهُمْصلى وَمَا هُمْ بِخَارِجِينَ مِنَ النَّارِ🡑 (*Roḥ*)
39.	--- وَلَا يُكَلِّمُهُمُ اللَّهُ يَوْمَ الْقِيَامَةِ وَلَا يُزَكِّيهِمْ وَلَهُمْ عَذَابٌ أَلِيمٌ 🡑 (البقره 2: 174) *Al-Qur'an (Qirā'at al-'Aammah)* --- وَلَا يُكَلِّمُهُمُ اللَّهُ يَوْمَ الْقِيَامَةِ وَلَا يُزَكِّيهُمْ وَلَهُمْ عَذَابٌ أَلِيمٌ 🡑 (*Roḥ*)
40.	لَيْسَ الْبِرَّ أَنْ تُوَلُّوا وُجُوهَكُمْ--- 🡑 (البقره2: 177) *Al-Qur'an (Qirā'at al-'Aammah)* لَيْسَ الْبِرُّ أَنْ تُوَلُّوا وُجُوهَكُمْ--- 🡑 (البقره2: 177) (*Shuba*)، (*Warsh*)، (*Roḥ*)، (*Qalon*)، (*Douri*)
41.	--- يُرِيدُ اللَّهُ بِكُمُ الْيُسْرَ وَلَا يُرِيدُ بِكُمُ الْعُسْرَ وَلِتُكْمِلُوا الْعِدَّةَ--- 🡑

	Al-Qur'an (Qirā'at al-'Aammah) (البقره2: 185) ---يُرِيدُ اللَّهُ بِكُمُ الْيُسْرَ وَلاَ يُرِيدُ بِكُمُ الْعُسْرَ وَلِتُكَمِّلُوا الْعِدَّةَ--- *(Roḥ)، (Shuba)*
42.	--وَعَلَى الَّذِينَ يُطِيقُونَهُ فِدْيَةٌ طَعَامُ مِسْكِينٍ --- (البقره2: 184) *Al-Qur'an (Qirā'at al-'Aammah)* --وَعَلَى الَّذِينَ يُطِيقُونَهُ فِدْيَةٌ طَعَامِ مَسَاكِينَ --- *(Warsh)، (Qalon)*
43.	أَلْحَجُّ أَشْهُرٌ مَعْلُومَاتٌ فَمَن فَرَضَ فِيهِنَّ الْحَجَّ فَلاَ رَفَثَ وَلاَ فُسُوقَ وَلاَ جِدَالَ فِي الْحَجِّ --- (البقره2: 197) *Al-Qur'an (Qirā'at al-'Aammah)* أَلْحَجُّ أَشْهُرٌ مَعْلُومَاتٌ فَمَن فَرَضَ فِيهِنَّ الْحَجَّ فَلاَ رَفَثٌ وَلاَ فُسُوقٌ وَلاَ جِدَالَ فِي الْحَجِّ --- *(Roḥ)* أَلْحَجُّ أَشْهُرٌ مَعْلُومَاتٌ فَمَن فَرَضَ فِيهِنَّ الْحَجَّ فَلاَ رَفَثٌ وَلاَ فُسُوقٌ وَلاَ جِدَالَ فِي الْحَجِّ --- *(Douri)*
44.	--- وَإِلَى اللَّهِ تُرْجَعُ الأُمُورُ (البقره2: 210) *Al-Qur'an (Qirā'at al-'Aammah)* --- وَإِلَى اللَّهِ تَرْجِعُ الأُمُورُ *(Roḥ)*
45.	يَسْأَلُونَكَ عَنِ الْخَمْرِ وَالْمَيْسِرِ قُلْ فِيهِمَا إِثْمٌ كَبِيرٌ وَمَنَافِعُ لِلنَّاسِ --- (البقره2: 219) *Al-Qur'an (Qirā'at al-'Aammah)* يَسْأَلُونَكَ عَنِ الْخَمْرِ وَالْمَيْسِرِ قُلْ فِيهِمَا إِثْمٌ كَبِيرٌ وَمَنَافِعُ لِلنَّاسِ --- *(Roḥ)*
46.	--- وَلَهُنَّ مِثْلُ الَّذِي عَلَيْهِنَّ بِالْمَعْرُوفِ وَلِلرِّجَالِ عَلَيْهِنَّ دَرَجَةٌ وَاللَّهُ عَزِيزٌ حَكِيمٌ (البقره2: 228) *Al-Qur'an (Qirā'at al-'Aammah)* --- وَلَهُنَّ مِثْلُ الَّذِي عَلَيْهِنَّ بِالْمَعْرُوفِ وَلِلرِّجَالِ عَلَيْهِنَّ دَرَجَةٌ وَاللَّهُ عَزِيزٌ حَكِيمٌ *(Roḥ)*
47.	--وَلاَ يَحِلُّ لَكُمْ أَن تَأْخُذُوا مِمَّا آتَيْتُمُوهُنَّ شَيْئاً إِلاَّ أَن يَخَافَا أَلاَّ يُقِيمَا حُدُودَ اللَّهِ فَإِنْ خِفْتُمْ أَلاَّ يُقِيمَا حُدُودَ اللَّهِ فَلاَ جُنَاحَ عَلَيْهِمَا فِيمَا افْتَدَتْ بِهِ --- (البقره2: 228) *Al-Qur'an (Qirā'at al-'Aammah)* --وَلاَ يَحِلُّ لَكُمْ أَن تَأْخُذُوا مِمَّا آتَيْتُمُوهُنَّ شَيْئاً إِلاَّ أَن يَخَافَا أَلاَّ يُقِيمَا حُدُودَ اللَّهِ فَإِنْ خِفْتُمْ أَلاَّ يُقِيمَا حُدُودَ اللَّهِ فَلاَ جُنَاحَ عَلَيْهِمَا فِيمَا افْتَدَتْ بِهِ --- *(Roḥ)*
48.	---فَإِن طَلَّقَهَا فَلاَ جُنَاحَ عَلَيْهِمَا أَن يَتَرَاجَعَا إِنْ ظَنَّا أَن يُقِيمَا حُدُودَ اللَّهِ --- (البقره2:

(230)	*Al-Qur'an (Qirā'at al-'Aammah)*
	...فَإِنْ طَلَّقَهَا فَلاَ جُنَاحَ **عَلَيْهُمَا** أَنْ يَتَرَاجَعَا إِنْ ظَنَّا أَنْ يُقِيمَا حُدُودَ اللهِ ⌂... *(Roḥ)*
49.	... لاَ تُكَلَّفُ نَفْسٌ إِلاَّ وُسْعَهَا **لاَ تُضَارَّ** وَالِدَةٌ بِوَلَدِهَا وَلاَ مَوْلُودٌ لَهُ بِوَلَدِهِ... **وَتَشَاوُرٍ** فَلاَ جُنَاحَ **عَلَيْهِمَا**... ⌂ (البقره 2: 233) *Al-Qur'an (Qirā'at al-'Aammah)* ... لاَ تُكَلَّفُ نَفْسٌ إِلاَّ وُسْعَهَا **لاَ تُضَارُّ** وَالِدَةٌ بِوَلَدِهَا وَلاَ مَوْلُودٌ لَهُ بِوَلَدِهِ...**وَتَشَاوُرٍ** فَلاَ جُنَاحَ **عَلَيْهُمَا**... ⌂ *(Douri)* ، *(Roḥ)*
50.	... وَمَتِّعُوهُنَّ عَلَى الْمُوسِعِ **قَدَرُهُ** وَعَلَى الْمُقْتِرِ **قَدَرُهُ** مَتَاعاً بِالْمَعْرُوفِ حَقّاً عَلَى الْمُحْسِنِينَ⌂ (البقره 2: 236) *Al-Qur'an (Qirā'at al-'Aammah)* ... وَمَتِّعُوهُنَّ عَلَى الْمُوسِعِ **قَدْرُهُ** وَعَلَى الْمُقْتِرِ **قَدْرُهُ** مَتَاعاً بِالْمَعْرُوفِ حَقّاً عَلَى الْمُحْسِنِينَ⌂ *(Warsh)* ، *(Douri)* ، *(Shuba)* ، *(Qalon)* ، *(Jamahiriya)* ، *(Roḥ)*
51.	وَالَّذِينَ يُتَوَفَّوْنَ مِنْكُمْ وَيَذَرُونَ أَزْوَاجاً **وَصِيَّةً** لِأَزْوَاجِهِم مَتَاعاً إِلَى الْحَوْلِ غَيْرَ إِخْرَاجٍ--- ⌂ (البقره 2: 240) *Al-Qur'an (Qirā'at al-'Aammah)* وَالَّذِينَ يُتَوَفَّوْنَ مِنْكُمْ وَيَذَرُونَ أَزْوَاجاً **وَصِيَّةٌ** لِأَزْوَاجِهِم مَتَاعاً إِلَى الْحَوْلِ غَيْرَ إِخْرَاجٍ--- ⌂ *(Warsh)* *(Qalon)* ، *(Jamahiriya)* ، *(Roḥ)*
52.	مَنْ ذَا الَّذِي يُقْرِضُ اللهَ قَرْضاً حَسَناً **فَيُضَاعِفَهُ** لَهُ وَ أَضْعَافاً كَثِيرَةً وَاللهُ يَقْبِضُ وَيَبْصُطُ وَإِلَيْهِ **تُرْجَعُونَ**⌂ (البقره 2: 245) *Al-Qur'an (Qirā'at al-'Aammah)* مَنْ ذَا الَّذِي يُقْرِضُ اللهَ قَرْضاً حَسَناً **فَيُضَاعِفَهُ** لَهُ وَ أَضْعَافاً كَثِيرَةً وَاللهُ يَقْبِضُ وَيَبْصُطُ وَإِلَيْهِ **تُرْجَعُونَ** ⌂ مَنْ ذَا الَّذِي يُقْرِضُ اللهَ قَرْضاً حَسَناً **فَيُضَاعِفُهُ** لَهُ وَ أَضْعَافاً كَثِيرَةً...⌂ *(Douri)* ، *(Warsh)* *(Qalon)* مَنْ ذَا الَّذِي يُقْرِضُ اللهَ قَرْضاً حَسَناً **فَيُضَعِّفَهُ** لَهُ وَ أَضْعَافاً كَثِيرَةً وَاللهُ يَقْبِضُ وَيَبْصُطُ وَإِلَيْهِ **تَرْجِعُونَ**⌂ *(Roḥ)*
53.	... فَلَمَّا كُتِبَ **عَلَيْهِمُ** الْقِتَالُ تَوَلَّوْا إِلاَّ قَلِيلاً مِنْهُمْ وَاللهُ عَلِيمٌ بِالظَّالِمِينَ⌂ (البقره 2: 246) *Al-Qur'an (Qirā'at al-'Aammah)* ... فَلَمَّا كُتِبَ **عَلَيْهِمُ** الْقِتَالُ تَوَلَّوْا إِلاَّ قَلِيلاً مِنْهُمْ وَاللهُ عَلِيمٌ بِالظَّالِمِينَ⌂ *(Douri)*

	‫--- فَلَمَّا كُتِبَ عَلَيْهِمُ الْقِتَالُ تَوَلَّوْا إِلاَّ قَلِيلاً مِنْهُمْ وَاللَّهُ عَلِيمٌ بِالظَّالِمِينَ‬ **(Roḥ)**
54.	‫--- وَلَوْلاَ دَفْعُ اللَّهِ النَّاسَ بَعْضَهُمْ بِبَعْضٍ لَفَسَدَتِ الأَرْضُ ---‬ (‫البقره‬2: 251) *Al-Qur'an (Qirā'at al-'Aammah)* ‫--وَلَوْلاَ دِفْعُ اللَّهِ النَّاسَ بَعْضَهُمْ بِبَعْضٍ لَفَسَدَتِ الأَرْضُ ---‬ **(Warsh)** ، **(Qalon)** ، **(Jamahiriya)** ، **(Roḥ)**
55.	‫يَا أَيُّهَا الَّذِينَ آمَنُوا أَنْفِقُوا مِمَّا رَزَقْنَاكُمْ مِنْ قَبْلِ أَنْ يَأْتِيَ يَوْمٌ لاَ بَيْعٌ فِيهِ وَلاَ خُلَّةٌ وَلاَ شَفَاعَةٌ وَالْكَافِرُونَ هُمُ الظَّالِمُونَ‬ (‫البقره‬2: 254) *Al-Qur'an (Qirā'at al-'Aammah)* ‫يَا أَيُّهَا الَّذِينَ آمَنُوا أَنْفِقُوا مِمَّا رَزَقْنَاكُمْ مِنْ قَبْلِ أَنْ يَأْتِيَ يَوْمٌ لاَ بَيْعٌ فِيهِ وَلاَ خُلَّةٌ وَلاَ شَفَاعَةٌ وَالْكَافِرُونَ هُمُ الظَّالِمُونَ‬ **(Douri)** ، **(Roḥ)**
56.	‫--- يَعْلَمُ مَا بَيْنَ أَيْدِيهِمْ وَمَا خَلْفَهُمْ---‬ (‫البقره‬2: 255) *Al-Qur'an (Qirā'at al-'Aammah)* ‫--- يَعْلَمُ مَا بَيْنَ أَيْدِيهُمْ وَمَا خَلْفَهُمْ---‬ **(Roḥ)**
57.	‫--وَانْظُرْ إِلَى الْعِظَامِ كَيْفَ نُنْشِزُهَا ---‬(‫البقره‬ 2: 260) *Al-Qur'an (Qirā'at al-'Aammah)* ‫وَانْظُرْ إِلَى الْعِظَامِ كَيْفَ نُنْشِرُهَا---‬ **(Warsh)** ، **(Douri)** ، **(Qalon)** ، **(Jamahiriya)** ، **(Roḥ)**
58.	‫وَإِذْ قَالَ إِبْرَاهِيمُ رَبِّ أَرِنِي كَيْفَ تُحْيِي الْمَوْتَى ---‬ (‫البقره‬ 2: 260) *Al-Qur'an (Qirā'at al-'Aammah)* ‫وَإِذْ قَالَ إِبْرَاهِيمُ رَبِّ أَرِنِي كَيْفَ تُحْيِي الْمَوْتَى ---‬ **(Roḥ)**
59.	‫--- وَاللَّهُ يُضَاعِفُ لِمَنْ يَشَاءُ وَاللَّهُ وَاسِعٌ عَلِيمٌ‬ (‫البقره‬2: 261) *Al-Qur'an (Qirā'at al-'Aammah)* ‫--- وَاللَّهُ يُضَعِّفُ لِمَنْ يَشَاءُ وَاللَّهُ وَاسِعٌ عَلِيمٌ‬ **(Roḥ)**
60.	‫--- لَهُمْ أَجْرُهُمْ عِنْدَ رَبِّهِمْ وَلاَ خَوْفٌ عَلَيْهِمْ وَلاَ هُمْ يَحْزَنُونَ‬ (‫البقره‬2: 262) *Al-Qur'an (Qirā'at al-'Aammah)* ‫--- لَهُمْ أَجْرُهُمْ عِنْدَ رَبِّهُمْ وَلاَ خَوْفٌ عَلَيْهُمْ وَلاَ هُمْ يَحْزَنُونَ‬ **(Roḥ)**
61.	‫وَمَثَلُ الَّذِينَ يُنْفِقُونَ أَمْوَالَهُمُ ابْتِغَاءَ مَرْضَاةِ اللَّهِ وَتَثْبِيتاً مِنْ أَنْفُسِهِمْ كَمَثَلِ جَنَّةٍ بِرَبْوَةٍ ---‬ (‫البقره‬2: 265) *Al-Qur'an (Qirā'at al-'Aammah)*

	وَمَثَلُ الَّذِينَ يُنفِقُونَ أَمْوَالَهُمْ ابْتِغَاءَ مَرْضَاةِ اللهِ وَتَثْبِيتاً مِنْ أَنْفُسِهِمْ كَمَثَلِ جَنَّةٍ بِرُبْوَةٍ --- 🔼 (Warsh)، (Douri)، (Qalon)، (Jamahiriya)، (Roḥ)
62.	يُؤْتِي الْحِكْمَةَ مَنْ يَشَاءُ وَمَنْ يُوْتَ الْحِكْمَةَ فَقَدْ أُوتِيَ خَيْراً كَثِيراً وَمَا يَذَّكَّرُ إلاَّ أُوْلُوا الْأَلْبَابِ 🔼 (البقره2: 269) Al-Qur'an (Qirā'at al-'Aammah) يُؤْتِي الْحِكْمَةَ مَنْ يَشَاءُ وَمَنْ يُوْتِ الْحِكْمَةَ فَقَدْ أُوتِيَ خَيْراً كَثِيراً وَمَا يَذَّكَّرُ إلاَّ أُوْلُوا الْأَلْبَابِ 🔼 (Roḥ)
63.	إنْ تُبْدُوا الصَّدَقَاتِ فَنِعِمَّا هِيَ وَإنْ تُخْفُوهَا وَتُؤْتُوهَا الْفُقَرَاءَ فَهُوَ خَيْرٌ لَكُمْ وَيُكَفِّرُ عَنْكُمْ مِنْ سَيِّئَاتِكُمْ وَاللَّهُ بِمَا تَعْمَلُونَ خَبِيرٌ 🔼 (البقره2: 271) Al-Qur'an (Qirā'at al-'Aammah) إنْ تُبْدُوا الصَّدَقَاتِ فَنِعِمَّا هِيَ وَإنْ تُخْفُوهَا وَتُؤْتُوهَا الْفُقَرَاءَ فَهُوَ خَيْرٌ لَكُمْ وَنُكَفِّرُ عَنْكُمْ مِنْ سَيِّئَاتِكُمْ وَاللَّهُ بِمَا تَعْمَلُونَ خَبِيرٌ 🔼 (Shuba)، (Douri)، (Warsh)، (Qalon)، (Jamahiriya)، (Roḥ)
64.	لِلْفُقَرَاءِ الَّذِينَ أُحْصِرُوا فِي سَبِيلِ اللهِ لاَ يَسْتَطِيعُونَ ضَرْباً فِي الأَرْضِ يَحْسَبُهُمُ الْجَاهِلُ أَغْنِيَاءَ مِنَ التَّعَفُّفِ--- 🔼 (البقره2: 273) Al-Qur'an (Qirā'at al-'Aammah) لِلْفُقَرَاءِ الَّذِينَ أُحْصِرُوا فِي سَبِيلِ اللهِ لاَ يَسْتَطِيعُونَ ضَرْباً فِي الأَرْضِ يَحْسِبُهُمُ الْجَاهِلُ أَغْنِيَاءَ مِنَ التَّعَفُّفِ--- 🔼 (Warsh)، (Douri)، (Qalon)، (Jamahiriya)، (Roḥ)
65.	...فَلَهُمْ أَجْرُهُمْ عِنْدَ رَبِّهِمْ وَلاَ خَوْفٌ عَلَيْهِمْ وَلاَ هُمْ يَحْزَنُونَ 🔼 (البقره2: 274) Al-Qur'an (Qirā'at al-'Aammah) ...فَلَهُمْ أَجْرُهُمْ عِنْدَ رَبِّهِمْ وَلاَ خَوْفٌ عَلَيْهِمْ وَلاَ هُمْ يَحْزَنُونَ 🔼 (Roḥ)
66.	--- وَلاَ خَوْفٌ عَلَيْهِمْ وَلاَ هُمْ يَحْزَنُونَ 🔼 (البقره2: 277) Al-Qur'an (Qirā'at al-'Aammah) --- وَلاَ خَوْفٌ عَلَيْهِمْ وَلاَ هُمْ يَحْزَنُونَ 🔼 (Roḥ)
67.	--- وَأَنْ تَصَدَّقُوا خَيْرٌ لَكُمْ إنْ كُنتُمْ تَعْلَمُونَ 🔼 (البقره2: 280) Al-Qur'an (Qirā'at al-'Aammah) --- وَأَنْ تَصَدَّقُوا خَيْرٌ لَكُمْ إنْ كُنتُمْ تَعْلَمُونَ 🔼 (Warsh)، (Douri)، (Qalon)، (Jamahiriya)، (Roḥ)
68.	وَاتَّقُوا يَوْماً تُرْجَعُونَ فِيهِ إلَى اللهِ --- 🔼 (البقره2: 281)

	Al-Qur'an (Qirā'at al-'Aammah) وَاتَّقُوا يَوْماً تَرْجِعُونَ فِيهِ إِلَى اللهِ --- 🔼 (Douri) ، (Roḥ)
69.	--- فَإِنْ لَمْ يَكُونَا رَجُلَيْنِ فَرَجُلٌ وَامْرَأَتَانِ مِمَّنْ تَرْضَوْنَ مِنَ الشُّهَدَاءِ أَنْ تَضِلَّ إِحْدَاهُمَا فَتُذَكِّرَ إِحْدَاهُمَا الأُخْرَى وَلاَ يَأْبَ الشُّهَدَاءُ إِذَا مَا دُعُوا--- 🔼 (البقره2: 282) *Al-Qur'an (Qirā'at al-'Aammah)* --- فَإِنْ لَمْ يَكُونَا رَجُلَيْنِ فَرَجُلٌ وَامْرَأَتَانِ مِمَّنْ تَرْضَوْنَ مِنَ الشُّهَدَاءِ أَنْ تَضِلَّ إِحْدَاهُمَا فَتُذَكِّرَ إِحْدَاهُمَا الأُخْرَى وَلاَ يَأْبَ الشُّهَدَاءُ إِذَا مَا دُعُوا--- 🔼 (Douri) ، (Roḥ)
70.	--- ذَلِكُمْ أَقْسَطُ عِنْدَ اللهِ وَأَقْوَمُ لِلشَّهَادَةِ وَأَدْنَى أَلاَّ تَرْتَابُوا إِلاَّ أَنْ تَكُونَ تِجَارَةً حَاضِرَةً تُدِيرُونَهَا بَيْنَكُمْ--- 🔼 (البقره2: 282) *Al-Qur'an (Qirā'at al-'Aammah)* --- ذَلِكُمْ أَقْسَطُ عِنْدَ اللهِ وَأَقْوَمُ لِلشَّهَادَةِ وَأَدْنَى أَلاَّ تَرْتَابُوا إِلاَّ أَنْ تَكُونَ تِجَارَةً حَاضِرَةً تُدِيرُونَهَا بَيْنَكُمْ--- 🔼 (Warsh) ، (Douri) ، (Qalon) ، (Jamahiriya) ، (Roḥ)
71.	وَإِنْ كُنتُمْ عَلَى سَفَرٍ وَلَمْ تَجِدُوا كَاتِباً فَرِهَانٌ مَقْبُوضَةٌ --- (البقره2: 283) *Al-Qur'an (Qirā'at al-'Aammah)* وَإِنْ كُنتُمْ عَلَى سَفَرٍ وَلَمْ تَجِدُوا كَاتِباً فَرُهُنٌ مَقْبُوضَةٌ --- (Douri)
72.	آمَنَ الرَّسُولُ بِمَا أُنزِلَ إِلَيْهِ مِن رَبِّهِ وَالْمُؤْمِنُونَ كُلٌّ آمَنَ بِاللهِ وَمَلاَئِكَتِهِ وَكُتُبِهِ وَرُسُلِهِ لاَ نُفَرِّقُ بَيْنَ أَحَدٍ مِنْ رُسُلِهِ وَقَالُوا سَمِعْنَا وَأَطَعْنَا غُفْرَانَكَ رَبَّنَا وَإِلَيْكَ الْمَصِيرُ 🔼 (البقره2: 285) *Al-Qur'an (Qirā'at al-'Aammah)* آمَنَ الرَّسُولُ بِمَا أُنزِلَ إِلَيْهِ مِن رَبِّهِ وَالْمُؤْمِنُونَ كُلٌّ آمَنَ بِاللهِ وَمَلاَئِكَتِهِ وَكُتُبِهِ وَرُسُلِهِ لاَ يُفَرِّقُ بَيْنَ أَحَدٍ مِنْ رُسُلِهِ وَقَالُوا سَمِعْنَا وَأَطَعْنَا غُفْرَانَكَ رَبَّنَا وَإِلَيْكَ الْمَصِيرُ 🔼 (Roḥ)
73.	قَدْ كَانَ لَكُمْ آيَةٌ فِي فِئَتَيْنِ الْتَقَتَا فِئَةٌ تُقَاتِلُ فِي سَبِيلِ اللهِ وَأُخْرَى كَافِرَةٌ يَرَوْنَهُم مِثْلَيْهِمْ رَأْيَ الْعَيْنِ --- 🔼 (آل عمران3: 13) *Al-Qur'an (Qirā'at al-'Aammah)* قَدْ كَانَ لَكُمْ آيَةٌ فِي فِئَتَيْنِ الْتَقَتَا فِئَةٌ تُقَاتِلُ فِي سَبِيلِ اللهِ وَأُخْرَى كَافِرَةٌ تَرَوْنَهُم مِثْلَيْهِمْ رَأْيَ الْعَيْنِ --- 🔼 (Warsh) ، (Qalon) ، (Jamahiriya) ، (Roḥ) قَدْ كَانَ لَكُمْ آيَةٌ فِي فِئَتَيْنِ الْتَقَتَا فِئَةٌ تُقَاتِلُ فِي سَبِيلِ اللهِ وَأُخْرَى كَافِرَةٌ تَرَوْنَهُم مِثْلَيْهِمْ رَأْيَ الْعَيْنِ --- 🔼 (Roḥ)

74.	فَإِنْ حَاجُّوكَ فَقُلْ أَسْلَمْتُ **وَجْهِيَ** لِلَّهِ وَمَنِ اتَّبَعَنِ---🏛 (آل عمران3: 20) *Al-Qur'an (Qirā'at al-'Aammah)* فَإِنْ حَاجُّوكَ فَقُلْ أَسْلَمْتُ **وَجْهِى** لِلَّهِ وَمَنِ اتَّبَعَنِ---🏛 *(Douri)*، *(Shuba)*، *(Roḥ)*
75.	لَا يَتَّخِذِ الْمُؤْمِنُونَ الْكَافِرِينَ أَوْلِيَاءَ مِنْ دُونِ الْمُؤْمِنِينَ وَمَنْ يَفْعَلْ ذَلِكَ فَلَيْسَ مِنَ اللَّهِ فِي شَيْءٍ إِلاَّ أَنْ تَتَّقُوا مِنْهُمْ **تُقَاةً** ---🏛 (آل عمران3: 28) *Al-Qur'an (Qirā'at al-'Aammah)* لَا يَتَّخِذِ الْمُؤْمِنُونَ الْكَافِرِينَ أَوْلِيَاءَ مِنْ دُونِ الْمُؤْمِنِينَ وَمَنْ يَفْعَلْ ذَلِكَ فَلَيْسَ مِنَ اللَّهِ فِي شَيْءٍ إِلاَّ أَنْ تَتَّقُوا مِنْهُمْ **تَقِيَّةً** ---🏛 *(Roḥ)*
76.	فَلَمَّا وَضَعَتْهَا قَالَتْ رَبِّ إِنِّي وَضَعْتُهَا أُنْثَى وَاللَّهُ أَعْلَمُ بِمَا **وَضَعَتْ** ---🏛 (آل عمران3: 36) *Al-Qur'an (Qirā'at al-'Aammah)* فَلَمَّا وَضَعَتْهَا قَالَتْ رَبِّ إِنِّي وَضَعْتُهَا أُنْثَى وَاللَّهُ أَعْلَمُ بِمَا **وَضَعْتُ** ---🏛 *(Shuba)*، *(Roḥ)*
77.	فَتَقَبَّلَهَا رَبُّهَا بِقَبُولٍ حَسَنٍ وَأَنْبَتَهَا نَبَاتاً حَسَناً **وَكَفَّلَهَا زَكَرِيَّا** ﷺ كُلَّمَا دَخَلَ عَلَيْهَا زَكَرِيَّا الْمِحْرَابَ وَجَدَ عِنْدَهَا رِزْقاً---🏛 (آل عمران3: 37) *Al-Qur'an (Qirā'at al-'Aammah)* فَتَقَبَّلَهَا رَبُّهَا بِقَبُولٍ حَسَنٍ وَأَنْبَتَهَا نَبَاتاً حَسَناً **وَكَفَّلَهَا زَكَرِيَّاءُ** ﷺ كُلَّمَا دَخَلَ عَلَيْهَا زَكَرِيَّاءُ الْمِحْرَابَ وَجَدَ عِنْدَهَا رِزْقاً---🏛 *(Warsh)*، *(Douri)*، *(Qalon)*، *(Jamahiriya)*، *(Roḥ)* فَتَقَبَّلَهَا رَبُّهَا بِقَبُولٍ حَسَنٍ وَأَنْبَتَهَا نَبَاتاً حَسَناً وَكَفَّلَهَا زَكَرِيَّاءُ ﷺ كُلَّمَا دَخَلَ عَلَيْهَا زَكَرِيَّاءُ الْمِحْرَابَ وَجَدَ عِنْدَهَا رِزْقاً---🏛 *(Shuba)*
78.	ذَلِكَ مِنْ أَنْبَاءِ الْغَيْبِ نُوحِيهِ إِلَيْكَ وَمَا كُنْتَ **لَدَيْهِمْ** إِذْ يُلْقُونَ أَقْلاَمَهُمْ أَيُّهُمْ يَكْفُلُ مَرْيَمَ وَمَا كُنْتَ لَدَيْهِمْ إِذْ يَخْتَصِمُونَ🏛 (آل عمران3: 44) *Al-Qur'an (Qirā'at al-'Aammah)* ذَلِكَ مِنْ أَنْبَاءِ الْغَيْبِ نُوحِيهِ إِلَيْكَ وَمَا كُنْتَ **لَدَيْهُمْ** إِذْ يُلْقُونَ أَقْلاَمَهُمْ أَيُّهُمْ يَكْفُلُ مَرْيَمَ وَمَا كُنْتَ لَدَيْهُمْ إِذْ يَخْتَصِمُونَ🏛 *(Roḥ)*،
79.	وَأَمَّا الَّذِينَ آمَنُوا وَعَمِلُوا الصَّالِحَاتِ **فَيُوَفِّيهِمْ** أُجُورَهُمْ وَاللَّهُ لاَ يُحِبُّ الظَّالِمِينَ🏛 (آل عمران3: 56) *Al-Qur'an (Qirā'at al-'Aammah)* وَأَمَّا الَّذِينَ آمَنُوا وَعَمِلُوا الصَّالِحَاتِ **فَنُوَفِّيهِمْ** أُجُورَهُمْ وَاللَّهُ لاَ يُحِبُّ الظَّالِمِينَ🏛 *(Roḥ)*

80.	وَمِنْ أَهْلِ الْكِتَابِ مَنْ إِنْ تَأْمَنْهُ بِقِنطَارٍ يُؤَدِّهِ إِلَيْكَ وَمِنْهُم مَّنْ إِنْ تَأْمَنْهُ بِدِينَارٍ لاَ يُؤَدِّهِ إِلَيْكَ إِلاَّ مَا دُمْتَ عَلَيْهِ قَائِماً...⏎(آل عمران3: 75) *Al-Qur'an (Qirā'at al-'Aammah)* وَمِنْ أَهْلِ الْكِتَابِ مَنْ إِنْ تَأْمَنْهُ بِقِنطَارٍ يُؤَدِّهِ إِلَيْكَ وَمِنْهُم مَّنْ إِنْ تَأْمَنْهُ بِدِينَارٍ لاَ يُؤَدِّهِ إِلَيْكَ إِلاَّ مَا دُمْتَ عَلَيْهِ قَائِماً...⏎ *(Qalon)*، *(Jamahiriya)*، *(Roḥ)* وَمِنْ أَهْلِ الْكِتَابِ مَنْ إِنْ تَأْمَنْهُ بِقِنطَارٍ يُؤَدِّهِ إِلَيْكَ وَمِنْهُم مَّنْ إِنْ تَأْمَنْهُ بِدِينَارٍ لاَ يُؤَدِّهِ إِلَيْكَ إِلاَّ مَا دُمْتَ عَلَيْهِ قَائِماً...⏎ *(Douri)* *(Shuba)*
81.	إِنَّ الَّذِينَ يَشْتَرُونَ بِعَهْدِ اللّهِ وَأَيْمَانِهِمْ ثَمَناً قَلِيلاً أُوْلَئِكَ لاَ خَلاَقَ لَهُمْ فِي الآخِرَةِ وَلاَ يُكَلِّمُهُمُ اللّهُ وَلاَ يَنظُرُ إِلَيْهِمْ يَوْمَ الْقِيَامَةِ وَلاَ يُزَكِّيهِمْ وَلَهُمْ عَذَابٌ أَلِيمٌ⏎ (آل عمران3: 77) *Al-Qur'an (Qirā'at al-'Aammah)* إِنَّ الَّذِينَ يَشْتَرُونَ بِعَهْدِ اللّهِ وَأَيْمَانِهِمْ ثَمَناً قَلِيلاً أُوْلَئِكَ لاَ خَلاَقَ لَهُمْ فِي الآخِرَةِ وَلاَ يُكَلِّمُهُمُ اللّهُ وَلاَ يَنظُرُ إِلَيْهِمْ يَوْمَ الْقِيَامَةِ وَلاَ يُزَكِّيهِمْ وَلَهُمْ عَذَابٌ أَلِيمٌ⏎ *(Roḥ)*
82.	وَإِنَّ مِنْهُمْ لَفَرِيقاً يَلْوُونَ أَلْسِنَتَهُم بِالْكِتَابِ لِتَحْسَبُوهُ مِنَ الْكِتَابِ وَمَا هُوَ مِنَ الْكِتَابِ...⏎ (آل عمران3: 78) *Al-Qur'an (Qirā'at al-'Aammah)* وَإِنَّ مِنْهُمْ لَفَرِيقاً يَلْوُونَ أَلْسِنَتَهُم بِالْكِتَابِ لِتَحْسِبُوهُ مِنَ الْكِتَابِ وَمَا هُوَ مِنَ الْكِتَابِ...⏎ *(Warsh)*، *(Douri)*، *(Qalon)*، *(Jamahiriya)*، *(Roḥ)*
83.	...وَلَكِنْ كُونُوا رَبَّانِيِّينَ بِمَا كُنْتُمْ تُعَلِّمُونَ الْكِتَابَ وَبِمَا كُنْتُمْ تَدْرُسُونَ⏎ (آل عمران3: 79) *Al-Qur'an (Qirā'at al-'Aammah)* ... وَلَكِنْ كُونُوا رَبَّانِيِّينَ بِمَا كُنْتُمْ تَعْلَمُونَ الْكِتَابَ وَبِمَا كُنْتُمْ تَدْرُسُونَ⏎ *(Warsh)*، *(Douri)*، *(Qalon)*، *(Jamahiriya)*، *(Roḥ)*
84.	أَفَغَيْرَ دِينِ اللّهِ يَبْغُونَ وَلَهُ أَسْلَمَ مَن فِي السَّمَاوَاتِ وَالأَرْضِ طَوْعاً وَكَرْهاً وَإِلَيْهِ يُرْجَعُونَ ⏎ (آل عمران3: 83) *Al-Qur'an (Qirā'at al-'Aammah)* أَفَغَيْرَ دِينِ اللّهِ يَبْغُونَ وَلَهُ أَسْلَمَ مَن فِي السَّمَاوَاتِ وَالأَرْضِ طَوْعاً وَكَرْهاً وَإِلَيْهِ يُرْجِعُونَ⏎ *(Roḥ)* أَفَغَيْرَ دِينِ اللّهِ يَبْغُونَ لَهُ أَسْلَمَ مَن فِي السَّمَاوَاتِ وَالأَرْضِ طَوْعاً وَكَرْهاً وَإِلَيْهِ تُرْجَعُونَ⏎ *(Warsh)*، *(Douri)*، *(Shuba)*، *(Qalon)*، *(Jamahiriya)*
85.	أُوْلَئِكَ جَزَاؤُهُمْ أَنَّ عَلَيْهِمْ لَعْنَةَ اللّهِ وَالْمَلآئِكَةِ وَالنَّاسِ أَجْمَعِينَ⏎ (آل عمران3: 87) *Al-Qur'an (Qirā'at al-'Aammah)*

	أُوْلَئِكَ جَزَاؤُهُمْ أَنَّ **عَلَيْهِمْ** لَعْنَةَ اللَّهِ وَالْمَلَائِكَةِ وَالنَّاسِ أَجْمَعِينَ⊞ **(Roḥ)**
86.	كُلُّ الطَّعَامِ كَانَ حِلاًّ لِبَنِي إِسْرَائِيلَ إِلاَّ مَا حَرَّمَ إِسْرَائِيلُ عَلَى نَفْسِهِ مِن قَبْلِ أَن تُنَزَّلَ **التَّوْرَاةُ**...⊞ (آل عمران3: 93) *Al-Qur'an (Qirā'at al-'Aammah)* كُلُّ الطَّعَامِ كَانَ حِلاًّ لِبَنِي إِسْرَائِيلَ إِلاَّ مَا حَرَّمَ إِسْرَائِيلُ عَلَى نَفْسِهِ مِن قَبْلِ أَن تُنَزَّلَ **التَّوْرَاةُ**...⊞ *(Douri)*، *(Roḥ)*
87.	...وَلِلَّهِ عَلَى النَّاسِ **حِجُّ الْبَيْتِ** مَنِ اسْتَطَاعَ إِلَيْهِ سَبِيلاً...⊞ *Al-Qur'an (Qirā'at al-'Aammah)* (97 :آل عمران3) ...وَلِلَّهِ عَلَى النَّاسِ **حَجُّ الْبَيْتِ** مَنِ اسْتَطَاعَ إِلَيْهِ سَبِيلاً...⊞ *(Warsh)*، *(Douri)*، *(Shuba)*، *(Qalon)*، *(Jamahiriya)*، *(Roḥ)*
88.	وَلِلَّهِ مَا فِي السَّمَاوَاتِ وَمَا فِي الْأَرْضِ وَإِلَى اللَّهِ **تُرْجَعُ الْأُمُورُ**⊞ (109 :آل عمران3) *Al-Qur'an (Qirā'at al-'Aammah)* وَلِلَّهِ مَا فِي السَّمَاوَاتِ وَمَا فِي الْأَرْضِ وَإِلَى اللَّهِ **تَرْجِعُ الْأُمُورُ**⊞ *(Roḥ)*
89.	ضُرِبَتْ **عَلَيْهِمُ** الذِّلَّةُ أَيْنَ مَا ثُقِفُوا إِلاَّ بِحَبْلٍ مِنَ اللَّهِ وَحَبْلٍ مِنَ النَّاسِ وَبَاءُوا بِغَضَبٍ مِنَ اللَّهِ وَضُرِبَتْ **عَلَيْهِمُ** الْمَسْكَنَةُ...⊞ (112 :آل عمران3) *Al-Qur'an (Qirā'at al-'Aammah)* ضُرِبَتْ **عَلَيْهُمُ** الذِّلَّةُ أَيْنَ مَا ثُقِفُوا إِلاَّ بِحَبْلٍ مِنَ اللَّهِ وَحَبْلٍ مِنَ النَّاسِ وَبَاءُوا بِغَضَبٍ مِنَ اللَّهِ وَضُرِبَتْ **عَلَيْهُمُ** الْمَسْكَنَةُ...⊞ *(Roḥ)* ضُرِبَتْ **عَلَيْهِمُ** الذِّلَّةُ أَيْنَ مَا ثُقِفُوا إِلاَّ بِحَبْلٍ مِنَ اللَّهِ وَحَبْلٍ مِنَ النَّاسِ وَبَاءُوا بِغَضَبٍ مِنَ اللَّهِ وَضُرِبَتْ **عَلَيْهِمِ** الْمَسْكَنَةُ...⊞ *(Douri)*
90.	وَمَا **يَفْعَلُوا** مِنْ خَيْرٍ فَلَنْ **يُكْفَرُوهُ** وَاللَّهُ عَلِيمٌ بِالْمُتَّقِينَ⊞ (115 :آل عمران3) *Al-Qur'an (Qirā'at al-'Aammah)* وَمَا **تَفْعَلُوا** مِنْ خَيْرٍ فَلَنْ **تُكْفَرُوهُ** وَاللَّهُ عَلِيمٌ بِالْمُتَّقِينَ⊞ *(Warsh)*، *(Douri)*، *(Shuba)*، *(Qalon)*، *(Jamahiriya)*، *(Roḥ)*
91.	...وَإِنْ تَصْبِرُوا وَتَتَّقُوا **لاَ يَضُرُّكُمْ** كَيْدُهُمْ شَيْئاً...⊞ (120 :آل عمران3) *Al-Qur'an (Qirā'at al-'Aammah)* ...وَإِنْ تَصْبِرُوا وَتَتَّقُوا **لاَ يَضِرْكُمْ** كَيْدُهُمْ شَيْئاً...⊞ *(Warsh)*، *(Douri)*، *(Qalon)*، *(Jamahiriya)*، *(Roḥ)*
92.	لَيْسَ لَكَ مِنَ الْأَمْرِ شَيْءٌ أَوْ يَتُوبَ **عَلَيْهِمْ** ...⊞ (128 :آل عمران3) *Al-Qur'an (Qirā'at al-'Aammah)*

	لَيْسَ لَكَ مِنَ الْأَمْرِ شَيْءٌ أَوْ يَتُوبَ **عَلَيْهُمْ** --- 🕌 (*Roḥ*)
93.	يَا أَيُّهَا الَّذِينَ آمَنُوا لَاَ تَأْكُلُوا الرِّبَا أَضْعَافاً **مُضَاعَفَةً** --- 🕌 (آل عمران 3: 130) *Al-Qur'an (Qirā'at al-'Aammah)* يَا أَيُّهَا الَّذِينَ آمَنُوا لَاَ تَأْكُلُوا الرِّبَا أَضْعَافاً **مُضَعَّفَةً** --- 🕌 (*Roḥ*)
94.	وَكَأَيِّنْ مِنْ نَبِيٍّ **قَاتَلَ** مَعَهُ رِبِّيُّونَ كَثِيرٌ --- 🕌 (آل عمران 3: 146) *Al-Qur'an (Qirā'at al-'Aammah)* وَكَأَيِّنْ مِنْ نَبِيٍّ **قُتِلَ** مَعَهُ رِبِّيُّونَ كَثِيرٌ --- 🕌 (*Warsh*) ، (*Douri*) ، (*Qalon*) ، (*Jamahiriya*) ، (*Roḥ*)
95.	سَنُلْقِي فِي قُلُوبِ الَّذِينَ كَفَرُوا **الرُّعْبَ** بِمَا أَشْرَكُوا بِاللَّهِ مَا لَمْ **يُنَزِّلْ** بِهِ سُلْطَاناً 🕌 --- (آل عمران 3: 151) *Al-Qur'an (Qirā'at al-'Aammah)* سَنُلْقِي فِي قُلُوبِ الَّذِينَ كَفَرُوا **الرُّعْبَ** بِمَا أَشْرَكُوا بِاللَّهِ مَا لَمْ **يُنْزِلْ** بِهِ سُلْطَاناً --- 🕌 (*Roḥ*) سَنُلْقِي فِي قُلُوبِ الَّذِينَ كَفَرُوا الرُّعْبَ بِمَا أَشْرَكُوا بِاللَّهِ مَا لَمْ **يُنْزِلْ** بِهِ سُلْطَاناً --- 🕌 (*Douri*)
96.	---قُلْ إِنَّ الْأَمْرَ **كُلَّهُ** لِلَّهِ يُخْفُونَ فِي أَنْفُسِهِمْ--- قُلْ لَوْ كُنْتُمْ فِي بُيُوتِكُمْ لَبَرَزَ الَّذِينَ كُتِبَ **عَلَيْهُمُ الْقَتْلُ** --- 🕌 (آل عمران 3: 154) *Al-Qur'an (Qirā'at al-'Aammah)* ---قُلْ إِنَّ الْأَمْرَ **كُلَّهُ** لِلَّهِ يُخْفُونَ فِي أَنْفُسِهِمْ--- قُلْ لَوْ كُنْتُمْ فِي بُيُوتِكُمْ لَبَرَزَ الَّذِينَ كُتِبَ **عَلَيْهُمُ الْقَتْلُ** --- 🕌 (*Roḥ*) ---قُلْ إِنَّ الْأَمْرَ **كُلَّهُ** لِلَّهِ يُخْفُونَ فِي أَنْفُسِهِمْ--- قُلْ لَوْ كُنْتُمْ فِي بُيُوتِكُمْ لَبَرَزَ الَّذِينَ كُتِبَ **عَلَيْهِمُ الْقَتْلُ** --- 🕌(*Douri*)
97.	وَلَئِنْ قُتِلْتُمْ فِي سَبِيلِ اللَّهِ أَوْ مُتُّمْ لَمَغْفِرَةٌ مِنَ اللَّهِ وَرَحْمَةٌ خَيْرٌ مِمَّا **يَجْمَعُونَ** 🕌 (آل عمران 3: 157) *Al-Qur'an (Qirā'at al-'Aammah)* وَلَئِنْ قُتِلْتُمْ فِي سَبِيلِ اللَّهِ أَوْ مُتُّمْ لَمَغْفِرَةٌ مِنَ اللَّهِ وَرَحْمَةٌ خَيْرٌ مِمَّا **تَجْمَعُونَ** 🕌 (*Warsh*) (*Douri*) (*Shuba*) (*Qalon*) ، (*Jamahiriya*) ، (*Roḥ*)
98.	وَمَا كَانَ لِنَبِيٍّ أَنْ **يَغُلَّ** وَمَنْ يَغْلُلْ --- (آل عمران 3: 161) *Al-Qur'an (Qirā'at al-'Aammah)* وَمَا كَانَ لِنَبِيٍّ أَنْ **يُغَلَّ** وَمَنْ يَغْلُلْ --- (*Warsh*) ، (*Qalon*)
99.	لَقَدْ مَنَّ اللَّهُ عَلَى الْمُؤْمِنِينَ إِذْ بَعَثَ **فِيهِمْ** رَسُولاً مِنْ أَنْفُسِهِمْ يَتْلُوا **عَلَيْهِمْ** آيَاتِهِ

	وَيُزَكِّيهِمْ ---🏛 (آل عمران3: 164) *Al-Qur'an (Qirā'at al-'Aammah)* لَقَدْ مَنَّ اللَّهُ عَلَى الْمُؤْمِنِينَ إِذْ بَعَثَ فِيهُمْ رَسُولاً مِنْ أَنْفُسِهِمْ يَتْلُوا عَلَيْهُمْ آيَاتِهِ وَيُزَكِّيهُمْ ---🏛 (*Roḥ*)
100.	وَلاَ تَحْسَبَنَّ الَّذِينَ قُتِلُوا فِي سَبِيلِ اللَّهِ أَمْوَاتاً --- (آل عمران3: 169) *Al-Qur'an (Qirā'at al-'Aammah)* وَلاَ تَحْسِبَنَّ الَّذِينَ قُتِلُوا فِي سَبِيلِ اللَّهِ أَمْوَاتاً --- (*Warsh*) (*Douri*)، (*Qalon*)، (*Roḥ*)
101.	--- أَلاَّ خَوْفٌ عَلَيْهِمْ وَلاَ هُمْ يَحْزَنُونَ🏛 (آل عمران3: 170) *Al-Qur'an (Qirā'at al-'Aammah)* --- أَلاَّ خَوْفَ عَلَيْهُمْ وَلاَ هُمْ يَحْزَنُونَ🏛 (*Roḥ*)
102.	وَلاَ يَحْسَبَنَّ الَّذِينَ كَفَرُوا أَنَّمَا نُمْلِي لَهُمْ خَيْرٌ لِأَنْفُسِهِمْ ---🏛 (آل عمران3: 178) *Al-Qur'an (Qirā'at al-'Aammah)* وَلاَ يَحْسِبَنَّ الَّذِينَ كَفَرُوا أَنَّمَا نُمْلِي لَهُمْ خَيْرٌ لِأَنْفُسِهِمْ ---🏛 (*Warsh*)، (*Douri*)، (*Qalon*)، (*Jamahiriya*) (*Roḥ*)
103.	مَا كَانَ اللَّهُ لِيَذَرَ الْمُؤْمِنِينَ عَلَى مَا أَنْتُمْ عَلَيْهِ حَتَّى يَمِيزَ الْخَبِيثَ مِنَ الطَّيِّبِ ---🏛 (آل عمران3: 179) *Al-Qur'an (Qirā'at al-'Aammah)* مَا كَانَ اللَّهُ لِيَذَرَ الْمُؤْمِنِينَ عَلَى مَا أَنْتُمْ عَلَيْهِ حَتَّى يُمَيِّزَ الْخَبِيثَ مِنَ الطَّيِّبِ---🏛 (*Roḥ*)
104.	وَلاَ يَحْسِبَنَّ الَّذِينَ يَبْخَلُونَ بِمَا آتَاهُمُ اللَّهُ مِنْ فَضْلِهِ هُوَ خَيْراً لَهُمْ --- وَاللَّهُ بِمَا تَعْمَلُونَ خَبِيرٌ 🏛 (آل عمران3: 180) *Al-Qur'an (Qirā'at al-'Aammah)* وَلاَ يَحْسِبَنَّ الَّذِينَ يَبْخَلُونَ بِمَا آتَاهُمُ اللَّهُ مِنْ فَضْلِهِ هُوَ خَيْراً لَهُمْ --- وَاللَّهُ بِمَا يَعْمَلُونَ خَبِيرٌ 🏛 (*Douri*)، (*Roḥ*) وَلاَ يَحْسِبَنَّ الَّذِينَ يَبْخَلُونَ بِمَا آتَاهُمُ اللَّهُ مِنْ فَضْلِهِ هُوَ خَيْراً لَهُمْ --- وَاللَّهُ بِمَا تَعْمَلُونَ خَبِيرٌ 🏛 (*Warsh*)، (*Qalon*)، (*Jamahiriya*)
105.	لاَ تَحْسَبَنَّ الَّذِينَ يَفْرَحُونَ بِمَا أَتَوا وَيُحِبُّونَ أَنْ يُحْمَدُوا بِمَا لَمْ يَفْعَلُوا فَلاَ تَحْسَبَنَّهُمْ بِمَفَازَةٍ مِنَ الْعَذَابِ وَلَهُمْ عَذَابٌ أَلِيمٌ 🏛 (آل عمران3: 188)، *Al-Qur'an (Qirā'at al-'Aammah)*

	لاَ يَحْسِبَنَّ الَّذِينَ يَفْرَحُونَ بِمَا أَتَوا وَيُحِبُّونَ أَنْ يُحْمَدُوا بِمَا لَمْ يَفْعَلُوا فَلاَ تَحْسِبَنَّهُمْ بِمَفَازَةٍ مِنَ الْعَذَابِ وَلَهُمْ عَذَابٌ أَلِيمٌ ۩ *(Roḥ)، (Jamahiriya)، (Qalon)، (Warsh)* لاَ يَحْسِبَنَّ الَّذِينَ يَفْرَحُونَ بِمَا أَتَوا وَيُحِبُّونَ أَنْ يُحْمَدُوا بِمَا لَمْ يَفْعَلُوا فَلاَ يَحْسِبَنَّهُمْ بِمَفَازَةٍ مِنَ الْعَذَابِ وَلَهُمْ عَذَابٌ أَلِيمٌ ۩ *(Douri)،*
106.	وَإِنَّ مِنْ أَهْلِ الْكِتَابِ لَمَنْ يُؤْمِنُ بِاللهِ وَمَا أُنْزِلَ إِلَيْكُمْ وَمَا أُنْزِلَ إِلَيْهِمْ خَاشِعِينَ لِلّهِ ---۩ (آل عمران3: 199)، *Al-Qur'an (Qirā'at al-'Aammah)* وَإِنَّ مِنْ أَهْلِ الْكِتَابِ لَمَنْ يُؤْمِنُ بِاللهِ وَمَا أُنْزِلَ إِلَيْكُمْ وَمَا أُنْزِلَ إِلَيْهُمْ خَاشِعِينَ لِلّهِ ---۩ *(Roḥ)*
107.	---وَاتَّقُوا اللهَ الَّذِي تَسَآءَلُونَ بِهِ وَالأَرْحَامَ إِنَّ اللهَ كَانَ عَلَيْكُمْ رَقِيباً ۩ (النساء: 1)، *Al-Qur'an (Qirā'at al-'Aammah)* ---وَاتَّقُوا اللهَ الَّذِي تَسَآءَلُونَ بِهِ وَالأَرْحَامَ إِنَّ اللهَ كَانَ عَلَيْكُمْ رَقِيباً ۩ *(Roḥ)، (Jamahiriya)، (Qalon)، (Douri)، (Warsh)* --- وَاتَّقُوا اللهَ الَّذِي تَتَسَاءَلُونَ بِهِ وَالأَرْحَامَ إِنَّ اللهَ كَانَ عَلَيْكُمْ رَقِيباً ۩ *https://www.islamawakened.com/quran//roots/Zay-Waw-Jiim.html*
108.	--- فَإِنْ آنَسْتُمْ مِنْهُمْ رُشْداً فَادْفَعُوا إِلَيْهِمْ أَمْوَالَهُمْ --- فَإِذَا دَفَعْتُمْ إِلَيْهِمْ أَمْوَالَهُمْ فَأَشْهِدُوا عَلَيْهِمْ وَكَفَى بِاللهِ حَسِيباً ۩ (النساء: 6) *Al-Qur'an (Qirā'at al-'Aammah)* --- فَإِنْ آنَسْتُمْ مِنْهُمْ رُشْداً فَادْفَعُوا إِلَيْهُمْ أَمْوَالَهُمْ --- فَإِذَا دَفَعْتُمْ إِلَيْهُمْ أَمْوَالَهُمْ فَأَشْهِدُوا عَلَيْهُمْ وَكَفَى بِاللهِ حَسِيبا ۩ *(Roḥ)،*
109.	وَلْيَخْشَ الَّذِينَ لَوْ تَرَكُوا مِنْ خَلْفِهِمْ ذُرِّيَّةً ضِعَافاً خَافُوا عَلَيْهِمْ--۩ (النساء: 9)، *Al-Qur'an (Qirā'at al-'Aammah)* وَلْيَخْشَ الَّذِينَ لَوْ تَرَكُوا مِنْ خَلْفِهِمْ ذُرِّيَّةً ضِعَافاً خَافُوا عَلَيْهُمْ--۩ *(Roḥ)*
110.	---مِنْ بَعْدِ وَصِيَّةٍ يُوصَى بِهَا أَوْ دَيْنٍ غَيْرَ مُضَارٍّ ---(النساء4: 12) *Al-Qur'an (Qirā'at al-'Aammah)* ---مِنْ بَعْدِ وَصِيَّةٍ يُوصَى بِهَا أَوْ دَيْنٍ غَيْرَ مُضَارٍّ --- *(Roḥ)، (Qalon)، (Douri)، (Warsh)،*
111.	وَمَنْ يَعْصِ اللهَ وَرَسُولَهُ وَيَتَعَدَّ حُدُودَهُ يُدْخِلْهُ نَاراً--- ۩ (النساء4: 14) *Al-Qur'an (Qirā'at al-'Aammah)*

	وَمَنْ يَعْصِ اللَّهَ وَرَسُولَهُ وَيَتَعَدَّ حُدُودَهُ **نُدْخِلْهُ** نَاراً --- 🏛 (Qalon)، (Warsh)
112.	وَاللَّائِي يَأْتِينَ الْفَاحِشَةَ مِنْ نِسَائِكُمْ فَاسْتَشْهِدُوا **عَلَيْهِنَّ** أَرْبَعَةً مِنْكُمْ 🏛--- (النساء4: 15) *Al-Qur'an (Qirā'at al-'Aammah)* وَاللَّائِي يَأْتِينَ الْفَاحِشَةَ مِنْ نِسَائِكُمْ فَاسْتَشْهِدُوا **عَلَيْهِنَّ** أَرْبَعَةً مِنْكُمْ 🏛--- *(Roḥ)*،
113.	--- فَأُوْلَائِكَ يَتُوبُ اللَّهُ **عَلَيْهِمْ** وَكَانَ اللَّهُ عَلِيماً حَكِيماً 🏛 (النساء4: 17) *Al-Qur'an (Qirā'at al-'Aammah)* --- فَأُوْلَائِكَ يَتُوبُ اللَّهُ **عَلَيْهِمْ** وَكَانَ اللَّهُ عَلِيماً حَكِيماً *(Roḥ)*
114.	وَالْمُحْصَنَاتُ مِنَ النِسَاءِ إِلَّا مَا مَلَكَتْ أَيْمَانُكُمْ كِتَابَ اللَّهِ عَلَيْكُمْ **وَأُحِلَّ** لَكُمْ مَا وَرَاءَ ذَلِكُمْ --- 🏛 (النساء4: 24) *Al-Qur'an (Qirā'at al-'Aammah)* وَالْمُحْصَنَاتُ مِنَ النِسَاءِ إِلَّا مَا مَلَكَتْ أَيْمَانُكُمْ كِتَابَ اللَّهِ عَلَيْكُمْ **وَأُحِلَّ** لَكُمْ مَا وَرَاءَ ذَلِكُمْ --- 🏛 (Shuba) *(Qalon)، (Douri)، (Warsh) (Roḥ)*
115.	--- فَإِذَا أُحْصِنَّ فَإِنْ أَتَيْنَ بِفَاحِشَةٍ **فَعَلَيْهِنَّ** نِصْفُ مَا عَلَى الْمُحْصَنَاتِ مِنَ الْعَذَابِ 🏛--- (النساء4: 25) *Al-Qur'an (Qirā'at al-'Aammah)* --- فَإِذَا أُحْصِنَّ فَإِنْ أَتَيْنَ بِفَاحِشَةٍ **فَعَلَيْهُنَّ** نِصْفُ مَا عَلَى الْمُحْصَنَاتِ مِنَ الْعَذَابِ ---🏛 *(Roḥ)*
116.	يَا أَيُّهَا الَّذِينَ آمَنُوا لَا تَأْكُلُوا أَمْوَالَكُمْ بَيْنَكُمْ بِالْبَاطِلِ إِلَّا أَنْ تَكُونَ **تِجَارَةً** عَنْ تَرَاضٍ مِنْكُمْ 🏛--- (النساء4: 29) *Al-Qur'an (Qirā'at al-'Aammah)* يَا أَيُّهَا الَّذِينَ آمَنُوا لَا تَأْكُلُوا أَمْوَالَكُمْ بَيْنَكُمْ بِالْبَاطِلِ إِلَّا أَنْ تَكُونَ **تِجَارَةً** عَنْ تَرَاضٍ مِنْكُمْ 🏛--- *(Warsh)، (Douri)، (Qalon)، (Roḥ)*
117.	--- وَالَّذِينَ **عَقَدَتْ** أَيْمَانُكُمْ فَآتُوهُمْ نَصِيبَهُمْ إِنَّ اللَّهَ كَانَ عَلَى كُلِّ شَيْءٍ شَهِيداً 🏛 (النساء4: 33) *Al-Qur'an (Qirā'at al-'Aammah)* --- وَالَّذِينَ **عَاقَدَتْ** أَيْمَانُكُمْ فَآتُوهُمْ نَصِيبَهُمْ إِنَّ اللَّهَ كَانَ عَلَى كُلِّ شَيْءٍ شَهِيداً 🏛 *(Roḥ)، (Douri)، (Warsh)*
118.	--- فَإِنْ أَطَعْنَكُمْ فَلَا تَبْغُوا **عَلَيْهِنَّ** سَبِيلاً إِنَّ اللَّهَ كَانَ عَلِيّاً كَبِيراً 🏛 (النساء4: 34) *Al-Qur'an (Qirā'at al-'Aammah)* --- فَإِنْ أَطَعْنَكُمْ فَلَا تَبْغُوا **عَلَيْهِنَّ** سَبِيلاً إِنَّ اللَّهَ كَانَ عَلِيّاً كَبِيراً 🏛 *(Roḥ)*

119.	---وَٱلْجَارِ الْجُنُبِ **وَالصَّاحِبِ** بِالْجَنْبِ وَابْنِ السَّبِيلِ--- 🔼
	Al-Qur'an (Qirā'at al-'Aammah) (النساء:4: 36)
	---وَٱلْجَارِ الْجُنُبِ **وَالصَّاحِب** بِالْجَنْبِ وَابْنِ السَّبِيلِ--- 🔼 *(Roḥ)*
120.	وَمَاذَا **عَلَيْهُمْ** لَوْ آمَنُوا بِاللَّهِ وَالْيَوْمِ الآخِرِ --- 🔼 (النساء:4: 39)
	Al-Qur'an (Qirā'at al-'Aammah)
	وَمَاذَا **عَلَيْهُمْ** لَوْ آمَنُوا بِاللَّهِ وَالْيَوْمِ الآخِرِ --- 🔼 *(Roḥ)*
121.	إِنَّ اللَّهَ لاَ يَظْلِمُ مِثْقَالَ ذَرَّةٍ وَإِنْ تَكُ حَسَنَةً **يُضَاعِفْهَا** وَيُؤْتِ مِنْ لَدُنْهُ أَجْراً عَظِيماً 🔼 (النساء:4: 39) *Al-Qur'an (Qirā'at al-'Aammah)*
	إِنَّ اللَّهَ لاَ يَظْلِمُ مِثْقَالَ ذَرَّةٍ وَإِنْ تَكُ حَسَنَةً **يُضَعِّفْهَا** وَيُؤْتِ مِنْ لَدُنْهُ أَجْراً عَظِيماً 🔼 *(Roḥ)*
122.	إِنَّ الَّذِينَ كَفَرُوا بِآيَاتِنَا سَوْفَ **نُصْلِيهِمْ** نَاراً --- 🔼
	Al-Qur'an (Qirā'at al-'Aammah) (النساء: 4: 56)
	إِنَّ الَّذِينَ كَفَرُوا بِآيَاتِنَا سَوْفَ **نُصْلِيهُمْ** نَاراً --- 🔼 *(Roḥ)*
123.	فَكَيْفَ إِذَا أَصَابَتْهُمْ مُصِيبَةٌ بِمَا قَدَّمَتْ **أَيْدِيهِمْ** --- 🔼
	Al-Qur'an (Qirā'at al-'Aammah) (النساء: 4: 62)
	فَكَيْفَ إِذَا أَصَابَتْهُمْ مُصِيبَةٌ بِمَا قَدَّمَتْ **أَيْدِيهُمْ** --- 🔼 *(Roḥ)*
124.	وَلَوْ أَنَّا كَتَبْنَا **عَلَيْهِمْ** أَنِ اقْتُلُوا أَنْفُسَكُمْ أَوِ **اخْرُجُوا** مِنْ دِيَارِكُمْ --- 🔼
	Al-Qur'an (Qirā'at al-'Aammah) (النساء: 4: 66)
	وَلَوْ أَنَّا كَتَبْنَا **عَلَيْهُمْ** أَنِ اقْتُلُوا أَنْفُسَكُمْ أَوِ **اخْرُجُوا** مِنْ دِيَارِكُمْ --- 🔼 *(Roḥ)*
	وَلَوْ أَنَّا كَتَبْنَا عَلَيْهِمْ أَنِ اقْتُلُوا أَنْفُسَكُمْ أَوِ **اخْرُجُوا** مِنْ دِيَارِكُمْ --- 🔼
	(Roḥ) ، *(Qalon)* ، *(Douri)* ، *(Warsh)*
125.	وَمَنْ يُطِعِ اللَّهَ وَالرَّسُولَ فَأُولَئِكَ مَعَ الَّذِينَ أَنْعَمَ اللَّهُ **عَلَيْهِمْ** --- 🔼
	Al-Qur'an (Qirā'at al-'Aammah) (النساء:4: 69)
	وَمَنْ يُطِعِ اللَّهَ وَالرَّسُولَ فَأُولَئِكَ مَعَ الَّذِينَ أَنْعَمَ اللَّهُ **عَلَيْهُمْ** --- 🔼 *(Roḥ)*
126.	وَلَئِنْ أَصَابَكُمْ فَضْلٌ مِنَ اللَّهِ لَيَقُولَنَّ **كَأَنْ لَمْ تَكُنْ** بَيْنَكُمْ وَبَيْنَهُ مَوَدَّةٌ --- 🔼 (النساء:4:
	Al-Qur'an (Qirā'at al-'Aammah) (73
	وَلَئِنْ أَصَابَكُمْ فَضْلٌ مِنَ اللَّهِ لَيَقُولَنَّ **كَأَنْ لَمْ يَكُنْ** بَيْنَكُمْ وَبَيْنَهُ مَوَدَّةٌ --- 🔼
	(Roḥ) ، *(Shuba)* ، *(Qalon)* ، *(Douri)* ، *(Warsh)*

127.	ـــ فَلَمَّا كُتِبَ **عَلَيْهِمُ** الْقِتَالُ إِذَا فَرِيقٌ مِّنْهُمْ يَخْشَوْنَ النَّاسَ كَخَشْيَةِ اللَّهِ أَوْ أَشَدَّ خَشْيَةً ـــ قُلْ مَتَاعُ الدُّنْيَا قَلِيلٌ وَالْآخِرَةُ خَيْرٌ لِّمَنِ اتَّقَى **وَلاَ تُظْلَمُونَ** فَتِيلاً 🢁 (النساء4: 77) *Al-Qur'an (Qirā'at al-'Aammah)*
	ـــ فَلَمَّا كُتِبَ **عَلَيْهُمُ** الْقِتَالُ إِذَا فَرِيقٌ مِّنْهُمْ يَخْشَوْنَ النَّاسَ كَخَشْيَةِ اللَّهِ أَوْ أَشَدَّ خَشْيَةً ـــ قُلْ مَتَاعُ الدُّنْيَا قَلِيلٌ وَالْآخِرَةُ خَيْرٌ لِّمَنِ اتَّقَى وَلاَ **يُظْلَمُونَ** فَتِيلاً *(Roḥ)* 🢁
128.	مَن يُطِعِ الرَّسُولَ فَقَدْ أَطَاعَ اللَّهَ وَمَن تَوَلَّى فَمَا أَرْسَلْنَاكَ **عَلَيْهِمْ** حَفِيظاً 🢁 (النساء4: 80) *Al-Qur'an (Qirā'at al-'Aammah)*
	مَن يُطِعِ الرَّسُولَ فَقَدْ أَطَاعَ اللَّهَ وَمَن تَوَلَّى فَمَا أَرْسَلْنَاكَ **عَلَيْهُمْ** حَفِيظاً *(Roḥ)* 🢁
129.	ـــ أَوْ جَاءُوكُمْ **حَصِرَتْ** صُدُورُهُمْ ـــ فَمَا جَعَلَ اللَّهُ لَكُمْ عَلَيْهِمْ سَبِيلاً 🢁 (النساء4: 90) *Al-Qur'an (Qirā'at al-'Aammah)*
	ـــ أَوْ جَاءُوكُمْ **حَصِرَةً** صُدُورُهُمْ ـــ فَمَا جَعَلَ اللَّهُ لَكُمْ **عَلَيْهُمْ** سَبِيلاً *(Roḥ)* 🢁
130.	ـــ وَأُولَئِكُمْ جَعَلْنَا لَكُمْ **عَلَيْهِمْ** سُلْطَانًا مُّبِينًا 🢁 (النساء4: 90) *Al-Qur'an (Qirā'at al-'Aammah)*
	ـــ وَأُولَئِكُمْ جَعَلْنَا لَكُمْ **عَلَيْهُمْ** سُلْطَانًا مُّبِينًا *(Roḥ)* 🢁
131.	وَإِذَا كُنتَ **فِيهِمْ** فَأَقَمْتَ لَهُمُ الصَّلاَةَ ـــ 🢁 (النساء4: 102) *Al-Qur'an (Qirā'at al-'Aammah)*
	وَإِذَا كُنتَ **فِيهُمْ** فَأَقَمْتَ لَهُمُ الصَّلاَةَ ـــ *(Roḥ)* 🢁
132.	ـــ فَمَن يُجَادِلُ اللَّهَ عَنْهُمْ يَوْمَ الْقِيَامَةِ أَم مَّن يَكُونُ **عَلَيْهِمْ** وَكِيلاً 🢁 (النساء4: 109) *Al-Qur'an (Qirā'at al-'Aammah)*
	ـــ فَمَن يُجَادِلُ اللَّهَ عَنْهُمْ يَوْمَ الْقِيَامَةِ أَم مَّن يَكُونُ **عَلَيْهُمْ** وَكِيلاً *(Roḥ)* 🢁
133.	وَمَن يُشَاقِقِ الرَّسُولَ مِن بَعْدِ مَا تَبَيَّنَ لَهُ الْهُدَى وَيَتَّبِعْ غَيْرَ سَبِيلِ الْمُؤْمِنِينَ **نُوَلِّهِ** مَا **تَوَلَّى وَنُصْلِهِ** جَهَنَّمَ وَسَاءَتْ مَصِيراً 🢁 (النساء4: 109) *Al-Qur'an (Qirā'at al-'Aammah)*
	وَمَن يُشَاقِقِ الرَّسُولَ مِن بَعْدِ مَا تَبَيَّنَ لَهُ الْهُدَى وَيَتَّبِعْ غَيْرَ سَبِيلِ الْمُؤْمِنِينَ **نُوَلِّهْ** مَا **تَوَلَّى وَنُصْلِهْ** جَهَنَّمَ وَسَاءَتْ مَصِيراً 🢁 *(Douri)*، *(Shuba)*
134.	يَعِدُهُمْ وَيُمَنِّيهِمْ وَمَا يَعِدُهُمُ الشَّيْطَانُ إِلاَّ غُرُوراً 🢁 (النساء4: 120) *Al-Qur'an (Qirā'at al-'Aammah)*

	يَعِدُهُمْ وَيُمَنِّيهُمْ وَمَا يَعِدُهُمُ الشَّيْطَانُ إِلاَّ غُرُوراً (*Roḥ*)
135.	۔۔وَعْدَ اللَّهِ حَقّاً وَمَنْ أَصْدَقُ مِنَ اللَّهِ قِيلاً (النساء4: 122) *Al-Qur'an (Qirā'at al-'Aammah)* ۔۔وَعْدَ اللَّهِ حَقّاً وَمَنْ أَصْدَقُ مِنَ اللَّهِ قِيلاً (*Warsh*)
136.	۔۔۔ فَأُوْلَـٰئِكَ يَدْخُلُونَ ٱلْجَنَّةَ وَلاَ يُظْلَمُونَ نَقِيراً (النساء4: 124) *Al-Qur'an (Qirā'at al-'Aammah)* ۔۔۔ فَأُوْلَـٰئِكَ يُدْخَلُونَ ٱلْجَنَّةَ وَلاَ يُظْلَمُونَ نَقِيراً (*Douri*)، (*Shuba*)، (*Roḥ*)
137.	وَيَسْتَفْتُونَكَ فِي النِّسَاءِ قُلِ اللَّهُ يُفْتِيكُمْ فِيهِنَّ۔۔۔ (النساء4: 127) *Al-Qur'an (Qirā'at al-'Aammah)* وَيَسْتَفْتُونَكَ فِي النِّسَاءِ قُلِ اللَّهُ يُفْتِيكُمْ فِيهُنَّ ۔۔۔ (*Roḥ*)
138.	وَإِنِ امْرَأَةٌ خَافَتْ مِنْ بَعْلِهَا نُشُوزاً أَوْ إِعْرَاضاً فَلاَ جُنَاحَ عَلَيْهِمَا بَيْنَهُمَا صُلْحاً ۔۔۔ (النساء4: 128) *(Al-Qur'an (Qirā'at al-'Aammah)* وَإِنِ امْرَأَةٌ خَافَتْ مِنْ بَعْلِهَا نُشُوزاً أَوْ إِعْرَاضاً فَلاَ جُنَاحَ عَلَيْهُمَا۔۔۔ (*Roḥ*) ۔۔۔أَنْ يَّصَّلَحَا بَيْنَهُمَا صُلْحاً ۔۔۔ (*Warsh*)، (*Douri*)، (*Qalon*)، (*Roḥ*)
139.	إِنَّ الْمُنَافِقِينَ فِي الدَّرْكِ الأَسْفَلِ مِنَ النَّارِ وَلَن تَجِدَ لَهُمْ نَصِيراً (النساء4: 145) *Al-Qur'an (Qirā'at al-'Aammah)* إِنَّ الْمُنَافِقِينَ فِي الدَّرَكِ الأَسْفَلِ مِنَ النَّارِ وَلَن تَجِدَ لَهُمْ نَصِيراً (*Warsh*)، (*Douri*)، (*Qalon*)، (*Roḥ*)
140.	۔۔۔ أُوْلَـٰئِكَ سَوْفَ يُؤْتِيهِمْ أُجُورَهُمْ وَكَانَ اللَّهُ غَفُوراً رَّحِيماً (النساء4: 152) *Al-Qur'an (Qirā'at al-'Aammah)* ۔۔۔ أُوْلَـٰئِكَ سَوْفَ نُؤْتِيهِمْ أُجُورَهُمْ ۔۔ (*Roḥ*) ۔۔۔ أُوْلَـٰئِكَ سَوْفَ نُؤْتِيهِمْ أُجُورَهُمْ ۔۔ (*Warsh*)، (*Douri*)، (*Shuba*)، (*Qalon*)،
141.	يَسْأَلُكَ أَهْلُ الْكِتَابِ أَنْ تُنَزِّلَ عَلَيْهِمْ كِتَاباً مِنَ السَّمَاءِ فَقَدْ سَأَلُوا مُوسَى أَكْبَرَ مِنْ ذَلِكَ فَقَالُوا أَرِنَا اللَّهَ جَهْرَةً ۔۔۔ (النساء4: 153)

	Al-Qur'an (Qirā'at al-'Aammah) --- تَنْزِلُ عَلَيْهُمْ --- (*Roḥ*) --- تُنْزِلَ عَلَيْهُمْ --- (*Douri*)، --- أَرْنَا اللَّهَ --- (*Roḥ*)، (*Douri*)
142.	--- فَبِمَا نَقْضِهِمْ مِيثَاقَهُمْ وَكُفْرِهِمْ بِآيَاتِ اللَّهِ وَقَتْلِهِمُ الْأَنْبِيَاءَ بِغَيْرِ حَقٍّ --- (النساء4: 155) *Al-Qur'an (Qirā'at al-'Aammah)* --- وَقَتْلِهِمِ الْأَنْبِيَاءَ --- (*Roḥ*)، (*Douri*)
143.	--- وَيَوْمَ الْقِيَامَةِ يَكُونُ عَلَيْهِمْ شَهِيداً (النساء4: 159) *Al-Qur'an (Qirā'at al-'Aammah)* --- وَيَوْمَ الْقِيَامَةِ يَكُونُ عَلَيْهِمْ شَهِيداً (*Roḥ*)
144.	فَبِظُلْمٍ مِنَ الَّذِينَ هَادُوا حَرَّمْنَا عَلَيْهِمْ طَيِّبَاتٍ أُحِلَّتْ لَهُمْ وَبِصَدِّهِمْ عَنْ سَبِيلِ اللَّهِ كَثِيراً (النساء4: 160) *Al-Qur'an (Qirā'at al-'Aammah)* --- عَلَيْهُمْ --- (*Roḥ*)
145.	وَأَخْذِهِمُ الرِّبَا وَقَدْ نُهُوا عَنْهُ --- (النساء4: 161) *Al-Qur'an (Qirā'at al-'Aammah)* --- وَأَخْذُهُمُ الرِّبَا وَقَدْ نُهُوا عَنْهُ --- (*Roḥ*)
146.	--- أُوْلَائِكَ سَنُؤْتِيهِمْ أَجْراً عَظِيماً (النساء4: 162) *Al-Qur'an (Qirā'at al-'Aammah)* --- أُوْلَائِكَ سَنُؤْتِيهُمْ أَجْراً عَظِيماً (*Roḥ*)
147.	فَأَمَّا الَّذِينَ آمَنُوا وَعَمِلُوا الصَّالِحَاتِ فَيُوَفِّيهِمْ أُجُورَهُمْ وَيَزِيدُهُمْ مِنْ فَضْلِهِ --- (النساء4: 172) *Al-Qur'an (Qirā'at al-'Aammah)* --- فَيُوَفِّيهِمْ أُجُورَهُمْ --- (*Roḥ*)
148.	--- وَيَهْدِيهِمْ إِلَيْهِ صِرَاطاً مُسْتَقِيماً (النساء4: 175) *Al-Qur'an (Qirā'at al-'Aammah)* --- وَيَهْدِيهُمْ --- (*Roḥ*)
149.	--- وَامْسَحُوا بِرُءُوسِكُمْ وَأَرْجُلَكُمْ إِلَى الْكَعْبَيْنِ --- وَإِنْ كُنْتُمْ مَرْضَى أَوْ عَلَى سَفَرٍ أَوْ جَاءَ أَحَدٌ مِنْكُمْ مِنَ الْغَائِطِ --- (المائده5: 6)

	Al-Qur'an (Qirā'at al-'Aammah)
	--- وَأَرْجُلَكُمْ إِلَى الْكَعْبَيْنِ --- *(Douri)*، *(Shuba)*
	---أَوْ جَا أَحَدّ--- *(Warsh)*، *(Douri)* *(Qalon)*
150.	وَيُخْرِجُهُم مِنَ الظُّلُمَاتِ إِلَى النُّورِ بِإِذْنِهِ **وَيَهْدِيهِمْ** إِلَى صِرَاطٍ مُسْتَقِيمٍ ⬆ (المائده5: 16)　*Al-Qur'an (Qirā'at al-'Aammah)* --- **وَيَهْدِيهُمْ** --- *(Roḥ)*
151.	قَالَ رَجُلَانِ مِنَ الَّذِينَ يَخَافُونَ أَنْعَمَ اللَّهُ **عَلَيْهِمَا** ادْخُلُوا **عَلَيْهِمُ** الْبَابَ --- (المائده5: 23) *Al-Qur'an (Qirā'at al-'Aammah)* ---**عَلَيْهُمَا** ادْخُلُوا **عَلَيْهُمُ** الْبَابَ --- *(Roḥ)*
152.	قَالَ فَإِنَّهَا مُحَرَّمَةٌ **عَلَيْهِمْ** أَرْبَعِينَ سَنَةً ⬆ (المائده5: 26) *Al-Qur'an (Qirā'at al-'Aammah)* قَالَ فَإِنَّهَا مُحَرَّمَةٌ **عَلَيْهُمْ** أَرْبَعِينَ سَنَةً --- ⬆ *(Roḥ)*
153.	وَاتْلُ **عَلَيْهِمْ** نَبَأَ ابْنَيْ آدَمَ بِالْحَقِّ --- ⬆ (المائده5: 27) *Al-Qur'an (Qirā'at al-'Aammah)* --- وَاتْلُ **عَلَيْهُمْ** --- *(Roḥ)*
154.	لَئِنْ بَسَطتَ إِلَيَّ يَدَكَ لِتَقْتُلَنِي مَا أَنَا بِبَاسِطٍ **يَدِيَ** إِلَيْكَ--- ⬆ (المائده5: 28) *Al-Qur'an (Qirā'at al-'Aammah)* لَئِنْ بَسَطتَ إِلَيَّ يَدَكَ لِتَقْتُلَنِي مَا أَنَا بِبَاسِطٍ **يَدِي** إِلَيْكَ--- ⬆ *(Shuba)*، *(Roḥ)*
155.	إِنَّمَا جَزَاءُ الَّذِينَ يُحَارِبُونَ اللَّهَ وَرَسُولَهُ --- أَوْ يُصَلَّبُوا أَوْ تُقَطَّعَ **أَيْدِيهِمْ** وَأَرْجُلُهُم مِنْ خِلَافٍ --- ⬆ (المائده5: 33) *Al-Qur'an (Qirā'at al-'Aammah)* --- أَوْ تُقَطَّعَ **أَيْدِيهُمْ** وَأَرْجُلُهُمْ --- *(Roḥ)*
156.	إِلَّا الَّذِينَ تَابُوا مِنْ قَبْلِ أَنْ تَقْدِرُوا **عَلَيْهِمْ** --- ⬆ (المائده5: 34) *Al-Qur'an (Qirā'at al-'Aammah)* إِلَّا الَّذِينَ تَابُوا مِنْ قَبْلِ أَنْ تَقْدِرُوا **عَلَيْهُمْ**--- ⬆ *(Roḥ)*

157.	سَمَّاعُونَ لِلْكَذِبِ أَكَّالُونَ لِلسُّحْتِ ---🏛 (المائده5: 42) *Al-Qur'an (Qirā'at al-'Aammah)* سَمَّاعُونَ لِلْكَذِبِ أَكَّالُونَ لِلسُّحْتِ ---🏛 *(Douri)*
158.	وَكَتَبْنَا **عَلَيْهُمْ** فِيهَا أَنَّ النَّفْسَ بِالنَّفْسِ ---🏛 (المائده5: 42) *Al-Qur'an (Qirā'at al-'Aammah)* وَكَتَبْنَا **عَلَيْهُمْ** فِيهَا أَنَّ النَّفْسَ بِالنَّفْسِ ---🏛 *(Roḥ)*
159.	فَتَرَى الَّذِينَ فِي قُلُوبِهِمْ مَرَضٌ يُسَارِعُونَ **فِيهِم** ---🏛 (المائده5: 52) *Al-Qur'an (Qirā'at al-'Aammah)* فَتَرَى الَّذِينَ فِي قُلُوبِهِمْ مَرَضٌ يُسَارِعُونَ **فِيهِم** ---🏛 *(Roḥ)*
160.	**وَيَقُولُ الَّذِينَ** آمَنُوا أَهَاؤُلَاء الَّذِينَ أَقْسَمُوا بِاللَّهِ جَهْدَ أَيْمَانِهِمْ ---🏛 (المائده5: 53) *Al-Qur'an (Qirā'at al-'Aammah)* ---**وَيَقُولَ الَّذِينَ** آمَنُوا--- *(Douri)*، *(Roḥ)* **يَقُولُ الَّذِينَ**--- *(Warsh)*، *(Qalon)*
161.	يَا أَيُّهَا الَّذِينَ آمَنُوا مَنْ **يَرْتَدَّ مِنْكُمْ** عَنْ دِينِهِ ---🏛 (المائده5: 54) *Al-Qur'an (Qirā'at al-'Aammah)* --- **يَرْتَدِدْ مِنْكُمْ** *(Warsh)*، *(Qalon)*
162.	يَا أَيُّهَا الَّذِينَ آمَنُوا لَا تَتَّخِذُوا الَّذِينَ اتَّخَذُوا دِينَكُمْ **هُزُوًا** --- **وَالْكُفَّارَ أَوْلِيَاءَ** ---🏛 (المائده5: 57) *Al-Qur'an (Qirā'at al-'Aammah)* --- **وَالْكُفَّارِ** --- *(Douri)*، *(Roḥ)*
163.	وَتَرَى كَثِيراً مِنْهُمْ يُسَارِعُونَ فِي الْإِثْمِ وَالْعُدْوَانِ **وَأَكْلِهِمُ السُّحْتَ** لَبِئْسَ مَا كَانُوا يَعْمَلُونَ🏛 (المائده5: 62) *Al-Qur'an (Qirā'at al-'Aammah)* --- **وَأَكْلِهِم السُّحْتَ** --- *(Douri)*، *(Roḥ)*
164.	لَوْلَا يَنْهَاهُمُ الرَّبَّانِيُّونَ وَالْأَحْبَارُ عَنْ قَوْلِهِمُ الْإِثْمَ **وَأَكْلِهِمُ السُّحْتَ** لَبِئْسَ مَا كَانُوا يَصْنَعُونَ🏛 (المائده5: 63) *Al-Qur'an (Qirā'at al-'Aammah)* --- عَنْ قَوْلِهِمُ الْإِثْمَ **وَأَكْلِهِمُ السُّحْتَ** --- *(Douri)*، *(Roḥ)*

165.	وَقَالَتِ الْيَهُودُ يَدُ اللَّهِ مَغْلُولَةٌ غُلَّتْ أَيْدِيهِمْ وَلُعِنُوا بِمَا قَالُوا ٮ--ⴲ (المائده5: 64) *Al-Qur'an (Qirā'at al-'Aammah)* ---أَيْدِيهُمْ--- *(Roḥ)*
166.	وَلَوْ أَنَّهُمْ أَقَامُوا التَّوْرَاةَ وَالإِنْجِيلَ وَمَا أُنزِلَ إِلَيْهِم مِّن رَّبِّهِمْ---ⴲ (المائده5: 66) *Al-Qur'an (Qirā'at al-'Aammah)* --- وَمَا أُنزِلَ إِلَيْهُمْ مِن رَبِّهِمْ--- *(Roḥ)*
167.	يَا أَيُّهَا الرَّسُولُ بَلِّغْ مَا أُنزِلَ إِلَيْكَ مِن رَّبِّكَ وَإِن لَّمْ تَفْعَلْ فَمَا بَلَّغْتَ رِسَالَتَهُ و ---ⴲ (المائده5: 67) *Al-Qur'an (Qirā'at al-'Aammah)* --- فَمَا بَلَّغْتَ رِسَالَتِهِ ـﻰ --- *(Warsh)*، *(Shuba)*، *(Qalon)*،*(Roḥ)*
168.	إِنَّ الَّذِينَ آمَنُوا وَالَّذِينَ هَادُوا وَالصَّابِئُونَ وَالنَّصَارَىٰ مَنْ آمَنَ بِاللَّهِ وَالْيَوْمِ الآخِرِ وَعَمِلَ صَالِحا فَلاَ خَوْفٌ عَلَيْهِمْ وَلاَ هُمْ يَحْزَنُونَⴲ (المائده5: 69) *Al-Qur'an (Qirā'at al-'Aammah)* --- وَالصَّابُونَ--- *(Warsh)*، *(Qalon)*، --- فَلاَ خَوْفَ عَلَيْهُمْ--- *(Roḥ)*
169.	لَقَدْ أَخَذْنَا مِيثَاقَ بَنِي إِسْرَائِيلَ وَأَرْسَلْنَا إِلَيْهِمْ رُسُلاً ---ⴲ (المائده5: 70) *Al-Qur'an (Qirā'at al-'Aammah)* لَقَدْ أَخَذْنَا مِيثَاقَ بَنِي إِسْرَائِيلَ وَأَرْسَلْنَا إِلَيْهُمْ رُسُلاً ---ⴲ *(Roḥ)*
170.	وَحَسِبُوا أَلاَّ تَكُونَ فِتْنَةٌ فَعَمُوا وَصَمُّوا ثُمَّ تَابَ اللَّهُ عَلَيْهِمْ---ⴲ (المائده5: 71) *Al-Qur'an (Qirā'at al-'Aammah)* ---- أَلاَّ تَكُونُ فِتْنَةٌ --- *(Douri)*، *(Roḥ)* --- عَلَيْهُمْ --- *(Roḥ)*
171.	أَن سَخِطَ اللَّهُ عَلَيْهِمْ وَفِي الْعَذَابِ هُمْ خَالِدُونَ---ⴲ (المائده5: 80) *Al-Qur'an (Qirā'at al-'Aammah)* أَن سَخِطَ اللَّهُ عَلَيْهُمْ --- *(Roḥ)*
172.	---إِن تُبْدَ لَكُمْ تَسُؤْكُمْ وَإِن تَسْأَلُوا عَنْهَا حِينَ يُنَزَّلُ الْقُرْآنُ تُبْدَ لَكُمْ عَفَا اللَّهُ عَنْهَا وَاللَّهُ غَفُورٌ حَلِيمٌ ⴲ (المائده5: 101) *Al-Qur'an (Qirā'at al-'Aammah)*

	--- حِينَ يُنَزَّلُ الْقُرْآنُ --- (Douri)، (Roḥ)
173.	فَإِنْ عُثِرَ عَلَى أَنَّهُمَا اسْتَحَقَّا إِثْماً فَآخَرَانِ يَقُومَانِ مَقَامَهُمَا مِنَ الَّذِينَ اسْتَحَقَّ عَلَيْهِمُ الْأَوْلَيَانِ فَيُقْسِمَانِ بِاللَّهِ لَشَهَادَتُنَا --- (المائده5: 107) *Al-Qur'an (Qirā'at al-'Aammah)* الَّذِينَ اسْتُحِقَّ عَلَيْهِمُ الْأَوْلَيَانِ (Warsh)، الَّذِينَ اسْتُحِقَّ عَلَيْهِمُ الْأَوْلَيَانِ (Douri)، الَّذِينَ اسْتُحِقَّ عَلَيْهِمُ الْأَوَّلِينَ --- (Shuba) الَّذِينَ اسْتُحِقَّ عَلَيْهِمُ الْأَوَّلِينَ --- (Roḥ)
174.	--- وَإِذْ تَخْلُقُ مِنَ الطِّينِ كَهَيْئَةِ الطَّيْرِ بِإِذْنِي فَتَنْفُخُ فِيهَا فَتَكُونُ طَيْراً بِإِذْنِي --- (المائده5: 110) *Al-Qur'an (Qirā'at al-'Aammah)* --- فَتَكُونُ طَائِراً بِإِذْنِي --- (Warsh)، (Qalon)، (Roḥ)
175.	إِذْ قَالَ الْحَوَارِيُّونَ يَا عِيسَى ابْنَ مَرْيَمَ هَلْ يَسْتَطِيعُ رَبُّكَ أَنْ يُنَزِّلَ عَلَيْنَا مَائِدَةً مِنَ السَّمَاءِ --- (المائده5: 112) *Al-Qur'an (Qirā'at al-'Aammah)* أَنْ يُنْزِلَ عَلَيْنَا مَائِدَةً --- (Douri)، (Roḥ)
176.	قَالَ اللَّهُ إِنِّي مُنَزِّلُهَا عَلَيْكُمْ فَمَنْ يَكْفُرْ بَعْدُ مِنْكُمْ فَإِنِّي أُعَذِّبُهُ عَذَاباً لاَ أُعَذِّبُهُ أَحَداً مِنَ الْعَالَمِينَ (المائده5: 115) *Al-Qur'an (Qirā'at al-'Aammah)* قَالَ اللَّهُ إِنِّي مُنْزِلُهَا عَلَيْكُمْ --- (Douri)، (Roḥ)
177.	وَإِذْ قَالَ اللَّهُ يَا عِيسَى ابْنَ مَرْيَمَ أَأَنْتَ قُلْتَ لِلنَّاسِ اتَّخِذُونِي وَأُمِّيَ إِلَهَيْنِ مِنْ دُونِ اللَّهِ --- (المائده5: 116) *Al-Qur'an (Qirā'at al-'Aammah)* --- أَأَنْتَ قُلْتَ لِلنَّاسِ اتَّخِذُونِي وَأُمِّي إِلَهَيْنِ --- (Roḥ)
178.	لِلَّهِ مُلْكُ السَّمَاوَاتِ وَالْأَرْضِ وَمَا فِيهِنَّ وَهُوَ عَلَى كُلِّ شَيْءٍ قَدِيرٌ (المائده5: 120) *Al-Qur'an (Qirā'at al-'Aammah)* لِلَّهِ مُلْكُ السَّمَاوَاتِ وَالْأَرْضِ وَمَا فِيهِنَّ --- (Roḥ)

179.	وَمَا تَأْتِيهِمْ مِنْ آيَةٍ مِنْ آيَاتِ رَبِّهِمْ إِلاَّ كَانُوا عَنْهَا مُعْرِضِينَ (الانعام6: 04) *Al-Qur'an (Qirā'at al-'Aammah)* --- وَمَا تَأْتِيهُمْ --- *(Roḥ)*
180.	فَقَدْ كَذَّبُوا بِالْحَقِّ لَمَّا جَاءَهُمْ فَسَوْفَ يَأْتِيهِمْ أَنْبَاءُ مَا كَانُوا بِهِ يَسْتَهْزِئُونَ (الانعام6: 05) *Al-Qur'an (Qirā'at al-'Aammah)* --- يَأْتِيهُمْ --- *(Roḥ)*
181.	--- وَأَرْسَلْنَا السَّمَاءَ عَلَيْهِمْ مِدْرَاراً --- (الانعام6: 06) *Al-Qur'an (Qirā'at al-'Aammah)* --- عَلَيْهُمْ --- *(Roḥ)*
182.	وَلَوْ نَزَّلْنَا عَلَيْكَ كِتَاباً فِي قِرْطَاسٍ فَلَمَسُوهُ بِأَيْدِيهِمْ --- (الانعام6: 07) *Al-Qur'an (Qirā'at al-'Aammah)* --- فَلَمَسُوهُ بِأَيْدِيهُمْ --- *(Roḥ)*
183.	مَنْ يُصْرَفْ عَنْهُ يَوْمَئِذٍ فَقَدْ رَحِمَهُ وَذَلِكَ الْفَوْزُ الْمُبِينُ (الانعام6: 16) *Al-Qur'an (Qirā'at al-'Aammah)* --- مَنْ يَصْرِفْ عَنْهُ --- *(Shuba)*، *(Roḥ)*
184.	وَيَوْمَ نَحْشُرُهُمْ جَمِيعاً ثُمَّ نَقُولُ لِلَّذِينَ أَشْرَكُوا أَيْنَ شُرَكَاؤُكُمُ الَّذِينَ كُنتُمْ تَزْعُمُونَ (الانعام6: 22) *Al-Qur'an (Qirā'at al-'Aammah)* --- وَيَوْمَ يَحْشُرُهُمْ جَمِيعاً ثُمَّ يَقُولُ --- *(Roḥ)*
185.	ثُمَّ لَمْ تَكُنْ فِتْنَتُهُمْ إِلاَّ أَنْ قَالُوا وَاللَّهِ رَبِّنَا مَا كُنَّا مُشْرِكِينَ (الانعام6: 23) *Al-Qur'an (Qirā'at al-'Aammah)* --- لَمْ يَكُنْ فِتْنَتَهُمْ --- *(Roḥ)*، --- وَ لَمْ تَكُنْ فِتْنَتَهُمْ --- *(Warsh)* --- لَمْ تَكُنْ فِتْنَتَهُمْ --- *(Douri)*، *(Qalon)*
186.	فَلَمَّا نَسُوا مَا ذُكِّرُوا بِهِ فَتَحْنَا عَلَيْهِمْ أَبْوَابَ كُلِّ شَيْءٍ --- (الانعام6: 44) *Al-Qur'an (Qirā'at al-'Aammah)*

	--- عَلَيْهُمْ --- (Roḥ) --- عَلَيْهُمْ وَ --- (Warsh)
187.	وَمَا نُرْسِلُ الْمُرْسَلِينَ إِلاَّ مُبَشِّرِينَ وَمُنْذِرِينَ فَمَنْ آمَنَ وَأَصْلَحَ فَلاَ **خَوْفٌ عَلَيْهِمْ** وَلاَ هُمْ يَحْزَنُونَ﴿ (الانعام6: 48) *Al-Qur'an (Qirā'at al-'Aammah)* --- فَلاَ **خَوْفَ عَلَيْهُمْ** --- (Roḥ)
188.	وَمَا مِنْ حِسَابِكَ عَلَيْهِمْ مِنْ شَيْءٍ فَتَطْرُدَهُمْ فَتَكُونَ مِنَ الظَّالِمِينَ﴿ (الانعام6: 52) *Al-Qur'an (Qirā'at al-'Aammah)* --- عَلَيْهُمْ --- (Roḥ)
189.	وَكَذَلِكَ فَتَنَّا بَعْضَهُمْ بِبَعْضٍ لِيَقُولُوا أَهَاؤُلاَءِ مَنَّ اللهُ مِنْ بَيْنِنَا أَلَيْسَ اللهُ بِأَعْلَمَ عَلَيْهِمْ بِالشَّاكِرِينَ﴿ (الانعام6: 53) *Al-Qur'an (Qirā'at al-'Aammah)* --- عَلَيْهُمْ --- (Roḥ)
190.	---إِنِ الْحُكْمُ إِلاَّ لِلَّهِ **يَقُصُّ الْحَقَّ** وَهُوَ خَيْرُ الْفَاصِلِينَ﴿ (الانعام6: 57) *Al-Qur'an (Qirā'at al-'Aammah)* --- **يَقْضِ الْحَقَّ** --- (Douri)، (Roḥ)
191.	قُلْ مَنْ يُنَجِّيكُم مِّنْ ظُلُمَاتِ الْبَرِّ وَالْبَحْرِ تَدْعُونَهُ تَضَرُّعاً وَخُفْيَةً لَئِنْ **أَنْجَانَا** مِنْ هَذِهِ لَنَكُونَنَّ مِنَ الشَّاكِرِينَ ﴿ (الانعام6: 63) *Al-Qur'an (Qirā'at al-'Aammah)* قُلْ مَنْ يُنْجِيكُم --- (Roḥ) --- لَئِنْ **أَنْجَيْتَنَا** مِنْ هَذِهِ --- (Warsh)، (Douri)، (Qalon)
192.	قُلِ اللهُ يُنَجِّيكُم مِّنْهَا وَمِنْ كُلِّ كَرْبٍ ثُمَّ أَنْتُمْ تُشْرِكُونَ ﴿ (الانعام6: 64) *Al-Qur'an (Qirā'at al-'Aammah)* قُلِ اللهُ يُنْجِيكُم --- (Warsh)، (Douri)، (Roḥ)، (Qalon)
193.	وَكَيْفَ أَخَافُ مَا أَشْرَكْتُمْ وَلاَ تَخَافُونَ أَنَّكُمْ أَشْرَكْتُمْ بِاللهِ مَا لَمْ يُنَزِّلْ بِهِ عَلَيْكُمْ سُلْطَانًا --- (الانعام6: 81) *Al-Qur'an (Qirā'at al-'Aammah)* --- مَا لَمْ يُنْزِلْ بِهِ --- (Warsh)، (Douri)، (Roḥ)

194.	وَزَكَرِيَّا وَيَحْيَى وَعِيسَى وَإِلْيَاسَ كُلٌّ مِنَ الصَّالِحِينَ ⚱ (الانعام6: 85) Al-Qur'an (Qirā'at al-'Aammah) وَزَكَرِيَّآءَ وَيَحْيَى وَعِيسَى وَإِلْيَاسَ كُلٌّ مِنَ الصَّالِحِينَ ⚱ (Warsh)، (Douri) (Shuba)، (Qalon)، (Roḥ)
195.	--- وَلَوْ تَرَى إِذِ الظَّالِمُونَ فِي غَمَرَاتِ الْمَوْتِ وَالْمَلَائِكَةُ بَاسِطُوا أَيْدِيهِمْ أَخْرِجُوا أَنفُسَكُمُ--- ⚱ (الانعام6: 93) Al-Qur'an (Qirā'at al-'Aammah) --- بَاسِطُوا أَيْدِيهُمْ --- (Roḥ)
196.	--- لَقَدْ تَقَطَّعَ بَيْنُكُمْ وَضَلَّ عَنكُم مَّا كُنتُمْ تَزْعُمُونَ ⚱ (الانعام6: 94) Al-Qur'an (Qirā'at al-'Aammah) --- لَقَدْ تَقَطَّعَ بَيْنُكُمْ وَضَلَّ عَنكُم مَّا كُنتُمْ تَزْعُمُونَ ⚱ (Roḥ)
197.	فَالِقُ الْإِصْبَاح وَجَعَلَ اللَّيْلَ سَكَناً ⚱ (الانعام6: 96) Al-Qur'an (Qirā'at al-'Aammah) فَالِقُ الْإِصْبَاح وَجَاعِلُ اللَّيْلَ سَكَناً ⚱ (Warsh)، (Douri) (Qalon)، (Roḥ)
198.	وَهُوَ الَّذِي أَنشَأَكُم مِّن نَّفْسٍ وَاحِدَةٍ فَمُسْتَقَرٌّ وَمُسْتَوْدَعٌ قَدْ فَصَّلْنَا الْآيَاتِ لِقَوْمٍ يَفْقَهُونَ ⚱ (الانعام6: 98) Al-Qur'an (Qirā'at al-'Aammah) وَهُوَ الَّذِي أَنشَأَكُم مِّن نَّفْسٍ وَاحِدَةٍ فَمُسْتَقِرٌّ وَمُسْتَوْدَعٌ قَدْ فَصَّلْنَا الْآيَاتِ لِقَوْمٍ يَفْقَهُونَ ⚱ (Douri)، (Roḥ)
199.	وَكَذَلِكَ نُصَرِّفُ الْآيَاتِ وَلِيَقُولُوا دَرَسْتَ وَلِنُبَيِّنَهُ لِقَوْمٍ يَعْلَمُونَ ⚱ Al-Qur'an (Qirā'at al-'Aammah) (الانعام6: 105) وَكَذَلِكَ نُصَرِّفُ الْآيَاتِ وَلِيَقُولُوا دَارَسْتَ وَلِنُبَيِّنَهُ لِقَوْمٍ يَعْلَمُونَ ⚱ (Douri)، (Roḥ)
200.	وَلَوْ شَاءَ اللَّهُ مَا أَشْرَكُوا وَمَا جَعَلْنَاكَ عَلَيْهِمْ حَفِيظاً وَمَا أَنتَ عَلَيْهِم بِوَكِيلٍ ⚱ (الانعام6: 107) Al-Qur'an (Qirā'at al-'Aammah) وَلَوْ شَاءَ اللَّهُ مَا أَشْرَكُوا وَمَا جَعَلْنَاكَ عَلَيْهُمْ حَفِيظاً وَمَا أَنتَ عَلَيْهُمْ بِوَكِيلٍ ⚱

	(Roḥ)
201.	وَلاَ تَسُبُّوا الَّذِينَ يَدْعُونَ مِنْ دُونِ اللَّهِ فَيَسُبُّوا اللَّهَ **عَدْواً** بِغَيْرِ عِلْمٍ ---⇑ (6الانعام: 108) *Al-Qur'an (Qirā'at al-'Aammah)* --- **عُدُوّاً** --- **(Roḥ)**
202.	--- وَمَا يُشْعِرُكُمْ **أَنَّهَا** إِذَا جَاءَتْ لاَ يُؤْمِنُونَ⇑ (6الانعام: 109) *Al-Qur'an (Qirā'at al-'Aammah)* --- وَمَا يُشْعِرُكُمْ **إِنَّهَا** --- **(Douri)**، **(Roḥ)** ---وَمَا يُشْعِرُكُمْ وَ --- **(Warsh)**
203.	وَلَوْ أَنَّنَا نَزَّلْنَا إِلَيْهِمُ الْمَلاَئِكَةَ وَكَلَّمَهُمُ الْمَوْتَى وَحَشَرْنَا **عَلَيْهِمْ** كُلَّ شَيْءٍ قُبُلاً --- ⇑ (6الانعام: 111) *Al-Qur'an (Qirā'at al-'Aammah)* وَلَوْ أَنَّنَا نَزَّلْنَا إِلَيْهِمُ الْمَلاَئِكَةَ وَكَلَّمَهُمُ الْمَوْتَى وَحَشَرْنَا **عَلَيْهُمْ** كُلَّ شَيْءٍ قُبُلاً --- ⇑ **(Roḥ)**
204.	--- وَالَّذِينَ آتَيْنَاهُمُ الْكِتَابَ يَعْلَمُونَ أَنَّهُ **مُنَزَّلٌ** مِنْ رَبِّكَ بِالْحَقِّ فَلاَ تَكُونَنَّ مِنَ الْمُمْتَرِينَ⇑ (6الانعام: 111) *Al-Qur'an (Qirā'at al-'Aammah)* --- أَنَّهُ **مُنْزَلٌ** مِنْ رَبِّكَ بِالْحَقِّ --- **(Warsh)**، **(Douri)**، **(Shuba)**، **(Qalon)**، **(Roḥ)**
205.	وَتَمَّتْ **كَلِمَتُ** رَبِّكَ صِدْقاً وَعَدْلاً لاَ مُبَدِّلَ لِكَلِمَاتِهِ وَهُوَ السَّمِيعُ الْعَلِيمُ⇑ (6الانعام: 115) *Al-Qur'an (Qirā'at al-'Aammah)* وَتَمَّتْ **كَلِمَاتُ** رَبِّكَ صِدْقاً وَعَدْلاً لاَ مُبَدِّلَ لِكَلِمَاتِهِ وَهُوَ السَّمِيعُ الْعَلِيمُ⇑ **(Warsh)**، **(Douri)**، **(Qalon)**، **(Roḥ)**
206.	وَإِنَّ كَثِيراً **لَيُضِلُّونَ** بِأَهْوَائِهِمْ بِغَيْرِ عِلْمٍ إِنَّ رَبَّكَ هُوَ أَعْلَمُ بِالْمُعْتَدِينَ⇑ (6الانعام: 119) *Al-Qur'an (Qirā'at al-'Aammah)* --- وَإِنَّ كَثِيراً **لَّيَضِلُّونَ** بِأَهْوَائِهِمْ --- **(Warsh)**، **(Douri)**، **(Qalon)**، **(Roḥ)**

207.	أَوَمَنْ كَانَ **مَيْتاً** فَأَحْيَيْنَاهُ وَجَعَلْنَا لَهُ نُوراً يَمْشِي بِهِ ---🏛 (الانعام6: 122) *Al-Qur'an (Qirā'at al-'Aammah)* ---أَوَمَنْ كَانَ **مَيِّتاً** --- (Warsh) ، (Qalon) ، (Roḥ)
208.	وَإِذَا جَاءَتْهُمْ آيَةٌ قَالُوا لَنْ نُؤْمِنَ حَتَّى نُؤْتَى مِثْلَ مَا أُوتِيَ رُسُلُ اللَّهِ اللَّهُ أَعْلَمُ **حَيْثُ** **يَجْعَلُ** رِسَالَتَهُ و --- 🏛 (الانعام6: 124) *Al-Qur'an (Qirā'at al-'Aammah)* --- اللَّهُ أَعْلَمُ **حَيْثُ** **يَجْعَلُ** رِسَالَتِهِ ے --- (Warsh) ، (Douri) ، (Shuba) ، (Qalon) ، (Roḥ)
209.	وَكَذَلِكَ زَيَّنَ لِكَثِيرٍ مِنَ الْمُشْرِكِينَ قَتْلَ أَوْلَادِهِمْ شُرَكَاؤُهُمْ لِيُرْدُوهُمْ وَلِيَلْبِسُوا **عَلَيْهِمْ** دِينَهُمْ---🏛 (الانعام6: 137) *Al-Qur'an (Qirā'at al-'Aammah)* --- وَلِيَلْبِسُوا **عَلَيْهُمْ** دِينَهُمْ --- (Roḥ)
210.	--- **سَيَجْزِيهِمْ** بِمَا كَانُوا يَفْتَرُونَ🏛 (الانعام6: 139) *Al-Qur'an (Qirā'at al-'Aammah)* --- **سَيَجْزِيهُمْ** بِمَا كَانُوا يَفْتَرُونَ🏛 (Roḥ)
211.	ثَمَانِيَةَ أَزْوَاجٍ مِنَ الضَّأْنِ اثْنَيْنِ وَمِنَ **الْمَعْزِ** اثْنَيْنِ (الانعام6: 143) *Al-Qur'an (Qirā'at al-'Aammah)* --- وَمِنَ **الْمَعِزِ** اثْنَيْنِ --- (Douri) ، (Roḥ)
212.	وَعَلَى الَّذِينَ هَادُوا حَرَّمْنَا كُلَّ ذِي ظُفُرٍ وَمِنَ الْبَقَرِ وَالْغَنَمِ حَرَّمْنَا **عَلَيْهِمْ** شُحُومَهُمَا ---🏛 (الانعام6: 146) *Al-Qur'an (Qirā'at al-'Aammah)* --- حَرَّمْنَا **عَلَيْهُمْ** شُحُومَهُمَا --- (Roḥ)
213.	---فَاعْدِلُوا وَلَوْ كَانَ ذَا قُرْبَى وَبِعَهْدِ اللَّهِ أَوْفُوا ذَلِكُمْ وَصَّاكُمْ بِهِ لَعَلَّكُمْ **تَذَكَّرُونَ**🏛 *Al-Qur'an (Qirā'at al-'Aammah)* (152 :6الانعام) --- لَعَلَّكُمْ **تَذَّكَّرُونَ** --- (Warsh) ، (Douri) ، (Shuba) ، (Qalon) ، (Roḥ)

214.	مَنْ جَاءَ بِالْحَسَنَةِ فَلَهُ عَشْرُ أَمْثَالِهَا وَمَنْ جَاءَ بِالسَّيِّئَةِ فَلاَ يُجْزَى إِلاَّ مِثْلَهَا وَهُمْ لاَ يُظْلَمُونَ (الانعام6: 160) *Al-Qur'an (Qirā'at al-'Aammah)* --- عَشْرُ أَمْثَالُهَا --- *(Roḥ)*
215.	قُلْ إِنَّنِي هَدَانِي رَبِّي إِلَى صِرَاطٍ مُسْتَقِيمٍ دِيناً قِيَماً مِلَّةَ إِبْرَاهِيمَ حَنِيفاً وَمَا كَانَ مِنَ الْمُشْرِكِينَ (الانعام6: 161) *Al-Qur'an (Qirā'at al-'Aammah)* دِيناً قَيِّماً مِلَّةَ إِبْرَاهِيمَ حَنِيفا--- *(Warsh)*، *(Douri)*، *(Qalon)*، *(Roḥ)*
216.	إِنَّ الَّذِينَ كَذَّبُوا بِآيَاتِنَا وَاسْتَكْبَرُوا عَنْهَا لاَ تُفَتَّحُ لَهُمْ أَبْوَابُ السَّمَاءِ--- (الاعراف7: 40) *Al-Qur'an (Qirā'at al-'Aammah)* إِنَّ الَّذِينَ كَذَّبُوا بِآيَاتِنَا وَاسْتَكْبَرُوا عَنْهَا لاَ تُفْتَحُ لَهُمْ أَبْوَابُ السَّمَاءِ--- *(Douri)*
217.	--- وَدَمَّرْنَا مَا كَانَ يَصْنَعُ فِرْعَوْنُ وَقَوْمُهُ وَمَا كَانُوا يَعْرِشُونَ (الاعراف 7: 137) *Al-Qur'an (Qirā'at al-'Aammah)* --- وَدَمَّرْنَا مَا كَانَ يَصْنَعُ فِرْعَوْنُ وَقَوْمُهُ وَمَا كَانُوا يَعْرُشُونَ *(Shuba)*
218.	إِذْ يُغَشِّيكُمُ النُّعَاسَ أَمَنَةً مِنْهُ --- (الانفال8: 11) *Al-Qur'an (Qirā'at al-'Aammah)* إِذْ يُغْشِيكُمُ النُّعَاسَ أَمَنَةً مِنْهُ --- *(Warsh)*، *(Qalon)* إِذْ يَغْشُكُمُ النُّعَاسَ أَمَنَةً مِنْهُ --- *(Douri)*،
219.	مَا كَانَ لِنَبِيٍّ أَنْ يَكُونَ لَهُ أَسْرَىٰ حَتَّى يُثْخِنَ فِي الأَرْضِ --- (الانفال8: 67) *Al-Qur'an (Qirā'at al-'Aammah)* مَا كَانَ لِنَبِيٍّ أَنْ تَكُونَ لَهُ أَسْرَىٰ حَتَّى يُثْخِنَ فِي الأَرْضِ --- *(Douri)*
220.	--- مِنْ أَعْنَابٍ وَزَرْعٌ وَنَخِيلٌ صِنْوَانٌ وَغَيْرُ صِنْوَانٍ --- (الرّعد 13: 4) *Al-Qur'an (Qirā'at al-'Aammah)* --- مِنْ أَعْنَابٍ وَزَرْعٍ وَنَخِيلٍ صِنْوَانٍ وَغَيْرِ صِنْوَانٍ --- *(Warsh)*، *(Douri)*، *(Qalon)*، *(Shuba)*

THE RECONSTRUCTION OF ISLAMIC THEOLOGY

221.	رُبَمَا يَوَدُّ الَّذِينَ كَفَرُوا لَوْ كَانُوا مُسْلِمِينَ ﴿الحجر15: 2﴾ *Al-Qur'an (Qirā'at al-'Aammah)* --- رُبَّمَا يَوَدُّ الَّذِينَ كَفَرُوا لَوْ كَانُوا مُسْلِمِينَ **(Douri)**
222.	مَا نُنَزِّلُ الْمَلَائِكَةَ إِلاَّ بِالْحَقِّ وَمَا كَانُوا إِذاً مُنْظَرِينَ ﴿الحجر15: 08﴾ *Al-Qur'an (Qirā'at al-'Aammah)* مَا تُنَزَّلُ الْمَلَائِكَةَ إِلاَّ بِالْحَقِّ وَمَا كَانُوا إِذاً مُنْظَرِينَ **(Douri)**، **(Qalon)**
223.	--- لَأَجِدَنَّ خَيْراً مِنْهَا مُنقَلَباً --- ﴿الكهف18: 36﴾ *Al-Qur'an (Qirā'at al-'Aammah)* --- لَأَجِدَنَّ خَيْراً مِنْهُمَا مُنقَلَبا --- **(Warsh)**، **(Qalon)**
224.	وَأُحِيطَ بِثَمَرِهِ فَأَصْبَحَ يُقَلِّبُ كَفَّيْهِ --- ﴿الكهف18: 42﴾ *Al-Qur'an (Qirā'at al-'Aammah)* وَأُحِيطَ بِثُمُرِهِ فَأَصْبَحَ يُقَلِّبُ كَفَّيْهِ --- **(Warsh)**، **(Qalon)** وَأُحِيطَ بِثُمُرِهِ فَأَصْبَحَ يُقَلِّبُ كَفَّيْهِ --- **(Douri)**،
225.	---قَالَ لَوْ شِئْتَ لاَ تَّخَذْتَ عَلَيْهِ أَجْراً ﴿الكهف 18: 77﴾ *Al-Qur'an (Qirā'at al-'Aammah)* --- قَالَ لَوْ شِئْتَ لاَ تَخِذتَّ عَلَيْهِ أَجْراً **(Douri)**
226.	تَكَادُ السَّمَاوَاتُ يَتَفَطَّرْنَ مِنْهُ ---﴿مريم19: 90﴾ *Al-Qur'an (Qirā'at al-'Aammah)* تَكَادُ السَّمَاوَاتُ يَنفَطِرْنَ مِنْهُ --- **(Douri)**، **(Shuba)**
227.	طَاهَا/ طَهَ ﴿طه 20: 1﴾ *Al-Qur'an (Qirā'at al-'Aammah)* طَاه/ طَهَ **(Warsh)** طَهَ--- **(Qalon)** طَهِ--- **(Douri)**
228.	قَالُوا إِنْ هَذَانِ لَسَاحِرَانِ---﴿طه20: 63﴾ *Al-Qur'an (Qirā'at al-'Aammah)*

	قَالُوا إِنَّ **هَٰذَانِ** لَسَاحِرَانِ--🔼 (Warsh)، (Qalon)، (Shuba) قَالُوا إِنَّ **هَٰذَيْ** نِ لَسَاحِرَانِ--🔼 (Douri)،
229.	**قَالَ** رَبِّي يَعْلَمُ الْقَوْلَ فِي السَّمَاءِ وَالْأَرْضِ وَهُوَ السَّمِيعُ الْعَلِيمُ🔼 Al-Qur'an (Qirā'at al-'Aammah) (الانبياء 21: 04) **قُلْ** رَبِّي يَعْلَمُ الْقَوْلَ فِي السَّمَاءِ وَالْأَرْضِ وَهُوَ السَّمِيعُ الْعَلِيمُ🔼 (Warsh)، (Douri)، (Qalon)، (Shuba)
230.	بَلْ قَالُوا أَضْغَاثُ أَحْلَامٍ بَلِ **افْتَرَاهُ** بَلْ هُوَ شَاعِرٌ --- 🔼 (الانبياء 21: 05) Al-Qur'an (Qirā'at al-'Aammah) بَلْ قَالُوا أَضْغَاثُ أَحْلَامٍ بَلِ **افْتَرَايَهُ** بَلْ هُوَ شَاعِرٌ ---🔼 (Warsh)، (Qalon)،
231.	أُذِنَ لِلَّذِينَ **يُقَاتَلُونَ** بِأَنَّهُمْ ظُلِمُوا وَإِنَّ اللَّهَ عَلَىٰ نَصْرِهِمْ لَقَدِيرٌ 🔼 Al-Qur'an (Qirā'at al-'Aammah) (الحج 22: 39) أُذِنَ لِلَّذِينَ **يُقَاتِلُونَ** بِأَنَّهُمْ ظُلِمُوا وَإِنَّ اللَّهَ عَلَىٰ نَصْرِهِمْ لَقَدِيرٌ 🔼 (Douri)، (Shuba)،
232.	--وَلَوْلَا **دَفْعُ** اللَّهِ النَّاسَ بَعْضَهُمْ بِبَعْضٍ--🔼 (الحج 22: 40) Al-Qur'an (Qirā'at al-'Aammah) --وَلَوْلَا **دِفْعُ** اللَّهِ النَّاسَ بَعْضَهُمْ بِبَعْضٍ--🔼 (Warsh)، (Qalon)
233.	مُسْتَكْبِرِينَ بِهِ سَامِرًا **تَهْجُرُونَ**🔼 (المؤمنون 23: 67) Al-Qur'an (Qirā'at al-'Aammah) مُسْتَكْبِرِينَ بِهِ سَامِرًا **تُهْجِرُونَ**🔼 (Warsh) (Qalon)
234.	قَالَ كَمْ لَبِثْتُمْ فِي الْأَرْضِ عَدَدَ سِنِينَ🔼 (المؤمنون 23: 112) Al-Qur'an (Qirā'at al-'Aammah) قَالَ كَمْ لَبِثْتُمْ فِي الْأَرْضِ عَدَدَ سِنِينَ🔼 (Douri)
235.	وَتَوَكَّلْ عَلَى الْعَزِيزِ الرَّحِيمِ🔼 (الشعراء 26: 217) Al-Qur'an (Qirā'at al-'Aammah) فَتَوَكَّلْ عَلَى الْعَزِيزِ الرَّحِيمِ🔼 (Warsh)، (Qalon)،
236.	وَمَا رَبُّكَ بِغَافِلٍ عَمَّا **تَعْمَلُونَ**🔼 (النمل 27: 93)

	Al-Qur'an (Qirā'at al-'Aammah) وَمَا رَبُّكَ بِغَافِلٍ عَمَّا **يَعْمَلُونَ** (*Douri*)، (*Shuba*)
237.	وَمِنْ آيَاتِهِ خَلْقُ السَّمَاوَاتِ وَالأَرْضِ وَاخْتِلافُ أَلْسِنَتِكُمْ وَأَلْوَانِكُمْ إِنَّ فِي ذَلِكَ لَآيَاتٍ **لِلْعَالِمِينَ** (الروم30: 22) *Al-Qur'an (Qirā'at al-'Aammah)* وَمِنْ آيَاتِهِ خَلْقُ السَّمَاوَاتِ وَالأَرْضِ وَاخْتِلافُ أَلْسِنَتِكُمْ وَأَلْوَانِكُمْ إِنَّ فِي ذَلِكَ لَآيَاتٍ **لِلْعَالَمِينَ** (*Warsh*)، (*Douri*)، (*Shuba*)، (*Qalon*)
238.	اللَّهُ الَّذِي خَلَقَكُمْ مِنْ **ضُعْفٍ** ثُمَّ جَعَلَ مِنْ بَعْدِ **ضُعْفٍ** قُوَّةً ثُمَّ جَعَلَ مِنْ بَعْدِ قُوَّةٍ **ضُعْفاً** وَشَيْبَةً---(الروم30: 54) *Al-Qur'an (Qirā'at al-'Aammah)* اللَّهُ الَّذِي خَلَقَكُمْ مِنْ **ضَعْفٍ** ثُمَّ جَعَلَ مِنْ بَعْدِ **ضَعْفٍ** قُوَّةً ثُمَّ جَعَلَ مِنْ بَعْدِ قُوَّةٍ **ضَعْفاً** وَشَيْبَةً --- (*Narrarion of Madina*)
239.	رَبَّنَا آتِهِمْ ضِعْفَيْنِ مِنَ الْعَذَابِ وَالْعَنْهُمْ لَعْناً **كَبِيراً** (الاحزاب33: 68) *Al-Qur'an (Qirā'at al-'Aammah)* رَبَّنَا آتِهِمْ ضِعْفَيْنِ مِنَ الْعَذَابِ وَالْعَنْهُمْ لَعْناً **كَثِيراً** (*Qalon*)، (*Warsh*)، (*Douri*)
240.	فَقَالُوا رَبَّنَا **بَاعِدْ** بَيْنَ أَسْفَارِنَا وَظَلَمُوا أَنْفُسَهُمْ--- (سبا34: 19) *Al-Qur'an (Qirā'at al-'Aammah)* فَقَالُوا رَبَّنَا **بَعِّدْ** بَيْنَ أَسْفَارِنَا وَظَلَمُوا أَنْفُسَهُمْ--- (*Douri*)،
241.	لِيَأْكُلُوا مِنْ ثَمَرِهِ وَمَا **عَمِلَتْهُ** أَيْدِيهِمْ أَفَلاَ يَشْكُرُونَ (يسين36: 35) *Al-Qur'an (Qirā'at al-'Aammah)* لِيَأْكُلُوا مِنْ ثَمَرِهِ وَمَا **عَمِلَتْ** أَيْدِيهِمْ أَفَلاَ يَشْكُرُونَ (*Shuba*)،
242.	وَلَقَدْ أَضَلَّ مِنْكُمْ **جِبِلّاً** كَثِيراً أَفَلَمْ تَكُونُوا تَعْقِلُونَ (سوره يسين36: 62) *Al-Qur'an (Qirā'at al-'Aammah)* وَلَقَدْ أَضَلَّ مِنْكُمْ **جُبْلاً** كَثِيراً أَفَلَمْ تَكُونُوا تَعْقِلُونَ (*Douri*)
243.	**لاَ** يَسَّمَّعُونَ إِلَى الْمَلإِ الأَعْلَى ---(الصَّافَّات37: 08) *Al-Qur'an (Qirā'at al-'Aammah)*

	لَا يَسَّمَّعُونَ إِلَى الْمَلَإِ الْأَعْلَى ---⇧ (Warsh) ، (Douri) ، (Qalon) ، (Shuba)
244.	وَمَا أَصَابَكُمْ مِنْ مُصِيبَةٍ **فَبِمَا كَسَبَتْ** أَيْدِيكُمْ وَيَعْفُو عَن كَثِيرٍ ⇧ (الشورى42: 30) Al-Qur'an (Qirā'at al-'Aammah) وَمَا أَصَابَكُمْ مِنْ مُصِيبَةٍ **بِمَا كَسَبَتْ** أَيْدِيكُمْ وَيَعْفُو عَن كَثِيرٍ ⇧ (Warsh) ، (Qalon)
245.	--- وَمَنْ يُطِعِ اللَّهَ وَرَسُولَهُ **يُدْخِلْهُ** جَنَّاتٍ ---⇧ (الفتح48: 17) Al-Qur'an (Qirā'at al-'Aammah) --- وَمَنْ يُطِعِ اللَّهَ وَرَسُولَهُ **نُدْخِلْهُ** جَنَّاتٍ تَجْرِي --- ⇧ (Warsh) ، (Qalon)
246.	فَشَارِبُونَ **شُرْبَ** الْهِيمِ ⇧ (الواقعه56: 55) Al-Qur'an (Qirā'at al-'Aammah) فَشَارِبُونَ **شَرْبَ** الْهِيمِ ⇧ (Douri)
247.	وَمَا هُوَ عَلَى الْغَيْبِ **بِضَنِينٍ** ⇧ (التكوير81: 24) Al-Qur'an (Qirā'at al-'Aammah) وَمَا هُوَ عَلَى الْغَيْبِ **بِضَنِينٍ / بِظَنِينٍ** ⇧ (Douri)
248.	الَّذِي خَلَقَكَ فَسَوَّاكَ **فَعَدَلَكَ** ⇧ (الانفطار 82: 07) Al-Qur'an (Qirā'at al-'Aammah) الَّذِي خَلَقَكَ فَسَوَّاكَ **فَعَدَّ لَكَ** ⇧ (Warsh) ، (Douri) ، (Qalon)
249.	كَلَّا بَل لَا **تُكْرِمُونَ** الْيَتِيمَ ⇧ وَلَا **تَحَاضُّونَ** عَلَى طَعَامِ الْمِسْكِينِ ⇧ **وَتَأْكُلُونَ** التُّرَاثَ أَكْلًا لَمًّا ⇧ **وَتُحِبُّونَ** الْمَالَ حُبًّا جَمًّا ⇧ (الفجر 89: 17- 20) Al-Qur'an (Qirā'at al-'Aammah) كَلَّا بَل لَّا **يُكْرِمُونَ** الْيَتِيمَ ⇧ وَلَا **يَحُضُّونَ** عَلَى طَعَامِ الْمِسْكِينِ ⇧ **وَيَأْكُلُونَ** التُّرَاثَ أَكْلًا لَمًّا ⇧ **وَيُحِبُّونَ** الْمَالَ حُبًّا جَمًّا ⇧ (Douri) وَلَا **تَحُضُّونَ** عَلَى طَعَامِ الْمِسْكِينِ ⇧ (Warsh) ، (Qalon)
250.	**يَحْسَبُ** أَنَّ مَالَهُ أَخْلَدَهُ ⇧ (الهمزة 104: 03) Al-Qur'an (Qirā'at al-'Aammah) **يَحْسِبُ** أَنَّ مَالَهُ أَخْلَدَهُ ⇧ (Warsh) ، (Douri) ، (Qalon)

Some verses from the above table have been selected to draw the readers' attention to notice whether the replacements, alterations, interpolations, additions, deletions, change of voice, tense, gender, grammatical mode, number (singular or plural) or the type (quality, quantity) etc. made in the Universal Reading of the Qur'an (popularly known as Qirā'at-i-Ḥafṣ) severely affect change in the meanings of the Qur'an (including change in the divine imperatives at some places), or they merely reflect a change in the manner of recitation of the Holy Text?

Al-Fatiḥa (1): 3;

Al-Baqara (2): 9, 48, 58, 96, 119, 140, 144, 158, 165, 182, 184, 210, 228, 236, 251, 260, 269, 271, 273, 281, 282, 283, 285;

Āl-i-Imran (3): 13, 36, 49, 75, 78, 79, 83, 109, 115, 120, 146, 157, 161, 169, 178;

Al-Nisā (4): 12, 14, 24, 33, 73, 77, 124;

Al-Maidah (5): 6, 69, 107;

Al-An'ām (6): 16, 22, 57, 96, 108, 115, 119, 124;

Al-Ḥij'r (15): 08;

Al-Kahf (18): 36;

ṬāHā (20): 63;

Al-Ḥajj (22): 39, 40;

Al-Mu'minūn (23): 67;

An-Naml (27): 93;

Ar-Rūm (30): 22;

Yā Sīn (36): 35, 62;

Al-Shurā (42): 30;

Al-Fatḥ (48): 17;

Al-Takwīr (81): 24;

Al-Infiṭār (82): 7;

Al-Fajr (89): 17-20;

Al-Humazah (104): 3;

I leave it on the readers to decide,

Do these changes really make the recitation of the Qur'an easy?

Do these alterations/distortions in the Holy Text really not affect the meaning and sanctity of Allah's Word?

Can such changes in the Holy Text of Allah's Word (*Kalam Allah*) be admitted on any pretext?

Is the doctrine of Variant Readings not more harmful and damaging to the authenticity of the Qur'an than the doctrine of abrogation——the abrogation of muḥkamāt (the cornerstone verses of the Qur'an) by the muḥkamāt—— propounded by the Ash'arites?

Is this, not a very unfortunate implication of the un-Qur'anic view of the status of *Hadīth* that the absolute authenticity of the Qur'anic Text, the most authentic document of Islam, has been put at stake?

Institutions in the garb of centres of research in 'Islamic or the Qur'anic sciences' or 'Teaching of Tajwid-o-Qirā'at', Majlas-e-Teḥqiqāt Islami, Kulliya-tut-Teḥqiqāt–e-Islami, Centre for Research in Islamic Social Sciences etc., in various countries including Pakistan, Kuwait, Libya, Jordan, Tunis and some North African countries, are working for the promotion of 'variant reading' of the Qur'an and for the promotion of more such versions. A responsible person in such a centre situated in Model Town Lahore told the author that up to eighty such versions of the Qur'an can be prepared based on the 'Usmanic Script. They are working on this project in collaboration with a centre based in Kuwait. This centre has already made an attempt in 2009-10 to publish sixteen such versions as the Qur'an from Pakistan. They failed in their attempt because the Publication of Holy Qur'an, Printing & Recording Errors Act No.LIV of 1973 of the Constitution of the Islamic Republic of Pakistan does not allow the publication of any such text as the Qur'an from Pakistan which differ with the Qirā'at al-Aamā Version declared as the Standard copy of the Qur'an in the Constitution.[121]

Copies of the Qur'an in Variant Readings are being printed as the Qur'an and distributed free of cast or on a very low price, to replace centuries old copies of Muṣāḥif (in Ḥafṣ Narration) in the houses of Muslims, to weaken Muslim belief in the absolute authenticity of the Qur'anic text. Copies of the Qur'an in narrations of Qalun, Douri, Warsh, Shuba, Roḥ and Jamahiriya etc. are being spread from these countries to promote a belief in the relative authenticity of the Qur'an among Muslims, and to defeat the Muslim's claim that the Qur'an is the only Scripture extant on earth, which is absolutely intact as to its Text. All these variant readings and some more are available on various websites.[122] Majma' al-Malik Fahd (King Fahd Complex for the Printing of the Holy Quran, Medina tul Munawwarah) publishes the Qur'an in Arabic and many other languages. It publishes the Qur'an in Qalon, Douri, Warsh Narrations. Of course, it publishes the Universal Reading of the Qur'an (Qur'an in *Qirā'at al-'Aammah*) too, but with the title of Qirā'at-i-Hafṣ as if it were just one more of the variant readings and at par with them. The Qur'anic text in Qirā'at-i-Shuba can also be seen at the archives of Majma al-Malik Fahd. The company produces millions of copies of these versions a year. As given on the website of Majma al-Malik Fahd

> "The complex began distributing its versions of the Qur'an, ... since 1405 AH [1985 AD] and this is done to Muslims inside and outside the Kingdom, and the quantities distributed amounted to hundreds of millions."[123]

Qirā'at conferences and competitions are funded and convened by such institutions to introduce variant readings and to promote belief in the relative authenticity of the Qur'anic Text among common Muslims at national and international level. The institute in Lahore Pakistan issues a research journal 'Rushd' for this purpose and has published its special Qirā'at Numbers in previous years.

Dr. Shehzad Saleem in his opus magnum 'History of the Qur'an: A Critical Study' critically examines around seventeen main (and several secondary) traditional narratives, surmised or fabricated to support 'variant readings' doctrine based on *saba' aḥruf ḥadīth*. The main narratives include the following:

i) "Narratives that four people belonging to the Anṣār were the only ones who collected the Qur'an in the lifetime of the Prophet (pbuh).

ii) Narratives on the collection of the Qur'an by Abū Bakr (rta).

iii) Narratives on the collection of the Qur'an by 'Usman (rta).

iv) Narratives on the collection of the Qur'an by 'Ali (rta).

v) Narratives on the Muṣaḥif of Ubayy (rta) and Ibn Mas'ud (rta).

vi) Narratives on 'Abdullah Ibn Mas'ud's rejection of the Mu'awwidhatayn.

vii) A narrative on the Placement of Sūrah Anfāl (8) and Sūrah Taubah (9).

viii) Narratives on 'Abdullah Ibn Mas'ud's Refusal to surrender his Muṣḥaf.

ix) Narratives on Laḥn in the Qur'an.

x) A narrative on the Schematic Arrangement of the Qur'an.

xi) Narratives on Usṭuwanah al-Muṣḥaf.

xii) Narratives on the changes made in the Qur'an by al-Ḥajjaj Ibn Yūsuf.

xiii) Narratives on the variations found in 'Usmānic Copies.

xiv) Two Narratives on the Incompleteness of the Qur'an.

xv) Critical Evaluation of Early Developments in Qur'anic Orthography.

xvi) Narratives on the Revelation of the Qur'an on *Seven Aḥruf*

xvii) Narratives on the Seven Canonical Readings."[124]

Dr. Shehzad Saleem observes that on almost all occasions the traditional interpretation of these narratives was found unconvincing and was interpreted afresh. Keeping his guard up from committing the epistemic fallacies identified by him in most previous work on this topic,[125] the overall conclusion as summarised by him is that the Qur'an that exists today in the vast majority of the Muslim Ummah is the very one revealed to the Prophet Muhammad (pbuh). Though revealed piecemeal, it was collected and re-arranged in the lifetime of the Prophet Muhammad (pbuh). Then its recital called *al-qirā'at al-'ammah* was consigned by him (pbuh), through the Companions (rta) and earlier scholars, to the living tradition of the Muslims. Thus, in accordance with the promise of protection made by Allah in the Qur'an, the Qur'an exists in the very form it was descended to the Last Prophet (pbuh).

———————

THE QUR'ANIC COSMOLOGY

CHAPTER 7

THE DILEMMA OF AN INTERVENTIONIST DEITY, AND ISLAM — SCIENCE RELATIONSHIP

The Qur'an is Qawl (Word): It consists of Allah's revealed information, worldview, precept, principles, teachings, commandments and guidance etc. Besides whatever else, the Qur'an gives principles of its own interpretation too. The worldview and the guidance derived from the Qur'an following Qur'anic principles of interpretation, merit to be called 'God-given revealed knowledge' though scope for the better interpretation of the Qur'an within the Qur'anically prescribed parameters is always there. As compared to it, theories of science and philosophy, methodology of science, principles of research, presuppositions of scientific and philosophic theories, discoveries of science, the worldview based on science, and philosophy arising in its wake, may be called empirical and rational knowledge based on human research and experimentation.

Reconciliation between Islam and science means reconciliation between 'God-given revealed knowledge' and 'knowledge gained through research in science and philosophy' i.e., 'man-made knowledge'. However, the main focus of study in this chapter will be on Islam and science relationship.

No doubt, nature is the creation of Allah. To call it 'Work of God' as compared to 'Creation of God' is dubious because of its vague connotation. Yet examining Sir Syed Ahmad Khan's thought, this study has used it in the same manner. [126]

'Science' as a study of the 'Work of God', is a purely human endeavour. It studies the Work of God in its empirical aspect alone. Its methodology admits no source of knowledge other than the empirical one and the rationality compatible with it.

Methodology of science, principles of research and basic presuppositions are not coherent with the Scripture. Besides its ultimate focus on the empirical aspect of reality alone, it has its own self-made concepts of natural and the supernatural. So we are justified using the term 'man-made knowledge' for the methodology of science, discoveries regarding structure and nature of the universe, the worldview based on science, and the philosophy arising in its wake. Reconciliation between Islam and science means reconciliation between 'God-given revealed knowledge' and 'empirical knowledge of science'.

Dr. Pervez Amirali Hoodbhoy (b.1369/1950), a Pakistani nuclear physicist, in his book *'Islam and Science: Religious Orthodoxy and the Battle for Rationality'* identifies a very genuine problem that lies beneath the failure of all Muslim attempts at bringing about reconciliation between Islam and science. Professor Hoodbhoy formulates this problem as 'The Dilemma of an Interventionist Deity'. Dr. Hoodbhoy argues that until the problem identified in the dilemma is satisfactorily addressed, no attempt at the reconciliation between Islam and science, or for that matter, developing an Islamic Science, Islamization of

Science, or Islamization of Knowledge etc. is destined to succeed.[127] Dr. Hoodbhoy highly deserves our appreciation for this contribution.

This study examines the dilemma and strives to meet the challenge. The study argues that all traditional Muslim attempts at reconciliation between Islam and science, from Ibn Sina to Iqbal, and the contemporary schools and scholars after Iqbal, invariably suffer from a very serious flaw in their ontology and the cosmology.[128]

The study argues that Islam, being a monotheistic religion, is based on faith in the absolute Oneness of Allah (God)——the Absolute Originator of everything——and its ontology given in the Qur'an consists of,

Allah's *Khalq* (the Creation), and

Allah's *Amr* (the Command)

as compared to traditional Muslim ontology prevalent since centuries which recognizes Allah and His creation, or eternal (*qadīm*) and contingent (*ḥādith*) as ontological categories. According to the Qur'anic ontology, as propounded in this study, Allah does not comprise the ontological category Himself except that He is the Absolute Originator of *Khalq* and *Amr* both. *'Nothing is like Him.'* (Q. 42:11) He is Singularly Unique and Supremely Transcendent. Similarly the Qur'anic cosmology as propounded in this study, consists of a divinely-administered universe in which there remains no question of Divine intervention, as compared to the modern version of traditional Muslim cosmology which conceives the universe to be mechanically running in accordance with the laws of nature; and God, who has set these laws, can intervene in the order of the universe if He so Wills.[129]

The problem identified in 'the dilemma of an interventionist deity' actually arises in the backdrop of this traditional Muslim ontology and modern version of its cosmology. Until these are reconstructed in a Qur'anic perspective, neither the dilemma can be resolved, nor the much needed and much sought after reconciliation be accomplished.

The Conception of a Divinely Administered Universe

Before we start examining the dilemma, let us pronounce as preliminary remarks that the Qur'an gives the conception of a 'divinely administered universe' and of God as Creator and Administrator of the universe when it says:

'Verily your Lord is Allah, Who created the heavens and the earth in six Days. Then He established Himself on the Throne (of authority). He covers the night and the day with each other, each seeking the other in rapid succession. He created the sun, the moon, and the stars; (all) subservient [to the laws of nature] under His Command (Amr). Behold! His is the Creation (Khalq) and His is the Command (Amr). The Giver of blessings is Allah, the Cherisher and Sustainer of the worlds!' (Q. 7:54) (Tafseer-e-Fazli)

Traditional Muslim view of the universe

As compared to conceiving Allah as Administrator of the universe, the traditional Muslim view of the universe sees God as an ontological entity as well as an interventionist deity. This study asserts that Allah does not comprise any ontological category Himself as argued above. The dilemma, as we shall see, actually assumes the traditional Muslim conception of God (as interventionist deity) in His relationship with the universe, as is given below:

'That the universe is created by Allah, its laws are set by Him, and it is autonomously running in accordance with these laws of nature. The laws of nature are subservient to Allah's Power and not the vice versa. Being the Creator of the universe and Setter of its laws, and being All-Knowing, All-Powerful, and The Wise, He can intervene in the system of the universe if He so Wills; and He does intervene.'

The study argues that the above view of the nature and structure of the universe and of relation between its parts (cosmology) based on traditional Muslim ontology is not in accordance with the Qur'anic teachings. The objection formulated in the dilemma is directed towards this mistaken view of the universe. Until it is reconstructed in accordance with the Qur'anic teachings, the dream of developing a science in line with the Qur'anic teachings cannot be fulfilled.

Are Islam, and Science Compatible?

Examining instances of traditional Muslim paradigms towards Islam-science relationship, extending from Ibn Sina (369-428AH/980-1037), Sir Syed Ahmad Khan (d.1898), Allama Muhammad Iqbal (d.1938) and contemporary Islamization of science schools and scholars of the first quarter of the 23rd century (1421-1444AH), we have reached the conclusion that the question: 'Are Islam, and science compatible? If so, how can they be reconciled?' is a false question. To attempt at proving them harmonious means striving in the wrong direction. A worldview derived from the Qur'an, in line with its own revealed principles of interpretation, and a worldview derived from science——which admits nothing except empirical knowledge (or rationality based on it) as the only source of knowledge, are two drastically different and irreconcilable worldviews. Any attempt at harmonising them is necessarily bound to fail.

The Real Problem and Its Formulation

What is the real problem and how should it have been genuinely formulated? Taking insight from several instances where the Prophet (pbuh) taught his followers to benefit from time-tested, beneficial knowledge based on human experience,[130] and taking guidance from the Qur'anic principle of *innovation* (*Bid'at*) we argue that the real problem is,

What are the Qur'anic parameters for relating 'man-made knowledge' of science (& philosophy) with the 'God-given revealed knowledge' of the Qur'an?

and the way it should have been formulated as a question is that:

What are the Qur'anic parameters for relating 'time-tested, beneficial, well researched knowledge' of science with 'the God-given revealed knowledge'? So that if at any time a prevalent view of science is replaced by a new theory of science, as the Ptolemaic theory of Science was replaced by the Newtonian mechanics; which in turn is replaced by the Einsteinian theory of relativity Physics, the Muslims are not compelled to make the same effort of relating them anew. As Ibn Sina attempted to reconcile the Qur'an with the Ptolemaic science, Sir Syed Ahmad Khan attempted to reconcile it with the Newtonian mechanics, and Iqbal tried for 'the construction of a scientific form of religious knowledge' in the Einsteinian perspective.

The study argues that to respond to the challenge we need to keep in mind following five points:

1. Innovation (*Bid'at*)

Bid'at is a Qur'anic principle for relating the outcome of beneficial, time-tested man-made knowledge with the revealed knowledge within the Qur'anic parameters. *Bid'at* is that Qur'anic principle which guarantees the applicability of Qur'anic teachings in all circumstances with the change of time, place, quantity and capacity until the Last Day. This is the principle that makes Islam as the most progressive revealed religion of the world. Unfortunately, because of the short-sightedness of religious scholars in Muslim history, *bid'at* happens to have acquired a highly undesirable connotation since centuries and the Muslims are unaware of its significance as a Qur'anic principle for relating beneficial, timetested, empirical knowledge with the 'God-given revealed knowledge'. No innovation (*bid'at*) in fundamentals of Dīn (Islam) and in respect of prohibitions is allowed. Not everyone is qualified for carrying out this job. The sound in knowledge (*ar-rasikhūna fil-'ilm*) are the ones who are best qualified for working out an appropriate relationship between Islam and the man-made knowledge in line with the Divine decree: *la talbisul Ḥaqqa bil batili …* (Mix not falsehood with truth!) (Q. 02:42) It is the Qur'anic principle of innovation (*bid'at*) which provides basis for ijtihād.[131]

2. The Qur'anic Ontology

The ontology, developed by traditional Muslim theologians under the impress of Greeks, comprises (i) God and (ii) His Creation. The worldview or the cosmology based on this traditional Muslim ontology acknowledges only two categories of being: Allah who is eternal (*qadīm*), and His Creation (*Khalq*) which is contingent (حادث *ḥādith*).[132] The ontology propounded in this book, conceives the Qur'anic ontology comprising of the categories of Allah's *Khalq* (Creation) and Allah's *Amr* (Command) as explained in the previous chapters. It does not conceive Allah as an ontological category but as the Absolute Originator of everything who is Singularly Unique and Supremely Transcendent. This ontology conceives *Khalq* (Creation) and *Amr* (Command) as originated ontological realities having no likeness or comparison with Allah in any way or participation in His divinity.[133]

All traditional Muslim paradigms for relating Islam and Science assume ontology borrowed from Greeks through Christians. We have discussed some instances of the formulation of theological problems and doctrines by the Mu'tazilites and the Ash'arites both based on this un-Qur'anic ontology in previous chapters.

We have already discussed in previous chapters, that the Qur'an is neither 'created (contingent)' as held by the Mu'tazilites, nor 'eternal *(qadīm)* as held by the Ash'arites. It is Allah's Word descended as *Al-Ḥaqq* (The Truth) on Prophet Muhammad (pbuh) and belongs to the ontological category of Allah's *Amr* (Command). Let us see the case of *rūḥ* *(soul/spirit) as* another instance of misperceiving its nature. The Qur'an says:

"And they ask you about the rūḥ (soul/spirit). Say please: Soul belongs to [the category of] my Lord's Command (amr), and you have been given but very little knowledge of it." (Q. 17:85) (TF).

'The creation' and 'the command' are two distinguished categories. Allah is the Originator of both ontological categories. *Rūḥ* (soul or spirit) belongs to the category of Allah's Command (*amr*). Life (*ḥayāt*) does not belong to the category of Allah's Command. Life and death both belong to the ontological category of Allah's *khalq*. Allah has created death and life to see what type of moral actions the people perform. (Q. 67:2)

He determines the purpose of creation of everything, grants whatever is needed to anything for its actualization, and His command (*amr*) is infused or installed in everything to make it operative and functional according to its purpose of creation. *Fiṭrah* (enduring nature / innate disposition) is a manifestation of Allah's *amr* (command) instilled in things. In verse 30 of Surah ar-Rūm (30) Allah uses the word '*fiṭrah*' for the enduring nature / natural disposition which He has set up in humankind and uses the word '*fatara*' for bestowal of *fiṭrah* to humankind. (Q. 30:30) Similarly, in verse one of Surah Fāṭir (35) Allah says:

"Glory be to Allah, the Originator [the Fāṭir, the Creator and Bestower of fiṭrah] of the heavens and the earth, Who made the angels messengers; having wings, two or three or four. He adds to the creation as He Wills. Verily Allah has Power over all things." (Q. 35:1) (Tafseer-e-Fazli)

This implies that origination of things by Allah is always with a specific *fiṭrah* (nature).

The root meaning of the term '*fiṭrah*' is 'to split' or 'to cleave' and hence implies 'opening up' and 'coming out'. The verb *fatara* is employed to mean "to bring forth" or "to originate". The idea that human beings recognize *tawḥīd* innately is often expressed by using the term *fiṭrah,* which is commonly translated as 'innate disposition'. Some people use the word 'primordial nature' to mean *fiṭrah.* If the term 'primordial nature' is used as a synonym for 'inner disposition' and Allah's *amr*, it is correct. If it is used to mean something eternal——beyond having beginning, or as something having any likeness or special relationship with God, it is not correct. Neither *khalq* nor *amr* is eternal. Allah's *amr* (Command) always functions as '*innate nature*' or '*innate disposition*' in His *khalq*. 'The Qur'ān employs the word *fiṭrah* itself only once, and says:

"So set your face towards religion as a man of pure faith. This is the natural disposition Allah has instilled in humankind. [... فِطْرَةَ اللهِ الَّتِي فَطَرَ النَّاسَ عَلَيْهَا ... Fiṭrata Allāhi Allatī Faṭara An-Nāsa `Alayhā.] There is no altering in Allah's creation, and this is the right religion. Most of the people do not realise it." (Q. 30: 30) (TF)

Oneness of Allah, no doubt, is innate in everything. The universe is replete with the signs of Allah's Oneness. It requires that humankind give no importance to one's own or anyone's desires as against Allah's Pleasure. Legislating and implementing one's own or anyone else's desire at par with Allah's injunctions is to change the *fiṭrah/innate nature* of humankind and altering Allah's creation. Legislating and implementing one's own or anyone else's desire at par with Allah's injunctions is *shirk (polytheism/associating partners with Allah.)* Allah forbids it, and decrees to set one's face directed towards the true faith single-mindedly.

Allah's *amr* manifests itself in things as their *fiṭrah*. It is *fiṭrah* of things which interlink them together. They are never discrete as the Ash'arite Atomism conceives them. It is Allah's *Amr* (command) as *Fiṭrah* (nature) in things, which holds up the system of the universe together. Spirit (*rūḥ*) which Allah infuses or instils in man, endows *fiṭrah* to humankind.[134]

3. The Qur'an and *Ḥadīth* Relationship

The Qur'an is *Qawl* i.e., the standard of truth as word, information, teaching, precept, command, guidance, message and speech. *Ḥadīth* is *'amal* (action/ implementation). To work out parameters for the implementation of Qur'anic injunctions in changing circumstances is *Fiqh* (jurisprudence). So *Fiqh* corresponds to discernment (*ḥikma*) and knowledge.

The Qur'an is Allah's Command /Injunction (*ḥukam*).[135] *Ḥadīth* reports implementation of Divine injunctions (*ḥukam*) ascribed to the Prophet (pbuh), on the authority of a chain of narrators. The Qur'an as Divine Command is absolute. What the Muslims have failed to understand is that the implementation of absolute Command cannot be absolute; it must correspond with the requirements of time, place, quantity and capacity. To work out the conditions of its implementation, within Qur'anic parameters, as said earlier, is *Fiqh*.

The Qur'an is the source of *sharī'ah* (divine law) and is ultimate, absolute and universal. The implementation of *sharī'ah* cannot be a source of *sharī'ah* itself. *Ḥadīth* is the precedent of the implementation of a divine law, set by the Prophet (pbuh) in particular circumstances when it was being revealed. Ijtehād of the rightly-guided caliphs, the honourable companions of the Prophet (pbuh) and the jurists of earlier centuries, too, have the status of being the precedent. To associate absoluteness and universality with them is to close the Muslim minds and to close the doors of ijtehād.

Allah calls the Qur'an '*Aḥsan-al-Ḥadīth Kitāb*' (The Fairest of Texts Book) when He says:

"Allah has revealed the Fairest of Texts Book, a Scripture consistent [Aḥsan-al-Ḥadīth Kitāb] (Q. 39:23); (It is) the Qur'an in Arabic, containing no crookedness [i.e., inconsistency]...." (Q. 39:28). (TF)

Allah also calls the Qur'an '*Ḥadīth-e-Aṣdaq*' (the most authentic *Ḥadīth*). (Q. 4:87) 'The Fairest of Texts Book' cannot be other than 'the most authentic and fully consistent.' It is as necessary for the interpretation of *Ḥadīth* (of *Ḥadīth-e-Qudsi* and *Ḥadīth-e-Nabvi* both) to be coherent with the *muḥkamāt* as it is necessary for the interpretation of the *mutashābihāt* to be coherent with the Qur'an. Allah holds those who try to interpret *the mutashābihāt* arbitrarily, as perverse at heart and mischief-makers.(Q. 3:7) By implication, the same judgement applies to those who do not examine the text of *ḥadīth* in the light of the *muḥkmāt* of the *Aḥsan al-Ḥadith Kitāb* and do not keep the interpretation of *ḥadīth* subservient to them. *Ḥadīth* is neither *authority* (qazi) over the Qur'an nor is it irrelevant to its interpretation. If it reports implementation of a Divine injunction by the Prophet (pbuh) it must be taken as precedent, and if it elaborates any verse, it must reconcile with the *muḥkamāt*. To make a divine *ḥadith* (*ḥadīth-e-qudsi*) or a prophetic *ḥadith* (*ḥadith-e-Nabvi*) judge (*authority*) over the interpretation of the *Aḥsan al-Ḥadith,* is to upturn the order.

4. Revealed Version of Truth Vs. Rational Version of Truth

The principle 'Truth cannot contradict truth.' devised by philosophers of religion for relating knowledge of science & philosophy' with the 'revealed God-given Qur'anic knowledge' is a false principle. It elevates knowledge of science & philosophy at par with the Qur'an as truth. The epithet *Al-Ḥaqq* is ascribed to the Qur'an by Allah. It is Allah Who says that what has been revealed to Haḍrat Muhammad (pbuh) is *Al-Ḥaqq* (The Truth). (Q. 47:02, also see Q. 34:6; and Q. 38:29.) The revealed knowledge of the Qur'an is 'the standard of truth'. Only that which is coherent with *Al-Ḥaqq* is *ḥaqq*. To assert knowledge of science & philosophy as 'rational version of truth', is false, void, having no authority at its back. Reinterpreting the Qur'an to make it compatible with science & philosophy is unjustified and tantamount to making the revealed Qur'anic knowledge subservient to human knowledge.

5. Theory vs. Truth

Science, and philosophy too‹ consist of theories whereas the Qur'an consists of 'revealed truth'. It is highly unfair and unlawful and illogical to strive for reconciling 'truth' with 'theory'. A further distinction exists in science itself between 'scientific theories' and 'established scientific facts'. A 'scientific theory' and an 'established scientific fact' differ with each other as to their epistemological status and with respect to their bearing for the teachings of the Qur'an. An 'established scientific fact' can never be inconsistent with the Qur'an. A philosophico-scientific worldview is a theory only. It never is an 'established scientific fact'. A scientific theory, how well accredited may it be considered by some philosophers, scientists or religious scholars, is after all a theory. What the Qur'an presents are not theories, they are revealed as ultimate truth.[136]

Scientists' Conception of the Universe —— First Horn of the Dilemma

First horn of the dilemma of the Qur'an and science relationship, formulates scientists' conception of the universe which is as follows:

'Science has no concern with whether God exists or not; or whether any divine agency has ever created it, set its laws and made it running or not.

Even if any such agency has created it, set its laws, and made it running, the divine agency has no role any more in it or can intervene in the order of nature in any way. The universe is autonomous and running in accordance with its laws of nature. Science is an empirical study of nature.

Every event that happens in the universe has a natural cause. That no event in the universe ever takes place without a cause, no matter whether we could ever identify it or not.

Traditional Muslim Perception of the Universe —— Second Horn of the Dilemma

This horn of the dilemma formulates conception of the universe traditionally believed in by Muslims as Islamic worldview which can be stated as follows:

Allah has created the universe, and set its laws according to which it is running.

He is All-Powerful. The laws of nature are subservient to His Power, and not the vice versa.

Being the Creator of the universe and Setter of its laws, and being All-Knowing, All-Powerful, and The Wise, He can intervene in the system of the universe if He so Wills.

The upholders of the dilemma argue that the problem of bringing about harmony between the Qur'an and science actually lies in harmonising above divergent horns of the dilemma. They further argue that belief in an Interventionist Deity in traditional Muslim perception, contradicts with basic suppositions of modern empirical science, shakes man's conviction in the immutability of the laws of nature, harms the tendency for the scientific explanation of phenomena, and pushes man towards explaining events and happenings with reference to a supernatural agency. It, in turn, weakens science's ability to predict and control the events of nature.

Proponents of the dilemma argue that the above Muslim belief in an Interventionist God is sufficient to make the Qur'an and science essentially incompatible. Until and unless the Muslims resolve this dichotomy, no viable reconciliation between Islam and science is possible.

Ibn e Sina (369-428AH/980-1037), Sir Syed Ahmad Khan (1232-1315AH/1817-1898) and Dr. Muhammad Iqbal (1294-1357AH/1877-1938) have strived to resolve this problem in their respective epochs. International Institute of Islamic Thought (IIIT, established in 1981 in Virginia), Ijmali school led by Dr. Ziauddin Sardar (b.1371AH/1951), traditionalist school of Syed Hussain Nasr (b.1351AH/1933), Bucailleism starting from Maurice Bucaille (1338-1418AH/1920-1998) have made efforts to prove the revealed origin of the Qur'an, and superiority of its knowledge concerning scientifically verifiable facts by showing compatibility of established facts of modern science with Qur'anic revelations. Dr. Muhammad Basil Altaie and many other scholars, schools and Islamic centres in the world are exerting their best abilities in the Islamization of Science or Islamization of Knowledge project in their individual capacities or as a team. Ibn Sina, taking the Aristotelian philosophy and the Ptolemaic view of the world as 'the rational version of truth' and the teachings of the Qur'an as 'the revealed version of truth' tried to bring about reconciliation between the two based on the principle *'Truth cannot contradict truth.'* Imam Abu Hamid al-Ghazali (450-505AH/1058–1111) about seventy years later, rejects Avicennian reconstruction of Muslim philosophy in terms of Aristotle, Ptolemy and Plotinus with very solid arguments.[137]

In the second half of the seventeenth century, the Ptolemaic science is replaced by the Newtonian, mathematically supported empirical mechanics, which prevails all over scientific horizons for about two centuries and provides scientific foundations to a great scientific and industrial revolution.[138] In the 19th century, Sir Syed Ahmad Khan comes forward to reconcile Islam with Newtonian mechanics and the philosophy of naturalism arising in its wake. He terms the rational interpretation of the Qur'an as the study of the 'Word of God' and the Newtonian mechanics as the empirical scientific study of the 'Work of God', and argues that the disharmony between the two is not possible. He further argues that in case of conflict between the outcomes of these two studies, the Work of God will override the Word of God. It means that in such case the Qur'an (Word of God) will be metaphorically reinterpreted to make it reconcile with the findings of Newtonian mechanics (and philosophy of naturalism).[139]

This theory propounded by Sir Syed Ahmad Khan as a solution for the problem of reconciling the Qur'an and science together, makes the interpretation of the revealed Qur'anic knowledge subservient to the findings of Newton's theory of mechanical science (the man-made knowledge). Look at the irony of fate, Sir Syed Ahmad Khan died in 1898 and only seven years later, Einstein's 'special theory of relativity' superseded Newtonian mechanics in 1905, and his 'general theory of relativity' in 1916. The effort made by Sir Syed Ahmad Khan in reinterpreting the Qur'an to make it harmonise with classical mechanics and the classical naturalism becomes null and void just seven years after he has passed away.

The Muslims find themselves once again confronted with the challenge to prove that the Qur'anic view of the structure and nature of the universe, they believed in as part of their faith, harmonises with the 'scientific worldview' propounded by the Theory of Relativity Physics and such other modern sciences. Here Iqbal comes forth to the rescue. Dr. Muhammad Iqbal in his lectures *The Reconstruction of Religious Thought in Islam* takes up the same problem, now arising in the perspective of the theory of relativity physics. These lectures were published in 1933, just five years prior to his demise. We can justifiably consider Iqbal at maximum maturity of thought while publishing these lectures. Iqbal propounds 'the construction of a scientific form of religious knowledge' as a solution to the problem.[140]

This study argues that the solution offered by Iqbal is based on two presuppositions:

i) Conceiving Allah as Absolute Ego on the analogy of finite human ego;

ii) Identification of Allah with Time (ad-Dahr).

This study further argues that both these presuppositions are contrary to the teachings of the Qur'an as is discussed in detail in the next chapter.[141] This is why Iqbal, too, does not succeed in giving a viable philosophy of science based on Qur'anic teachings.

We have also examined the views offered by some contemporary schools of thought and celebrated scholars after Iqbal on this problem but have found that none of the mediaeval, modern and contemporary institutes, schools, Islamic centres and scholars have yet been able to find a viable concept of science in line with the teachings of the Qur'an, which meets the objection genuinely identified and formulated by Dr. Hoodbhoy as the dilemma of an interventionist deity.

This study argues that the principle of 'truth cannot contradict truth' or the assertion that 'Word of God and Work of God cannot conflict with each other.' and 'the conception of a scientific form of religious knowledge' or 'Islamization of science' are false principles, assertions or projects/programs based on un-Qur'anic ontology and un-Qur'anic cosmology.

These principles, concepts or premises are false because 'theories of science' for not admitting revelation as the higher source of knowledge can never reach to the level of 'truth' at par with the Qur'anic knowledge. Any attempt at harmonising Islam and science based on these principles, concepts or premises, is necessarily bound to fail. This only shows that the problem is not rightly identified, understood or formulated on genuine lines.

Divinely Administered Universe vs. Mechanically Running Autonomous Universe.

This study argues that besides assuming un-Qur'anic ontology(gies), all traditional Muslim paradigms for reconciling Islam and science, also assume un-Qur'anic cosmology(gies). Since the dilemma is prepared in the backdrop of this traditional Muslim position, it also assumes the same cosmological misconception too. Cosmology is that branch of philosophy which deals with the general structure of the universe besides dealing with its origin, laws, characteristics such as space, time, causality and God-universe relationship.

When we examine the horn of dilemma which describes traditional Muslim position, we see, it is based on a misconceived cosmological notion of a universe autonomously running in accordance with the laws of nature, with Allah as an Interventionist Deity Who can intervene in the order of the universe when He Wills. It is a misrepresentation of Qur'anic cosmological doctrine. It is based on the conception of an un-Qur'anic ontology. The dilemma could not arise, had it not assumed the same misconceived cosmological doctrine.

The Qur'anic cosmology gives the conception of a divinely administered universe, based on Qur'anic ontology consisting of Allah's *khalq* and Allah's *amr*. According to Qur'anic ontology, the universe (the physical reality) is not mere *khalq* (creation), Allah's *amr* subsists in it. Allah's *amr* (command) is issued, infused, descended, blown into or installed in it. Allah Almighty Himself is neither *khalq* nor *amr*, neither physical nor non-physical, neither *natural* nor *supernatural*.[142] Being the absolute Originator of everything, He supremely transcends from all analogy and likeness or comparison with whatever he has brought about as *khalq* or *amr*. He also transcends from their participation in His Divinity, in any way, as holds between ocean and the waves, soul and the body, ink and its differentiation into letters, words and the writing, and from all comparisons e.g. in polar concepts like infinite and finite, uncaused first cause and efficient cause etc. He encompasses everything in His Knowledge and in His Power. He is Omnipresent, but transcends any kind of immanence in (*suryaniat*), unicity with (*ittehad*), emanation (*ṣadūr or faizān*), all-inclusiveness or in-givenness (*halool*) in anything or anyone. Allah encompasses everything in His Knowledge and in His Power, but does not include anything in His Holy Being. The Qur'anic concept of nearness to Allah is that of *'with-ness' or 'togetherness' with Allah* (معیت *m'aiyat*) of His servants.[143]

The Qur'anic notion of God is that of the absolute Originator of both *khalq* and *amr*, the Creator and the Administrator of the universe. The order of the universe runs in accordance with the laws of nature only because Allah's command (*amr*) instilled in everything and in the universe sets its laws, gives it direction, keeps it running and sustains it according to Allah's Knowledge, Wisdom and Will. As Administrator of the order of the universe, Allah's *amr* (command) descends in the heavens as He Wills. (Q. 65:12) Laws of nature operate as the function of His Command (*amr*). The Qur'an states everything in the universe as replete with signs of His Oneness, Will, Wisdom, Knowledge, Power, Presence and whatever as stated by His Goodly Names. Whenever He Wills to bring about anything, He issues the command *'KUN!'* (*Be!*), and there it is! It does not necessarily mean coming into being of a thing, event or change instantaneously. To say *'KUN'* means putting the *caption* for the origination of something. As soon as Allah puts the *caption (unwān* عنوان*)* of a thing, event or change, factors begin to integrate, causes start to take shape, and everything begins to operate in the execution of Allah's command. Execution of His Command takes no time. (*'Innamā Qawlunā Lishay'in 'Idhā 'Aradnāhu 'An Naqūla Lahu KUN Fayakūnu.* Q. 16:40) It is the Dignity of the Absolute Master that He creates with means (already originated things) as well as without means (*ex-nihilo*).[144] The Volition (*Irādah*) of the Absolute Knower is the hidden form of a thing; the Command of Allah (*Amr*) puts its caption, and the origination takes place as Willed by Allah. (Q. 16:40) Allah's command is always obeyed. (Q. 36:82) To hold the origination of the universe as manifestation or operation of Allah's attributes (*ṣiffah*) is to take a style of expression, not approved by Allah in the Qur'an. This un-Qur'anic style of expression provides basis to the doctrine of *waḥdat al-wujud*.[145] Nowhere in the Qur'an does Allah Almighty talk about His Holy Person in terms of His attributes (*ṣifa*) or coming into being of the universe as a result of the manifestation of His attributes. Rather He ordains the believers to call upon Him by His *al-Asmā' al-Ḥusnā'* (Comely Names). The origination of the universe (creation and command both, and their coordination with each other) is by way of Allah's *al-Asmā' al-Ḥusnā* (Comely Names). Allah operates in the universe by way of His Comely Names.

Occasionalism (The Ash'arite Atomism)

The study does not claim that none amongst the Muslims has ever visualised the concept of a divinely administered universe, nor does it suggest that this is the first time that such a view is being promulgated. Not at all! The Ash'arite theologians, in the very early centuries of Muslim civilization, grappling with the problem of the creation of the world, have contrived a very ingenious theory known as 'the Ash'arite atomism' known in the west as 'the Ash'arite occasionalism'. This Ash'arite theory was initiated by al-Ash'ari and completed by Qadi Abu Bakr al-Baqillani.

Bakar defines occasionalism as

The belief in the exclusive efficacy of God, of whose direct intervention into the events in nature are regarded as the overt manifestation or occasion. Occasionalism implies that all things and events in nature are substantially discontinuous by nature. The world is a domain of discrete entities which are independent of each other. There is no link whatsoever between them, save through the Divine Will. It is conceived that the Ash'arites postulated the existence of indivisible non-material particles. These particles are the most fundamental units that could exist, and out of which the whole world is created. Accordingly, these are referred to as 'the Ash'arite *Jawahar* [atoms].' The world, which the Ash'arites define as 'everything other than God' consists of two distinct elements, *jawahar* [wrongly translated as atoms] and *a'raḍ* (accidents). *Jawhar* (sing. of *jawahar*) is the locus which gives subsistence to the accidents. An *'arḍ* (accident) cannot exist in another *'arḍ* (accident) but only in a *jawhar* or a body composed of these *jawahar* with *a'raḍ* subsisting in them. Conversely, a body cannot be stripped of accidents, positive or negative, such as colour, smell, life, knowledge, or their opposites."[146]

The first major characteristic of the Ash'arite *jawahar* (non-material atoms) is that they are devoid of size or magnitude (*kam*), and are completely homogeneous. In other words, they are entities without length or breadth, but which combine to form bodies possessing dimensions.

The Ash'arite *jawahar* cannot have magnitude because extension is a property of physical space, involving the idea of boundary or surface. Since space too is atomized, and their theology demands that the *jawahar* be completely independent of one another, there can be no question of the *jawahar* occupying physical space.'[147]

The Ash'arite occasionalism is a very original and ingenious attempt to give a worldview based on the idea of a divinely administered universe in line with how they understood Qur'anic teachings, unconsciously presuming Greek ontology in their ideas. They explained everything *i.e.,* time, space, causality, laws of nature etc. on the basis of this theory. The Ash'arites conceived the universe restless and continuously developing; nothing in the universe would stay two instants in a stationary state.[148] Altaie summarises the Ash'arite 'theology of nature' (or *Daqīq al-Kalam* as they called it) as based on five theological principles given below.

Temporality

This stipulates that the world is temporal, finite and limited and that the creation took place ex nihilo i.e., out of nothing.

Discreteness

This stipulates that the structure of space, time, energy and matter and every associated property is discrete.

Continual creation

This stipulates that the world has to be re-created every moment anew.[149] In the words of al-Baqillani, *'arḍ* (the accident) 'perishes in the second instant of its coming-to-be.' This perishability of *jawahar* (non-material atoms) and *'ar'arḍ* (accidents) is a direct consequence of their theological belief that God directly intervenes not only in the coming of things into being, but also in their persistence in being from one instant to another.

Indeterminism:

This stipulates that the laws of nature that we recognize are contingent and undetermined. (Altaie sees this notion resonating in the Copenhagen interpretation of quantum theory.)

Space-time integrity

This stipulates that space has no meaning of its own and would exist only if a body existed, and that time has no meaning of its own without an event taking place in space.'

Professor Muhammad Basil Altaie asserts that it is incorrect to conceive *jawahar* as atoms. It is the *jawahar* (with *'arādh* recreated in them) associated with each other to make a body which can be called atom in modern parlance. Altaie contends that *jawhar* (singular of *jawahar*) according to *Kalam* is an abstract entity. Professor Altaie asserts that many renowned scholars have committed fallacy in understanding that it is the *a'radh* which are annihilated and recreated each moment and not the *jawahar*. *Jawahar*, though ever enduring, cannot persist without *a'rādh* subsisting in them. It is the necessary association of *jawahar* with *'arādh* that comprise recreation. [150]

The present study conceives the five basic theological principles stated above with reference to Professor Altaie, as five basic presuppositions of the Ash'arite atomism, and argues that so far as ontology is concerned, it makes no difference whether the *jawahar*, before the recreation of *arādh* (accidents) in them, can be rightly labelled as atoms, or the vice versa. The ontology, presupposed in both cases, is equally un-Qur'anic. [151]

The writer does not agree with converting philosophico-scientific theories into creed as done by Baqilani. Such approach attaches finality with speculations and close minds for centuries from further investigation into theological doctrines. This study argues that had the Ash'arites not committed epistemic fallacy in perceiving their ontological and cosmological principles as Qur'anic, which actually were rooted in Greek philosophy, and had left behind the doors for further investigations opened, they would have brought about a great revolution in all spheres of knowledge, including empirical and rational sciences, for all times to come.

The Qur'anic Ontology

Detailed study of the Ash'arite 'theory of nature', bewilders a serious reader. How grand a theory, the Ash'arites were able to construct to provide a metaphysical basis to Islamic theological principles just in the third century of Islamic civilization. But why could they not succeed in developing a methodology of science? The reason lies not in their cosmology, but in their misperceived ontology. The Ash'arites, like all other Muslim theological, philosophical, exegetical schools, and schools of jurisprudence failed to identify *'amr'* (Allah's command) as a basic principle of Islamic ontology like *khalq* (creation). Had they visualised Qur'anic ontology from verse Q. 7:54 as consisting of Allah's *khalq* (creation) and Allah's *amr'* (command) instead of conceiving God and Creation as sole ontological entities, and eternity (*qidm*) and contingency (*hudūth*) as their category distinction, they would have saved from generating confusion, doubt and dissension in theology. It would have saved them from creating serious impediments in the development of empirical sciences and rationality in Islamic civilization.[152]

As has been stated earlier, *Al-Ḥaqq'* (The Truth) is the title used in the Qur'an by Allah for The Qur'an descended by Him to His Messenger (pbuh). So, Allah is stated in the Qur'an to be 'The Descender of *'Al-Ḥaqq'*. (Q. 47:02. Also see 34:6; and 38:29) The Ash'arites confounded the use of *'Al-Ḥaqq'* (The Truth) as title in the identical sense with the Descender of *Al-Ḥaqq.* This was clearly unjustified, unlawful and unfair of them.

These theologians have committed exactly the same epistemic fallacy in the formulation of their cosmology. The scriptures including the Qur'an, the *sharī'ah*, *rūh* (soul), *fiṭrah* and Allah's *amr* which descends in the heavens and the earth etc, all belong to the category of Allah's *amr* (command), as distinguished from Allah's *khalq* (creation). Since the Ash'arites did not identify *amr* (*command*) as an ontological reality like *khalq*, they identified the Qur'an with Allah's attribute of Knowledge and Will to prove that it was not contingent.

Interpreting verse 29 of Surah al-Hijr of the Qur'an, it is usually said that after creating Adam (pbuh), Allah blew some of the divine spirit into him, and ordered the Angels that

> *"when I have proportioned him and breathed into him of My [created] soul, then fall down to him in prostration." (Q. 15:29) (Sahih International)*

Commenting on this Altaie says:

> "Thanks to the infusion of the *divine* spirit, which has become an essential part of his [*humankind's*] makeup. I believe that one manifestation of this divine infusion is the ability to think conceptually and construct things to enable humankind to explore the world with such ingenuity. It is as if man has acquired, by that divine infusion, some of the divine attributes. This makes it possible to view man's mission in this world to build up his own understanding of the Creator through investigating the world." (Altaie, ibid, 154)

This study argues that the concept of *ruh* (soul or spirit) as something divine is reminiscent of un-Qur'anic ontology. Allah's *khalq* is as divine as Allah's *amr* as Allah says: "...*all creation and command belong to Him*." (Q. 07:54) Allah refers to 'creation' as belonging to Him before He refers to 'command'. *Ruh* (spirit) relates to the ontological category of Allah's Command (*amr*) and equally belongs to the originated order, as the body, the physical reality, the life and death belong to the ontological category of Creation (*khalq*). Neither *khalq* nor *amr* participate in the Divinity of Allah to the least.

In the case of the problem of 'eternity vs. createdness of the Qur'an', as we have seen, the Ash'arite theologians identified the Qur'an with Allah through His Attributes of Knowledge and Will.[153]

In the case of creation of the universe and sustaining it, the theologians identified Allah's *amr* (*KUN!*) with Allah through His attribute of Power and Will as is clear from the quotation given below from Bakar.

> "If the atoms and accidents perish in the second instant of their coming-to-be, if they are created and annihilated at every instant, then how do we explain the fact that, as far as our ordinary experience tells us, it is the same world that continues to exist?"

Osman Bakar presents Kalam's answer to this question well summarised by Professor al-Attas that is as follows:

> "The world, after its initial existence, does not endure or continue to exist (*baqa*), but passes out of existence (*fana*); it ceases to exist at every moment of time, and what we observe of its continuance in existence is in reality the continuous renewal of its similars. The divine activity of 'perpetually bringing forth similar worlds from non-existence into existence' takes place at the atomic level, and may be explained as follows:
> 'When God creates an atom of a body, He also creates in it the accidents that cast it into being. The moment this atom passes out of existence He replaces it with a similar atom by creating in it similar accidents, that is, accidents of the same species as the one subsisting in the preceding atom, so long as He wills the same body to continue in existence. If He wills otherwise, then He would cease creating the accidents in question.' "[154]

As is evidently clear from the above that the Ash'arite 'theory of nature' (their cosmology), though very much based on the conception of a divinely administered universe, did not allow them to believe in the objective reality of *fiṭrah* (enduring nature / innate nature / natural disposition of things) and in the objective reality of 'the laws of nature' because of believing in an un-Qur'anic ontology. They did not have any ontological category corresponding to the *fiṭrah* of things. The question is: how could they refuse to accept the objective reality of the *fiṭrah* (an enduring *nature*) and of the laws of nature when the Qur'an says:

> *'So set your face towards religion [dīn] as a man of pure faith. This is the natural disposition (fiṭrah) set up / instilled in humankind by Allah. (*...فِطْرَةَ اللَّهِ الَّتِي فَطَرَ النَّاسَ عَلَيْهَا*) There is no altering in Allah's creation; and this is the right religion (dīn al-ḥanīf). But most of the people do not realise it.' (Q. 30:30) (Tafseer-e-Fazli)*[155]

What is evident from the above is that

Allah has created humankind on the *fiṭrah* of 'pure faith'. This is the basic make up, the enduring nature, the innate nature, the natural disposition instilled in humankind.

Creation on the *fiṭrah* of 'pure faith' implies that Allah creates everyone in 'a holy state'.

Allah commands humankind not to legislate at individual, social, national and global level for altering the *fiṭrah* (natural disposition) of Allah's creation. The same command is to be observed in education, research in science, development of technology, human rights and all other fields. This is what the Qur'an calls dīn-al-ḥanīf (the right religion). Allah states Haḍrat Ibrahim (pbuh) as a prototype of being on the *fiṭrah* of dīn-al-ḥanīf. (Q. 3:67)

The scriptures which Allah descended for humankind consisted of guidance, most appropriate to the '*fiṭrah*' of humankind. The Qur'an is the last of the scriptures, and for all humankind, and is intact. Allah calls it 'The Truth' (*Al-Ḥaqq*).[156]

To legislate for the implementation of human likes and dislikes at an individual, social or international level, or in the system of education, research in sciences or development of technology as opposed to Allah's revealed truth, is to legislate for altering the *fiṭrah* of humankind. To value human likes and dislikes at par with Allah's prescribed values and disvalues is polytheism (shirk) and opposite to what the Qur'an calls ad-Dīn al-Ḥanīf.'

Allah has created everything on *fiṭrah,* endowed by Him. The heavens and the earth, and everything within them have also been created on *fiṭrah* instilled in them. Allah calls Himself as 'The Bestower of *Fiṭrah*' when He says:

> *"Say, 'Shall I take for myself a patron anyone other than Allah, 'The Bestower of Fiṭrah' to the heavens and the earth, (*..فَاطِرِ السَّمَاوَاتِ وَالأَرْضِ*). Fāṭiri As-Samāwāti Wa Al-'Arḍi)?" (Q. 6:14)*

> *"Verily I have turned my face as a true believer towards Him Who 'created and bestowed innate nature (Fiṭrah)' to the heavens and the earth (*..فَطَرَ السَّمَاوَاتِ وَالأَرْضَ*). Fāṭara As-Samāwāti Wa Al-'Arḍi). I am certainly not of those who associate partners in His Divinity." (Q. 6:79)*

> *'Praise be to Allah, the Originator of the heavens and earth (Fāṭiri As-Samāwāti Wa Al-'Arḍi), who made angels messengers having three, four [pairs of] wings. He adds to the creation as He Will: God has power over everything.' (Q. 35:1)*

Traditional Muslim perception of the universe i.e., contemporary version of the Ash'arite occasionalism which, constrained by the development of modern empirical science, affirms enduring nature of things and objective reality of laws of nature and physical reality of the universe, but still believes Allah to be an Interventionist Deity, is as contrary to the Qur'anic concept of a divinely administered universe as the classical Ash'arite occasionalism which denied enduring nature (*fitra*) to things, objective reality of laws of nature and physical reality of the universe. The Qur'an disapproves the views mentioned above as the second horn of the dilemma.

According to the Qur'an, Allah is the Originator (and 'The Bestower of nature' —*The Fātir*) to the heavens and the earth, but He has not originated the world once for all and has bestowed the laws of nature, with which it is autonomously running forever.

> *"Surely your Lord is Allah, Who created the heavens and the earth in six days, … Surely His is the Creation (Khalq) and the Command (Amr)…" (Q. 7:54) (Tafseer-e-Fazli)*

> *"He adds to the creation as He Will: God has power over everything." (Q. 35:1) (Tafseer-e-Fazli)*

Creation and administration of the order of the universe is with Allah's Knowledge and Power. He encompasses everything in His Knowledge and with His Might He established on the Throne (for administering the order of reality) when He says:

> *"He manages and regulates every affair from the heavens to the earth." (Q. 32:5)*

> *"It is Allah Who has created seven heavens and of the earth the like thereof. His amr (Command) descends throughout them that you may realise that Allah has Power over all things and that Allah surrounds all things in His Knowledge." (Q. 65:12)*

What do the above verses mean! Allah has created everything in the heavens and the earth on a *fitrah* (enduring nature). He is *'The Fātir*—The Bestower of a distinctive nature (*fitrah*)' to species and genres He has created. Everything is infused with Allah's *amr* (Command) as its *fitrah* (nature). Everything is active in the domain prescribed by its *fitrah*. Everything is governed by the laws of nature prescribed by its *fitrah*. Belief in the descension of Allah's command (*amr*) throughout heavens and the earth, suggests that

> the universe is not the locus of arbitrary intervention of a capricious deity but the administration of All-Powerful and All-Knowing Allah, whose *amr*, instilled in everything, is active in the universe as a guiding principle, and Who is running the universe by His Command (*amr*).

The universe is lit and luminous with Allah's light of guidance. (Q. 24:26) That all consequences flow from the Will of Allah manifests His Power. That His Will is based on His Knowledge, manifests His Omniscience and Omnipresence. Allah encompasses everything in His Knowledge and Power. So far, Allah's *amr* as ontological principle of reality is concerned, Allah says:

> *'They ask you about the soul [rūh]. Please say to them: "Soul [rūh] belongs to [the ontological category of] your Lord's Command [amr]. 'You have been given but a little knowledge of this [category].' (Q. 17:85)*

The search for *laws of nature* means striving to discover *fitrah* (the innate nature) regulating a specific species of phenomena. Optimums and measures are included in *fitrah* of every being. As has been said above, *'His Command descends throughout the seven heavens and the parts of the earth like thereof.'* As much as man will discover, it will give him better prediction and control over *nature*, but he will ever find himself confronted with the challenge to know much more about nature and its laws. Man's knowledge will never be ultimate, and will never encompass Allah's Command (*amr*). Man's knowledge about 'the nature' of reality will always remain to be little, and his struggle to discover it will never end. The more he comes to know, the more new vistas of knowledge will open before him to discover further.

The Ash'arite denial of the objective reality of objects and of their *fiṭrah* is incoherent with the verses mentioned above. The Ash'arite denial of causation is also contrary to the Qur'anic teachings for Allah's *amr* instilled in things links them together. To interpret the Divine Command '*KUN*' (Be!) necessarily to mean instantaneous coming into being of a thing, is not correct. Allah creates with means as well as without means (*ex nihilo*). His Command '*KUN*' determines a caption, and affairs begin to take place according to the *fiṭrah* (nature) as prescribed by Allah's Will.[157] He directs all affairs. (*yudabbir ul amr*). (Q. 10:3) 'Allah created the heavens and the earth in six days, and then established on the Throne. (Q. 7:54) '*Ársh* (Throne) is the central place from which the universe is being administered. Allah is 'the Nourisher of the *Throne*' (*Rabb ul-'Arsh*) too. (Q. 9:129) *Throne* belongs to the ontological category of *Khalq*. Six days are *the past* and are still (i.e., inactive) and saved in Allah's Knowledge. Seventh day, *the present day,* is active. The Qur'an specifies that the world is created within a finite period of time by Allah, the Omnipotent Creator. 'Established on the Throne' means that on *the seventh day* He made the creation active with His command (*amr*) and set on the administration of the Universe. The Qur'an does not give the idea of an autonomously running order of reality. The universe is running as per Allah's *amr* infused in it as *fiṭrah* (or laws of its nature) in accordance with Allah's *amr* which descends in the heavens and the earth. (Q. 10:3)

Another very important corollary of this view is that nothing whatsoever is discrete, as opposed to visualised by the Ash'arite atomism. Everything is interlinked as required by their *fiṭrah* (enduring nature). The universe is founded on *truth* (*ḥaqq*). The Qur'an is the statement of *Truth* as Word (*Qawl*). 'The Truth' (*Al-Ḥaqq*) is real. The untruth, evil (*al-bāṭil*) is unfounded. *Al-Bāṭil* has no parallel existence with *Al-Ḥaqq* from ever. Deviation from the truth (*Al-Ḥaqq*) is *al-bāṭil* (evil). *Al-Bāṭil or evil* has no reality of its own accept in a relative manner.

The Qur'an does not give the conception of a universe that is unreal and ephemeral or of a universe, which does not have any well-defined *fiṭrah*. The Qur'an states the present order of reality as *dār-al-'amal* (the world meant for proving oneself true by doing good deeds). This is the accumulative *fiṭrah* of the present order of reality. The order of the universe as a whole, and each thing in its individual capacity too, operates coherently to this purpose. The Qur'an also does not give the conception of a closed universe, created once and for all, running autonomously in accordance with the laws set for it. The Qur'an gives the conception of a divinely administered and perpetually expanding universe when it says:

"With Power did We construct Heaven: and We are extending it." (Q. 51:47). (TF)

The Qur'an explicitly stipulates that the universe (heavens and earth) will collapse at its final stage:

'The Day that We roll up the heavens like a scroll rolled up for letters; even as We produced the first Creation, so shall We re-produce a new one: a Promise We have undertaken: truly shall We fulfil it.' (Q. 24:104). (TF)

The order of reality to be created anew will be meant for requital (*dār-al-Jaza*). This end will determine the *nature* of the life hereafter. Activity of everything in that world will be directed towards the fulfilment of this end. The Qur'an neither supports the Ash'arite denial of *fiṭrah* (enduring nature) for things and the universe giving them perpetually renewed existence in less than a moment, nor Sir Syed Ahmad Khan's created closed Newtonian universe mechanically running in accordance with immutable laws of nature. Allah has not used the word *miracle* (*mu'jiza*) in the Qur'an for the extraordinary happenings. Instead, Allah has used the word *signs* (*āyāt*) for them. The events commonly called *miracles* (*signs/āyāt*), as subservient to Allah's command (*amr*), are certainly as natural as other events and part of the universe as *dār-al-'amal*. These are a manifestation of the Glory of Allah's Names. We must strive to find their explanation in terms of laws of nature. If we fail to discover their causal conditions, it will simply show that capabilities of man are limited and cannot encompass Allah's Knowledge. It is possible that in this struggle some other important aspects of *nature* (*fiṭra*), realms of existence, layers of reality and their laws become exposed to us.

There are various spheres of nature, orders of existence and layers of reality. Chemistry, physics, biology, zoology, sociology, psychology, genetics, classical mechanics, quantum mechanics, oceanology, astronomy and whatever known and unknown disciplines of natural, biological, psychological and sociological and all possible types of sciences, occult or non-occult, deal with various but interrelated, interlinked spheres of phenomena. Each domain of existence or sphere of reality has its own (but interlinked) laws. Dividing phenomena into *natural* and *supernatural* is the outcome of un-Qur'anic ontology, classical mechanical cosmology and Newtonian naturalism. According to Qur'anic ontology if *khalq* denotes to the basic structure or substratum (like *hardware*), and the *amr* denotes to *the fiṭrah* infused and instilled in *khalq* (like a software) which subsists in it as enduring nature, determining its purpose, defining orbit of activity and the optimums, giving direction to its activity, the *khalq* and the *amr* operating together as one, constitute the phenomena called *'natural'*.[158] *'Supernatural'* is nothing. A thing beyond having a *nature* (*fiṭrah*), means conceiving a thing without having a, purpose, direction, orbit of activity and Allah's *amr*. This is a logical impossibility. There is no concept of the supernatural (i.e., beyond having any *nature* or *fiṭrah*,) in the Qur'an. Is subatomic phenomena studied by quantum physics supernatural? Can anyone claim that he knows all layers of existence, all orders of reality and their orbits of activity?

The Qur'an mentions a self-conscious creature, living in this very world with human beings, called jinni. The Qur'an verifies that they are created out of fire. (Q. 14:27) They also have moral-consciousness, as the scriptures tell us, and will be held accountable for their deeds. Fire is a physical object. Humankind in all phases of their existence on earth, have come across such events which verify the existence of this creature. Can any scientist with any stretch of mind conceive the creation out of fire of such a creature! They definitely have been endowed with a *fiṭrah* (nature). Their activity is very much *natural*. But for most of humankind, jinni and their activity is *supernatural*. The same may be conceived about the angels. At around eighty-eight places the Qur'an mentions them.[159] They are a self-conscious creature who have not been endowed with freedom of will. They do not do anything of their own accord. They have been assigned various duties by Allah. *'They do not disobey Allah in what He commands them but do what they are commanded. (Q. 66:6)* Allah knows whether they belong to the category of Allah's creation or to the category of His command but purpose of their life as stated in the Qur'an is *Yaf'alūna Mā Yu'umarūna* . يَفْعَلُونَ مَا يُؤْمَرُونَ *(to do what they are commanded by Allah).' (Q. 66:6)* There is no mention in the Qur'an of what elements they are composed of; however to believe in them is as much a part of faith as the belief in scriptures and prophets (pbut). *They are honoured servants of Allah. (Q. 21:26)* Ḥadīth narrates them to be made up of Nūr (Light).

The Qur'an states that Haḍrat Sulemān (pbuh) had Jinni and birds, too, in the ranks of his armies and in the position of his courtiers. (Q. 27.17) [160] Jinni also performed various other jobs for Haḍrat Sulemān (a.s.), too. They were made subservient to Haḍrat Sulemān (pbuh). Allah had given him (pbuh) knowledge to communicate with them and assign them duties. (Q.27:20-24, 27-28) He also heard the chief of ants communicating to its clan. (Q.27:18) *'Whatever there is in the heavens and earth submit to Him [Allah] willingly or unwillingly.' (Q. 3:83; Q. 13:15)* Everything is directed by the command (*amr*) infused in it as its *nature* or descended to it, to act accordingly. This is its submission to Allah. Allah administers the universe with His *Amr;* His *amr* (command) descends throughout the universe as He Wills; and His *Amr* is obeyed. (cf. Q.65:12 and cf. Q.41:11-12)

He created the earth in two Days. In further two days Allah set mountains on earth and bestowed blessings on earth and managed provisions for all things in due measure, then He turned towards heavens and perfected them as seven firmaments in two Days, and He assigned to each heaven its duty and command (amr / guiding principle). (Q. 41: 9-11) The Qur'an also tells us that while creating the heavens Allah turned to the sky which was then smoke, and to the earth too, and said to them:

> *"Come, willingly or unwillingly,' and they said, 'We come willingly'—and in two Days He formed seven heavens, and assigned to each its amr (Command) [nature]." (Q. 41:11-12) (TF)*

There are many other instances, which show that consciousness is given to all creatures. It is possible that at some point in time science may discover *the mind* or *consciousness* as another dimension of reality. Will it not change our whole perception of reality as has been changed with the discovery of interconvertibility of matter and energy, acceptance of *time* as the fourth dimension of reality, or with the discovery of indeterministic probabilistic behaviour of the wave-particles of quantum physics?

The Qur'an refers to special kinds of knowledge.

A courtier, a human being, in the court of Haḍrat Suleman (pbuh), was able to fetch a very heavy throne from the court of the Queen of Sheba (A.S.) to the court of Haḍrat Suleman (pbuh), in the twinkling of an eye (i.e., in a nano-second). Allah did not say that he accomplished something *supernatural*. Allah Almighty calls him the one *'who had a special knowledge from the Scripture.'* (Q. 27:39-40) It further shows that the scriptures contain possibilities for special knowledge too.

The seemingly extraordinary action he performed was based on a special knowledge endowed to him from the Scripture. Allah may grant any kind of special knowledge to any of His servants as He Wills. Allah grants His *signs* (*āyāt*) to His servants and Messengers whom He chooses. This extraordinary knowledge of utilising provisions of reality not reachable by anyone with his effort, is a special blessing from Allah. It is an instance of making extraordinary things, so supernatural for most of humankind, but very much natural for the one who has been endowed with knowledge of the laws governing that specific realm of existence or layer of reality. Jinni are supernatural for most of us, and some of us may not even believe in them. But their existence is very much natural for those who have been bestowed with a special knowledge relating their 'realm of existence' and 'orbit of activity'. Man's knowledge about the nature, structure and expansions of reality is so little that man's big claims about it do not deserve to be called knowledge. Science and philosophy had been arguing for the eternity of the universe for centuries until in the beginning of twentieth century, with the introduction of the theory of relativity and the concept of big-bang, science changed its stance and pronounced the world to be contingent, having a beginning in time at a limited temporal distance in the past. Before the advent of relativity physics, religious belief in a contingent universe was considered unscientific. To believe the universe to be three-dimensional was scientific and believing other than this was unscientific in Newtonian mechanics. Now science believes in a four dimensional universe. Is it not possible that in the future we can identify many more dimensions in nature?

In the Newtonian classical universe, things were considered static and enduring. With the 'time' perceived as fourth and essential dimension of reality in 'relativity physics', and discovery of the structure of atom, the concept of a *'thing'* transformed into an *'event'*, transforming the concept of universe into *a cosmic event*, yet everything was still believed to be determined by law of universal causation. Less than a century ago, we did not have the idea of *probability laws* and of a universe running under laws of quantum physics. The advent of quantum mechanics has radically changed our perception of the past and future. Quantum universe is probabilistic as compared to classical universe which is causal and fully determined under law of causation such that complete knowledge of the past allows computation of the future; likewise, complete knowledge of the future allows precise computation of the past. But it is not so in quantum physics. Given complete knowledge of the past, quantum physics allows only probabilistic predictions of the future.[161]

Quantum physics studies subatomic objects. They are neither particles nor waves; they manifest wave-particle duality. Their location is indeterminable. They manifest their location at more than one place at a time. They change their position as soon as they are perceived. Big-Bang has acquired the status of a standard cosmology, as Newtonian classical mechanics had been considered previously for two centuries. 'Singularity' is the term used to describe that unprecedented situation in which the Bing-bang is perceived to have taken place——a situation when there was neither *time* nor *space;* neither *matter* nor *energy* nor *causation.* Since no physics is possible in the absence of *time* and *space* to study that unique situation, nothing could be said about it with certainty. Dark matter, super energy, anti-matter, virtual particles, black-holes are the new concepts introduced under quantum theory. These concepts radically differ from concepts of classical mechanics. Theories of science change with the passage of time. Concept of wave-particle duality has superseded the classical particle concept; indeterminism of quantum measurement has replaced the determinism of classical physics. With the change of perspective, how can the concept of 'laws of nature' remain unchanged! Laws of nature may not need God in a deterministic classical mechanically running, three-dimensional universe, except for giving first motion to this cosmic machine; but an indeterministic four dimensional, expanding quantum universe very much needs God to coordinate different and at times diverse, layers of the order of reality. Nature follows the laws set for it by Allah, but what we discover or formulate, as laws of nature, are neither ultimate nor mere constructs of our own mind. They depict present status of our knowledge of the *fiṭrah* (*nature*) of things and interpretation of phenomena unaided by the guidance of revelation.

The scriptures have always been telling us that the universe is contingent and created, as the Qur'an has very clearly declared it. Following the Ptolemaic cosmology, the Muslim philosophers al-Farabi (872-950) and Ibn Sina (980-1037), argued in favour of the eternity of the universe.[162] The Qur'an has been telling us that Allah is ('فَعَّالٌ لِمَا يُرِيدُ' *Fa`ālun Limā Yurīdu) 'The Accomplisher of what He Will'.* (Q. 11:107; also see: Q. 85:19) But the Muslim philosophers, having accepted Aristotelian philosophical argument for the denial of 'volition' (*Iradah*) as divine attribute, were compelled to pronounce 'volition' —— as not worthy of Allah's Dignity. It was al-Ghazali (1058-1111) who refuted their argument in his *Tahafat-al-Flasifa* and established 'volition' as Allah's Glory.[163] Dr. Altaie argues that

> "For two hundred years we used to conceive the law of gravity to be God's mechanism for controlling the solar system. In spite of the fact that the astronomers are still accurately measuring the orbits of the planets and making predictions, yet neither the mathematical formulation nor the concept of Newtonian law of gravity has been found correct."[164]

We must keep in mind that our concepts always accord with our present knowledge of the 'nature of things'. How much of the universe we know, is a question whose answer carries least accuracy. If we were to claim that we know about 4% of the universe that we know it; about 44% of the remaining 96% of the universe, we know that we do not know it; and about the remaining 52% we do not even know what it is that we do not know. None can guess what will be our concepts when we have discovered new realms of reality and layers of existence and dimensions of the universe yet unknown to us.

———————

THE QUR'AN, SCIENCE AND PHILOSOPHY

EVOLVING A QUR'ANIC PARADIGM FOR RELATING SCIENCES AND PHILOSOPHY WITH ISLAM

Philosophical doctrines and the scientific worldview of an epoch from which a scholar gets too much impressed, attain the status of the standard of rationality for him. He begins to think that to believe these ideas as compared to the ones believed by past generations, is more rational and logical. If one already believes in a revealed religion the problem of reconciliation of revealed and rational versions of truth takes utmost importance. On the contrary, *iman bil-ghaib* (faith in the unseen) is the foundation of religion. This is the prime quality of the *muttaqīn* (those who qualify for attaining guidance from the Qur'an.)[165] The *muttaqīn* firmly believe that if any metaphysical notion, principle of logic, or scientific worldview is contrary to the teachings of the revealed truth, fault lies not with the assertions of faith but with the metaphysical notion, logic, or science. Al-Farabi and Ibn Sina, the renowned Muslim philosophers of the 10th and the 11th century are very close to each other in their philosophical views but Ibn Sina (Avicenna) developed these ideas much more than al-Farabi did. In the history of Muslim philosophy, they both are referred to as Muslim philosophers.[166] The Muslim philosophers got so impressed by Plato and Aristotle that they accepted their philosophical views as the standard of rational truth reconciling their philosophical differences by reinterpreting their views. As Muslim they believed religion as the revealed truth. In the history of religious philosophy, the desire for reconciliation has emerged in the form of reconstruction of religious thought in terms of prevalent philosophical and scientific theories. This is undertaken with the apparently avowed purpose to make the rational face of religion more bright. But in the end it is the religion that suffers. In their attempt at the reconciliation of religion and philosophy, Muslim philosophers had to deny all the major beliefs of Islam. To quote just one example here: Volition has been ascribed in the Qur'an to God as His Dignity and Majesty. The God-fearing one's believe that Allah has created the universe at Will and has created it ex-nihilo. They find no contradiction in believing Volition to be Allah's Glory. Since volition had been denied by Aristotle to be an attribute worthy of God, Muslim philosophers too had to deny it; and with it they too had to deny the creation of the universe by God at His Will and Command. Imam Ghazali, with great philosophical acumen, locates the presuppositions which made them deviate from standard Qur'anic beliefs and reconstructs them so as to prove Islamic beliefs fully rational. Averroes did his best to defend Avicenna against al-Ghazali's criticism but could not succeed.

Controversy between these thinkers is not merely an intellectual heritage of Muslim history, but also has intimate relevance with our own times. This provides us with a criterion to examine succeeding attempts as well as our own approach towards evolving a Qur'anic paradigm for defining the relationship between religion and the philosophico-scientific worldview of our own times. Rational supernaturalism and theology of modernity propounded by Sir Syed Ahmad Khan, construction of a scientific form of religious thought by Dr. Muhammad Iqbal, sociological interpretation of Islam and especially presentation of tawhid as worldview by Dr. Ali Sharī'ahti, blending creationism and evolutionism into a harmonious whole by Dr. Israr Ahmed, bifurcating the personality of the Prophet (pbuh) into various facets by Dr. Israr Ahmed, Dr. Ishaq Zafar Ansari and Maulana Abdul Waheed, making distinction between 'scientific theories' and 'established scientific facts' and correlating the latter with the Qur'an by Maurice Bucaille to prove the divine origin of the Qur'an, Islamization of Knowledge theories by IIIT, Ziauddin Sardar, Seyyed Hossein Nasr and similar attempts by various contemporary scholars need to be seen and evaluated in this perspective.

The writer considers attempts in the history of Muslim civilization from Avicenna to the contemporary scholars at the reconstruction of religious thought, not to be on appropriate lines, and proposes that the Muslim philosophers should be on their guard against such attempts and resist such irrationalities presented in the garb of rationality.

By 'reconstruction of religious thought' we mean taking a scientific theory (e.g., the Ptolemaic, the Newtonian or the Einsteinian) and the worldview arising in its wake (i.e., philosophy) as the standard of rationality, and setting on to reinterpret religious doctrines in philosophico-scientific terminology so as to prove them harmonious with these standards. History of Muslim philosophy is replete with such attempts. Failing to find anything in the Qur'an that could support their contention, either they insert un-Qur'anic terminologies, identifications, analogies or metaphorical interpretations in the Qur'an or they try to search out a Divine or Prophetic *Hadīth* in the corpus of traditions or a tradition ascribed to any of the companions of the Prophet (r.a.) based on which they could insert their own suggestion in the Qur'an to read in it their desired meaning.

Philo of Alexandria (also called Judaeus Philo c.20 BCE—40 CE)ᐟ a Jewish religious scholar, is the originator of religious reconstruction, in the known history. He is among those scholars of the early period who got too impressed by Platonic philosophy. Believing Judaism as the revealed truth, and the Platonic philosophy as the standard of rationality, Philo set himself to developing a speculative justification for Judaism in terms of its harmonisation with Plato. In the history of philosophy, this was the first attempt at the rational reconstruction of religious thought. This created scope for Hellenistic interpretation of religious thought and laid foundations for the philosophical and theological development of Christianity as we see it today.

The Ptolemaic model of the world which consisted of nine heavens with the earth in the centre presented the scientific worldview of Ibn-e-Sina's times (Circa 980–1037 A.D.). The Ptolemaic cosmology prevailed for 1400 years. The Qur'anic model of the universe consists of seven heavens and is irreconcilable with the Ptolemaic model.[167] Remaining true to the Qur'an, Ibn-e-Sina could not accept the Ptolemaic model. Then he had to reject the Ptolemaic model as false, or prove it doubtful. Which he could not do. He surrendered his belief in Qur'anic cosmology consisting of seven heavens in favour of the Ptolemaic cosmology consisting of nine heavens. Ibn Sina was as much impressed by Aristotelian metaphysics as Philo was by Platonic metaphysics. Ibn Sina could not prove his mettle in locating flaws in Aristotelian logic which was based on dualistic metaphysics, his concept of 'will' as implying imperfection, his concept of 'cause–effect relationship' as logical necessity, and his concept of 'perfection' as immutability etc. Accepting the Ptolemaic cosmology, the Aristotelian metaphysics, and the neo-Platonic concept of god as standards of rationality of his times, he set himself on the reconstruction of Islamic religious thought. This marred Ibn-e-Sina's whole metaphysics with inconsistency and self-contradiction. He had to surrender his belief in the Qur'anic cosmology consisting of seven heavens in favour of the Ptolemaic cosmology consisting of nine heavens,[168] he had to surrender his belief in the creation of the universe in favour of eternal emanation, belief in Allah's Knowledge of particulars in favour of God's all-encompassing eternal knowledge, belief in human freedom in favour of logical determinism, belief in bodily resurrection in favour of spiritual resurrection, belief in miracles in favour of absoluteness of efficient causation and so on.

Ideas thrive upon terms and travel in history. If they are false they go on colouring the understanding and interpretation of other ideas. At times it may take centuries for someone to identify them and straighten them. It was around fourteen centuries after Aristotle when al-Ghazali (1058–1111) redefined the notion of Divine 'Will' to show that it was absolutely compatible with the Dignity and Majesty of the Qur'anic God and is Honour for Him. He also pointed out other inconsistencies in Ibn Sina's philosophy which arose as implication of accepting Aristotle's metaphysics, logic, concept of 'causation' and other ideas.[169]

Newtonian cosmology and naturalism

Expanding on the ideas of Galileo, Copernicus and Johannes Kepler, in 1687 Sir Isaac Newton presented a comprehensive worldview of an eternal, infinite, closed, static, steady state, clockwork universe, in which the total momentum of the Universe is conserved, interactions redistribute the momentum but the total never change. In this model, God was needed only to start the clockwork as the initial cause, and then it runs by itself for the rest of time.[170] There could be no role for God in this universe whose Goodly Names are mentioned in the Qur'an. Neither could there be any place in this universe for miracles, supernatural events, supernatural entities or divine intervention which the traditional Muslim theology believes.[171] Prayer and supplication has no real meaning. Laws of nature are sufficient to account for everything relating matter, life, mind, soul, freewill, personal identity or whatever. "Prophecies and so-called miraculous events either are explicable by the known or hitherto unknown laws of nature; if they are not thus explicable, their happening itself must be denied. Since, for religious and moral as well as for scientific truth, human reason is the only source of knowledge, the fact of a Divine Revelation is to be explained in natural terms if it is to be believed. The contents of such revelations can be accepted only as far as they are rational according to the prevalent standards. If human beings have a religion at all, it is only that, which his reason dictates. In short, it can be said that Newtonian naturalism contradicts with the most vital doctrines of Islam; the doctrines, which rest essentially on the existence of a Person God, His so many Attributive Names, the Creator at Will of the universe and nature, the Originator of creation (*khalq*) and command (*amr*), and the idea of an organised system of Divinely administered universe;[172] angels, prophets, the soul (*ruḥ*) and its immortality; human freedom and responsibility; resurrection, judgement, reward and the life hereafter.

Basic Principle of Sir Syed's Theology of Modernity

The philosophy of naturalism evolved from Newtonian empirical mechanical science, constituted the standard of rationality of Sir Syed Ahmad Khan's times. The challenge he had in the second half of the 19th century in the British occupied India was the following:

Either to prove naturalism to be wrong, or

to show its assumptions to be doubtful, or

to keep on believing what he believed as a traditional believer and ignore the challenge of modernity; or

following Philo and Ibn Sina, to reconstruct his religious beliefs to demonstrate that they were compatible with the standard of rationality of his own times.

Khan opts for the last and formulates a 15 point framework comprising, what he calls, his 'theology of modernity' (*jadid ilm al-kalam*) to reinterpret the Islamic Scripture to demonstrate its harmonisation with the assumptions, implications and consequences of Newtonian naturalism.[173] Like Ibn Sina, Khan justifies his belief in God, based on the cosmological argument as First Cause; conceives this First Cause as Absolute Existence in the sense of *waḥdat al wujud*; interprets His Attributes in the Mu'tazilites' sense. This comprises his Rational Supernaturalism. How can God conceived as Uncaused First Cause be a Creator at Will, how can a First Cause descend revelation, how can He be the Command Giver and the Administrator of the world etc! Conceiving God as First Cause, how could you believe in angels, prophets, the soul, spirituality and immortality, human freedom and responsibility, bodily resurrection, judgement and reward and the life hereafter! How can a First Cause claim to have created the earth in two days, and in two days to have created the provisions on earth, and in two days to have created the seven heavens!(Q. 41:9-12)

The Qur'an is the basic source of teachings in Islam. It is believed by Muslims to be revealed, the standard of truth, authority in matters of *deen* (*Al-Ḥaqq*). What conforms to it is true (*ḥaqq*), what contradicts it is false (*bāṭil*), what is said in violation to this is wrongful (*bi ghayr 'l Ḥaqq*), deviation from it is error (*al-ḍalāl*), to express views without reference to it is to follow conjecture (*ẓann*), and saying anything about Allah, not supported by the Qur'an, is concoction (*iftirā*). The Qur'an calls itself 'the Word of God'.

Sir Syed Ahmad Khan stipulates to call the created world (*i.e.*, the phenomena of nature,) 'the Work of God' as compared to the Qur'an which calls itself 'the Word of God'. In order to reconstruct teachings of the Qur'an to demonstrate its accordance with Newtonian naturalism, elaborating the close relationship between 'the Work of God' and 'the Word of God' he introduces a principle that in case of conflict between science and religion "'the Work of God' overrides 'the Word of God.'" Developing this hermeneutics he makes the revealed Word of God (the 'Standard of Truth' in Islam) subservient to human knowledge based on the study of nature, Newtonian scientific worldview being the best instance of it in Khan's times. As stated earlier, Sir Syed Ahmad Khan passed away in 1898, and Einstein's Special Theory of Relativity replaced Newtonian naturalism in 1905 and his General Theory of Relativity in 1916. These theories refuted the view of the world and the version of naturalism based on Newtonian mechanics and Sir Syed Ahmad Khan's interpretation of the Qur'an propounded to reconcile with it.

Einstein's cosmology and naturalism

Newtonian naturalism believed no connection between space and time. Physical space was held to be a flat, three-dimensional continuum (*i.e.*, an arrangement of all possible point locations—to which Euclidean postulates would apply.) Time was viewed as absolute—*i.e.*, independent of space, as a separate, one-dimensional continuum — completely homogeneous along its infinite extent.[174] So the Newtonian universe was an infinite space existing corresponding to absolute time.

Albert Einstein in his 'theory of relativity' suggested that time wasn't separate from space but connected to it. He visualised that time and space were combined to form *space-time*, and everyone measured his or her own experience in it differently. Einsteinian naturalism sees the fabric of space as four-dimensional. In it, *time* is not absolute; it is relative to the experiencing subject. The basic elements of space-time are *events* as compared to the Newtonian naturalism, which believes in a static and steady state universe with *things* as its elements. "In any given space-time, an event is a unique position at a unique time." Einstein also suggested that space-time wasn't flat, but curved or "warped" by the existence of matter and energy. Einsteinian naturalism states "that objects with large masses can warp [bend/twist] *time* by speeding it up or slowing it down. How many dimensions are needed to describe the universe is still an open question. According to some modern theories, the universe can only be adequately described by using a system with many more dimensions than were originally proposed by Einstein."[175]

Basic Principle of Iqbal's Theology of Modernity ——Construction of a Scientific Form of Religious Knowledge

Einstein's study of 'the Work of God' makes Sir Syed's reconstruction of Muslim theology outdated and incompatible with the newly arisen naturalism. As per his own principle that 'Work of God overrides the Word of God', a new Sir Syed was needed to reinterpret 'the Word of God' to show that it was still compatible with the naturalism of Einstein——Einstein who definitely did not believe in a Personal God and who was a determinist. Einstein argues that the natural scientists cannot legitimately believe in the reality of supernatural causes behind natural events.[176] Now Iqbal comes forward with a new interpretation of 'the Word of God' in his *Reconstruction of Religious Thought in Islam* in line with Einsteinian Naturalism and other modern sciences and philosophical theories. Basit Bilal Koshul in his article "Muhammad Iqbal's reconstruction of the philosophical arguments for the existence of God"[177] rightly sums up Iqbal's understanding of the relationship between religion and science in the following words which could be termed as first point of Iqbal's theology of modernity (*jadeed ilm al-kalam*):

[i] 'If religion aspires to attract seekers whose religious faith is based on personal experience (rather than tradition, culture and dogma), religion will have to open itself to science.

[ii] If science aspires to give a coherent and holistic account of experience (rather than partial and mutually irreconcilable accounts) science will have to open itself to religion.'[178]

According to Iqbal, faith is ultimately based on a special type of inner experience. Sufism has been providing this facility by developing special spiritual and psychological techniques for directing the evolution of this inner experience in an individual believer, but by becoming incapable of receiving fresh inspirations from the modern thought and experience, sufism has failed to fulfil this need. From here draws the second point of 'Iqbal's theology of modernity' that "Keeping in view the unique characteristics of modern culture, a scientific form of religious knowledge is but needed to make such inner experience possible."[179] By accomplishing a reconstruction of modern scientific understanding of experience in terms of, what Dr. Basit Bilal calls, Qur'anicaly informed perspective, Iqbal believes, we will provide that scientific form of religious knowledge which is essential for that special type of inner experience on which the faith is ultimately based on. Thus Iqbal sees the "harmonisation of religion and science as essential precondition for the possibility of such inner experience in the modern, scientific cultural setting."[180]

Qur'anicaly Informed Perspective

Qur'anicaly informed perspective Iqbal starts by examining religious experience to pave the way for opening religion towards science and science towards religion. As is evident from the very title of his work, Iqbal undertakes a philosophical discussion of some of the basic ideas of Islam, in order to attempt a reconstruction of Islamic religious thought in terms of modern science and philosophy, considering them standard of rationality. Iqbal considers that the essence of religion is faith, that faith is based on religious experience [revelation] or intuition, and that science is a systematisation of sense experience and philosophy an intellectual view of reality.[181] Developing an extended concept of thought, Iqbal persistently advocates his conviction that senses, reason and intuition are not independent sources of knowledge but aspects of one wider source which he calls 'thought'. They seek visions of the same reality, so they must be reconcilable. Intuition, however, a higher form of thought, is more basic than intellect and sense experience and is not devoid of cognitive elements. In the first lecture of *Reconstruction*, Iqbal examines the genuineness of intuition as a source of knowledge, and taking the Qur'an as the embodiment of religious experience, gives an account of reality revealed in it. In order to prove his contentions, he critically interprets and examines the accounts of reality discernible from scientists and philosophers with a view to discovering whether they ultimately lead us to the same character of reality as is revealed by religious experience. In this chapter he analyses religious experience as a source of knowledge and argues that intellectual thought and religious experience are not opposed to each other, they have common source and thus are complementary to each other. The second chapter examines this experience philosophically and concludes that judgement based on religious experience fully satisfies the intellectual test. Through philosophical discussions of levels of human experience, and the meaning of creation, the primacy of life and thought, the teleological character of reality and the meaning of teleology with reference to God, by the end of this lecture he is able to reach the idea of God (or Ultimate Reality). He reaches this idea by identifying *Time* with God, and the spatial aspects of reality with God's manifestation in serial time. In this chapter Iqbal examines modern philosophical and scientific theories of space and time to find that philosophical theories in fact come to agree with the religious experience of reality; however conceding the limitations of the intellectual view of life, Iqbal asserts that it cannot take us beyond a pantheistic view of life whereas intuition of one's own self reveals that the ultimate nature of reality is spiritual (*i.e.*, a Self) and must be conceived as an Ego. Further, the Qur'an emphasises the individuality of the Ultimate Ego and gives Him the proper name Allah.[182] The third chapter puts the religious experience of prayer to pragmatic test. Having reached and having identified the Ultimate Ego with the Qur'anic God citing Surat al-Ikhlas, which declares the incomparable uniqueness of God as Individual, in this chapter, Iqbal embarks upon drawing out either the characteristics of the Absolute Ego and reinterpreting the attributes of the Qur'anic God to reconcile them or the other way round." [183] "The fourth chapter relates religious experience with modern and Islamic 'theories of self and its freedom' from the perspectives of religion and philosophy. The fifth chapter explores prophecy as a fundamental of Islamic culture that demonstrates how religious experience transforms itself into a living world force. This particular perspective is possible only by disregarding the Greek classical metaphysical view of reason, matter and movement and by adopting the Qur'anic anti classical approach to the universe. The sixth lecture on *Ijtihad* illustrates how the dynamism within the structure of Islamic thought was lost by the adoption of classical methods of reasoning that led to *taqlid* and stagnation. The concluding chapter comes back to the question 'Is religion possible?' and argues that the religion and the scientific processes involve different methods but they are in a sense parallel to each other. In the scientific process, self stands outside, and in the religious experience the self develops an inclusive attitude. Both are descriptions of the same world but from different stand points."[184]

Iqbal, no doubt, makes an ingenious attempt in his lectures for the harmonisation of Islam and science and philosophy, and he lawfully deserves appreciation as do Abu al-Hassan Al-Ash'ari, al-Ghazali, Ibn Sina, Sir Syed Ahmad Khan and all those who spent their lives striving in this direction. But, this admission does not allow anyone to claim that it is on the correct lines. Attempts made by Abu al-Hassan Al-Ash'ari, Ibn Sina and Sir Syed Ahmad Khan, for the same purpose, too were equally ingenious in their own times! However, if the basic suppositions of their thought, as identified in previous chapters, were contrary to the Qur'anic teachings, should we not examine presuppositions of Iqbalian project for their accordance with the Qur'an! This alone will decide the merit of Iqbal thought.

In the second chapter of his *Reconstruction,* looking at Nature as a structure of interrelated events possessing the character of continuous creative flow, as presented by Einstein, Iqbal conceives it as a systematic mode of behaviour and as such organic to the Ultimate Self (*i.e.,*God), as character is [organic] to human self. (Iqbal, 28, 45) (Koshul, 101)

Conceiving God as Ultimate Ego on the Analogy of Man — One of the Two Fundamental Presuppositions

Conceiving the relationship between Nature and God on the analogy of character to man, is one of the two fundamental presuppositions which enable Iqbal to bring about that scientific form of religious knowledge which he considers necessary for making a special type of inner experience possible which according to him the faith is ultimately based on. Looking at Nature as the habit of Allah and considering Nature as organic to the Ultimate Self, as we shall see, has its own implications.

Any discussion on the negative or positive implications of the above idea drawn by Iqbal, will be pointless, unless the status of the basic idea is decided *i.e.,* whether it is correct or incorrect.

Our point is that if Nature (as theo-philosophically interpreted by Iqbal) is to God as character is to human self, if it is organic to the Ultimate Self as *habit,* then Nature is to be considered uncreated. Since Iqbal too believes in traditional Muslim ontology, what is uncreated, must mean eternal for him.

To perceive nature, as organic to God on the analogy of man, is absolutely contrary to the Message of the Qur'an. Does God not say in the Qur'an:

Nothing is like Him. (Q. 42:11)

Hence He is supremely and incomparably Unique and Transcendent of all analogies, likeness and comparisons! Then how could you justify conceiving the Life of God on the analogy of man!

The Qur'an says:

'If all the trees on the earth were pens and the sea, with seven seas behind it, were ink, still Allah's Words would not run out.' (Q. 31:27)

As creation (*khalq*) or command (*amr*), or a composition of both, Nature is replete with the Signs of its Originator. A Qur'anicaly informed scientific study of Nature is must to keep it within Qur'anicaly prescribed limits. [185]

Best example of 'what a Qur'anicaly informed scientific study of nature could genuinely mean' can be seen in Al-Ghazali's attempt at the refutation of al-Farabi and Ibn Sina's philosophy. This is in real sense the best instance in the history of Muslim thought of what Iqbal perceives as reconstruction of scientific [and philosophical] thought in terms of Qur'anicaly-informed perspective and a reconstruction of religious thought in terms of scientific [and philosophical] understanding of experience, which as Iqbal believes, will provide us that scientific form of religious knowledge which is essential for that special type of inner experience on which the faith is ultimately based on. Had al-Ghazali not entangled in un-Qur'anic ontology accepted by his predecessor Ash'arites, he would have produced such an excellent example of a Qur'anically informed scientific and philosophical study of nature and a reconstruction of religious thought in terms of scientific and philosophical understanding of experience, which Iqbal aspired in his lectures but could not accomplish!

Let us examine Iqbal's own case in this perceptive.

Naturalism arising out of Einstein's theory of relativity which sees reality as a space-time continuum taking *time* as a fourth dimension of space, is a modern scientific understanding of experience of the physical world. This brings to the fore the concept of *time* with its implications with reference to *simultaneity*. Bergson, a renowned philosopher of Iqbal's period, critically examines implications of Einstein's concept of *time* and, refusing to accept it, develops his own concept of *time* and of ultimate reality. Bergson conceives Ultimate Reality as *Time.* Thus *time* acquires central place in both scientific and philosophical deliberations of Iqbal's period. Biology and psychology also develop in this period and problems of the nature of life, nature of self and its autonomy, and their relationship with *time*, come to the forefront as the centre of discussions in these fields. Modernity exposes itself to Iqbal through concepts of *time, life, self* and *autonomy of self*. Being a Muslim thinker Iqbal aspires to reconstruct these objectifications of modernity in Islamic perspective ultimately to relate this scientific form of religious knowledge to scientific and philosophical understanding of reality. Iqbal gets impressed by the Bergsonian concept of *time* as the essence of ultimate reality. In psychology introspection as a method for the study of *self,* impresses Iqbal, and in it he sees the prospects of a philosophy of *self* (*falsafa-e-khudi*) and a new proof for the existence of God in place of traditional arguments, which he rejects. The question was how to relate *time* and *self* together. Iqbal conceives 'self' as ego (*khudi*) – an entity, which conceives itself as 'I-am'. He argues that life and ego-hood cannot be conceived without *time. Time* is the essence of everything. When on the analogy of human ego, he conceives God as the Absolute Ego, he identifies *Time* (as 'eternal now' or 'pure duration') as the permanent factor in the Being of God. Now he needs something from the Qur'an which could substantiate his above contention. Not finding anything in the Qur'an to this purpose, he turns towards the *tradition (Ḥadīth)* where he finds one, based on which maintaining God and *Time* identical, he attempts to reconstruct what he calls scientific form of religious knowledge. Can a *tradition* not verified by the Qur'an be a saying of the Prophet (pbuh)! Should such a thing bear authority! Can such an approach of harmonising religion and science be termed a move in the correct direction!

Iqbal's Identification of *Time* with God — Second Fundamental Preposition of Iqbal's Thought

If God is *time* or *time* is an essential factor in the Being of God, as Iqbal puts it, then at least Iqbal and Bergson both have been able to discover at least one ultimate factor of God's Being! If God is *Time* or the *vice versa*, can the universe be held contingent and created! Does this philosophy essentially differ from Ibn Sina or Sir Syed's views? Thus, the second fundamental presupposition of Iqbal's reconstruction of religious thought in Islam is his identification of God with *Time* (*al-Dahr*). From this identification Dr. Basit Bilal Koshul draws what he calls Iqbal's Qur'anic-scientific conception of *time*.[186]

Iqbal's Qur'anic-scientific Conception of *Time* —Elaboration and Justification by Basit Bilal Koshul

Iqbal quotes a Divine Ḥadīth (Ḥadīth-e-Qudsi) in which the Prophet says: "Allah says: Do not vilify *time* for *time* is God."[187] In order to justify Iqbal's identification of God with *time*, Dr. Koshul, refers to "the dynamism, creativity, and freedom—to the degree that these are characteristics of *time*, they also are characteristics of God." Dr. Koshul terms it as the Qur'anic-scientific conception of *time*.[188] In order to support above contentions Dr. Koshul refers to eight passages from the Qur'an *i.e.* Q. 3:190-1; 2:164; 24:44 and 10:6; 25:62; 31:29; 39:5; 23:80 as mentioned by Iqbal himself to point out that the Qur'an considers *time* to be one of the greatest symbols of God.[189] Iqbal conceives the real time as pure duration. He conceives God, his Absolute Ego, as the whole of Reality, which exists in pure duration. Thus, Iqbal asserts "*time* to be an essential element in the being of God."[190]

There is a difference between 'symbol' and 'sign'. "One thing, A, is a sign of another thing B, if A refers to B in some way or other. [And] there are different ways in which one thing can refer to another thing. But one thing A is a symbol of B if it is identical with B or some essential aspect of B. For example mathematical symbols are symbols not signs. In Islamic religious numerology the figure 786 is a symbol of the formula *Bismi-Allahi.* Basit Bilal is right in rendering Iqbal's assertion which sees "*time* to be an essential element in the being of God." as "Time is a greatest symbol of God." But in our view Iqbal's assertion and its rendering by Dr. Koshul both are absolutely un-Qur'anic. The correct thing would be to say that "*Time* is a sign of God." as mentioned in the following verses:

"Everything in the heavens and earth belongs to God. God is Self-Sufficient and Worthy of all Praise. If all the trees on earth were pens and all the seas, with seven more seas besides, [were ink,] still God's words [kalimātullah –signs] would not run out: God is Almighty and All Wise." (Q. 31:27)

Since this study does not consist of an exclusive examination of Iqbal's *Reconstruction of Religious Thought in Islam,* it is not possible to give a fuller examination of his work. Suffice it is to say that if his 'identification of God with Time' is verified from the Qur'an, attempt made by Iqbal must be accepted in the right direction and implications drawn by

Iqbal based on this principle should be taken as correct. However, if it is otherwise, then neither the attempt will be considered as rightly-directed nor the implications thereof will be considered correct. Let us examine this Iqbalian principle and Dr. Koshul's attempt to justify it.

This Divine tradition (*Ḥadīth-e-Qudsi*) which identifies God with time occurs in five versions, all narrated by Haḍrat Abu Huraira (r.a.). First and fourth versions clearly deny any identification between God and time. The second and the third versions are self-contradictory —— as they can be interpreted in both ways. Whereas the last version very clearly identifies Allah with time. Leaving the first four versions aside Iqbal chooses the last version.

Various versions of the Tradition of 'ad-dahr'

Following are the various versions of the above-mentioned tradition:

"(i) The Prophet (pbuh) said: "Allah says: Man vilifies time, whereas time is in My Hand. I control the day and night."

(ii) The Prophet (pbuh) said: "Allah says: Man tortures Me when he vilifies time, whereas I Myself am Time; I alter the day and night."

(iii) The Prophet (pbuh) said: "Allah says: Man tortures Me when he says: Woe to the Time! So none of you should say "Woe to the Time for I Myself am Time; I bring the day and night. I will suspend their coming if I would like."

(iv) The Prophet (pbuh) said: "Allah says: None of you should say, "Woe to the time; for time is in My Hand."

(v) The Prophet (pbuh) said: "Allah says: Do not vilify Time, for Allah is Time." [191]

The Qur'an consists of 6238 verses.[192] The text of the Qur'an is historically intact and throughout centuries, the same text in one and the same arrangement of verses and *surahs* is prevalent all over the world. It is not difficult to examine whether this alleged 'Qur'anic-scientific conception of time' derives anywhere from the Qur'an!

I) The word '*ad-dahr*' (meaning '*time*') is an Arabic word and occurs only at the following two places in the Qur'an:

Those who have taken their own desires as their god, those whom God lets to stray in the face of knowledge, sealing their ears and hearts and covering their eyes, they say:

'There is only our life in this world: we die, we live, nothing but time [ad-dahr الدَّهر] destroys us. They have no knowledge of this; they only follow conjecture.' (Q. 45:24)

II) Inviting man towards pondering over his own self, it has been said in Surah *Al-Insān* of the Qur'an (which is also known as Surah Ad-Dahr) that:

"Was there not a period of time [ad-dahr] when man was not anything to speak of!" (Q. 76:01)

Out of the five different versions of the same tradition, Iqbal picks up one, which explicitly contradicts with the *muḥkamāt* of the Qur'an. Let us now examine the eight passages of the Qur'an pointed out by Iqbal himself on the basis of which Dr. Koshul attempts to justify what he calls Iqbal's Qur'anic-scientific conception of time.

"In the creation of the heavens and earth; in the alternation of night and day; in the ships that sail the seas with goods for people; in the water which Allah sends down from the sky to give life to the earth when it has been barren, scattering all kinds of creatures over it; in the changing of the winds and clouds that run their appointed courses between the sky and earth: there are signs in all these for those who use their minds." (Q. 2:164)

'Control of the heavens and earth belongs to Allah; God has power over everything. There truly are signs in the creation of the heavens and earth, and in the alternation of night and day, for those with understanding; who remember Allah standing, sitting, and lying down, who reflect on the creation of the heavens and earth: 'Our Lord! You have not created all this without purpose–Your Glory is far above that!– so protect us from the torment of the Fire.' (Q. 3:189-91)

'Allah alternates night and day– there truly is a lesson in [all] this for those who have eyes to see.' (Q. 24:44)

'In the succession of night and day, and in what God created in the heavens and earth, there truly are signs for those who are aware of Him.' (Q. 10:6)

'It is He who made the night and day follow each other – so anyone who wishes, may be mindful or show gratitude.' (Q. 25:62)

'[Do you not see that God causes the night to merge into day and the day to merge into night; that He has subjected the sun and the moon, each to run its course for a stated term; that He is aware of everything you [people] do!' (Q. 31:29)

'He created the heavens and earth for a true purpose; He wraps the night around the day and the day around the night; He has subjected the sun and moon to run their courses for an appointed time; He is truly the Mighty, the Forgiving.' (Q. 39:5)

'It is He who gives life and death; the alternation of night and day depends on Him; will you not use your minds!' (Q. 23:80)

Is there even a slightest justification for taking *ad-dahr* to mean Allah at any of these places? Absolutely not. Can anybody else know the Holy Being of Allah better than Allah Himself? Absolutely not. When Allah Almighty has not used the word '*ad-dahr*' for Himself, on what authority can anybody hold Allah and '*ad-dahr*' (*time*) identical or defend such a view? The Qur'an forbids the believers from ascribing anything, not based on the Qur'anic authority, to Allah. The Qur'an calls it concoction (*iftrā*). The Qur'an says:

'So who does more wrong than he who fabricates lies against Allah, with no authority in knowledge, in order to lead people astray? God does not guide the evildoers.' (Q. 6:144)

The status of authority lies with the Qur'an as the Qur'an says:

'Those, who do not judge according to Allah's revelation, disbelieve Allah's revelations.' (Q. 5:44)

'Those, who do not judge according to what Allah has revealed, are doing grave wrong.' (Q. 5:45)

Those, who do not judge according to what Allah has revealed, are lawbreakers. (Q. 5:47)

It is clear from the above verses that the Qur'an gives no support to the contention that 'God is *time* or that *time* is God.' To consider *time* to be one of the greatest symbols of God, and to consider "dynamism, creativity, and freedom—to the degree that these are characteristics of time, they also are characteristics of God" is to identify God and *time* which the Qur'an does not sanction.

To translate *Sunnat Allah* as *the habit* of Allah is also incorrect. No doubt, to be a capricious deity does not suit the Majesty of Allah, but it too is not correct to ascribe *habits* to Allah. 'Ways of Allah' are based on His Knowledge and Wisdom. He has placed patterns and harmonies in nature but laws of nature (*Allah's amr*) are subservient to His Will, His Will is not subservient to the laws of nature. How highly Iqbal evaluates this supposition can be seen from the fact that according to him this view has the potential of investing science with new meaning and significance.[193] He observes this when he says: "The knowledge of Nature is the knowledge of God's behaviour. In our observation of Nature we are virtually seeking a kind of intimacy with the Absolute Ego, and this is only another form of worship."[194] Let us examine verses Q. 33:62, 35:43, 48:23 of the Qur'an, which he claims to endorse the above idea.

'Prophet, tell your wives, your daughters, and women believers to make their outer garments hang low over them so as to be recognized and not insulted: God is most forgiving, most merciful. If the hypocrites, the sick at heart, and those who spread lies in the city do not desist, We shall rouse you [Prophet] against them, and then they will only be your neighbours in this city for a short while. They will be rejected. Wherever they are found, they will be arrested and put to death. This has been God's practice with those, who went before. You will find no change in God's practices. سُنَّةَ اللَّهِ فِي الَّذِينَ خَلَوْا مِنْ قَبْلُ وَلَنْ تَجِدَ لِسُنَّةِ اللَّهِ تَبْدِيلًا (Q. 33:59-62)'*

'[The Children of Ishmael] swore their most solemn oath that, if someone came to warn them, they would be more rightly guided than any [other] community, but when someone did come they turned yet further away, became more arrogant in the land, and intensified their plotting of evil– the plotting of evil only rebounds on those who plot. Do they expect anything but what happened to earlier people? You will never find any change in God's practice; you will never find any deviation there. فَهَلْ يَنْظُرُونَ إِلَّا سُنَّةَ الْأَوَّلِينَ فَلَنْ تَجِدَ لِسُنَّةِ اللَّهِ تَبْدِيلًا وَلَنْ تَجِدَ لِسُنَّةِ اللَّهِ تَحْوِيلًا (Q. 35:42-43)'*

'If the disbelievers had fought against you, they would have taken flight and found no one to protect or support them: such was God's practice in the past and you will find no change in God's practices. سُنَّةَ اللَّهِ الَّتِي قَدْ خَلَتْ مِنْ قَبْلُ وَلَنْ تَجِدَ لِسُنَّةِ اللَّهِ تَبْدِيلًا (Q. 48:22-23)'*

The whole Iqbalian project of reconciliation of science and religion is based on purging modern scientific thought from materialistic, mechanistic, and reductionist philosophical concepts by replacing them with so-called Qur'anic-scientific concepts of Nature and *Time* through the above-mentioned two presuppositions. The good intention and sincerity of Iqbal and his interpreters admitted, we have placed all the references from the Qur'an for an intelligent reader to decide the epistemic merits of this attempt by himself.

Some Contemporary Scholars

Blending "Creation" and "Evolution" together —— Dr. Israr Ahmed

Following the same track Dr. Israr Ahmed (1932 – 2010) writes an Urdu Booklet *Ijād-o-Ibdā' i 'Alam sey 'Almi Nizam-e-Khilazfat tak Tanazzal-w-Irtiqa' kay Maraḥil* rendered into English by his younger brother, the renowned philosopher and religious scholar, Dr. Absar Ahmed (b. 1945) by the title *The Process of Creation: A Qur'anic Perspective.*[195] In Dr. Absar Ahmed's words "In this tract Dr. Israr Ahmed, by collecting and collating references primarily from the Qur'an and *Ḥadīth*, has endeavoured to put forth a theory which in essence blends 'Creation' and 'Evolution' together into one harmonious thread." Dr. Absar Ahmed further says: "The thrust of the venture is on presenting the Qur'anic position on questions pertaining to the realms of existence as distinct yet overlapping phases of creation and evolution, all brought into effect by the Omnipotent God, the Qur'an calls Allah."[196] He further observes: "Dr. Israr Ahmed puts in bold relief the ontological dualism of man by emphasising the evolutionary process only in the physical part of man." [197] Dr. Israr Ahmed states the problem in the following words:

'According to Islamic theistic belief, only Allah is the 'Necessary Being' and the 'Eternal Being'."[198] In "stark contrast, the vast expanse of space and time and the sum total of creation and existence (including human beings) are only 'potentialities', 'possibilities', and 'contingencies'. While there can be no dispute regarding these two beliefs, the process by which 'possibility' emerged from 'Necessity' and 'contingency from 'Eternity' remains a topic of debate and contestation among the theologians.' [199]

In response to this issue Dr. Israr Ahmed says:

'In this booklet, we will try to unravel the cosmogenesis, unfolded by a deeper reflection on the highly subtle and profoundly significant Qur'anic verses, and its convergence with certain points of modern cosmological, astrophysical and biological thought.'[200]

The epistemic fallacy committed by Dr. Israr Ahmad's thinking is manifest in the above para in the use of terms like 'possibility as opposite to necessity' and 'contingency [*hadūth*] as opposite to eternity [*qidm*]'. These terms presuppose an un-Qur'anic ontology as has been made clear at various places in the book. These are polar concepts and applicable to entities belonging to the same order of reality only, so not applicable to Allah, Who is incomparably Unique and transcends any likeness or comparison to anything. The point is that when you accept an un-Qur'anic notion about God or His attributes, and try to read it in the Qur'an, you cannot avoid facing inconsistencies. As has been said earlier that no Good-Name of God in Muslim tradition tantamount to the concept of 'eternity', 'timelessness', 'immutability', 'perfection' and 'uncaused cause'. Muslims borrowed these un-Qur'anic notions from Greeks either directly or through Christians. So far as Christians are concerned it has been admitted even by them that there is no evidence of these concepts being Divine Attributes in Christianity before Augustine (354-430), nor is there any evidence in the Old Testament for it.[201]

Basic Supposition of Dr. Israr Ahmed's Thesis

The nutshell of Dr. Israr Ahmed's attempt is that "the word *'KUN'* (Be!), the verbal imperative of Allah, is the basis and catalyst through which the process of Genesis or the event of Creation was initiated, and that whenever Allah decides on a matter, it is sufficient for Him to utter this verbal imperative and the matter is done."[202]

By a quite unjustified move, he translates the verbal imperative of Allah, the Word *'KUN'* (Be!) into *'Kalimah tu Allah'*. The translation of verses 2:117, 3:47, 19:35, 40:68, 16:40, 36:82 referred to by Dr. Israr Ahmed, themselves refer to the Word *KUN* as Command (*amr*) and not the KALIMA. We will quote just one of these here.

"…The (nature) of His *Amr* is such that when He wills a thing to be, He says to it, "Be" … and it is!" (Yaseen, 36:82)

The right rendering of the Word "*KUN*" is Command, and not the KALIMA (i.e., statement). Allah Himself does not call the Word *KUN* as "*Kalimah tu Allah*" as He calls Haḍrat Isa (pbuh) as "Kalimatum minho".[203]

Dr. Israr Ahmed further identifies the *'Kalimah tu Allah'* (with reference to verse nos. Q. 17:109, and Q. 31:27) with every single created being; hence every single being representing the manifestation of a Divine Imperative 'Be'. If each single created being would need the expression of the Divine imperative 'Be' then there will be no genera, species, organisation, classification or laws of nature etc. in the universe. So with reference to verse Q. 87:1-3 Dr. Israr Ahmed identifies 'Laws of Nature' or the 'Physical Laws' as the manifestation of Allah's promise of 'apportioning' and 'guiding' in the realm of inanimate matter, 'biological laws' in the sphere of biology and the 'instincts' in the sphere of animal life, and rules of logic in the realm of human beings etc. And beyond this normal functioning of the created order there is nothing but 'Revelation'.[204] Thus 'normal functioning of the created order does not require any additional expression of the Divine Word "Be!" "But wherever there is a need to alter the normal functioning of the created order — to alter the normal chain of 'cause and effect' in order that a special Divine Decree is enacted — then there is the need for a new Divine Word "Be!".[205] Thus identifying and translating the Word *'KUN'* into *Kalimah tu Allah,* Dr. Israr Ahmed enters into an endless process of drawing implications from this apparently illegitimate move. Then he explains the creation of angels, human souls, jinni and whatever else in a manner reminiscent of mythological periods in human civilization. Why is this illegitimate move, can be very easily comprehended by examining Al-Ash'ari's argument on the problem of the "createdness vs. eternity" of the Qur'an, as a parallel case given in this book at chapter "Acceptance of an un-Qur'anic Ontology".[206]

The views of the Mu'tazilites and the Ash'arites both did not correspond to the Qur'anic teachings. However, the case of the Ash'arites is more appropriate to refer here. Declaring *Kalamullah* inherent in Allah's Attribute of Speech[207] and drawing the conclusion that Allah's Word (*Kalamullah*) was with God from ever as unarticulated speech (*kalam-i nafsi*), was like Dr. Israr Ahmad's an illegitimate move. It was equivalent to the incarnation of the Divine Attribute of Speech in the form of the Qur'an. This will make the Qur'an co-eternal with God participating in His Divinity.

Dr. Israr's relevance with the above instance is that referring to the four verses mentioned above and "numerous others addressing the same theme" he says that

'...and the conclusion to be derived from this is that, whenever Allah decides on a matter, it is sufficient for Him to utter the verbal imperative "*KUN*" (i.e., Be!) and the matter is done.'

He further says:

'....the "Word of Allah" [?] is all that is needed in order to bring a thing or event into being.'

It is here that Dr. Israr Ahmed replaces what he calls 'the verbal imperative of Allah' by 'Word of Allah' or '*Kalima* of Allah'. He himself admits that "The relationship between the "*Kalima* of Allah" and bringing of a thing or event into being has a direct bearing on the issue of interpreting the meaning of '*kalimah*'." At the same time he further admits that

> "The Qur'an repeatedly refers to the legal injunctions, individual and social moral decrees, judicial decisions, and ordained laws set by Allah as the *Kalimaat* or "Words" of Allah, as all of these matters are indeed the outcome of the "Word of Allah"."[208]

Does this sentence bear any meaning? He goes further and with reference to verses Q. 17:109 and Q. 31:27 identifies every single thing and matter in the created order with "Words of my Lord" and then with the verbal imperative 'Be!' by holding it as manifestation of the verbal imperative 'Be!' This entire booklet is a meaningless quibble of such utterly confused talk.

Dr. Israr Ahmad's work relates to the interpretation of some verses of the Qur'an. Let us see what guidance the Qur'an gives concerning it. With reference to the verse 7 of Surah Āl-e-Imran 3, it has been made clear in the first chapter of this book that the Qur'an consists of two kinds of verses: the imperatival (*muḥkamāt*) and the non-imperatival (*mutashābihāt*). The imperatival (*muḥkamāt*) are the verses that are explicitly or implicitly in the form of commandments and are definite in meaning. The non-imperatival (*mutashābihāt*) are the verses that, on reading or listening, render an obligation on the reader or the listener according to what is stated or narrated in them. Only the imperatival verses are called the "Mother of the Book" (*Umm-ul-Kitab*). The imperatival verses are the standard in any decision. These are the cornerstone of the Book/Scripture. Whatever is to be inferred from the non-impertival verses, is necessarily to be verified by, and be coherent with the imperatival verses. The Qur'an pronounces those who leap towards arbitrary interpretation of *mutashābihāt* overlooking their accordance with the *muḥkamāt,* as diseased at heart and a mischief-monger.[209] Does Dr. Israr Ahmad follow this commandment in this enterprise?

Let us see the implications of Dr. Israr Ahmad's venture for the development of empirical science in Muslims.

> Does this theorising made by Dr. Israr Ahmad add any factual improvement in any present scientific theory of the origin of the world (i.e., big-bang theory), or gives a new theory on the origin of the world parallel to the prevalent scientific theories!

> Or does it give a new and better approach to scientific investigations!

> Does this effort introduce a scientifically verifiable kind of a new theory about the status of the laws of nature or laws governing social changes?

> Does it contain any concrete suggestion for the development of sciences in accordance with Qur'anic teachings?

Dr. Israr Ahmed, Dr. Zafar Ishaq Ansari (1932 – 2016) and   Maulana Wahiduddin Khan (b. 1925)

Dr. Israr Ahmed, Dr. Zafar Ishaq Ansari and Maulana Wahiduddin Khan are among those who trace the reason of Muslim's lagging behind in empirical science in improper understanding of Allah Almighty's injunction

"Say [O Prophet!]: If you aspire Allah's love, then follow me, and Allah will love you and forgive you your sins, for Allah is Oft-Forgiving Merciful" (3:31)

They think that a Muslim scientist does not do research openly and courageously for he fears lest anywhere he defies the above injunction. The solution they offer is in the shape of their classification of the holy person of the Prophet (pbuh) into various facets of authority. They assert his(pbuh) messenger-ship is only one among these aspects, and maintain that he (pbuh) is to be followed only in this respect, and even in this respect he (pbuh) is to be followed in matters pertaining to religion alone. They further assert that we are not necessarily obliged to follow him (pbuh) in matters pertaining to the mundane world. Referring to a *Ḥadīth* concerning the date palm, we have critically examined this view in our article "The Way of *Shahidīn*: The Construction of a Qur'anic Theology of Sufism in *Tafseer e Fāzlī*" included in our book *The Qur'anic Theology, Philosophy and Spirituality.*

Briefly speaking, how could such a person submit to the Prophet (pbuh) or follow him (pbuh) even if he happened to be in the lifetime of the Prophet (pbuh)! The Qur'an gives the idea of the indivisibility of the personality of a prophet or a messenger. Father, wife, son, relative or non-relative whoever believes in him, and follows him, belongs to him; (pbuh) and whoso does not follow him (pbuh), does not belong to him (pbuh). This is true of all *the messengers.*[210] Messengership is a whole time affair covering the whole life. A messenger (pbuh) is primarily a messenger, and then anything else. The reason for bifurcating the personality of the prophet into facets and holding messengership just one facet by such people, seems to be that they are attached to their likes and dislikes. Making *risalat* just a facet of the personality of the prophet(pbuh), they are trying to procure ample space for entering their likes and dislikes into the teachings of the Qur'an.

Correlating established Scientific Facts with the Qur'an — Maurice Bucaille (1920-98)

In his review article on Leif Stenberg's book, *The Islamization of Science: Four Muslim Positions, Developing an Islamic Modernity,* dilating upon bucailleism Muzaffar Iqbal says:

"The concern of this position is not to find an Islamic epistemological base for science nor is [it] concerned with moral or ethical issues of modern scientific research. People relating to this position are simply interested in correlating certain scientific "facts" with the Qur'anic verses."

He further says:

"Since the publication of the English translation of Maurice Bucaille's book, *La Bible, le Coran et la Science* (1976) as *The Bible, the Qur'an and Science* (1978), several studies have been devoted to "prove" the divine origin of the Qur'an on the basis that the Qur'an contains certain scientific facts which were unknown to humanity at the time of its revelation." [211]

'Scientific Theories' and 'Established Scientific Facts'

One can support his contentions with such other references but to make the Divine origin of the Qur'an dependent on certain scientific facts will not be the right approach. Bucaille is well aware of it. Bucaille does not state that the Qur'an is a book of science, but that modern science can clarify and give the full meaning of certain verses of the Qur'an. He offers a very fruitful idea in his writings that 'established scientific facts' should be distinguished from 'scientific theories'. He is so sure of the divine origin of the Qur'an that he asserts that an 'established scientific fact' has never contradicted with the Qur'an, nor shall it contradict the Qur'an ever. This is a very important point and we have used it in reformulating our own paradigm at the end of this chapter.[212]

IIIT, Ijmali School, Nasr's School of Sacred Science

Seyyed Hossein Nasr (b. 1933)

Seyyed Hossein Nasr (b. 1933) has advanced the notion of a "Sacred Science". He has untiringly advocated a reconstruction of Islamic scientific thought on the basis of revealed knowledge. He attempts to outline the philosophical foundation of a sacred science which will not focus on conquering nature but which will attempt to function within the limits set by Divine Commandments.[213] But no solid results, as we see it, have come about from this approach. He too, have committed several epistemic fallacies in the basic postulates of his paradigm as is shown below. Basic points of Nasr's paradigm can be stated as follows:

i. Man is a theomorphic (God-like) being. He believes that man is made in the image of God. [The Qur'an says: *'Not is to His likeness.'(Q. 42:11)*]

ii. Every revealed religion contains within itself "the Truth" and means of attaining the Truth.' Every revealed i.e., orthodox and integral religion possesses ultimately two essential elements, the Doctrine and the Method. They all possess the Doctrine though they differ in doctrinal language; they all possess the Method, though they differ depending upon their traditional climates.

The way the Qur'an teaches to the Muslims for arguing with the People of the Book is that 'the Muslims will not affirm anything said by them nor will they deny it; but they will say what Allah has revealed is The Truth.'

"Argue not with the people of the Scripture, but in the best way, except with those who do wrong. And say: We believe in what was revealed to us and revealed to you. Our Allah and your Allah is One, We are devoted to Him." (Q. 29:46)

Allah says:

وَمَا هُوَ إِلَّا ذِكْرٌ لِلْعَالَمِينَ ۝ *"It [the Qur'an] is not but the Advice for whole humankind."(Q. 68:52)*

Our view is that nothing except the Qur'an can bring the whole of humanity together. Nothing less than the absolute truth can entertain the status of authority; and it is the Qur'an about which it has been said in the Qur'an: *"This truly is a decisive statement* (إِنَّهُ لَقَوْلٌ فَصْلٌ) *'Innahu Laqawlun Faşlun). (Q, 86:13)"* Those who do not believe the Qur'an to be the Advice for the whole of humanity or the Decisive statement, do not act upon Allah's injunction stated in verse Q. 29:46 and consider world religions to be the different ways of truth.

Does Nasr not defy this injunction! He does not stop here; he includes Hinduism and Buddhism among orthodox and integral religions. Can he support this from the Qur'an!

iii. Only God is 'Real', 'Absolutely Real' or 'the Absolute'. 'The world' and for that matter 'man' and everything in the world is but 'the relative' or 'the relatively real" for it only 'appears to be real".

This distinction is un-Qur'anic. Fourth chapter of this book examines this assertion while examining the doctrine of *waḥdat al-wujud.*

iv. From Absolutely Real to the relatively real, there are grades of reality and degrees of universal existence.

This is Un-Qur'anic. What Seyyed Hossein Nasr calls grades of reality, either belong to the category of Allah's *khalq* or to the category of Allah's *amr*. Allah stands above and beyond as the Absolute Originator of all grades of reality, realms of existence and domains of experience, as Supremely Singular, Absolutely Unique, and Alone(*AḤAD*).

v. Method is a way of, a) concentrating upon the Real, b) of *attaching oneself to the Absolute, c) living according to the Will of Heaven in accordance with the purpose and meaning of human existence.*[214]

vi. Nasr calls his position 'Traditionalist School'. 'Tradition' for him denotes whatever is sacred. Everything received by man through revelation and by unfolding of revelation is sacred. As compared to it, philosophy and all man made sciences: technology, arts and civilization evolved out of it, are profane and unnatural. Nasr asserts that the purpose of wisdom and the sacred science is to discover and unfold sacrosanct aspect of nature, affirm oneness and inter-relatedness in nature. He aspires to develop a science which grants spiritual perfection to its seeker.

'Amr' as an ontological category infused in things as their nature is that aspect which Nasr calls sacrosanct and which he aspires sciences to discover. Since, he don't have the idea of Allah's *amr* instilled in Nature as *fiṭrah* (essence) of things, in his metaphysics, he has no option except to express himself in such vague terms.

vii. Nasr's whole philosophy consists of very unfamiliar, vague, ambiguous and complicated terms derived from different religions, traditions, languages and philosophies. Some of these are as follows:

Tradition, sapiential dimensions, symbolism, sophia perennis, philosophia perennis, traditional wisdom= al-hikma= theosophy, macrocosmos, microcosmos, prima materia. alchemy, horizontal, vertical, doctrine, method etc.

Our view is that to devise or insert un-Qur'anic terms in Dīn is conspiracy and treachery against Dīn. The Holy Qur'an narrates its content in easy to understand language. (Q 54: 17, 22, 32, 40) Allah also says: *"Allah intends for you ease and does not intend for you hardship..." (Q. 2:185)* Nasr is among scholars who devise abstract and complicated terms to make things difficult or to hide their real intent.

Seyyed Hossein Nasr has never been able to practically develop any sacred science, wisdom or technology better than, equal to, or comparable with the modern empirical science and philosophy that can grant perfection to the seekers of knowledge, except contributing some positive talk on ecology. According to our view nothing sacred could be developed based on doubtful, and confused premises and vague and complicated terminologies.

Ijmali School of Thought —— Ziauddin Sardar (b. 1951)

Ijmali School was a heterogeneous group of scholars who denied the objectivity of science perceiving it as a cultural activity connected to the scientist and his worldview. Led by Ziauddin Sardar as its chief propounder, it failed to offer any paradigm and has long been dissolved. Dr. Munawar A. Anees, one of its significant proponents, presently associated with the University of Management and Technology Lahore Pakistan, no longer owns it as a genuine approach. Sardar sums up in 12 short points what he thinks Nasr is telling us in his books. Leif Stenberg rightly thinks that they do expose some of the basic presuppositions underlying the ideas of both Sardar and Nasr. These points are as follows:

xviii) "All religions, including secular worldviews such as Buddhism are the same at a certain level of reality.

xix) Pythagorean cult, neo-Platonism, and other ancient esoteric mythologies are the basis of Islamic metaphysics.

xx) The Zoroastrian notion of a world perpetually in motion between the forces of light and darkness is a part of the Islamic metaphysical system.

xxi) The Hindu notion of a cyclic time, reincarnation and karma are also an integral part of Islamic metaphysical system.

xxii) Gnostics are somehow superior beings who know the truth.

xxiii) Islamic cosmology is essentially a combination of gnosticism and occultism.

xxiv) The history of Islamic sciences is basically a history of astrology and magic, numerology and alchemy, sacred geography and geometry, gnosis and Greek mystical mythology.

xxv) Islamic science has nothing to do with the practical realm; it is a purely abstract form of mysticism.

xxvi) Islamic science is divorced from ethics.

xxvii) The goal of Islamic science is unity, but in science the unity is so all pervasive that there is no distinction between the Creator and the created (waḥdat al-wajud); it is certainly an elusive goal.

xxviii)   Islamic science is the study of ontological reality.

xxix) Islamic science is hierarchical, which means that it must submit to the authority of the gnostics and others who know the truth so that the correct esoteric interpretation can be given to Islamic science."[215]

Nasr's critique of other perspectives is not direct. He seldom explicitly mentions persons, movements or regimes of which he is critical. However, in response to Sardar's criticism, Nasr's view as summed up by Leif Stenberg is as follows:

"Nasr's opinion is that Sardar is badly informed about the content of the various philosophical traditions within Islam in a historical as well as in a contemporary perspective. In his eyes, Sardar is unable to make the correct interpretation of Islamic traditions."[216]

IIIT [International Institute of Islamic Thought]

"The Position of IIIT is based on the premises that Muslim *ummah* is in a state of malaise; the roots of this malaise are to be found in influences from a world of ideas based on a vision foreign to Islam."

"According to this Position, the fundamental premises for establishing an Islamic science are based on the worldview which recognizes that 'the Word of God' [The Qur'an] is relevant in each and every sphere of human activity, that God has created this universe with a purpose, and has made Man, His [?] vice-regent for an appointed term. The model and example to be followed is that of Prophet Muhammad (SAW). Nature is not to be exploited, but should be understood and treated as a trust given to him by the Creator."[217]

They too have not been able to give a solid proposal or paradigm that could accelerate the scientific study of nature as worship of Allah as visualised by Sir Syed Ahmad Khan, Dr. Muhammad Iqbal, Seyyed Hossein Nasr, Dr. Israr Ahmed and many others. To underestimate the sincerity, honesty, acumen and devotion of any of the scholars or the schools of thought (including Al-Ash'ari, Avicenna, al-Ghazali, Ibn Arabi and Syyed Hossein Nasr) will be indecent and unbecoming. We should be grateful to them for identifying the significance of the problem, devoting their lives and capabilities in working out its solution, and for bearing the hardships they had to suffer, with perseverance. Nor have we any right to underrate their intentions, for only Allah knows the intentions. Through this study, we have tried to play our part, as per our ability and with no claim of finality, in enlightening the truth and to take the torch of knowledge ahead.

Analysis and Examination

Purpose of this study is not to underestimate the efforts of those who understand the significance of working out the principles of relationship between revealed knowledge and man-made knowledge in Islam. Rather the purpose is to take their work ahead. In the case of Sir Syed Ahmad Khan, it is stressed that the very principle "The Work of God overrides the Word of God" is not correct. By 'Word of God' he means the knowledge based on the rational interpretation of the Qur'an. What he calls 'The Work of God' is actually nothing other than the theories of science and the worldview based on the scientific study of nature along with philosophical investigation about nature. This is what we have called man-made knowledge. If these two spheres of knowledge dispute on some matter, which one of the two will override? If it is maintained, as Khan does, that the latter will take precedence, while the former will be interpreted metaphorically to accord with it, it simply means making the Qur'an subservient to a prevalent theory of science.

'What then is the appropriate theological principle for relating revealed knowledge with man-made knowledge?'

This principle that "The Work of God overrides the Word of God." is not something new introduced the first time by Sir Syed Ahmad Khan. The Ptolemaic cosmology consisting of nine heavens was the scientific worldview of Ibn Sina's times as the Newtonian cosmology without any concept of heavens presented the scientific worldview of Sir Syed Ahmad Khan's time. Aristotelian philosophy with uncaused First Cause as its concept of God, denial of Will as Attribute of God, logical necessity as its concept of cause-effect relationship, dualistic metaphysics with its primordial concept of matter etc., was the philosophy of Ibn Sina's times, as the Newtonian naturalism with its infinite space, absolute time, closed, mechanically autonomous eternal universe was the philosophy of Syed Ahmad Khan's times. Ibn Sina reinterpreted the Word of God to make it compatible with the dictates of the Ptolemaic Science and Aristotelian philosophy, as Syed Ahmad Khan did to harmonise it with the Newtonian cosmology and naturalism. The same is true of Iqbal with the difference that the Einsteinian cosmology and naturalism and the Bergsonian philosophical reconstruction of Einsteinian concept of time take the place of prevalent science and philosophy for him. He strives to reconcile the Word of God with the above objectifications of science and philosophy.

The standards of rationality change as science and philosophy change. The Qur'an, the embodiment of revealed knowledge, is 'The Truth' for all times to come. The question is why is it necessary for the Muslims to metaphorically interpret and reinterpret, every now and then, in each scientific epoch, to prove that the Qur'an is compatible with the theories of science and philosophy! The Ptolemaic science based on Aristotelian philosophical speculations, believed in nine heavens. There is no concept of heavens in Newton or in Einstein. Should we suspend our belief in the existence of seven heavens until science ever comes to prove it! While drowning, Pharaoh pronounces faith in the Lord of Haḍrat Musā and Haḍrat Hāroon (Peace be upon them.). Allah says:

"It is not accepted now. We shall preserve your dead body so that the coming generations take lesson." (Q. 10:91-92)

No one knew about the dead body of Pharaoh at the time of revelation of these verses until it was discovered in the last quarter of the 19th century. Should the Muslims suspend their belief in the contents of these verses till that time! Should they suspend their beliefs in many other things relating scientific facts till they are ever confirmed by science or philosophy! Shall a Muslim be held answerable for believing or not believing the correctness of Darwin's or Lamrck's theory of evolution, or a big-bang theory of the creation of the universe in the Hereafter!

Conclusion

We have seen in the previous chapter that: "Are Islam, and science compatible? If so, how can they be reconciled?" is a false question. Any attempt at harmonising Islam which, though gives due importance to rational and empirical data, admits revelation as higher source of knowledge, and science which admits nothing except rational and empirical data as source of knowledge, is necessarily bound to fail.

The study argues that

"What are the Qur'anic principles for relating knowledge acquired through science and philosophy, with the revealed knowledge acquired from the Qur'an?"

is the appropriate question to be asked. This study further argues that while discussing problem of the relationship of science (& philosophy) with Islam, following points are necessary to be kept in mind:

1. It should be accepted that Word of Allah (*Al-Ḥaqq*) alone is The Truth in all matters and for all times to come.

Allah has taken upon Him to ensure its protection.

Allah pronounces it as the Fairest of Texts Book (Aḥsan-al-*Hadīth*). So it is consistent par excellence. Seeing contradiction in it proves one's own inability, as well as disbelief that the Qur'an is from Allah. The Qur'an makes a very definite statement regarding its nature:

"Were it from someone other than God, they would have found many contradictions therein."
(Q. 4:82)

All its verses are to be categorised into two classes only: The imperatival and the Non- imperatival. The imperatival verses are the foundation of the Book; only that interpretation of the non-imperatival verses will be correct which is consistent with the former ones.

The Qur'an (*Aḥsan-al-Hadīth Kitab*) is authority over *Hadīth* and not the vice versa.

It is necessary for a valid *Hadīth* to be compatible with the imperatival verses (*muḥkamāt*) of the *Aḥsan-al-Hadīth Kitab*. Any interpretation of a *Hadīth* which does not accord with them, will not be correct.

The Qur'an is Ḥukam (Imperative) (Q. 13:37) and the *Hadīth* reports implementation of Ḥukam. Ḥukam is universal and the implementation always conforms to time, place, quantity and capacity.

2. It should be kept in mind that the theories of science (natural, rational, biological, social or whatever) and the intellectual view of reality (the worldview) are closely interlinked. Either a scientific theory is embedded in a philosophical worldview or a worldview gives rise to a theory.

'Established facts of science' should be differentiated from 'the theories of science.' 'Established facts of science' are the one-time theories of science, which have been scientifically verified and raised to the level of established facts. It should be made clear to a Muslim that until and unless anything establishes as a scientific fact, it will only be a conjecture even if it reaches to the level of a so-called well-accredited theory.

It should also be made clear to a Muslim that an 'established scientific fact' can never contradict with the Qur'an (The Truth). No instance from the past can be presented to refute this assertion. Keeping this difference in mind a Muslim can go to any level of study or research in science with full confidence.

Let us see some instances of Established Scientific Facts:

There was a time when the earth's being round was not an established fact. It was just a scientific theory. The invention of supersonic aircrafts and satellites irrevocably proved it to be an established fact. The earth's being round is no more a theory, but an established scientific fact.

Whether the matter was only divisible up to a limit (*i.e.*, atoms) or it was infinitely divisible without any limit was a question before the rise of modern science, to be answered by philosophical speculations and had given rise to many theories. Now matter's divisibility into atoms, but not further divisible into smaller material particles, is an established scientific fact.

There were various scientific theories regarding the nature of energy. The breakability of atoms and interconvertibility of matter and energy is now an established scientific fact.

3. That scientific worldviews are only scientifically supported cosmological theories regarding the nature and structure of reality. The Ptolemaic worldview prevailed for sixteen centuries, the Newtonian worldview prevailed for two centuries. If the theories in the past were replaced by other theories, present ones may also be replaced. It should be made clear on a Muslim that

holding an opinion based on scientific research, positive or negative, about a scientific or philosophical worldview e.g., the Ptolemaic, the Avicennian, the Newtonian, the Einsteinian, or the Bergsonian or of the Stephen Hawking's unless it contradicts with an explicit teaching of the Qur'an, has nothing to do with faith. The same applies to holding an opinion about a theory of the origin of species.

4. A scientific theory relates to some specific aspect of the universe for example: theory of causation, theory of gravitation, theory of quantum mechanics, theory of the origin of the world (i.e., the Big Bang etc.), or theories of the origin of life or origin of species. The same is true regarding the theories of social change, political administration or governance etc. These are all human endeavours to understand and discover the laws of social change, political administration and better governance and have the status of intelligent conjectures. A theory, even if it is considered a well-accredited theory, is a theory only and cannot hold the status of an 'established scientific fact.' Theories give us a control on nature. There is nothing unlawful in using them for a better control on forces of nature and society in the best interest of humanity. The benefit of humankind is how much dear to Allah is evident from the following verse where developing a similitude of *Al-Ḥaqq* (truth) and al-Baṭil (falsehood) Allah says:

> *"Al-Ḥaqq is to remain on the earth for it benefits humankind; al-bāṭil is to pass away like foam that scum on the bank." (Q. 13:17)*

5. As per Qur'anic cosmology discussed in the previous chapter, the universe is a divinely administered order of reality with fiṭrah (enduring nature) instilled in everything.

> Allah's *amr* (command) subsists in everything (of Allah's *khalq*) as enduring nature (*fitrah*). Allah's *amr* infused in everything as guiding principle regulates its activity as its law of nature.

> A divinely administered order of reality needs no intervention for it has Allah's *amr* innately working in it as its specific nature (*fiṭrah*). Allah administers the universe with His *amr*. Provisions are placed in the *fiṭrah* of things. Allah's *Amr* descends at present too, as He Will, within the orbit of naturality as Allah says:

> *His amr descends in the heavens and the earth.(Q. 10:03; 65:12)*

6. The empirical facet of reality, as identified by contemporary science, is not the only facet of reality. There are various facets of reality with laws of their own.

> (a) The Qur'an narrates a person who could bring a huge throne within the blinking of an eye. Allah says: *"He had a knowledge of the Book."* (Q. 27:40) This apparently supernatural phenomenon was based on a special knowledge endowed to him.

> (b) The Qur'an narrates the creation of a living and self-conscious creature (Jinni) from fire. This creature also has moral-consciousness and is accountable for their deeds. Can anyone with any stretch of imagination conceive the creation from fire of such a creature! Fire is a physical entity. It can be asked from Dr. Israr Ahmed: Were the Jinni came into being through a kind of process of evolution like human beings or were they created directly as Jinni? What were the necessary steps in the evolution of this species in its final form, and what are the laws governing this process if they had come into being through a process of evolution! Which species is immediately prior to the Jinni? Does the status of ontological dualism apply to the Jinni too? If they were created from fire as such, why can't Allah create Adam from

mud as such? Each sphere of knowledge has its own laws. All reality is an organised but administered system.

If we as Muslim are never embarrassed in believing freedom of will and accountability at the face of the psychological determinism, why should we feel embarrassed in believing the creationism, the seven heavens, the judgement and reward and the divinely prescribed moral values and limits in the face of a Ptolemaic, Newtonian, Einsteinian naturalism, or Darwinian evolutionism etc?

7. Philosophers have not been able to devise a substantial proof for their own existence and for how they maintain their own self-identity, over the years. Phenomenalism, perspectivism, relativism and the like show that philosophers have not been able to prove the existence of the external world, too, in which they live. All their views about self-identity, about nature and structure of reality are mere conjectures. Why should a Muslim be embarrassed over believing Allah, the Prophets (May peace be upon them all!) and the revelation, if man with lofty claims of knowledge has not been able to prove his own self-existence, self-identity, nature of time, nature of void, existence of the external world, freedom of will, nature of mind, nature of mind-body relationship and moral-consciousness.

8. The sphere of empirical science relates to the orbit of *khalq* and *amr* both. Regarding '*amr* (command) it has been said that "you have been given but little knowledge of it." (Q. 17:85) So man's knowledge of certain things will always remain little. A Muslim researcher must realise this limit to his knowledge. But it does not bar him from doing research on it.

9. Three things emerge from scientific research: worldview, theories, technology. What attitude should be taken by a Muslim scientist or scholar, about the scientific or philosophical worldviews as well as theories of science and facts of science has been discussed above. So far as scientific technology or institutions arising from social theories are concerned, Islam does not leave us to wander in darkness. The Qur'an gives us the principle of innovation (*bid'at*) to relate man-made knowledge with revealed knowledge. *Bid'at* (innovation) can be of two types: lawful (*bid'at-e ḥasana*) and unlawful (*bid'at-e-sayyia'*). Working out appropriate limits for relating man-made knowledge with revealed knowledge in Qur'anic parameters is ijtihād. 'No *bid'at* (innovation) in respect of prohibitions is allowed' is the basic principle of ijtihād. Not everyone is qualified for carrying out this job.[218] The Qur'an qualifies 'the sound in knowledge' for working out the limits and scope of lawful and comely innovations to help people in coming towards righteousness.[219] 'The sound in knowledge' are the ones who are best qualified for working out an appropriate relationship between revealed knowledge and man-made knowledge keeping in accordance with the *muḥkamāt*.[220]

Firmly believing that postulates of man-made knowledge are against Islamic paradigm, we cannot conceive of living without the outcomes of science. Already acting upon the principle of innovation, we are making use of them. We are making use of them with a feeling of doubt or a sense of guilt. Why not make use of these products with an open heart in the light of religious sanction of innovation (*bid'at*).[221] *Bid'at-e ḥasana* has always been part of Islam, and it will remain so. This is the Qur'anic principle for using knowledge generated by human research, experience and speculation. Muslims have disregarded this principle because of short sightedness and have kept on considering that the door of ijtihad was closed.

10. It is a very sad reality that the Muslims have not been able to translate commandments, insights, values and disvalues stated in the Qur'an into systems, institutions, approaches, technologies, models, methodologies, sciences and disciplines covering all occupations and areas to demonstrate their worth on laboratory bench of a global society because of disregarding the principle of innovation. In the present global scenario, making use of the principle of *bid'at-e ḥasana* is the right way for the above purpose.

11. Purpose of research in science, philosophy or technology is not the implementation of our desires against truth; it is to seek the Pleasure of Allah by providing convenience to human beings in fulfilment of their obligations with reference to truth. The Qur'an says:

> *"So set your face towards religion as a man of pure faith. This is the natural disposition Allah has instilled in humankind. There is no altering in Allah's creation, and this is the right religion. Most of the people do not realise it." (Q. 30:30)*

Prohibition in this verse relates to altering the natural disposition of human beings. Natural disposition of human beings relates to piety. To keep the fulfilment of our desires within Allah's prescribed limits is piety. Implementing our desires against truth and legislating for it, will mean altering Allah's creation. That is absolutely forbidden. Theories regarding biomedical ethics, amputations, organ-donation, organ transplant, genetic engineering and geno-modification etc., are to be seen in the light of the principle of innovation by committees of enlightened Muslim religious scholars and experts of related sciences.

12. Finally yet importantly, man has been sent on earth as *khalifa*. Usually it is translated as vicegerent of God. Being Omnipresent, Omnipotent and Omniscient, Allah transcends any need for a kind of second-in-command to run the affairs on earth. Man is given a mandate for using the provision placed on earth in accordance with divine guidance in the face of having been given freedom to follow his desires. Everything in the universe is made subservient to man. The Qur'anic science will entrust man with freedom to make research in any sphere of life as *khalifa* not defying any imperative of Allah. It is an obligation on a Muslim as *khalifa* to do his best to innovate ways and means to make use of earthly provisions in the best interest of humanity. Pleasure of Allah will be the ultimate motive behind all his activity. If he is given authority in the land, he will invent ways and means to judge between the people with truth and seal the ways leading towards injustice. (Q. 38:26) The knowledge to govern people is that matters between the people should be decided according to the truth and personal desires must not have any influence over the judgement. One's liking when mixed with the truth pushes the person away from the right path. Allah has appointed man as *khalifa* on earth to see how they behave. (Q.10:14)[222]

SUMMARY, MAIN ISSUES AND CONCLUSION

CHAPTER 9

SUMMARY

This study identifies the formulation of false theological doctrines constructed on un-Qur'anic philosophical terms, application of Aristotelian logic on the Holy Being of the Qur'anic God, discussion on God in terms of His attributes instead of His Comely Names/*al-Asmā' al-Ḥusnā*, acceptance of Greek ontology in place of Qur'anic ontology, development of cosmology based on this un-Qur'anic ontology, acceptance of such terms from Greeks or Christianity as Divine attributes, which have no basis in the Qur'an, as the root cause of doubt and contradiction in Qur'anic discourse and theological polemics among Muslims since the eleventh century. About eleven centuries have passed now.

This book is indirectly a critical review on Robert R. Reilly's views about Ash'arite theology, presented in his book *Closing of the Muslim Mind.*

It is admitted that Ash'arite theology prevalent in the Muslim world since centuries has many flaws in it, but the reason identified by Robert Reilly, is inaccurate and the solution suggested by him is misleading. He identifies dehellenization of theology by the Ash'arites as their basic fault. In our view, this is absolutely incorrect. Idealising Greek philosophical ways of thinking, the Mu'tazilites acknowledged the primacy of reason over revelation, whereas the Ash'arites did the opposite, which deserves appreciation. The epistemic fallacy, the Ash'arites committed, was that while borrowing terms from speculative theologians in the formulation of their theological doctrines, they failed to realise that they were also allowing un-Qur'anic ontology (rooted in Greek philosophy) to enter into their theological system. This fallacy marred their theology with contradictions. The second fallacy they committed was that they gave equal importance to dogmas handed over to them by tradition, which they should have given to the beliefs derived from the Qur'an alone. For instance a term 'the non-recital revelation' (*wahi-i-ghair matlaw* وحيّ غير مَتلو) devised by traditional theologians put *Hadīth* over and above the *muḥkamāt* of the *Ahsan-al-Hadīth Kitāb* and paved the way for insertion of any kind of unauthentic dogma's, traditions (*rawayāt*) and baseless stories in the commentary of the Qur'an and in theology. To further support their contention they devised another un-Qur'anic term '*Nass*' (نصّ text) to bracket tradition with the verses of the Qur'an, to bring compilations of *Hadīth* at par with the Qur'an. Though apparently they did not give philosophical speculations primacy over revelation, they committed an epistemic fallacy by giving generally accepted unauthentic dogmatic beliefs primacy over the revelation. Another fallacy they committed was that they accepted un-Qur'anic terms like eternity, infinity, timelessness and immutability, coined in Greek ontology, as attributes of Allah to employ in the formulation of their theological doctrines, used them in the translation and commentary of the Qur'an too, and these are still in use in every dimension of Islamic discourse.

The solution suggested by Robert Reilly that the Muslims should turn towards philosophy if they want to come out of intellectual decline, is absolutely misleading.[223] The minds become closed when dogma, tradition, rituals, and superstitions are raised to the level of faith, speculations get the status of creed, rationalisation is given preference over reasoning, and principles of the interpretation of the Qur'an given in the Qur'an itself are disregarded.

It is necessary that the Muslims reopen their minds and reconstruct their theology based on the Qur'anic ontology and terms coined in it, and focus on Qur'anic principles for translation and commentary of the Qur'an.

MAIN ISSUES

First Section "How Doubt and Inconsistency Enter Into Qur'anic Commentary and Theology!" consists of 4 chapters. These chapters identify a few, but very important, epistemic fallacies committed by the Ash'arite theologians, translators of the Qur'an and the exegetes. It also traces the origin of these fallacies and their unfortunate implications. The author develops a concept of ontology in Qur'anic perspective, as visualised by him, and shows how the traditional un-Qur'anic concept of ontology has been the source of creating doubt and contradiction in theology and theological doctrines since centuries, on the problems of 'the ontological status of Divine attributes', 'eternity vs createdness of the Qur'an', 'problems relating freewill and predestination', 'relation of the contingent with 'the eternal', and differences in translation and commentary of the Qur'an, and especially using the epithet Al-Haqq in the sense of 'The Truth' both for the Qur'an as well as for the Descender of the Qur'an.

One of the main issues discussed in the First Chapter relates to the question: Whether the epithet *Al-Ḥaqq* can genuinely be used in the sense of 'The Truth' both for Allah and the Qur'an (at places where the phrase 'huw I Ḥaqq) occurs in the Qur'an, as has been the practice of theologians and the Qur'an scholars since centuries? The study argues that it needs no proficiency in logic to discern that the epithet *Al-Ḥaqq* (The Truth) cannot be used for the Qur'an and the Descender of the Qur'an in the identical sense. If this distinction is not kept in view, it is necessary to create confusion and contradiction.

Another issue discussed in this chapter relates to the question: How did this contradiction enter in Islam as a creed? The study traces the conversion of this un-Qur'anic dogma into religious doctrine to become prevalent as creed, in Haḍrat Abu al-Hassan Al-Ash'ari's book *Al- Ibanah an Usul Ad-Diyaanah,* (Eng. tr. The Elucidation of Islam's Foundation by Walter C. Klein), American Oriental Society, New Haven, 1940) at pages p. 67, 76 and translator's introduction at page 66. Instances from nine renowned translators and exegetes of the Qur'an have been presented in this chapter to show how this epistemic fallacy gives rise to confusion and contradiction in theology and commentary of the Qur'an.

The Qur'an is descended by Allah in the style of Speech and not in the style of text composed as 'Writing'. Another issue discussed in this chapter relates to the question: Is it epistemically appropriate to apply rules of grammar and syntax meant for making out the meaning of a sentence in a text composed in the style of 'writing', to a text delivered as

'Divine Speech' and that too, extending over a long period of about 23 years? Another question discussed in this chapter relates to the question: What is the epistemic difference between the two styles, and what is the methodology appropriate for the interpretation of a Text delivered in the style of 'Divine Speech' as distinguished from the one delivered in the style of 'Writing'?

In response to these questions the study argues that being revealed in Clear Arabic language (*Arabi-yim-mubeen*), rules of grammar and syntax are basic and necessary for determining the meaning of the verses of the Qur'an. But keeping in view the unique character of the Qur'anic revelation delivered piecemeal in the style of Speech, the significance of the rules of Arabic grammar and syntax become secondary and the significance of the Qur'anic principles given in the Qur'an itself for the interpretation of the Qur'an, and comprehension of the objectives intended by the Deliverer of Speech becomes primary and necessary. This factor has never been recognised throughout Islamic history by the theologians and the Qur'an scholars till today. The study strives to explain the difference in 'meaning of a sentence' and the 'objective of a part of Speech' with examples.

The issue discussed in the Second Chapter relates to the question: "Whether 'address in 'second person singular' or in 'third person singular' in the Qur'an particularly refers to the Prophet (pbuh) as has been mistakenly understood by the Qur'an scholars since centuries, as is evident from the translation of two verses given below from Pickthall:

'It is the Truth from thy Lord (O Muhammad), so be not thou of those who waver.' (Q. 2:147) and

'(This is) the truth from thy Lord (O Muhammad), so be not thou of those who waver.'(Q. 3:60)." (Pickthall)

The study argues that it is a specific feature of Qur'anic Speech that at times addressing in second person singular, it addresses each and every individual, present as well as non-present, including those who are yet to come in the world till the Last Day. Therefore, it is not necessarily addressed to the Prophet (pbuh). Not keeping in mind this difference is another important source of inserting doubt, dissension and contradiction in the interpretation of the Qur'an and in theology.

The traditional Ash'arite ontology, which is the cornerstone of all their theological doctrines, perceives everything, including God and whatever else, either as eternal or as created (contingent). Hence it conceives 'anything uncreated as eternal.' The issue discussed in the Third Chapter relates to the question: Whether this ontology is Qur'anic or un-Qur'anic? Does it accord with the *muḥkamat* of the Qur'an? The study in this chapter argues that this ontology is un-Qur'anic and a source of immense confusion, contradiction, dissension, sectarianism, disorientation in Muslim civilization and of intellectual decline. The study constructs ontology in Qur'anic perspective, which perceives everything other than God, in two ultimate but originated categories of Allah's *khalq* (creation) and *Allah's amr* (command), with God (Allah) as the absolute Originator of these categories at His Will and Decree and supremely Singular and Unique as Self.

Study in the Fourth Chapter discusses the question: Where does the origin of this ontology lie if it is un-Qur'anic? The book uncovers its origin in Greek philosophers' doctrines. It also works out the unfortunate implications of this un-Qur'anic ontology for the Muslim thought in this chapter.

Second section deals with 'The Misperceptions of Qur'anic Hermeneutics. The study in Chapter Five "Non-Classification of Verses into *Muḥkamāt* (imperatival) and *Mutashābihāt* (non-imperatival) examines the question: Whether, the Qur'anic categorisation of its verses into *muḥkamāt* and *mutashābihāt* and Allah's pronouncing the *muḥkamāt* as *umm ul-Kitāb* (Cornerstone of the Scripture) is only meant for recitation, and for holding it as belief, as has been considered by Muslims since centuries; or it contains a very important Divine principle and guidance to avoid doubt and contradiction in the interpretation of the Qur'an? Study in this chapter identifies repercussions of showing disregard to this Qur'anic hermeneutical principle by theologians and the Qur'an scholars and overlooking the fact that the interpretation of *mutashābihāt* must accord with the *muḥkamāt*. Declaring the *muḥkamāt* as *Umm ul-Kitāb*, this Divine guidance further illuminates that even to imagine that the Cornerstone verses of Allah's revealed Word can conflict, delete, or abrogate each other, will be highly obnoxious, disgusting and fallacious. Translations of verse 35 of Surah Al-Nūr (24) and verse 3 of Surah al-Ḥadīd (57), made by nine renowned scholars, have been examined as two typical instances of the translation of *mutashābih* verses, to make clear the difference if the Qur'anic principle of the interpretation of *mutashābihāt* under discussion is overlooked, and in case it is followed.

Chapter Six, "Revisiting the Ontological Status of *Ḥadīth*" in the next section examines the question: Whether the '*Aḥsan-al-Ḥadīth Kitāb*' [The Fairest of Texts] should hold primacy over the *Ḥadīth*, or can *Ḥadīth* be held *authority* (*qazi*) over the '*Aḥsan-al-Ḥadīth Kitāb*'? Another issue discussed in this chapter is: Whether *Ḥadīth* can ever insert any addition, deletion or alteration in the *muḥkamāt* of the *Aḥsan-al-Ḥadīth Kitāb*?" Another issue discussed in this concern is that: Whether the *Ḥadīth* too, can be considered source of Divine law as the Qur'an or it is neither source of Divine law nor irrelevant to the Qur'an; rather it is precedent of the implementation of Divine law? Another issue discussed in this regard is that: Whether *Ḥadīth* as precedent of the implementation of Divine law is universal like the Divine law, or the implementation of Divine law is bound to accord with the requirements of time, place, quantity and capacity?

The study argues that the *Ḥadīth* cannot hold primacy over the *muḥkamāt* of the *Aḥsan-al-Ḥadīth Kitāb*' (i.e., the Qur'an). The study further argues that to hold that *Ḥadīth* can ever insert any addition, deletion or alteration in the Qur'an is to challenge the status of the Qur'an as 'The Truth— *Al-Ḥaqq*' and as *Aḥsan-al-Ḥadīth Kitāb*' and to challenge the status of *muḥkamāt* as *Umm al-Kitāb* ('The Foundation of the Book').

Dr. Pervez Amirali Hoodbhoy, in his book *Islam and Science: Religious Orthodoxy and the Battle for Rationality*, identifies a very genuine problem that lies beneath the failure of all Muslim attempts at bringing about reconciliation between Islam and science. Hoodbhoy formulates this problem as *'The Dilemma of an Interventionist Deity'*. Hoodbhoy argues: How can the traditional Muslim perception of God as Interventionist Deity, be reconciled with the perception of modern empirical science which admits no role for God in the universe and sees the universe as autonomously running in accordance with immutable laws of nature?

Highlighting the fundamental dichotomy between traditional Muslim cosmology and modern scientific cosmology Dr. Hoodbhoy argues that until the problem identified in the dilemma is satisfactorily addressed, no attempt at the reconciliation between Islam and science & philosophy, or for that matter, developing an Islamic Science, Islamization of Science or Islamization of Knowledge etc. is destined to succeed. It really is a thought-provoking question. Chapter Seven in Section 'Qur'anic Cosmology' examining the dilemma develops a cosmology based on ontology constructed in Qur'anic perspective to meet the challenge.

The classical Ash'arite cosmology i.e., the Ash'arite atomism, too, is examined in this chapter and has been found contrary to the *muḥkamāt* of the Qur'an. It has been reconstructed in this chapter keeping in view its accordance with the *muḥkamāt*, and making sure that it does not hinder the development of empirical science on Qur'anic foundations.

Modern scientific cosmology conceives empirical knowledge as the only source of knowledge dependable in science. Cosmology deals with nature and structure of the universe and God-universe relationship etc. Islam does not deny the significance of empirical knowledge, but gives ultimate primacy to revelation as source of knowledge. Muslims believe the Qur'an to be The Truth. They hold that basic principles of Islamic ontology and cosmology are given in the Qur'an. Last Chapter "Evolving a Qur'anic Paradigm of Science and Philosophy" discusses the question: In case scientific perception of nature in an era, happens to conflict with the perception of nature traditionally believed in by Muslims (based on the interpretation of the Qur'an), which perception will override the other and on what grounds? The same question may be asked in the following way too: How to relate the outcome of empirical and rational sciences with the revealed Qur'anic knowledge and what are the principles given in the Qur'anic in this regard?

Examining the attempts of renowned Muslim scholars Ibn Sina, Sir Syed Ahmad Khan, Dr. Muhammad Iqbal, and contemporary scholars on Islamization of Science or Islamization of Knowledge, the study in this chapter argues that no reconciliation between Islam (which acknowledge revelation as superior source of knowledge) and science (which does not acknowledge revelation as a source of knowledge at all) is possible. The above scholars were misdirected in their approach. The real question they should have asked was: How to relate the outcome of empirical and rational sciences with the revealed Qur'anic knowledge and what are the principles given in the Qur'anic in this regard. Study in this section develops a paradigm to this purpose based on Qur'anic ontology, Qur'anic cosmology, the concept of Ḥadith as precedent of the Divine law, introducing the concept of *Bid'ah* (Innovation) as a Qur'anic principle for relating empirical and rational knowledge of science and philosophy with Scriptural knowledge of the Qur'an. This chapter is an abridged but updated version of an extended article published in our book *The Qur'anic Theology, Philosophy and Spirituality.* It is included here because of its intimate relevance with the central theme of this book.

CONCLUSION

This study identifies the formulation of false theological doctrines based on un-Qur'anic philosophical terms, application of Aristotelian logic on the Being of Qur'anic God, discussion on God in terms of His attributes (*ṣifā*) instead of His *al-Asmā' al-Ḥusnā* and acceptance of such terms from Greeks or Christianity as Divine attributes which have no basis in the Qur'an; and most of all the acceptance of un-Qur'anic Greek ontology as foundation of Islamic theology, and development of cosmology in its wake, committing epistemic fallacy in identifying the difference in the interpretation of a Kalam delivered as Speech and a Kalam delivered as 'Writing', disregard for Qur'anic hermeneutics by non-classification of Qur'anic verses into *muḥkamāt* and *mutashābihāt*, misperceiving the ontological status of *Ḥadīth* vis-à-vis the Qur'an, shortsightedness in understanding the significance of the Qur'anic principle of innovation (*bid'at*), as the root cause of doubt and contradiction in Qur'anic discourse, theological polemics, sectarian division in the ummah, disorientation of Muslim civilization and intellectual decline of the Muslim world.

In conclusion, this study suggests a reconstruction of Islamic theology through radical reform in prevalent key conceptualisation frameworks (i.e., its ontology, cosmology, hermeneutics, *Ḥadīth* as precedent of divine law) based upon Qur'anic epistemology and principle of *innovation* (*bid'at*). It critiques the earlier frameworks suggested by traditional Muslim theologians and suggests a new framework of Qur'anic epistemology, ontology hermeneutics, and *Ḥadīth* as precedent of divine law that opens up avenues of innovation and ijtehad for future researchers. It aims to endorse a constructivist episteme for redefining Muslim theological discourse.

SOME CONTEMPORARY, MODERN AND CLASSICAL COMPETING WORKS —— AN OVERVIEW

CHAPTER 10

SOME CONTEMPORARY COMPETING WORKS

1. The Closing of the Muslim Mind

Robert R. Reilly. *The Closing of the Muslim Mind: How Intellectual Suicide Created the Modern Islamist Crisis.* Forward by Roger Scruton. Wilmington: Intercollegiate Studies Institute Books, 2010. 244 pages.

Robert Reilly identifies dehellenization of theology by the Ash'arites, as their basic fault. According to this manuscript, it is incorrect. This study agrees with Robert Reilly that the Ash'arites have committed fallacies in their theology. However, this study does not agree with Robert Reilly as far as the reason identified by him is concerned. The fault, the Ash'arites committed, was that while borrowing philosophical terms from speculative theologians in the formulation of their theological doctrines, they failed to realise that they were also allowing un-Qur'anic ontology (rooted in Greek philosophy) to enter into their theological system. This fault marred their theology with contradictions. This study does not agree with Robert Reilly, as to the solution suggested by him that Muslims should turn towards philosophy if they want to come out of intellectual decline. This study finds this solution absolutely misleading. The minds become closed when dogma, tradition, rituals, superstitions and speculations are given the status of faith; rationalisation is given preference over reasoning; and principles of the interpretation of the Qur'an given by the Qur'an itself are disregarded, and terms coined in alien metaphysics are accepted in Qur'anic discourse. This study suggests that the Muslims should reconstruct their theology based on the Qur'anic terms and the Qur'anic ontology focusing on the Qur'anic principles for the interpretation of the Qur'an.

2. Islam and Science: Religious Orthodoxy and the Battle for Rationality

Dr. Pervez Amirali Hoodbhoy, Islam and Science: Religious Orthodoxy and the Battle for Rationality, (London: ZED Books, 1991)

Hoodbhoy identifies a very genuine problem that lies beneath failure of all Muslim attempts at bringing about reconciliation between Islam and science. Hoodbhoy formulates this problem as 'The Dilemma of an Interventionist Deity. Highlighting the fundamental dichotomy between traditional Muslim cosmology and modern scientific cosmology Dr. Hoodbhoy argues that until the problem identified in the dilemma is satisfactorily addressed, no attempt at the reconciliation between Islam and science & philosophy, or for that matter, developing an Islamic Science, Islamization of Science or Islamization of Knowledge etc. is destined to succeed. Hoodbhoy highly deserves appreciation for this thought-provoking contribution. Chapter Seven in Section 'Qur'anic Cosmology' of this book, develops a cosmology in Qur'anic perspective to meet the challenge.

3. The Cambridge Companion to Classical Islamic Theology, 2008

4. The Oxford Handbook of Islamic Theology , 2016

5. The Oxford Handbook of ISLAMIC PHILOSOPHY Edited by KHALED EL-ROUAYHEB and SABINE SCHMIDTKE, Published in 2017 by OXFORD UNIVERSITY PRESS USA.

6. Routledge Handbook of Islamic Law, Edited by Khaled Abou El Fadl, Ahmad Atif Ahmad, and Said Fares Hassan, Routledge London and New York: Taylor & Francis Group, 2019 [26 Chapters by 24 Contributors besides separate 'Introductions' by the editors]

7. The Oxford Handbook of Qur'anic Studies edited by Mustafa Shah and Muhammad Abdel Haleem, published by Oxford University Press UK, in 2020

8. Leah Kinberg, "*Muḥkamāt* and Mutashābihāt (The Qur'an 3/7): Implication of a Qur'anic Pair of Terms in Mediaeval Exegesis", in Arabica, T. 35, Fasc. 2 (Jul., 1988), 143-172, Published by: BRILL

The Cambridge Companion to Classical Islamic Theology, 2008

Edited by Tim Winter published by Cambridge University Press in 2008, consists of fifteen chapters written by fifteen renowned scholars. First five chapters see classical Muslim theology, in historical perspectives. Next ten chapters deal with selected theological themes relating to classical theology.

The Oxford Handbook of *Islamic Theology,* 2017

Edited by Sabine Schmidtke, published in 2017, consists of 41 chapters contributed by 37 renowned experts of the respective fields. This book explores the history of Islamic theology, extending from the 'Formative and the Early Middle Period' to 'the Later Middle and the Early Modern Period', and from 'the End of the Early Modern Period to the Modern Period' giving brief account of various Muslim/Islamic theologies, with particular emphasis on the doctrinal thought of all the various Islamic intellectual strands. An attempt has also been made, as rightly stated by the editor, to cover the doctrinal thought of all the various intellectual strands of Islam engaged with theological concerns, including the philosophers and the Ismāʿīlīs. (p.1)

The Oxford Handbook of Qur'anic Studies, 2020

Edited by Mustafa Shah and Muhammad Abdel Haleem, published in 2020 consists of 57 chapters contributed by 52 renowned Qur'an scholars.

Routledge Handbook of Islamic Law, 2019

Edited by Khaled Abou El Fadl, Ahmad Atif Ahmad, and Said Fares Hassan, published in 2019 consists of 26 chapters by 24 contributors besides separate 'Introductions' by the editors.

(i) None of these well researched chapters included in above mentioned Handbooks shows that any of the scholars belonging to any of these schools or strands has ever realised that the ontology, on which the foundations of these Muslim/Islamic theologies have been laid down was contrary to the ontology given in the Qur'an as argued in our book.

(ii) Similarly, none of the articles included in these books, contributed by any scholar shows that Muslim scholars have ever visualised *hadīth* as precedent of the implementation of the divine law, and that as such it neither is source of divine law nor universal; and that though the divine law is universal and immutable, the way of its implementation as reported in *hadīth* is must to accord with the time, place, quantity and capacity. Most of the discussions, extending over centuries, including M. A. S. Abdel Haleem, "Qur'an and hadīth" in *The Cambridge Companion to Classical Islamic Theology* delve upon the problem of its status whether *Hadīth* is to be called revelation or not; or that whether *hadīth*, too, is source of divine law or not. None of the authors delves upon the ontological status of *hadīth* vis-à-vis the Qur'an that it reports the implementation of divine law in the holy hands of the Prophet (pbuh). None of them delves upon the fact that *hadīth* entertains the status of precedent of divine law; that it is not universal like divine law, and that the way of implementation of divine *hadīth* law is bound to accord with the time, place, quantity and capacity.

(iii) In most of the articles included in these books, and especially in *The Oxford Handbook of Qur'anic Studies*, the Qur'an scholars use the word 'Speech' for the Qur'an. But they use it in the sense of 'Allah's Word' or 'Kalām'. None of them ever realise that the Qur'an is delivered in the style of 'Address' and not in the style of 'Writing'. Therefore, it occurs to none of them that the rules meant for the interpretation of the Qur'anic Text, taken as 'Address' (*Khaṭāb*) must differ from the rules taking the Qur'anic Text as if delivered in the style of 'Writing'. None of the worthy contributors in the Handbooks have visualised this difference as has been discussed in this study. The present book not only points out this difference of style, but also elaborates the appropriate approach in the interpretation of the Qur'an taken as 'Address' with examples.

(iv) As per Allah's Word, what has been revealed on Haḍrat Muhammad (pbuh) is The Truth (*Al-Ḥaqq*) (Q. 13:1; Q. 47:2; Q.32:2-3) so Allah is the Descender of 'The Truth' (*Al-Ḥaqq*), Allah is the One whose 'Word' revealed on the Holy Heart of Haḍrat Muhammad (pbuh) through the ArchAngel is 'The Truth'. '

It can be asserted, with full confidence, on the authority of the above mentioned books that none of the theologians from the formative, mediaeval and modern period till date, as discussed in the Handbooks under-discussion, has realised that to use epithet '*Al-Ḥaqq*' (The Truth) both for 'the Qur'an' and 'The Descender of the Qur'an' in the identical sense is to insert a sheer contradiction in the translation and commentary of the Qur'an as well as in theology. Untoward implications of inserting this contradiction in Muslim theology have also been pointed out in the book.

Classical occasionalist cosmology, rising in the wake of un-Qur'anic ontology (and its modern version till date) still based on the same ontology stressing the idea of an Interventionist deity, neither can give an accurate Qur'anic worldview nor develop empirical and rational sciences. None of the theologians belonging to any of the schools or strands of Muslim/Islamic theology(gies) or schools of philosophy, as can be argued on the authority of the above mentioned Handbooks and many others published by Cambridge, Oxford or Rutledge, has been able to trace the root-cause of the failure of Muslim classical and traditional cosmology in the un-Qur'anic ontology on which it is based. The question of reconstructing a cosmology on Qur'anic lines could not arise until the un-Qur'anic nature of ontology, presupposed in all Islamic/ Muslim theologies, is identified and reconstructed accordingly on Qur'anic lines.

'Eternity', 'infinity', 'timelessness', and 'immutability' as defined by Greek philosophers and Christian theologians, accepted by Muslim theologians, translators of the Qur'an, the Qur'an commentators and religious scholars, which is prevalent till date, because of being based on un-Qur'anic ontology and cosmology, are contrary to the Qur'anic concept of God. The root-cause of many perennial problems of Islamic/Muslim theology can be traced back to the acceptance of these un-Qur'anic terms as Divine attributes in Islamic discourse. On the authority of the Handbooks and Readings mentioned above, it can be argued that none in the history of Muslim theology and Islamic sciences has pointed to the un-Qur'anic nature of these terms as Divine attributes.

Many worthy contributors in these books, have discussed the problem of the ontological status of Divine attribute vis-à-vis Essence of God, but none of them realise that Allah has not used the word 'Sifa' (attribute) or any other derivative of the root 'w-ṣ-f' while talking on His Own Exalted Person. On the other hand Allah has stated that 'His are the Most Goodly Names' (al-Asmā' al-Husnā) and ordains the Muslims to call upon Him by His Goodly Names and refrain from blaspheming in His Names.

Therefore, it can be argued on the authority of the Handbooks under-discussion, that throughout the history of Muslim theology, the theologians have remained unmindful of the fact that to talk on the Person of God in terms of 'essence and attributes', in any way, was contrary to the teachings of the Qur'an. Working out of a logic based on the relationship of 'The Name and The Named' would have been the right approach for the Muslim theologians and philosophers, had they realised it.

The Qur'an in verse Q. 3:7, with absolute clarity, divides the verses of the Qur'an into two exclusive categories: *Muḥkamāt* and the *Mutashābih*āt. Giving the status of Umm al-Kitāb to the *Muḥkamāt*, the Qur'an makes it clear in the same verse that anyone who will leap towards the interpretation of the *Mutashābih*āt will prove himself to be diseased in heart and a mischief monger. Does it mean that Allah likes that the believers do not strive for the interpretation of verse Q. 3:7 and take it as a part of the Qur'an solely meant for recitation? The whole of the Qur'an (the *muḥkamāt* and the *mutashābihāt* both) has been sent for guidance and teaching of humankind. Verse Q. 3:7, very clearly is a *muḥkam* verse. There is no ambiguity in it. It consists of a very important Qur'anic principle for the interpretation of the Qur'an and implies an imperative to keep the interpretation of the *mutashābihāt* subservient to the *muḥkamāt*. A translator or the commentator should first of all decide whether the verse under consideration is a *muḥkam* or a *mutashābih* verse as per his understanding; and if it were a *mutashābih* verse, he will make sure that its interpretation must accord with the *muḥkamāt* of the Qur'an as identified by him. He will not make big claims about the firmness and finality of his interpretation, and will pray before God that only He knows the real meaning of the verse.

Leh Kinberg in his article "*Muḥkamāt* and Mutashābihāt (The Qur'an 3/7): Implication of a Qur'anic Pair of Terms in Mediaeval Exegesis" published by Brill in Arabica, T. 35, Fasc. 2 (Jul., 1988) at 143-172, and Massimo Campanini in his article "Modern Qur'anic Hermeneutics: Strategies and Development" included as chapter in "The Oxford Handbook of Qur'anic studies" give a very detailed survey of the discussions made by Muslim religious scholars, translators and commentators of the Qur'an in the mediaeval and modern era on the interpretation of verse Q. 3:7.

On the authority of these authors and on the authority of other material included in these Handbooks and research articles, it can be argued that none of the Muslim scholars, in the whole history of Islamic theology and of translation and commentary of the Qur'an, have accomplished the classification of the verses of the Qur'an in accordance with the Qur'anic categorisation given in verse Q. 3:7. Leh Kinzberg mentions only one book *Aḍwā" 'alā mutashābihāt al-qur'ān* in which ash-Shaykh Khalīl Yāsīn interprets the verses which he considers *mutashābihāt*. But, he gives no special criterion for distinguishing *muḥkamāt* from the *mutashābihāt*, developed by Leh Kinzberg if any. It is not clear from Leh Kinzberg's article whether ash-Shaykh Khalīl ensures the accordance of the interpretation of *mutashābihāt* with those which he identifies as *muḥkamāt,* or he makes a purely arbitrary interpretation of these verses. Arbitrary interpretation of *mutashābihāt,* as stated above, is not allowed.

Ghulam Ahmed Perwez (1903-1985), a Pakistani religious scholar in his Urdu article "Mafhoom ul-Qur'an" very clearly identifies a divine principle of Qur'anic interpretation in this verse. Since he too could not visualise that the ontology on which the Islamic theology is based, was un-Qur'anic and therefore, the cosmology arising in its wake, too, was contrary to Qur'anic teachings, so he too could not accomplish a commentary of the Qur'an which could attract the attention of the generality of the Muslims. He, too, did not accomplish a classification of the verses of the Qur'an into *muḥkamāt* and the *mutashābihāt.* He also could not understand the difference between the Qur'anic Text taken as 'Address' and taken as 'Writing'. He is not a denier of *Ḥadīth* as he is claims; however, as a critic of the authenticity of the compilations of *Ḥadīth*, he too fails to visualise the real status and significance of *Ḥadīth* as PRECEDENT of the implementation of divine law and that the way of implementation of divine law is not fixed once for all forever by *ḥadīth*.

'Innovation' (*bida'*) has been discussed in various chapters of the manuscript. Though the traditionalists make distinction between 'good innovation' and 'bad innovation', because of their adherence to the Qur'an, the sunna and the consensus as the basic reliable resources of divine law, they have always refrained from and opposed the concept of 'innovation'. On the authority of the survey of the history of Islamic sciences in above mentioned Handbooks and Readings, it can be said with full confidence that *bid'ah* (innovation) as presented in this book, as a positive and invaluable Qur'anic principle, which provides basis for relating knowledge, acquired through empirical and rational sciences and human experience with the God-given knowledge derived from revealed sources, has never been appreciated by Muslim communities because of the short-sightedness of traditionalist religious scholars.

9. God, Nature, and the Cause: essays in Islam and science, by Basil Altaie published in 2016 by KR&M

Professor Basil Altaie holds that the Qur'an certainly is the prime source of religious knowledge in Islam, yet he observes that in order to formulate the Islamic understanding of the Divine action in the world, we certainly need to investigate the historical background of theological issues in the works of earlier Islamic scholars. Though he gives very valuable analysis of the Ash'arites' 'philosophy of nature' and 'natural philosophy' in his books,[224] he too remains unable to identify the root cause of disagreement among Muslim theological sects in un-Qur'anic metaphysical presuppositions (especially the un-Qur'anic ontology) invariably inherent in the foundations of all Islamic/Muslim theology(ies).

Maintaining the Qur'an to be the prime source of religious knowledge in Islam, though he refers to Muslim scholars' disagreement in the interpretation of Qur'anic verses as another root-cause of dissension in theology, but here too, he fails to identify the need for a new hermeneutical framework suited to the Qur'anic Text taken as 'Divine Address' (*Khaṭāb*) as distinguished from taking it as 'delivered in the style of Writing'.

Though Professor Altaie gives very valuable analysis of the classical and traditional Ash'arite cosmology and its comparative study with the contemporary scientific cosmological theories, because of remaining confined to the traditional un-Qur'anic ontological framework, he too, remains unable to identify the un-Qur'anic nature of metaphysical presuppositions inherent in the foundations of Islamic theology and cosmology in Qur'anic perspective.

10. The Qur'an, Morality and Critical Reason: The Essential Muhammad Shahrur, translated, edited and with an introduction by Andreas Christmann, (Brill: Leiden.Boston, 2009)

The Qur'an, Morality, and Critical Reason presents for the first time in English a comprehensive account of Shahrur's approach to how to think about Islam and how to interpret Islam in the modern world. This book assembles the essential writings of Muhammad Shahrur. It is a compilation of texts, specifically rearranged and modified by Andreas Christmann for the purpose of this translation, in collaboration with and in the guidance of Muhammad Shahrur himself explaining his ideas for Christmann. So there is no doubt that it presents a most reliable source for Shahrur's ideas. This volume is an attempt to present Shahrur's entire intellectual output and (almost) the entire spectrum of his thought in a single book.

Dale F. Eickelman, in his 'Foreword' for this book, writes that Shahrur proclaims his faith in Islam but advocates a critical stance towards established conventions of authoritative learning. Shahrur's goal, as explained by Eickelman, is to redefine how Muslims and non-Muslims alike think about religion and sacred authority. Shahrur's ideas directly challenge the authority of traditional Qur'anic exegesis (*Tafseer*), collections of sayings of the prophet (*ḥadīth*), and Islamic jurisprudence (*fiqh*) as according to him these disciplines of learning have implicitly acquired an authority equal to that of the Qur'an itself. I agree with Shahrur that there definitely is a need to reinterpret ideas of religious authority and tradition, and to apply Islamic precepts to contemporary society notwithstanding the fact that popular resistance to such challenges to established authority has always been intense. But the same objections as raised by the author of the manuscript against above mentioned Handbooks, apply to Shahrur's books too. For example, "Read the Qur'an as if it was Revealed Last Night" is the title of the chapter written as "Introduction To Muhammad Shahrur's Life And Work". But, nowhere it shows that Shahrur was conscious of the fact that the Qur'an is revealed (piecemeal in about 22 years) in the style of 'Address' (*Khaṭāb*) and not in the style of 'Writing'; so the hermeneutical requirements for such type of revelation compiled as Book must be different from the traditional paradigms. Nowhere in his work, it is evident that Shahroor had any idea of 'what is the ontology which the Qur'an has given to the believers' and how it differs from the ontology 'that lies in the foundations of traditional theology, cosmology and Qur'anic translation and commentary, handed over to us through tradition, and presumed by Shahroor himself in his writings. It has been claimed in the Foreword that this publication of Shahrur's thought challenges a millennium of Islamic theological tradition. But this is not true. Shahrur's writings assume the same un-Qur'anic terms based on un-Qur'anic ontology, (as explained in this book) which have no place in the Qur'an; his works apply same Aristotelian logic on the Person of God, which being based on un-Qur'anic Aristotelian metaphysics, is inapplicable to the Qur'anic God. What is this critical reason for which he or his supporters make so big claims, when he has no idea that a hermeneutics appropriate for a Text delivered in the style of 'writing' will be inappropriate for the interpretation of a Text revealed as 'Address' (*Khaṭab*)! What is this 'critical reason' which does not make him perceive that the ontology in the foundation of Muslim theologies was un-Qur'anic.

Ibn Sina was impressed by Aristotelian metaphysics, and the Ptolemaic model of the universe, which was a kind of scientific worldview of his times. Ibn Sina asserts the Qur'an to be a revealed version of truth, and the Ptolemaic model of the universe as science of his times, and strives to reconcile the Qur'an with the standards of rationality of his times. Shahrur, so much impressed by dialecticism as he is, tries to articulate divine-human relationship on dialecticism. Dialecticism of the divine-human relationship, as Andreas Christmann puts it in the "Introduction", is at the heart of Shehrur's epistemological, hermeneutical, and legal theories. Thus instead of visualising Divine-human relationship in Qur'anic perspective and modelling his epistemological, hermeneutical and legal theories on it, he formulates them on dialecticism as anyone can model his understanding on idealism, empiricism, relativism etc.

He sees God as transcendental reality and perceives immortality, immutability, absoluteness, infinity, abstractness and sacrality as descriptions of this God. This is what he presents as a new interpretation of Islam. He considers his own speculations and arbitrary interpretations as the true version of Islam. The present book advocates a more critical stance towards established conventions of authoritative learning than Shahrur does, but the author's work presents everything on the authority of the Qur'an and nowhere follows arbitrary whims or speculations. The Qur'an identifies conjecturers as the ones Who are within a flood [of confusion] and are heedless. (Q. 51:9-10)

11. Shabbir Akhtar, The Quran and the Secular Mind: A Philosophy of Islam, London and New York: Routledge, 2008.

This book presents Shabbir Akhtar's major philosophical contribution to the study of the Qur'an. In this study Shabbir Akhtat argues that Islam is unique in its decision and capacity to confront, rather than accommodate, the challenge of secular belief. He encourages his Muslim co-religionists to assess the central Qur'anic doctrine at the bar of contemporary secular reason. Shabbir Akhtar claims to revive the tradition of Islamic philosophy, closed since the work of 12th century Muslim thinker and commentator on Aristotle, Ibn Rushd (Averoes). He argues that reason, in the aftermath of revelation, must be exercised critically, rather than merely to extract and explicate Qur'anic dogma. As rightly observed by Carool Kersten in his review article on Shabbir Akhtar's book, that

"To assess the relevance of the Qur'an in a secularising world, Akhtar explores the tension between scientific empiricism and revelation, the moral and epistemological dimensions of human nature, the role of reason, the complexities surrounding 'the history of the secular revolt against God', and 'the similarity between philosophy and religion'."

But, in the author's view, unless anyone identifies that the classical and traditional Muslim cosmology is based on an ontology not consistent with the teachings of the Qur'an, and reconstructs cosmology on an ontology based on the Qur'anic teachings, he cannot justify in the fullest sense, the relevance of the Qur'an in a secularising world and resolve the tension between scientific empiricism and the revelation. Unfortunately, Shabbir Akhtar too, in spite of his superb intellectual abilities, does not succeed in identifying un-Qur'anic presuppositions in the foundations of Muslim theology and philosophy.

SOME CLASSICAL AND MODERN COMPETING WORKS

1. Al-Ash'ari, Al- Ibanah an Usul Ad-Diyanah (Eng.tr)

Al-Ash'ari, *Al- Ibanah an Usul Ad-Diyanah* (Eng.tr with Introduction and Notes) by Walter.C. Klein, *The Elucidation of Islam's Foundation*, New York: Kraus Reprint Corporation, 1967. (Originally published in New Haven, Conn., American Oriental Society, 1940.)

This book laid down the foundations of Ash'arite theology in the last quarter of eleventh century A.D., which is still prevalent in the Muslim Ummah. It is in this book at p. 66, 67, and 76 that Al-Ash'ari accepts un-Qur'anic ontology in the foundations of the Ash'arites' Islamic theology. He commits this epistemic fallacy by identifying *Al-Ḥaqq* (The Truth) used in the Qur'an as epithet for the Qur'an itself, with Allah (the Descender of *Al-Ḥaqq*) in the identical sense as The Truth. He uses this unlawful move to hold the Qur'an to be un-created as opposed to the Mu'tazilites' stance. The present manuscript considers this unlawful move the root-cause of all confusion in Islamic theology and argues against it and reconstructs it in Qur'anic perspective.

2. Al-Ghazali's *'Tahafut al-Falasifa' (The incoherence of the philosophers)*

Al-Ghazali, *Tahafut al-Falasifa* (*The Incoherence of the Philosophers*), A parallel English-Arabic text translated, introduced, and annotated by Michael E. Marmura Institute of Global Cultural Studies Binghamton University, State University of New York, 2000.

The present book resembles the above mentioned book, in the sense that it, too, challenges the existing established works in the field, in a similar manner as Ghazali's book did. It denounces many established foundational frameworks as 'alien to Qur'an' and proposes new frameworks to replace them.

It differs from the work of Ghazali in the sense that this work does not condemn any previous work as heretical. The position it holds is that all previous theologians and philosophers have made important contributions to their respective fields with intellectual integrity and good intentions. The epistemic fallacies committed by them in their works originated because of accepting mismatched terms in Islamic discourse coined in mismatched ontological and epistemological alien frameworks.

3. *Reconstruction of Religious Thought in Islam* by Muhammad Iqbal,

Muhammad Iqbal, *Reconstruction of Religious Thought in Islam, (ann.* by Muhammad Saeed Sheikh), Iqbal Academy Pakistan, 1989. (Originally published in 1933.)

Iqbal realises that Muslim thought has remained stagnant for centuries, and thinks of reopening the Muslim mind through 'Ijtehad' and reconstructing religious thought in the present context, synthesising two seemingly opposing concepts of revelation and reason. These themes are similar to those discussed in this book. However, the proposed book (the manuscript) goes further and challenges some Iqbalian concepts as being based on un-Qur'anic ontology, and committing epistemic fallacies similar to those committed by ancient Muslim scholars.

CHAPTER 11

GLOSSARY

Ajl-e-musammā (Appointed term):

There is a concept of 'appointed term of life'(*ajl-e-musammā*) in the Qur'an. It has been stated in the Qur'an that when the appointed term of life comes for the disbelievers, the realities they had been denying throughout their life become manifest on them. Now they beg for respite promising that they will follow the guidance sent by Allah and will live according to it. It is said to them that neither the 'appointed term' comes in advance nor can it be delayed. An antinomy argument has been formulated by the predestinarians to prove that the libertarians' stand point was not correct. According to our research the dilemma of 'Free Will and the Appointed Term' is based on un-Qur'anic concept of the inexorability of the appointed term (*ajl-e-musammā*) and does not pose a challenge to human freewill. Span of 'life' or the term of 'death' are not appointed inexorably. Allah, the Creator of life can extend life and Allah, the Creator of death, can postpone death for as much time as He Will. Actually, it is the wrongdoers who entreat for respite when death reaches them, and it is they who are denied such respite.[ccxxv]

The Ash'arite Atomism (Occasionalism)

The Ash'arite atomism (as occasionalism) is a cosmology developed by the Ash'arites. Like their theory of the eternity of the Qur'an, it too, is developed based on their un-Qur'anic ontology. This theory denies any enduring/lasting nature (*fiṭrah*) to things. Therefore the question of the existence of any laws of nature regulating the phenomena could not arise. Denying the principle of universal causation, this view presents a most extreme form of Divine interactionism in the universe. It does not admit the real existence of the physical universe. Actually this is a cosmological theory presented by Muslim theologians in the early centuries but unfortunately, like some other such theories, it acquired the status of a creed (*'aqīda*) and played a crucial role in hampering the progress of empirical sciences in the Muslim communities. How could such cosmology endorse the development of a kind of empirical science in Muslim communities which do not acknowledge the role of laws of nature and significance of cause-effect relationship in nature! The Ash'arites have contrived this theory as an explanation to the creation and then administration of the universe. It, clearly instances, how much harm a theory (if it is not based on Qur'anic tenets) could mete out to the community if it enters in Islamic theology, turns into creed, and assumes sanctity.

Compelled by the success and strength of the Newtonian mechanics, and then with the advent of Einsteinian relativity physics and now the discoveries of quantum physics, it did not remain possible for the Muslims to deny natural characteristics of phenomena, the role of causation or laws of nature. So, the traditional Muslim cosmology has to admit the basic postulates of empirical science. Yet, their belief in God as an Interventionist Deity does not reconcile with the basic postulates of modern science. The Qur'anic cosmology developed in this book perceives the universe as a system, divinely administered with Allah's *amr* (command) subsisting in everything as its enduring nature, which interlinks everything with the whole universe.

Cosmology deals with nature and structure of the universe and God-universe relationship etc. Islam does not deny the significance of empirical knowledge, but gives ultimate primacy to revelation as source of knowledge and basic principles of Islamic ontology and cosmology are given in the Qur'an.

Al-Asmā al-Ḥusnā

Nowhere in the Qur'an Allah Almighty uses the word '*ṣifah*' (*attributes*) to talk about Himself. Rather the Qur'an ordains the believers to call on Allah by His Goodly Names (*al-Asmā' al-Husnā*) and to leave those who blaspheme against His Comely Names:

> *"And the Most beautiful Names belong to Allah; so invoke Him by them, and keep away from those who blaspheme His Names. They will be requited for what they used to do." (Surah al-A'raf, 7:180)*

The Personal Name of the Creator of all, the true Master, and the Sustainer of the worlds is Allah. All other Excellent Names are His attributive Names. His *al-Asmā' al-Husnā* are either mentioned in the Holy Qurān or derivable from it in line with the *muhkamāt*. To invoke any of His Names for the satisfaction of base desires or to fulfil an evil purpose, or to accomplish an evil design, or to make arbitrary addition or deletion in His Names are various ways to blaspheme His Names. It is strictly forbidden and Allah ordains to leave those who blaspheme against His Comely Names.

Whatever has originated from the Absolute Originator, belongs either to the category of His creation (*khalq*) or to the category of His command (*amr*). Even *amr* does not follow from Him because of any inner compulsion. No descensions (*tanazzalāt*) could ever ensue from Him without His Will and Command. His Goodly Names (and not the Attributes as perceived by *waḥdat al-wujud*) are the reason or the channel of the origination of *khalq* or *amr* from Him.

To hold the Origination of the universe as the manifestation of Allah's attributes (*ṣiffah*) is to take an un-Qur'anic style and a way of expression not approved by Allah. It has its unfortunate implications, too. This un-Qur'anic view provides basis to the doctrine of *Waḥdat al-Wujud*.

Eternal (*Azli*), Everlasting (*Abdi*), Infinite (*Lā-Maḥdūd*), Timeless (*Mawara-i-Zamān*) in the sense it implies determinism, Absolute Perfection (*Kamāl-e-Muṭliq*) in the sense it implies Immutability are un-Qur'anic names used in Muslim theology, translation and commentary of the Qur'an and other Islamic sciences. These are not translatable into any of the Goodly Names of Allah. These are the outcome of philosophical ontology derived from Greek philosophers and consist of polar concepts. They are un-Qur'anic and must not be attributed to Allah, in translation, exegesis or in the formulation of theological doctrines.

To argue that God is High above having any Names, or that no name matches His dignity, majesty and grandeur is known as the doctrine of the *ineffability* of God. It is clearly un-Qur'anic. Allah narrates His Own Goodly Names (*al-Asmā' al-Husna*) in the Qur'an and ordains to call upon Him by these Goodly Names.

Ad-Dahr (Time), too, is not Allah's Name. The Qur'an does not endorse it. The word '*ad-Dahr*' (Time) occurs only twice in the Qur'an, but nowhere it is used to denote God.

Bid'at (Innovation):

Bid'at is a Qur'anic principle for relating knowledge acquired through empirical or rational sciences or the time-tested beneficial human knowledge acquired in any other way, with the revealed knowledge within parameters defined in the Qur'an. No innovation which conflicts with the *muḥkamāt* is i.e., with the fundamentals of Dīn is ever allowed.

If we use the word 'Islam' for the religion revealed by Allah in its final form on Prophet Muhammad (pbuh) and approved by Him as a way of life for humankind, and if we use the word 'modernity' for all kinds of man-made knowledge (philosophy, and sciences—social as well as natural) it can be said that Islam and modernity are opposed to each other. Islam is a way of life which recommends fulfilment of desires within Allah's prescribed limits whereas modernity legislates for the maximum fulfilment of desires. Islam legislates to keep fulfilment of desires subservient to Allah's prescribed limits whereas modern societies legislate to keep their laws subservient to the free fulfilment of desires. One's free pursuit of desire does not harm the similar freedom of any other is the only limit before it. Thus Islam and man-made knowledge (sciences and philosophy) differ in their basic assumptions. Apparently, no viable understanding between the two seems possible. Should the Muslims then reject all human experiments in various fields as unholy and profane! As for the aspect of utilising the outcome of human knowledge is concerned, Islam does not leave us to wander in darkness. The Qur'an opens the way of *bid'ah* (Innovation). No innovation in respect of prohibitions is allowed. Not everyone is qualified for carrying out this job. The sound in knowledge (*ar-rasikhûn fil-ilm*) are the ones who are best qualified for working out an appropriate relationship between Islam and man-made knowledge in line with the Divine decree: *la talbisul Ḥaqqa bil batili ... (Mix not falsehood with truth!).* (02:42) It is the Qur'anic principle of innovation (*bid'ah*) which provides basis to *ijtihâd*. It is this principle which is meant to keep the revelation appropriately applicable in all circumstances and in all times to come. Unluckily because of the shortsightedness of some religious scholars, '*bid'ah*' has acquired a highly undesirable connotation since centuries. It is high time that the principle of *innovation* is revived as the basis of *ijtihad* and a framework is formulated for relating science, philosophy and time-tested beneficial human knowledge, with the knowledge derived form the Qur'an.

Epistemological Status of *Ḥadīth*:

The Qur'an is the source of Divine law (*sharī'ah*). *Ḥadīth* reports implementation of *sharī'ah* by the Prophet (pbuh). Divine law is universal. Implementation of a universal law cannot be universal. Implementation of the same divine law in different ways by the Prophet (pbuh) at various occasions proves that the way of the implementation of a divine law is bound to accord with the requirements of time, place, quantity and capacity. *Ḥadīth* is the PRECEDENT of the Divine law. *Ḥadīth* is neither *authority* (*qāzi*) over the dictates of *Aḥsan al-Ḥadīth Kitāb* nor is irrelevant to its interpretation. Interpretation of *Ḥadīth*, itself, is must to accord with the *muḥkamāt* (the pivotal, the cornerstone verses) of the *Aḥsan al-Ḥadīth Kitāb* as the interpretation of the *mutashābihāt* themselves is must to accord with them. *Ḥadīth* can neither alter nor delete or abrogate the content of of a *muḥkam* verse. It is the disharmony of *ḥadīth* with the *muḥkamāt* which can declare them fake or interposed.

Muḥkamāt and Mutashābihāt

As per verse 7 of surah Āl-e-Imran 3 the Qur'an categorises all verses of the Qur'an into *muḥkamāt* (explicitly imperatival) and *mutashābihāt* (non-imperatival ones) and characterises *muḥkamāt* as *Umm-ul-Kitab* (the cornerstone, pivotal, or the foundation of the Book). It is usually held that verses which are imperatival, decisive, precise, unambiguous and definite in meaning, are *muḥkamāt* and which are otherwise (i.e. ambiguous and liable to more then one interpretation) are *mutashābihāt.* However, this is not correct. A *muḥkam* verse must consist of an explicit divine imperative. This is the only essential characteristic of a *muḥkam* verse. Verse 07 of Surah Āl-e-Imran (3) itself is a *muḥkam* verse. It explicitly contains the divine imperative to keep the interpretation of a *mutashābih* verse to accord with the *muḥkamāt*. If a Qur'an scholar overlooks this imperative, and leaps towards an arbitrary interpretation of a *mutashābih* verse, it will prove him to be diseased at heart, and a mischief-monger.

The absence of a divine imperative is the essential characteristic of a *mutashābih* verse. Of course, *muḥkamat* are decisive, precise, unambiguous and definite in meaning, but these do not comprise the defining characteristics of being a *muḥkam* verse. There are many *mutashābih* verses, which are clear in statement, definite in meaning and are not liable to more than one interpretation. The Qur'an labels verses other than *muḥkamāt* (the *Umm-ul-Kitāb*) as *mutashābihāt. Mutashābihāt,* though, include all non-imperatival verses, yet these occur in the Qur'an in various ways as narratival (which state a story or an event), metaphorical, allegorical, metaphysical, or eschatological verses. Symbolic and abstract verses consisting of 'separate letters' also come in the same category. Verses containing Allah's promise, pledge, a glad-tiding or a threat, admonish or advice too are instances of *mutashābih* verses. Verses which Allah recommends or approves for the sake of making a prayer before Him, or for entreating or beseeching to Him are also *mutashābih* verses. Surah an-Noor (24) consists of 64 verses and it is stated in the very first verse that imperatives explicitly stated in its verses, or 'does' and 'don'ts' derivable from them as consequences, are obligatory. Yet it does not mean that all of its verses are necessarily considered to be *muḥkamāt*. This Surah also consists of *mutashābih* verses.

As per this Qur'anic categorisation of verses, one must firmly believe that classification of verses into *muḥkamāt* and *mutashābihāt* is definitely feasible. There definitely are verses which are so clearly *muḥkamāt* (for example verses which consist of divine laws or imperatives) and there are certain others which are so clearly *mutashābihāt* (the Light verse, the Chair verse, the Throne verse, verses consisting of Separate Letters etc). Other verses may be sorted out based upon them. It is not necessary that while translating a verse one determines whether it is Makki or Madinite. Keeping in view the universal nature of divine message in the Qur'an, it is necessary that while making translation or exposition of a verse, the Qur'an scholar must distinguish a verse as a *muḥkam* or a *mutashābih* verse before he proceeds further. If he distinguishes the verse in question as a *muḥkam* verse, he must be sure that no *muḥkam* verse (one of the Cornerstone verses) can ever conflict with any other *muḥkam* verse, or abrogate or cancel it. If the Qur'an scholar is certain that the verse in question is a *mutashābih* verse, he must make sure that its interpretation necessarily accords with the verses identified as *muḥkamāt*. It is very disappointing that the theologians and the Qur'an scholars have made no effort to classify verses of the Qur'an in accordance with this Qur'anic categorisation and have not followed this principle in their translation and commentary of the Qur'an.

The Mu'tazilites and the Ash'arites

The Mu'tazilites believed in the primacy of reason and held traditionally believed dogmas and revelation subservient to reason. The concept of reason or rationality they followed, of course, was actually based upon Aristotelian logic which in turn is based upon Aristotelian dualist metaphysics and ontology not compatible with the Qur'an. Though, the Ash'arites pronounced the primacy of revelation over reason, as opposite to the Mu'tazilites, yet they were no better than the Mu'tazilites in holding accordance with Aristotelian logic as the standard of rationality equally applicable to Allah and the Qur'an. Both theological schools failed to identify that the ontology in the foundation of their respective theologies was the same and that it was un-Qur'anic. Moreover, though the Ash'arites claimed to uphold the primacy of revelation over reason, they gave the same, rather more, importance to tradition and religious dogmas accepted from preceding generations, having no authority on their back from the Qur'an.

Ontological status of *Ḥadīth*

What is the nature of the relationship of *Ḥadīth* with the Qur'an? Does *Ḥadīth* hold primacy over the Qur'an and can delete, cancel or abrogate the content of a verse? Is the Qur'an alone the source of Divine law and as *Aḥsan-al-Ḥadith Kitāb (The Fairest of Texts Book)* holds primacy over *Ḥadīth;* and *Ḥadīth* only reports implementation of Qur'anic injunctions by the Prophet (pbuh) and is subservient to imperatival verses of the Qur'an for the validation of its interpretation? Is the injunctions of the Qur'an alone universal and final and the way of implementation of these injunctions bound to accord with the requirements of time, place, quantity and the capacity? What standpoint one takes on these questions will determine his position on the ontological status of *Ḥadīth.*

Significance of Ontology

Ontology is a genre of philosophy which investigates the ultimate categories of Reality. It is used as a synonym to metaphysics for one of the definitions of metaphysics is 'doing ontology'. No theology, religious or philosophical (or even mythological), can be conceived of as not based on a specific ontology. This is not a prerequisite of theology alone; all sciences—— natural, social, psychological, biological, mathematical or whatever, have their ontology. Literature and spirituality, too, are not free from it. Terms are never neutral; they are always coined in an ontological perspective. When terms coined in one ontological perspective are accepted or used in a discourse based on a different ontology without realising and stipulating the difference, it is necessary to give rise to confusion and contradictions. This is exactly what has happened to Muslim thought. Prevalent schools or strands of Islamic theology are based on an ontology which is contrary to the teachings of the Qur'an.

The traditional Ash'arite ontology, which is the cornerstone of all Sunnite theological doctrines, perceives everything, including God and whatever else, either as eternal or as created (contingent). Hence, it conceives 'anything uncreated as eternal.' This ontology is un-Qur'anic and a source of immense confusion, contradiction, dissension, sectarianism, disorientation in Muslim civilization and of intellectual decline. The ontology reconstructed in Qur'anic perspective, perceives everything other than God, in two ultimate but originated categories: Allah's *khalq* (creation) and Allah's *amr* (command). It perceives God (Allah) as the Absolute Originator of these categories at His Will and Decree and Supremely Singular and Unique as Self.

Cosmology is always based on ontology. The Qur'anic cosmology, as argued in this study, conceives the universe as divinely administered reality with Allah's *amr* (command) subsisting in everything (of Allah's *khalq*) and in the whole universe as enduring nature (*fitrah*) and as guiding principle giving rise to laws of nature. However, neither *khalq* nor *amr* participate in Allah's Divinity in any manner.

Shān-e-Nazool

Tradition narrating a particular circumstance, condition or event as presumed-cause of descension of a particular verse or verses. Accepting it as a principle of the interpretation of the Qur'an, harms the universality of Allah's Message. It gives a particular conjectural narrative, primacy over Allah's revealed Kalam, having the status of Authority as *The Truth.*

Tradition and Dogma

In theological perspective, tradition consists of religious dogmas. Without inquiring into its Qur'anic basis, tradition is accepted from preceding generations. It may include unfounded dogmas. When unfounded dogmas get formulated as doctrines, they acquire the status of creed and become part of the official interpretation of faith. Minds become closed when dogmas, traditions, rituals, superstitions and speculations become faith, rationalisation overrides reasoning, alien terms get incorporated in Qur'anic discourse and arbitrary paradigms are given preference over the Qur'anic principles of the interpretation of the Qur'an. Ummah gets divided into communities, and communities into sects giving birth to intellectual crises. This, in turn, results in intellectual decline and downfall of civilization.

NOTES AND REFERENCES

[1] *Surah an-Noor (24) consists of 64 verses. Status of this Surah as stated in the very first verse is that this Surah is obligatory (farz فرض). It means that imperatives explicitly stated in its verses, or 'does' and 'don'ts' derivable from them, are obligatory. Yet it does not mean that all of its verses are muḥkamāt. This Surah also consists of mutashabih verses.*

[2] ***Note:*** *Nine Eng. translations of the Qur'an by celebrated Qur'an scholars as given below are used in this book for comparative study. Qur'anic Arabic Corpus website (http://corpus.quran.com /translatiozn.jsp?, (prepared by Language Research Group, University of Leads) accessed during June 01 - 30, 2020 contains the following SEVEN parallel English translations of the Qur'an and makes the comparative study of the translation of verses very easy:*

(i) Sahih International, The Qur'ān (English Meanings) Abul-Qasim Publishing House, 1997 Al-Muntada Al-Islami, 2004;

ii) Pickthall; iii) Yusuf Ali; iv) Shakir; v) Muḥammad Sarwar; vi) Muḥsin Khan; and vii) Arberry.

Following, two more translations have been added to these by the writer:

1) Eng. tr. of Maulana Abu 'al A'la Maududi's Tafhīm–ul-Qur'an, at englishtafsir.com (https://www .englishtafsir .com /Quran/6/index.html;

2) M. A. S. Abdel Haleem, The Qur'an: A new translation, Oxford World's Classics, (New York: Oxford University Press, 2004, 2005) at Wordpress.com (https://islamiclegacy.files. wordpress.com /2018/07/ translation-of-the-quran-by-m-a-s-abdel-haleem .pdf).

A comparative study of these nine translations with each other as well as with a tenth one, the Urdu exegesis of Haḍrat Fazal Shah and Muhammad Ashraf Fazli, Tafseer-e-Fazli, 7 vols. (Lahore Pakistan: Fazli Foundation, 1982-1998) has been made. Eng. tr. of its six volumes has been published between 2002-2019 by Fazli Foundation. Rendering into English of the 7th volume is in progress.

Transliteration of a few verses used at some places has been taken from http//transliteration. org/Qur'an/website_cd/ mixpicthall /002.asp

The thought-contradiction (the root-cause of religious-factionalism) is, as the Qur'an says, the outcome of denial of truth (takzeeb-il-Ḥaqq): "But they belied the truth when it came to them, so they are entangled in thought-contradiction." (Q. 50:05) Haḍrat Fazal Shah and Muhammad Ashraf Fazli, Tafseer-e-Fazli, vol.7, (Urdu) Lahore: Fazli Foundation, 1998) 10.

[3] *Haḍrat Fazal Shah and Muhammad Ashraf Fazli, Tafseer-e-Fazli, vol.3, (Eng tr.), ed. Abdul Hafeez, Lahore: Fazli Foundation, 2008), 21.*

[4] " *...Wa Al-Ladhī 'Unzila 'llayka Min Rabbika Al-ḥaqqu..." (Q.13:1) Ibid, (eng. tr), 181*

[5] *Marmaduke Pickthall, Meaning of the Glorious Qur'an, (Q. 47:2), Qur'anic Arabic Corpus (QAC) (http://corpus.quran. Com /translation.jsp?*

[6] *Ibid, (Q. 32:2-3)*

[7] *Al-Ash'ari, Abu 'L-Hasan 'Ali Ibn Isma'il, Al- Ibanah an Usul Ad-Diyanah (Eng. tr. The Elucidation of Islam's Foundation by Walter C. Klein), (New Haven: American Oriental Society, 1940), 66, 67, 76; also see translator's note at page 66.*

[8] *At times, it addresses humankind, at other times it addresses the believers or the people of the Book, the Children of Israel, and the disbelievers and so on. At times, it addresses the Prophet (pbuh). At another time, it addresses in second person singular but not necessarily to the Prophet (pbuh). Still another place addressing in third person singular, apparently addressing a specific individual, it teaches to everyone how to impart a correction in anyone's behaviour without mentioning his name and harming his dignity.*

[9] *Tradition narrating a particular circumstance, condition or event as presumed-cause of descension of a particular verse or verses.*

[10] *M. A. S. Abdel Haleem, The Qur'an: A new translation, Oxford World's Classics, (New York: Oxford University Press, 2004, 2005), 200. at Wordpress.com (https://islamiclegacy.files. Wordpress .com /2018/07/ translation-of-the-quran-by-m-a-s-abdel-haleem .p df).*

[11] *Ibid,*

[12] *It should be noted that the calf worshippers did not deny prophethood of Mūsā (pbuh) or his God. Sāmri had told them that (carved calf) was their as well as Ḥaḍrat Mūsā's Lord, and Ḥaḍrat Mūsā (pbuh) had forgotten it. (Q. 20:88) So the observation of the writer contained here does not apply to those who deny the Finality of Ḥaḍrat Muhammad (pbuh) as the Last of the Prophets (pbuh).*

[13] *Abu al-Ā'lā Madudi, Tafheem ul-Qur'an, vol.3, (Urdu) (Lahore: Idara Tarjuman al-Qur'an, 2012), FN.72 at 118.*

[14] *In verses 13-14 of Surah Ash-Shurā Allah says:*

"In matters of faith, He has laid down for you [people] the same commandment that He gave to Noah; which, We have revealed to you [Muhammad] and, We enjoined on Abraham and Moses and Jesus: 'Uphold the faith and do not divide into factions within it'– what you [Prophet] call upon the idolaters [alá al-mushrikīna] to do is hard for them; God chooses whoever He pleases for Himself and guides towards Himself those who turn to Him." (Q. 42:13) Haleem, The Qur'an: A new translation, 312.

[15] *Allah says:*

"...do not join those who ascribe partners to God [al-mushrikīn]; those who divide their religion into sects, with each party rejoicing in their own." (Q. 30: 31-32) Ibid, 259.

[16] *Allah says:*

"Messengers! ... This community of yours is one – and I am your Lord: be mindful of Me – but they have split their community into sects, each rejoicing in their own. So [Muhammad] leave them for a while steeped [in their ignorance]." (Q. 23:51-54) Ibid, 217.

[17] *Allah says:*

"As for those who have divided their religion and broken up into factions, have nothing to do with the [Prophet]. Their case rests with God: in time He will tell them about their deeds." (Q. 6:159) Ibid, 93.

[18] *Ḥaḍrat Fazal Shah and Fazli, Tafseer-e-Fazli, vol.6 (Eng tr), 186. Similarly concerning the People of the Book the Qur'an says:*

"They did not split up into factions (tafarraqu) until after there had come to them the clear evidence." (Q. 98:4) Ibid, (Urdu) vol.7, p 458.

[19] *Allah says:*

"Say, 'He has power to send punishment on you from above or from under your very feet, or to divide you into discordant factions and make some taste the violence of others." (Q. 6:65) Ibid, TF, (Eng) vol. 2, 101

[20] *Dr. Muhammad Taqi-ud-Dīn Al-Hilāli and Dr. Muhammad Muhsin Khān, Translation of the Meanings of The Noble Qur'an in the English language, (Madina K.S.A.: King Fahad Complex), (Q. 7:150) 221. Also, Qur'anic Arabic Corpus website (http://corpus.quran .com/ translation. jsp?*

[21]

"Allah only forbids you from those who fight you (*qātalūkum*) because of religion and expel you from your homes and aid in your expulsion that you make allies of them..." (Q. 60:9) "... and you will never fight with me with an enemy (*walan tuqātilū*)..." (Q. 9:83, 111) Also see at Q. 4:76 (3 times), Q. 61:4, Q. 9:30, Q. 49:9 (2 times), Q. 59:11 *and some other places too.*

Sahih International, The Qur'an--English Meanings, (Jedda: Al-Muntada al-Islami, 2004)

[22] *Ibid,*

[23] *Abdel Haleem, Ibid, 222.*

[24] *Haḍrat Fazal Shah and Ashraf Fazli, TF, vol.4 (ed. 2012), 314. This translation does not contradict anywhere with the Qur'an.*

Sahih International translates this verse (Q. 24:26) as the following:

> "Evil words are for evil men, and evil men are [subjected] to evil words. And good words are for good men, and good men are [an object] of good words. Those [good people] are declared innocent of what the slanderers say. For them is forgiveness and noble provision."

It is much better than eight others mentioned above, though not so explicit yet is an attempt in the right direction.

[25] *See, Hafeez Fazli, "Paish Lafaẓ" in Muslim Fiker ki Qur'ani Jihāt, 27.*

[26] *The injunction 'to enjoin what is right and forbid what is wrong' (Amr bil Ma'rūf wa nahī 'anil Mukar) (Q. 3:104, Q. 9:71, Q. 9: 112 etc.) lays down an obligation on the individual, the community and the state in different manner as to their status. Mostly individuals and groups assume a role not matching their status and take the implementation of law in their hands because the translators and exegetes do not make the referent clear. Similar is the case of Jihād. No individual or the group can assume on his or her own to act upon this Divine commandment unless declared by the State.*

[27] *Arthur Arberry, The Holy Koran: A Translation, (1955), at Qur'anic Arabic Corpus, (Q. 33:57)*

[28] *Abdel Haleem, Allah ordained the angels that*

> 'When I have fashioned him [Adam] and breathed My spirit (rūḥ) into him, bow down before him,'. (Q. 15:29)

'My spirit' is objectionable. 'Spirit' belongs to the category of Allah's Amr. Moḥsin Khan translates it as 'the soul, which I created for him [Adam]…'.

If Abdel Haleem conceives rūḥ (spirit) as something having some special closeness with Allah's Being, Muhammad Moḥsin Khan conceives it as 'created'. Both these translations are contrary to Qur'anic ontology. Rūḥ (spirit) belongs to the category of Allah's command. There are others too, who draw from this verse that 'Allah has created man on His own Image.' They hold that the soul of man is of divine origin, for God has breathed a bit of His own spirit into him. M. M. Sharif, History of Muslim Philosophy, Vol.1, 178. "Ibn Arabi maintains that human beings owe their uniqueness to the fact that they were created in the image of God …" Seyyed Hossein Nasr and Oliver Leaman, History of Islamic Philosophy, Routledge: London and New York, 1996, 897. Nasr, Ideals And Realities of Islam, 2.

[29] *Abdul Hafeez Fāzli, "H. A. Wolfson and A. H. Kamali On the Origin of the Problem of Divine Attributes in Muslim Kalām", The Qur'anic Theology, Philosophy and Spirituality, (Lahore Pakistan: PU Press, 2016. Updated and published at Amazon 2019). 228-29.*

[30] *Aristotelian dualist metaphysics bifurcates Allah into His Being and Attributes. Ash'rites accepted this metaphysics; they also accepted logic based on it; they applied this logic on Qur'anic God and affirmed the independent reality of Divine attributes as superadded to the Being of God. Ṣifa (attributes of Allah) are real but not in Aristotelian sense. Allah has not used the word 'ṣifa' or any of the other derivatives of this root in the Qur'an, to talk about His own Holy Person. Nor does He approve that the believers talk about Him in terms of His ṣifah (divine attributes). The way to talk about Him, as prescribed by Allah, is by way of His Comely Names. All this discussion started because of accepting un-Qur'anic terms (i.e., 'being' and 'attribute') by the Mu'tazilites and the Ash'arites both.*

[31]

إِنَّ رَبَّكُمُ اللَّهُ الَّذِي خَلَقَ السَّمَاوَاتِ وَالأَرْضَ فِي سِتَّةِ أَيَّامٍ ثُمَّ اسْتَوَى عَلَى الْعَرْشِ يُغْشِي اللَّيْلَ النَّهَارَ يَطْلُبُهُ حَثِيثاً وَالشَّمْسَ وَالْقَمَرَ وَالنُّجُومَ مُسَخَّرَاتٍ بِأَمْرِهِ أَلاَ لَهُ الْخَلْقُ وَالأَمْرُ تَبَارَكَ اللَّهُ رَبُّ الْعَالَمِينَ "Inna Rabbakumu Allāhu Al-Ladhī Khalaqa As-Samāwāti Wa Al-'Arḍa Fī Sittati 'Ayyāmin Thumma Astawá `Alá Al-`Arshi Yughshī Al-Layla An-Nahāra Yaṭlubuhu Ḥathīthāan Wa Ash-Shamsa Wa Al-Qamara Wa An-Nujūma Musakhkharātin Bi'amrihi 'Alā Lahu Al-Khalqu Wa Al-'Amru Tabāraka Allāhu Rabbu Al-`Ālamīna."

[32] *Al-Ash'ari, Al- Ibanah an Usul Ad-Diyanah, 66.*

[33] *Ibid, 66, 67, 74, 76, 78; Klein writes as note (no.102) at page 66 that*

> *"In this section al-Ash'ari repeats himself frequently. He attempts to show, on the one hand, that the Qur'an is not created, because it has not the characteristics of a created thing and exists independently of creation, and, on the other hand, that it is eternal and uncreated because, it is in a sense, a predicate of God's, like His Knowledge and His Will....."*

The writer thinks that it is more probable that Ash'ari conceives the Qur'an with Allah from ever as predicate of His attribute of Knowledge and Will, as implied in his reply to Jahmiyyah when he says:

> *"Since the Will of God is eternal, it is uncreated, why do you not believe that His Word is uncreated.' At page 76 he quotes Abu Abdallah's [Ahmad bin Hanbal 780/164–855/241AH] comments presumably with approval that: 'The Qur'an is from God's Knowledge and in it are names of God; wherefore we do not doubt that it is uncreated. It is the Word of God [Kalamullah] and He discourses by it eternally." Ibid, 74.*

[34] *Cf. H. A. Wolfson, The Philosophy of the Kalam, Harvard University Press Cambridge, 1976, 263-74.*

[35] *There was a great controversy between the Ash'arites and the Mu'tazilites over the question whether the Speech is one of the attributes of God or not. The orthodox section including the Ash'arites held Speech as one of His seven rational attributes eternally held by Him, so they argued the Qur'an to be eternal too. M. M. Sharif, ibid, 316. It is argued in the book that Allah does not talk on His Holy Being in terms of His attributes (Siffat). He ordains that the believers call upon Him by His Holy Names. All this discussion on Allah's attributes is unfounded and out of place.*

[36] *Al-Ash'ari, Al- Ibanah an Usul Ad-Diyanah (Eng. tr.), 66, 67, 76. Also see translator's note at page 66. Refer to FN 34 above. For details see: Hafeez Fāzli, ibid.*

[37] *H. A. Wolfson, "Extradeical and Intradeical Interpretation of Platonic Ideas", Religious Philosophy: A Group of Essays, (Harvard University: The Belknap Press, 1961), 49. See also, A. H. Fāzli, "The Qur'an: Creation or Command!" in The Qur'anic Theology, Philosophy and Spirituality, 61-70.*

[38] *The origin of Kalām-i nafsi and Kalām-i lafẓi—terms used by the Ash'arites—does not lie in the Qur'an. Their origin lies in Philo's philosophy, which in turn can be traced back to the intradeical interpretation of Platonic Ideas. According to this interpretation,*

> *"the ideas of Plato's world of ideas' actually are the eternal ideas of god's mind, which are with god from ever. While creating the universe, god first created these eternal ideas apart from him in an intelligible form, and then created this intelligible world in physical form."*

Wolfson, Ibid, 42. Its origin can also be traced in the Ash'arites' conception of seven Divine attributes, eternal attribute of Speech one among them. Also see, Hafeez Fāzli, "H. A. Wolfson and A.H. Kamali on the Origin of the Problem of Divine Attributes in Muslim Kalam" in The Qur'anic Theology, Philosophy and Spirituality, 22-237

[39] *See: Hafeez Fāzli, "The Construction of a Qur'anic Theology **of** Sufism in Tafseer-e-Fāzli", in Ibid, 98*

[40] *Whereas the Qur'an says:*

> *"...And they believe in that, which has been descended to Muḥammad (pbuh)——for it is the truth (al-ḥaqq) from their Lord (Q. 47:2) "This is because the disbelievers follow falsehood, while the believers follow 'the truth (al-ḥaqq) from their Lord..." (Q. 47:3) Haḍrat Fazal Shah and Ashraf Fazli, TF vol.6 Eng. tr, 295.*

See, Hafeez Fāzli, "Is al-ḥaqq One of al-Asma' al-Ḥusnā", Qur'anic theology, Philosophy and Spirituality, 29–46; and "The Qur'anic Ontology and Status of al-ḥaqq" in Ibid, 80-101.

[41] *Basil Altaie, Creation and the Personal Creator in Islamic Kalām and Modern Cosmology, 154.*

[42] *Abdel Haleem, "The Role of Context in Interpreting and Translating the Qur'an", Journal of Qur'anic Studies, SOAS, University of London, 20.1, (2018), 60.*

[43] *Scholars like Abu Muslim Asfahāni, Ubaid ullah Sindhi, Haḍrat Fazal Shah (d.1978) and Muhammad Ashraf Fāzli (d.2016) [authors of Tafseer-e-Fazli] absolutely deny that any verse of the Qur'an is abrogated. (Tafseer-e-Fazli translates and explains all the verses, the way that shows no need for contriving any doctrine of abrogation.) Sayyuṭi, Shah Walliullah Dehlawi, and Maulana Qasmi support abrogation. Qasmi, Maulana Khurshid Anwer Qasmi Faizabadi, al-Fauz al-Azeem, (Sharah, Shah Walliullah Dehlawi, al-Fauz al-Kabīr), (Karachi: Qadeemi Kutab Khana) 254. Maulana Amīn Aḥsan Iṣlaḥi supports the doctrine of abrogation too.*

[44] *Pervez Amirali Hoodbhoy, Islam and Science: Religious Orthodoxy and the Battle for Rationality, (London: ZED Books, 1991), 14-15.*

[45] *Bakar defines Occasionalism as*

> *'The belief in the exclusive efficacy of God, of whose direct intervention the events in nature are regarded as the overt manifestation or occasion. Occasionalism implies that all things and events in nature are substantially discontinuous by nature. The world is a domain of separate, discrete entities that are independent of each other. There is no connection whatsoever between them, save through the Divine Will.'*

Osman Bakar, "The Atomistic Conception of Nature in Ash'arite Theology" in Tawhid and Science (Essays on the History and Philosophy of Science), (Kuala Lumpur: University of Malaysia & Nourine Enterprises, (1991)

[46] *M. B. Altaie, "Creation and the Personal Creator in Islamic Kalam and Modern Cosmology, in Humanity", The World and God, Studies in Science and Theology, Vol. 11, (Sweden: Lund University, 2008). 154.*

[47] *Claudius Ptolemy c. AD 90 – c. AD 168, was a Greek-Roman citizen of Egypt. He was a renowned mathematician, astronomer, geographer, astrologer, and poet. The Ptolemaic cosmology is emanationistic in nature. It conceives the universe eternal and denies the role of divine will and command in its coming into being. Ptolemy conceives an ontology and cosmology in line with Aristotelian philosophical physics (and gives a model of the universe based on nine heavenly spheres (with the earth in the centre), contrary to Qur'anic cosmology, which gives the view of a universe based on seven heavens. The Ptolemaic philosophical cosmology, after remaining prevalent as a philosophico-scientific worldview for about fifteen centuries was replaced by the Newtonian Mechanics in the second half of the 17th century. Newton (1642-1726 AD) is widely recognized as one of the most influential scientists of all times and a key figure in the scientific revolution. With the publication of his book Mathematical Principles of Natural Philosophy in 1687 he laid the foundations of 'classical mechanics'. 'The Newtonian mechanics' remained the dominant worldview till it was superseded by the worldview based on 'the theory of relativity'. Einstein's 'special theory of relativity' supersedes the Newtonian mechanics in 1905 and his 'general theory of relativity' in 1916 and is prevalent till today as the scientific cosmology. See, Hafeez Fāzli, "Evolving a Qur'anic Paradigm of Science and Philosophy: Ibn Sina, Sir Syed Ahmad Khan, Dr. Muhammad Iqbal, and Some Contemporary Scholars", in Ibid, 275-315.*

[48] *Founded by Ziauddin Sardar (b. 1951) and Dr. Munawwar Ahmad Anees' (b. 1948).*

[49] *Professor of Theoretical Physics at Yarmouk University. Dr. Basil Altaie is well versed in modern science tradition as well as in classical Islamic theology of Nature.*

[50]

وَالَّذِينَ آمَنُوا وَعَمِلُوا الصَّالِحَاتِ وَآمَنُوا بِمَا نُزِّلَ عَلَى مُحَمَّدٍ وَهُوَ الْحَقُّ مِنْ رَبِّهِمْ كَفَّرَ عَنْهُمْ سَيِّئَاتِهِمْ وَأَصْلَحَ بَالَهُمْ

(Wa Al-Ladhīna 'Āmanū Wa `Amilū Aṣ-Ṣāliḥāti Wa 'Āmanū Bimā Nuzzila `Alá Muḥammadin Wa Huwa Al-ḥaqqu Min Rabbihim Kaffara `Anhum Sayyi'ātihim Wa 'Aṣlaḥa Bālahum).

Sahih International:

> "And those who believe and do righteous deeds and believe in what has been sent down upon Muḥammad - and it is the truth from their Lord - He will remove from them their misdeeds and amend their condition."

Pickthall:

   "… that, which is revealed unto Muḥammad - and it is the truth from their Lord …"

Yusuf Ali:

   "… the (Revelation) sent down to Muḥammad - for it is the Truth from their Lord,- .."

Shakir:

   "… what has been revealed to Muḥammad, and it is the very truth from their Lord, …"

Muḥammad Sarwar:

   "…what is revealed to Muḥammad - which is the Truth from his Lord.

Moḥsin Khan:

   "…that which is sent down to Muḥammad (SAW), for it is the truth from their Lord,…"

Arberry:

   "… what is sent down to Muḥammad -- and it is the truth from their Lord -- …"

*Qur'anic Arabic Corpus website (*http://corpus.quran .com/translation .jsp?*)*

Abdel Haleem:

   "…what has been sent down to Muḥammad — the truth from their Lord …

Wordpress.com   (https://islamiclegacy.files.wordpress.com/2018/07/translation-of-the-quran-by-m-a-s-abdel-haleem.pdf)

Maududi:

   As for those who believed, and did' good works, and accepted that which has been sent down to Muḥammad, <u>and it is the very Truth from their Lord-</u>"

englishtafsir.com (https://www.englishtafsir.com/Quran/6/index.html

Qur'an website (http://www.quranwebsite.com/read/reading tafsir english. html)

51

الٓمٓرٰ ۚ تِلْكَ آيَاتُ الْكِتَابِ ۗ وَالَّذِي أُنزِلَ إِلَيْكَ مِن رَّبِّكَ الْحَقُّ وَلَٰكِنَّ أَكْثَرَ النَّاسِ لَا يُؤْمِنُونَ ۩ *Alif-Lām-Mīm-Rā Tilka 'Āyātu Al-Kitābi Wa Al-Ladhī 'Unzila 'Ilayka Min Rabbika Al-ḥaqqu Wa Lakinna 'Akthara An-Nāsi Lā Yu'uminūna.*

52

الٓمٓ ۩ تَنزِيلُ الْكِتَابِ لَا رَيْبَ فِيهِ مِن رَّبِّ الْعَالَمِينَ ۩ أَمْ يَقُولُونَ افْتَرَاهُ ۚ بَلْ هُوَ الْحَقُّ مِن رَّبِّكَ لِتُنذِرَ قَوْمًا مَّا أَتَاهُم مِّن نَّذِيرٍ مِّن قَبْلِكَ لَعَلَّهُمْ يَهْتَدُونَ ۩ *'Alif-Lām-Mīm. Tanzīlu Al-Kitābi Lā Rayba Fīhi Min Rabbi Al-`Ālamīna. 'Am Yaqūlūna Aftarāhu Bal Huwa Al-ḥaqqu Min Rabbika Litundhira Qawmāan Mā 'Atāhum Min Nadhīrin Min Qablika La`allahum Yahtadūna. (Q. 32:1-3) Also see Q. 2:2.*

53

   "…that which is revealed unto Muḥammad - and it is the truth [howa 'l- Ḥaqq] from their Lord…"(Q. 47:2) "That is because God is The Truth [howa 'l- Ḥaqq]. Lo! He brings the dead back to life, He has power over things;" (Q. 22:6), (Abdel Haleem) "So it will be, because it is God alone who is The Truth [howa 'l- Ḥaqq], and whatever else they invoke is sheer falsehood (howa 'l -Bāṭil); it is God who is the Most High, the Most Great." (Q. 22:62), (Abdel Haleem) [Prophet], those who have been given knowledge can see that what has been sent to you from your Lord is the truth [howa 'l- Ḥaqq],…(Q. 34:6) "But your people (O Muḥammad SAW) have denied it (the Quran) though it is the truth [howa 'l- Ḥaqq]. Say: "I am not responsible for your affairs." (Q. 6:66) "Or they say, he has fabricated it! It [the Scripture] 'is the truth [howa 'l- Ḥaqq] from your Lord',..(Q. 32:3)

54

   ذَٰلِكَ بِأَنَّ الَّذِينَ كَفَرُوا اتَّبَعُوا الْبَاطِلَ وَأَنَّ الَّذِينَ آمَنُوا اتَّبَعُوا الْحَقَّ مِن رَّبِّهِمْ ۚ كَذَٰلِكَ يَضْرِبُ اللَّهُ لِلنَّاسِ أَمْثَالَهُمْ ۩ *Dhālika Bi'anna Al-Ladhīna Kafarū Attaba`ū Al-Bāṭila Wa 'Anna Al-Ladhīna 'Āmanū Attaba`ū Al-ḥaqqa Min Rabbihim Kadhālika Yaḍribu Allāhu Lilnnāsi 'Amthālahum.*

55

(i)   Allah's Word is the truth (*Qaulo hul ḥaqq*). cf. 06:73.

What Allah has revealed is the truth. (cf. 02: 42, 91)

al-ḥaqq (the truth) is from your Lord. (cf. 02:147, 03:60)

al-ḥaqq (the truth) is from the Lord. cf. 22:54.

Say: Al-ḥaqq is from the Lord of you all. Then whosoever will, let him believe, and whosoever will, let him disbelieve. cf. 18:29.

What Allah descends unto His Messenger is al-ḥaqq (the truth). cf. 5:83, 84, 11:120, 13:01, 19, 21:55.

The disbelievers denied the truth when it came unto them; cf. 06:05, 66; 08:31-32, 21:24.

Allah's Injunctions are al-ḥaqq (the truth): cf. 02:149, 33:53,

Al-ḥaqq will be the measure of weighing on the Day of Judgement, cf. 07:08.

The Prophet of Allah is the best knower of the truth in any matter. Those who prefer their own understanding, actually dispute with the Prophet on the truth. Cf. 08:06.

Only Allah leads to the truth. cf. 10:35.

The truth (i.e., Scripture, Guidance) comes from the Lord, 10: 76-77, 94, 108, 11:17, 28:48, 57:16;

The truth comes from the Lord and only disbelievers, the enemy of God and of believers, deny it. cf. 60:01

What Allah has promised concerning the Day of Judgement and Requital or anything else is the truth. cf. 11:45, 14:22, 18:21, 28:13, 30:60, 31:33, 35:05, 40:25, 77, 42:18, 46:17.

To be on the right; rightful. 24:49

When the verses of the Qur'an are recited unto the people of the Book, they say: We believe; it is the truth (al-ḥaqq) from our Lord. cf. 28:52-53.

Those who disbelieve say of the truth when it reaches them that it is naught other than mere magic. cf. 34:43, 46:07.

Word of the Lord (al-ḥaqq) revealed in the past testifies the Word of the Lord (al-ḥaqq) revealed in the present, and Word of the Lord revealed in the present witnesses the Word of the Lord revealed in the past. 02:41, 89, 91; 03:03; 06:05; 35:31; 37:37.

The truthful narration of a similitude by Allah in the Qur'an, cf. 02:26. Al-ḥaqq in the sense of truth of an event; 12:51.

[56] *For al-bāṭil as opposite to al-ḥaqq (the Qur'an or its teachings), see, 02:42, 109, 144, 146, 213; 07:118, 18:56, 40:78; to confound falsehood with the truth to conceal al-ḥaqq: cf. 03:71; similitude of al-ḥaqq and al-bāṭil: Allah compares Al-ḥaqq to rain water and al-bāṭil to the swelling foam that the flood water bears on it. Coming of the foam over the surface is proof of its passing away. Al-ḥaqq is to remain on the earth for it benefits the humankind; al-bāṭil is to pass away like foam that scum on the bank. cf. 13:17. Allah casts the truth against falsehood so that it breaks its head and lo! it vanishes. cf. 17:81, 21:18; Allah wipes out the falsehood and establishes the truth with His Words. cf. 42:24; When al-ḥaqq is practically established at some point, it becomes so manifest that it cannot be denied; it completely nullifies falsehood; the guilty, the hypocrites dislike it, cf. 08:08, 09:48, 10:82, 23:70. The truth has come; and falsehood neither produce nor reproduce. Neither was there any falsehood at the beginning of creation nor has it any scope to show it at the end. cf. 34:49. (This means that 'evil' has no permanent place in reality.) Bāṭil is only the opinion of those who disbelieve. cf. 38:27; The disbelieving people ever tried to refute Al-ḥaqq with false argument, but they failed, then Allah seized them. cf. 40:05; And on the Day when those who disbelieve are exposed to the Fire (they will be asked): Is not this real! They will say: Yea, by our Lord ... cf. 46:34. For al-ḥaqq as opposite to aḍ-ḍalāl (error) see: After The Truth what is there saving error! 10:32. (This further proves that 'evil'is nothing except deviation from The Truth. For al-ḥaqq as opposite to ẓann (false suspicion, conjecture) see, Al-ḥaqq as opposite to ẓann, see, 03:154, 45:32, and 10:35; also see: 'Assuredly conjecture can by no means take the place of truth.' cf. 10:36; 53:28.*

[57] *For elaborate study of almost all places where any derivative of the root ḥā-qaf-qāff occurs in the Qur'an to confirm that there is no justification for using the word 'al-ḥaqq' (The Truth) to refer to Allah see, Hafeez Fāzli, "Is Al-ḥaqq One of Al-Asmā' Al-Ḥusnā!", Ibid, 29-46; also see: ibid, The Qur'anic Ontology and Status of al-Haqq", Ibid, 47-58.*

[58] *At the back of this un-Qur'anic creed lie the acceptance of un-Qur'anic Greek ontology, and the intradeical interpretation of Platonic ideas. (Wolfson, Religious Philosophy, 42.) All the three verses Q. 22:6, 22:62 and Q. 31:30 are non-imperatival (mutashābih) in kind and are liable to be misinterpreted if not based on muhkamāt. Besides these two factors also lies a third factor of overlooking the accordance of the interpretation of these mutashabih verses with the muhkamāt. This un-Qur'anic creed gets strengthened further by waḥdat al-wujud school, an offshoot of the Ash'arite theology on spiritual direction. The belief that 'Al-ḥaqq' is one of al-Asmā' al-Ḥusnā and to identify Allah with 'Al-ḥaqq' as His preferred name, is one of the two fundamental presuppositions of the doctrine of waḥdat al-wajūd. The waḥdat al-wajūd school use Al-ḥaqq (The Truth) as Allah's Name for translating God into The Reality, and 'Absolute Reality', and for translating 'what is other than God and His attributes' as relative reality, half-reality, or temporal, ephemeral manifestation of Reality. Waḥdat al-wujud school also use it for translating God into The Truth, or The Absolute Truth. Seyyed Hossein Nasr, "The Qur'an and Ḥadīth as source and inspiration of Islamic Philosophy', History of Islamic Philosophy part-1", Seyyed Hossein Nasr and Oliver Leaman (eds.), (London: Routledge, 1996), 29; Frithjof Schuon, Dimensions of Islam, (tr. Townsend), (Lahore Pakistan: Suhail Academy, 1999), footnotes at 33, 48, 50. William C. Chittick, "Waḥdat al-Wujud In Islamic Thought", The Bulletin (Jan.- Mar. 1999), 8.*

[59] *Nasr, Seyyed Hossein, Ideals and Realities of Islam, (Lahore Pakistan: Suhail Academy,1999),15-16; also see 135 where Nasr says: Waḥdat al-wujud asserts that "only God is absolutely Real; everything else is relative." See also: Muhyi-d-dīn Ibn 'Arabi, The Wisdom of the Prophets (Fuṣuṣ al-Ḥikam) tr. Titus Burkhardt, (Lahore Pakistan: Suhail Academy, 1999), 139. Explaining the word 'al-ḥaqq' in the Glossary the translator says: "al-ḥaqq: The Truth or the Reality...". And in the first line of the first chapter the translator equates God to al-ḥaqq when he says: "God (al-ḥaqq) wanted to see the essences ..." 8.*

[60] *As rūḥ is of the things of Allah's amr (Q. 17:85) They are asking thee concerning the Spirit [rūḥ]. Say: The Spirit [rūḥ] is by command of my Lord, and of knowledge ye have been vouchsafed but little.(17:85) (Pickthall) Sharia (Divine law) too is of the things of Allah's amr. (Q. 45:18)*

[61] *Pickthall translates these verses in the following manner:*

"That is because Allah, He is the truth, and because He quickens the dead, and because He is Able to do all things." (Q. 22:6) "That is because Allah, He is the True, and that whereon they call instead of Him, it is the False, and because Allah, He is the High, the Great." (Q. 22:62) "That (is so) because Allah, He is the True, and that which they invoke beside Him is the False, and because Allah, He is the Sublime, the Great." (Q. 31:30).

At one place, he calls Allah, 'the truth' and at other places, he calls Him 'the True'. 'Truth' is the property of a proposition whereas it is a person who can be true! At times Pickthall identifies Allah with His Word at other times he treats Him as a Person!

[62] *Similarly the right rendering of verses Q. 6:62, Q. 10:30, Q. 10:32 and Q. 18:44 as per Qur'anic ontology prescribed by us, can be as follows:*

"Then they shall be brought back to Allah, their Real Master (Mawlāhumu al-ḥaqq). Be aware, He ordains and He is Most Expeditious in reckoning." (Q. 6:62) (TF)

"Here every soul will perceive the significance of what he/she had done in the past. And all shall be brought back to Allah, their true Lord (Mawlāhumu al-ḥaqq), and all the falsehood they had invented will then abandon them." (Q. 10:30) (TF)

"Such, then, is Allah, your true Sustainer (Allah-o-Rabbukum 'l Ḥaqq). What then remains 'after the truth' (Ba`da al-ḥaqqi) save error (aẓẓalāl)! Where, then, are you turning away!" (Q. 10:32) (TF)

"So it becomes clear that the Real Accomplisher of affairs is Allah (Al-Walāyatu Lillāhi al-ḥaqqi). He is Best for reward, and Best for consequence." (Q. 18:44) (TF)

"Then exalted be Allah, the True King (Al-Mālik al-ḥaqq)! And hasten not (O Muḥammad) with the Qur'an ere its revelation hath been perfected unto thee, and say: My Lord! Increase me in knowledge." (Q. 20:114) (Pickthall)

"So Exalted is Allah, the Real King (Al-Mālik al-ḥaqq). There is no god but He. The Lord of the glorious throne." (Q. 23:116) (TF)

[63] *In verses Q. 24:22-24 preceding 24:25 Allah says that those who falsely accuse chaste women are cursed in this world as well as the Hereafter. On that Day Allah will give their own tongues, hands and feet the ability to talk and these will bear witness against them concerning their evil deeds. At verse 8 of Surah Al-A'raf 7 Allah says that al-ḥaqq (the Qur'an) will be the measure of weighing on the Day of Judgement for the purpose of Requital. Now in verse 24:25 Allah says that on that Day Allah will pay them what they really deserve, and they will come to know that Allah is the true Manifester of the piety of the virtuous women whom they had caused humiliation and disgrace by making malicious and false statements, and also that He is the true Manifester of al-ḥaqq (the Perfect in Justice) by giving the evil-doers their just due.*

[64] *Dr. Qazi Abdul Qadir, Kashhaf-e Iṣṭilaḥāt-e (Urdu-English), (Karachi: Shu'ba Talīf o Tarjama Karachi University, 1994), 239.*

[65] *Nelson Pike, God and Timelessness, (London: Routledge & Kegan Paul, 1970), ix-x.*

[66] *Richard Swinburne, The Coherence of Theism, (Oxford: Clarendon Press, 1977), 217.*

[67] *'al-Dahr' [Time] occurs twice in the Qur'an at Q. 45:24 and Q. 76:1 and nowhere it denotes Allah. Interpretation of a ḥadīth, which identifies Allah with Time, or the other way round, contradicts with the muḥkamāt of the Qur'an. Hafeez Fāzli, "Iqbal's View of Omniscience and Human Freedom", Ibid, 173.*

[68] *A. H. Fāzli, The Qur'anic Theology, Philosophy and Spirituality, Pp9,10, 125, and 248.*

[69] *Aristotelian philosophy conceives perfection as immutability. No change in God's knowledge whatsoever is possible. Admitting knowledge of particulars for God will introduce change in His knowledge and contradict with absolute perfection of God perceived in the perspective of Aristotelian philosophy. There is no concept of 'absolute perfection' as Divine attribute in Islam, as perceived in the Aristotelian sense. Fazli, 'The Qur'anic View of Omniscience and Human Freedom', 125.*

70 *Swinburne, Richard. The Coherence of Theism, 217*

[71] *Hafeez Fāzli, "Introduction" in The Qur'anic Theology…, 13-14.*

[72] *Q. 12:95, 36:39, 46:12.*

[73] *Plotinus argues that Allah is too great, high and perfect to be expressed, described, praised in words or called upon by any Name. No Name matches His dignity, majesty and grandeur. This is known as the doctrine of the ineffability of God. As is clear it is un-Qur'anic. Allah narrates His own Goodly Names (al-Asmā' al-Ḥusna) in the Qur'an and ordains to call upon Him by these Goodly Names. Hafeez Fāzli, "The Qur'anic view of omniscience and human freedom", 127-28 and 'Christian view of Omniscience and human freedom' 150-52 in The Qur'anic Theology, Philosophy and Spirituality.*

[74] *W.K.C. Guthrie, A History of Greek Philosophy Vol.1 The earlier Presocratics and the Pythagoreans, Cambridge: Cambridge University Press, 1962, 12. Also, cf. Dr. Naeem Ahmad, Tarikh e Falsfa-e Yunaan, (Urdu) Lahore: Ilmi Kitab Khana, 2005, 145.*

[75] *A doctrine of becoming, which perceives God as Absolute Existence and perceives the universe as its manifestation, remaining consistent with its premises, cannot perceive the universe as created and contingent. Similarly, a universe coming into being as a process of emanation can neither be contingent nor ex nihilo.*

[76] *Altaie, The Divine Word And The Grand Design: Interpreting the Qur'an in the Light of Science, UK: Beacon Books, 2019, 163.*

[77] *Richard Swinburne, The Coherence of Theism Oxford, Clarendon Press, 1977, 217.*

[78] *Fāzli, H.A. The Qur'anic Theology, Philosophy and Spirituality, 101-224. This book contains eight articles on various dimensions of the problem of predestination with reference to the Ash'arite theology*

including one article with reference to Christian theologians and philosophers' view on divine omniscience and human freedom. 'Introduction' of this contain valuable elaboration of these concepts, too. Also see, Hafeez Fazli, "Fateh Ullah Gullen ka Nazriya-e-Taqdīr" in Muslim Fiker ki Qur'ani Jihāt, [Urdu], (Lahore: PU Press, 2018), 93-122.

[79] *It took around fourteen centuries after Aristotle when al-Ghazali (1058–1111) reconstructed the notion of 'Allah's Volition' as a capacity to freely choose one, out of two absolutely identical possibilities without any principle of particularization / preference and showed that the concept of 'volition' was absolutely compatible with the perfection of the Qur'anic God and a sign of His Dignity and Majesty. He also pointed out other inconsistencies in Ibn-e-Sina's philosophy that arose as an implication of accepting Aristotle's concept of 'cause'. However, most of the Muslim theologians, the Qur'an scholars, translators and exegetes are still unaware of it. Hafeez Fazli, "Ibn Sina, al-Ghazali and Ibn Taymiyyah on the Origination of the World", The Qur'anic Theology, Philosophy and Spirituality, 247-267.*

[80] *Cf. Simon Van Den Berg (tr.), "Introduction" in Averoes, Tahafut Al-Tahafut (The Incoherence of the Incoherence), Vol. I, (London Lozac & Co, 1954), xix.*

[81] *Hafeez Fāzli, "H. A. Wolfson and A. H. Kamali on the Origin of the Problem of Divine Attributes in Muslim Kalām", in The Qur'anic Theology …228-29.*

[82] *Wolfson, "Extradeical and Intradeical Interpretation of Platonic Ideas", Religious Philosophy: A Group of Essays, 42.*

[83] *Hafeez Fāzli, The Qur'anic Theology, Philosophy and Spirituality. Also see Urdu book: Abdul Hafeez Fazli, Muslim Fiker ki Qur'ani Jihāt, (Lahore: PU Press, 2018), Pakistan.*

[84] *Wolfson, Religious Philosophy: A Group of Essays, 31.*

[85] *Ibid, 42-43.*

[86] *Abdul Hameed Kamali, "Mahiyat-e-Khud Agahi aur Khudi ki Tashkeel" (Urdu), Iqbal Review : July1963, (Lahore: Iqbal Academy Pakistan), 4*

[87] *Hafeez Fazli, "Ibn Sina, al-Ghazali and Ibn Taimiyya on the Origination of the World", p 252, 258, 282*

[88] *A.H. Kamali, ibid*

[89] *Problem of the relationship of Divine Essence and Attributes, and of the Createdness vs. Eternity of the Qur'an are two instances of such a kind of problems.*

[90] *Abu al-Hassan al-Alvi, "Nazriya-e-Waḥdat al-Wujud and Dr. Israr Ahmad", Mohaddith Forum Online, April 26, 2012. Accessed March, 2019.*

[91] *ibid*

[92] *Ibid*

[93] *Nasr, Ideals and Realities of Islam, 128.*

[94] *Iqbal considers that if this metaphor of Light is taken to suggest the omnipresence of God instead of His absoluteness, it is liable to a pantheistic interpretation. Therefore, Iqbal takes it as referring to the absoluteness of God. Iqbal, Reconstruction of Religious Thought in Islam, 51. However, the metaphor of light in this verse refers neither to God nor to His absoluteness, nor to His omnipresence even. This interpretation suits Iqbal because he conceives God as all-inclusive and immanent. Otherwise, this interpretation is not coherent with the Imperatival Verses (muhkamāt) of the Qur'an nor accords with the Qur'anic ontology. Hafeez Fazli, "Iqbal's View of Omniscience and Human Freedom", in Ibid, p167-68.*

Attributes of Allah are real but not in the sense conceived by traditional Muslim theologians and waḥdat-al-wujudi sufis following Aristotle. The universe neither is the manifestation of the Being of God (ذات/Person), nor of His Attributes. In both cases, it will imply sheer waḥdat al-wujud and make everything the temporal and ephemeral appearance of absolute existence/wujud-e-muṭliq (i.e., Allah). The universe (khalq and amr both) is the manifestation of the activity of Allah's al-Asmā al-Ḥusnā (The Goodly Names). Allah ordains the believers to call upon Him by His Goodly Names. Allah, nowhere in the Qur'an, has talked about His Own Holy Person in terms of the word Ṣifa (Attributes).

[95] *The Qur'an has also been called Nūr because it is Allah's sent guidance.* *Q. 64:8.*

[96] *Light (Nur) is one of the Goodly Names of Allah as there are other Names. The Qur'an says: Allah has created the heavens and the earth and whatever therein is in six days. Light, as a physical phenomenon, is part of it. Then how can it be a symbol for the absolute?*

[97] 'Have these people [of Mecca] not travelled through the land with hearts to understand [ya'qilūna] and ears to hear? It is not people's eyes that are blind, but their hearts within their breasts' Q. 22:46. *(Abdel Haleem)*

[98] Those who follow their desires go astray. (Q: 18:28; 25:43; 45:23;...) There reason ('aql) go blind. *(Q, 22:46)*

[99] *The holy person of the Prophet (pbuh) has been likened to a Lamp that gives light (Sirājan Munīran). Q. 33:46.*

[100] *Haḍrat Fazal Shah and Muhammad Ashraf Fazli, Tafseer-e-Fazli vol. 7, 139.*

[101] *Hafeez Fāzli, Iqbal's View of Omniscience and Human Freedom, Ibid, 173. Also see Urdu article, Hafeez Fāzli, "Kiya Allah Ad-Dahr Hai!", Muslim Fiker ki Qur'ani Jihāt, (Lahore: PU Press, 2018) 133-147.*

[102] *Iqbal, Ibid, note by editor at 160.*

[103] *Ibid, 46.*

[104] For detailed study of this point, please see section "Iqbal's Conception of Time and its Identification with God" in the last chapter.

[105] *Allah Almighty says:* "We shall make sure of its safe collection and recitation." *(Q. 75:17)*

[106] "We have sent down the Quran Ourself, and We Ourself will guard it." *(Q. 15:9) (TF vol.3)*

[107] *Whose veracity and trustworthiness had already been witnessed by the Prophet (pbuh) as they were from among the 'Ten Witnessed Ones' ('ashra-e-mubashra); then attested by the chain of witnessed successors (shāhidīn) of these shāhidīn till today.*

[108] *For detailed study of some such alleged instances, see Urdu book, Hafeez. Fāzli, Muslim Fiker ki Qur'ani Jihāt, 46-51*

[109] *In most of the translations and exegeses, this difference is not made clear, with the result that the individuals or groups on their own assume the obligation or authority that vests in the Ūlil-Amr (the administrator / administration) for the Implementation of a certain Divine commandment, which results in schism in the society.*

[110] *Sheikh-ul-Islam Dr. Muhammad Tahir al-Qadri, Taghayyir-e-Zamān sey Ijtehādi Aḥkām mein Riāyat awr Tabdīli,* (تغیّر زمان سے اجتہادی احکام میں رعایت اور تبدیلی), *36-72. Dr. Muhammad Tahir al-Qadri states various instances of the same in this book. He also states various instances of ijtehād concerning a Sunnah of the Prophet (pbuh) by His rightly guided successors (r.a.).*

[111] *Paradigms, which confine a Qur'anic word to its 'lexical meaning' and the statement to its syntactical purport (mafhoom) taking the Qur'anic text in the style of 'Writing'.*

[112] "God has been truly gracious to the believers in sending them a Messenger from among their own, to recite His revelations to them, to make them grow in purity, and to teach them the Scripture and wisdom— before that they were clearly astray." *(Q. 3:164) (Abdel Haleem)*

[113] *The Compilation of the Qur'an in Perspective - Answering Islam, https://www.answering-islam.org/Gilchrist/Jam/chap6.html. Accessed: Jan 10, 2023.*

[114] *Sam Shamoun, "The Seven Ahruf and Multiple Qiraat – A Qur'anic Perspective", https://www.answering-islam.org/authors/ shamoun/ ahruf_ quirat.html. Accessed: Jan 10, 2023.*

[115] *If a noun occurs as singular in the Universal Reading, it may occur as dual or plural in any variant reading; if a noun occurs as masculine in the Universal Reading, it may occur as the opposite gender in any other reading.*

[116] *The Qur'an says about such people:*

فَوَيْلٌ لِّلَّذِينَ يَكْتُبُونَ الْكِتَابَ بِأَيْدِيهِمْ ثُمَّ يَقُولُونَ هَذَا مِنْ عِندِ اللَّهِ... فَوَيْلٌ لَهُمْ مِمَّا كَتَبَتْ أَيْدِيهِمْ

🏛 (البقره2: 79)

"So woe to those who write the "scripture" with their own hands, then say, "This is from Allah ," in order to exchange it for a small price. Woe to them for what their hands have written and woe to them for what they earn." Sahih International: https://corpus.quran. com/ translation. jsp? chapter= 2&verse=79

[117] *Maulana Mufti Muhammad Shafi', Ma'arif ul Qur'an, Eng. tr. by Prof. M. Hassan Askari, Karachi: Maktaba-e-Darul Ulum, 1995, 14-15.*

[118] *Keeping this in view, why the Farahi school admits the doctrine of abrogation?*

[119] *In 1977, the name of Libya was changed to Socialist People's Libyan Arab Jamahiriya. Jamahiriya was a term coined by Gaddafi, usually translated as "state of the masses". The country was renamed again in 1986 as the Great Socialist People's Libyan Arab Jamahiriya, after the United States bombing that year. This version of the Variant Reading as been published by Libya.*

[120] *These versions are published by **Majma' al-Malik Fahd /King Fahd** Complex for the Printing of the Holy Quran based at Medina, and are available on their websites and archives, at www.qurancomplex .org - King Fahd Complex For Printing The Holy Quran Website. See also, https://dm.qurancomplex.gov.sa/en/*

[121] *Captain® Muhammad Siddique, Al-Qur'an il Karim Ki Qirā'ati Teḥrif (القرآن الكريم کی قراءتی تحریف), Karachi, 2018, 07. Captain® Muhammad Siddique has indexed copies of the relevant record in his book.*

[122] *www.qurancomplex .org - King Fahd Complex For Printing The Holy Quran Website. See also, https://dm.qurancomplex.gov.sa/en/, https://rushdjournal.com/index.php/rushd*

[123] *https://en.wikipedia.org/wiki/ King_Fahd_Complex_for_the_ Printing _of_the_Holy_Quran.*

[124] *Dr Shezad Saleem, History of the Qur'an: A Critical Study, (Lahore: Al-Mawrid, 2nd edition), 1180.*

[125] *Dr Shehzad Saleem observes that the collection history of the Qur'an has generally been compiled only on the basis of historical reports found in Ḥadīth anthologies instead of being compiled on the account given in the Qur'an on its own collection. He further observes that tools of historical criticism have not been fully employed to evaluate the content acquired from Ḥadīth anthologies with the result that far-reaching conclusions were at times drawn from data having questionable reliability. The third thing that has marred the value of previous works on this topic, is that the readings of the Qur'an [i.e. the variant readings] have been regarded acceptable along with its reading transmitted by certain (qat'ī) means against the verdict of the Qur'an itself. Dr Shehzad Saleem refers to the Muslim scholars' attitude of veneration toward akḥbār-I ahād (isolate reports) reported from or ascribed to the Prophet (pbuh). Thus, many scholars, instead of critically examining the historicity of the narratives based on these isolate reports, accepted these narratives even if they were not satisfied by their content and contentions. Dr Shehzad Saleem, History of the Qur'an: A Critical Study, 1179.*

[126] *'Creation of God' as compared to 'Work of God' presupposes Allah's Will and Command.*

[127] *Hoodbhoy, Islam and Science: Religious Orthodoxy and the Battle for Rationality, (London: ZED Books, 1991), 14-15.*

[128] *Ontology investigates the ultimate principles of reality. This is why one definition of metaphysics is 'doing ontology'. As per scientific ontology, the universe is a material universe (inter-convertible with energy) running according to laws of nature (laws of quantum mechanics being their latest manifestation). Religious and philosophical cosmology both deal with God-universe relationship, nature and structure of the universe etc. Since scientific ontology knows no god and has no role of god in its system, according to NASA, Cosmology: The Study of the Universe. 6 3, 2011 https://map.gsfc.nasa.gov /universe /WMAP_ Universe. pdf (7 28, 2019), modern science conceives cosmology as "a scientific study of the large scale properties of the universe as a whole. It uses the scientific method to understand the origin, evolution and ultimate fate of the entire universe. Like any field of science, modern scientific cosmology involves the formation of theories or hypotheses concerning the universe, which make specific empirically testable*

predictions about the phenomena. Depending on the outcome of the observations, the theories will need to be abandoned, revised or extended to accommodate the data. The prevailing theory about the origin and evolution of our Universe is known as the Big Bang theory.'

[129] Occasionalism, as predecessor of modern Muslim cosmology, is the most extreme form of interventionism, which neither admits the existence of enduring nature (fitrah) of things nor any stable and permanent laws of nature nor any objective existence of physical things and the universe.

[130] In the Battle of the Trench (also known as battle of the Confederates), approving the suggestion of Haḍrat Salman Fārsi (r.a.), the Prophet (pbuh) commanded the excavation of a trench around Madinah as a defence plan against the Arab confederates who were coming to launch a war against Muslims at Madinah. By giving approval to Haḍrat Salman Fārsi's suggestion, the Prophet (pbuh) taught His followers to make use of time-tested beneficial human knowledge within the Qur'anic parameters. In the Battle of Badr, the Prophet (pbuh) approving the suggestion of a companion (r.a.), shifted his camp to a place situated near water resource but the Prophet (pbuh) did not abandon the enemies from taking water as suggested by that companion (r.a.). Naeem Ahmad, Ayyam-e-Habib (Urdu), (Lahore: Ch. Muhammad Ayyub, 2004), 579.

[131] Fāzli, 'Introduction' in The Qur'anic Theology…, 21. Rahbaniyyat (monastic asceticism) was an innovation (bid'at) of the Christians; Allah did not enjoin it on them. They had initiated it with the purpose of seeking Allah's pleasure. [Allah does not disapprove of it.] They could not confine themselves within viable limits, as they should. (Q. 57:27) Let us see an instance of innovation:

'And proclaim the pilgrimage among men: they will come to thee on foot and (mounted) on every kind of camel, lean on account of journeys through deep and distant mountain highways.' (Q. 22:27)

Can the Muslims go on hajj as stated in this verse now? This is Bidat-e-hasana and now we go by air to act upon this injunction.

Stoning of the images of the devil (rami jamâr) is an essential component of Hajj. For centuries, people have been performing this ritual from sunrise until midday on 10th of Zil Hajj, and from midday till sunset on 11th and 12th of Zil Hajj. Though no Divine Injunction existed as to this effect, yet it had been a practice since centuries. With too much increase in the number of pilgrims, it did not remain possible for all to perform this ritual within these time limits. Since a few years the time for the performance of this ritual has been extended to the whole day i.e., from sunrise until sunset all the three days.

[132] Abu 'L-Hasan 'Ali Ibn Isma'il Al-Ash'ari, Al- Ibanah an Usul Ad-Diyanah, Eng. tr. The Elucidation of Islam's Foundation by Walter C. Klein. 66, 67, 76.

[133] The originated ontological categories of amr and khalq suggested by the Qur'an must not be confounded with ālam al-amr (celestial world) and ālam al-khalq (terrestrial world) of the Muslim waḥdat al-wujud Sufism, which they have accepted under the impress of Greeks and confirmed in their mystic experience.

[134] Cf. Haḍrat Fazal Shah and Muhammad Ashraf Fazli, Tafseer Fazli vol.5, Eng. tr. Ed. Abdul Hafeez, (Lahore: Fazli Foundation, 2015), 187, 292.

[135] The Qur'an says: " --- وَكَذَلِكَ أَنزَلْنَاهُ حُكْماً عَرَبِيّاً" (Wa Kadhalika 'Anzalnāhu Ḥukmāan `Arabīyāan) "And thus have We revealed this Judgement of Authority in Arabic." (Q. 13:37) With reference to its ontological status, the Qur'an too, belongs to the category of Allah's Command. It does not belong to the category of 'creation' (khalq). Hafeez Fāzli, "The Qur'an: Creation or Command!" 61-70.

[136] "Since the publication of the English translation of his book, La Bible, le Coran et la Science (1976) as The Bible, the Qur'an and Science (1978), [by] Bucaille …several studies have been devoted to 'prove' the divine origin of the Qur'an on the basis that the Qur'an contains certain scientific facts, which were unknown to humanity at the time of its revelation… [However,] Bucaille does not state that the Qur'an is a book of science, but that modern science can clarify and give the full meaning of certain verses of the Qur'an. He offers a very fruitful idea in his writings that 'established scientific facts' should be distinguished from 'scientific theories'. He is sure of the divine origin of the Qur'an when he asserts that an 'established

scientific fact' has never contradicted with the Qur'an, nor shall it contradict it ever." This is a very important point.

Also, see, Hafeez Fāzli, "Evolving a Qur'anic Paradigm …" 303. Review article by Muzaffar Iqbal on Leif Stenberg, The Islamization of Science : Four Muslim Positions, Developing an Islamic Modernity, (New York: Coronet Books, 1996), 240.

[137] *It is evident from his writings that Imam Ghazali firmly believed that the truth and the untruth could never be reconciled. He believed that any attempt at such a thing would necessarily give rise to contradictions. He wrote* Tahafatul Falasifa (Incoherence of the Philosophers) *in which he critically examined twenty selected problems from Al-Farabi and Ibn Sina's works and argued that*

(i) Either the very principles i.e., premises, on the basis of which, they reached their conclusions were wrong; or

(ii) In case the premises were correct, they had violated the principles of logic, which they themselves proclaimed; so the conclusions were incorrect.

(iii) If the conclusions stated by them were correct, these do not follow from their premises.

Imam Ghazali held that on sixteen out of these twenty problems the Muslim philosophers can be exonerated but they cannot be given leave on the remaining four problems, of deviation from established Islamic beliefs, which are as follows:

(1) The problem of the eternity of the world; (2) The problem of the denial of God's Knowledge of particulars; (3) The problem of the denial of miracles; (4) The problem of the denial of bodily resurrection."

Hafeez Fāzli, "Ibn Sina, "al-Ghazali and Ibn Taymiyyah on the Origination of the World", ibid, 251-71.

[138] *Newton (1642-1726 AD) is widely recognized as one of the most influential scientists of all times and a key figure in the scientific revolution. With the publication of his book Mathematical Principles of Natural Philosophy in 1687, he laid the foundations of 'classical mechanics'. 'The Newtonian mechanics' remained the dominant worldview till it was superseded by the worldview based on 'the special theory of relativity' in 1905 and on general theory of relativity in 2015.*

[139] *Cf. Muhammad Khalid Masud, "Iqbal's Approach to Islamic Theology of Modernity" Al-Hikmat (Research Journal of the Dept. of Philosophy, PU, Lahore, Pakistan 2007), 12.*

[140] *Allama Muhammad Iqbal, Reconstruction of Religious Thought in Islam, ed. & annotation, M. Saeed Sheikh, 1, 48-50. Also see, Basit Bilal Koshul, "Muhammad Iqbal's reconstruction of the philosophical arguments for the existence of God" in Muhammad Iqbal: A Contemporary, (edt.) Muhammad Suhail Umar and Basit Bilal Koshul, Lahore: Iqbal Academy Pakistan, 2010, 127.*

[141] *A. H. Fāzli, "Evolving a Qur'anic Paradigm…" Ibid, 284-295. Also, Fāzli, "Kiya Allah ad-Dahar hay!" (Urdu) [Is God Time!], Muslim Fiker ki Qur'ani Jihāt, 129-144.*

[142] *Sir Syed Ahmad Khan's Rational Supernaturalism is a typical example of un-Qur'anic ontology on Mu'tazilites' lines.*

[143] *Q. 2:153, 194; Q. 9:40; Q. 29:69 etc.*

[144] *If birth cannot take place without the means of a father or a mother, then how did the birth of Adam (pbuh), the first man, take place? Allah Almighty created Adam from clay and then He said, 'Be!' and he came into existence. Allah creates with means as well as without means.*

[145] *Ibn Arabi, Ibn Taimiyyah and Dr. Israr Ahmad and too many others hold the universe to be the manifestation of Divine attributes. This view provides basis to the doctrine of Waḥdat al-Wujud. However, Ibn Taimiyyah is a critic of Ibn al-'Arabi, his own view is tantamount to holding the universe as a manifestation of the activity of Divine attributes. For Ibn Taimiyya's doctrine of the universe as 'continuity of effects of Divine attributes' (doctrine of 'Tasalsal bil Āthār' نظریہ تسلسل بالآثار) See, A. H. Fazli, "Ibn Sina, Al-Gazali And Ibn Taymiyyah On The Origination Of The World", Ibid, 262. Also see: Muhammad Hanif Nadvi, Aqliyāt-e Ibn Tamiya, [Speculations of Ibn Taymiyyah] Lahore: Institute of Islamic Culture, Second*

reprint 2001,196. Also, see, Ibid, "Ibn Taimiya ka Tasawar-e Sifat", (Urdu) Pakistan Philosophical Journal, Vol. January 1962, Pakistan Philosophical Congress, Club Road Lahore, 45-46. Muhammad Hanif Nadvi develops Ibn-e Tamiyah's doctrine of the continuity of effects with reference to pages 71, 72, 188, 189, 190, 201, 209 of Ibn Tamiyah's Ar-Rasala tut Tadmuriyyah published by Husainiya of Egypt. Year of publishing is not given.

For Ibn al-Arabi and Dr. Israr Ahmad's doctrines of Divine attributes see, Abu al-Hassan al-Alvi, "Nazriya-e-Waḥdat al-Wujud and Dr. Israr Ahmad", Mohaddith Form Online, Placed on 26.4.2012 and accessed on 25.3.2019. Al-Alvi presents a very good summary of Haḍrat Ibn al-'Arabi and of Dr. Israr Ahmad's views on waḥdat al-wujud in this Urdu article.

Abu al-Hassan Alvi considers the descensions (tanazzalāt) from Allah's attribute of Kalām (Speech) in Dr. Israr Ahmad as compared to the view of descensions by way of Allah's attribute of Knowledge ('ilm) in Shaikh Ibn al-'Arabi, as the essential difference between the two versions of waḥdat al-wujud. (Abu al-Hassan al-Alvi, "Nazriya-e-Waḥdat al-Wujud and Dr. Israr Ahmad", Mohaddith Form Online, placed: on 26.4.2012, accessed on 25.3.2019.

[146] Osman Bakar, "The Atomistic Conception of Nature in Ash'arite Theology" in Tawhid and Science, 77-103. http://www .allamaiqbal. com /publications/journals/review/oct91/2.htm. Accessed: 7/18/2019. Besides Bakar one more, good account of this theory can be seen in M. Basil Altaie, "Creation and the Personal Creator in Islamic Kalam and Modern Cosmology", Humanity, 149-166.

[147] Osman Bakar, "The Atomistic Conception of Nature…", Ibid

[148] Altaie, "Creation and the Personal Creator…", Ibid, 151.

[149] Altaie states that, H. A. Wolfson in his The Philosophy of the Kalam, 149-166, gives a modern analysis and discussion of this principle. He also states that a very good account of this principle can be found in al-Juwayni, al-shamil Fi Usul al-Deen. Altaie, ibid, 154.

[150] Altaie, "Creation and the Personal Creator…" Ibid.

[151] Bakar, ibid. However, they believe principles of their cosmology as derived from the teachings of the Qur'an. This is why al-Baqillani, as already stated in some other chapter, and other fellow theologians transformed the doctrinal status of this 'theory of nature', from being a mere premise in support of specific religious beliefs, to an essential part of the Ash'arite creed.

[152] Hafeez Fāzli, "The Qur'anic Ontology and Status of al-ḥaqq", Ibid, 49-60; also Hafeez Fazli, "The Qur'an: Creation or Command!" Ibid, 61-70.

[153] Al-Ash'ari, Al- Ibanah an Usul Ad-Diyanah, Eng. tr. 66, 67, 76

[154] Bakar, 'The Atomistic Conception of Nature…'

[155] Haḍrat Fazal Shah, Muhammad Ashraf Fazli, Tafseer-e-Fazli, 7 vols. (Lahore: Fazli Foundation, 1985-1998) according to our knowledge, is 'the first ever complete Tafseer of the Qur'an accomplished on the Qur'anic principles of its interpretation.' The translation of verses given in this article is mostly taken from it or from the English translation of its six volumes published so far.

[156] Hafeez Fāzli, "The Qur'anic Ontology and Status of Al-Haqq", Ibid, 50-51.

[157] He decided to create the heavens and the earth in six days, as per His Knowledge. He will bring everything to naught with a single command within no time. The Day of Judgement will commence with a single command of His and all humankind will come out of their graves instantaneously. (Q. 25:25, 69:14, 78:40)

[158] This analogy is to have a crude idea only; about the amr (command) Allah says you have been but given a little knowledge only (Q. 17:85), and man's knowledge will ever remain little about it.

[159] Some of which are as follows: Q. 2:98, Q. 81:20, and Q. 53:5-6, Q. 43:77 etc. Q. 69:17, Q. 4:36 etc.

[160] "And before Solomon were organised his hosts- of Jinns and men and birds, and they were all kept in order and ranks." Q. 27.17.

[161] *Chad Orzel, "Six Things Everyone Should Know About Quantum Physics", 2015,7.8.2015, https://www.forbes.com/sites /chadorzel/ 2015/07/08/six-things-everyone-should-know-about-quantum-physics/ #8922ca7d4672 Accessed: 6.7.2017.*

[162] *G. F. Hourani, "The dialogue between Al-Ghazali and the philosophers on the origin of the world", part-I, in The Muslim World, vol.48 Issue 4(1958), 308.*

[163] *Ibid, 183; also see Hafeez Fāzli, "Ibn Sina, al-Ghazali and Ibn Taymiyyah on the Origination of the World" in Ibid, 9.*

[164] *Altaie, ibid, 164.*

[165] *Al-Qur'an, (02:2-3)*

[166] *"These two philosophers were Aristotelian. They were also Neoplatonists who had formulated two closely related but quite distinct emanative schemes. There are, moreover, differences between these two thinkers, not only in their emanative schemes, but also in their theories of the soul, epistemologies, and eschatologies. At the same time, however, there ideas overlap with each other, so that many of al-Ghazali's criticisms apply to both." Michael E. Marmura (tr.), "Translator's Introduction" in The Incoherence of the Philosophers, (Eng. tr. of Ghazali's Tahafut al-Falasfa), Provo, Utah: Brigham Young University Pmsi, 2000, xix.*

[155] *Claudius Ptolemy c. AD 90 – c. AD 168, was a Greek-Roman citizen of Egypt. He was a renowned mathematician, astronomer, geographer, astrologer, and poet.*

[168] *For Geocentric universe of Aristotle and Ptolemy see: http://www.cartage.org.lb/en/ themes/sciences/ mainpage.htm)*

[169] *For details and references, please see, Hafeez Fazli, "Ibn Sina, al-Ghazali and Ibn Taymiyyah on the Origination of the World", The Qur'anic Theology, Philosophy and Spirituality, 247-49.*

[170] *cf. The Physics of the Universe: Cosmological theories through history, http://physicsof the universe.com /cosmological.html*

[171] *"While naturalism has often been equated with materialism, it is much broader in scope. …Strictly speaking, naturalism has no ontological preference; i.e., no bias toward any particular set of categories of reality: dualism and monism, atheism and theism, idealism and materialism are all per se compatible with it. So long as all of reality is natural, no other limitations are imposed.' 'Naturalists point out that even when one scientific theory is abandoned in favour of another, man does not despair of knowing nature, nor does he repudiate the "natural method" in his search for truth. Theories change; methodology does not." (http://www.britannica.com/ EBchecked/ topic/ 406468/naturalism, last updated 9.11.2013)*

[172] *"Verily Allah keeps the heavens and the earth in place lest they leave their places. If they move from their places, no one can grasp them. Allah is Ever Most Forbearing, Oft-Forgiving." (35:41)*

[173] *"Naturalism did not exist as a philosophy before the nineteenth century, but only as an occasionally adopted and non-rigorous method among natural philosophers. It is a unique philosophy in that it is not ancient or prior to science, and that it developed largely due to the influence of science. Naturalism begins with Galileo and Isaac Newton, who began to explain nature by theoretical and experimental descriptions of matter and their motions. The outstanding success of this method led others to emulate them, and a comprehensive understanding of the universe was initiated. Galileo and Newton were not naturalists; they did not hesitate to attribute supernatural causes to things that they thought could not be explained by natural causes. Until the late eighteenth century, most scientists agreed with them, but the influence of the Enlightenment led scientists, such as Antoine Laurent Lavoisier, Pierre Simon de Laplace, and James Hutton to abandon all supernatural explanations in favour of natural ones. Biology was the last science to be so treated, by Jean Baptiste Lamarck and Charles Darwin. I am convinced that each of these men intentionally tried to be the Newton of his day--and science--by finding purely natural laws to explain natural processes and objects." "Naturalism is Today An Essential Part of Science", Conference paper by Prof. Steven D. Schafersman, at http://www.stephenjaygould.org/ ctrl/ schafersman nat.html. Accessed: August 04, 2022.*

[174] *Cf. Space-time in Encyclopaedia Britannica* http://www. Britannica .com/EBchecked/topic/557482/space-time *Last updated 19.2.13)*

[175] *Cf. (http://www.skwirk.com/p-c_s-4_u-138_t-400_c-1407/ einstein-s-theory-of-relativity-/nsw/einstein-s-theory-of-relativity-/the-big-bang-and-our-universe/the-origin-of-the-universe*

[176] *Science and Religion (1941), http://atheism.about.com/od/ einsteingodreligion/ a/ GodNature.htm*

[177] *Basit Bilal Koshul, "Muhammad Iqbal's reconstruction of the philosophical arguments for the existence of God" in Muhammad Iqbal: A Contemporary, 127.*

[178] *Ibid*

[179] *Ibid, 96.*

[180] *Ibid*

[181] *Allama Muhammad Iqbal, Reconstruction of Religious Thought in Islam, ed. & annotation, M. Saeed Sheikh (Lahore: Institute of Islamic Culture, reprint 1986), 1, 49.*

[182] *cf., ibid, 48-50.*

[183] *Abdul Hafeez, "Iqbal's View of Omniscience and Human Freedom", The Muslim World, vol. 95, Number 1, January 2005, 125-45, Hartford Seminary 77 Sherman Street Hartford CT 06105 USA*

[184] *Muhammad Khalid Masud, "Iqbāl's Approach to Islamic Theology of Modernity", Al-Hikmat, 27(2007), 12.*

[185] *For seeing, 'What a Qur'anicaly informed scientific study of nature could genuinely mean! See Abdul Hafeez, "Ibn Sina, Al-Ghazali and Ibn Taimiyyah on the Origination of the World", International Journal of Humanities and Religion, Vol 2, No 1 (2013), 27.*

[186] *Koshul, ibid, 110.*

[187] *Iqbal, Reconstruction ..., 8.*

[188] *Muhammad Iqbal: A Contemporary, 110.*

[189] *Koshul, ibid, 110.*

[190] *Iqbal, Reconstruction..., 46-7.*

[191] *Ṣaḥīḥ Muslim Sharif, (Urdu version) trans. Allama Waheed uz Zamān, Lahore: Mushtaq Book Corner Urdu Bazar, 1995, 421-22.*

[192] *Some Qur'an scholars divide the same holy text into 6236 verse and according to some it is divisible into 6238. But there is no difference as to the Holy Text. The Qur'anic Text, which has been declared as the Standard Copy In the 1973 Constitution of Pakistan, divides the holy text into 6236 verses. However, it is absolutely incorrect, that the verses of the Qur'an are 6666 in number.*

[193] *Koshul, 126.*

[194] *Iqbal, Reconstruction..., 45.*

[195] *Dr. Israr Ahmad, The Process of Creation: A Qur'anic Perspective, (tr. Dr. Absar Ahmad), Markazi Anjuman Khuddam ul Qur'an Lahore, 2013.*

[196] *Ibid, 5.*

[197] *Ibid., This is not the first ever attempt solely made by Dr. Israr Ahmad for blending the 'creation' and 'evolution' together in one thread.*

> *"In his encyclical* Humani Generis *(1950), [Pope] Pius XII had already stated that there was no opposition between evolution and the doctrine of the faith about man and his vocation, on condition that one did not lose sight of several indisputable points."*

Pope John Paul II in his address entitled Truth Cannot Contradict Truth to the Pontifical Academy of Sciences (October 22, 1996) admits that

"Today, almost half a century after the publication of the encyclical, new knowledge has led to the recognition of the theory of evolution as more than a hypothesis. It is indeed remarkable that this theory has been progressively accepted by researchers, following a series of discoveries in various fields of knowledge. The convergence, neither sought nor fabricated, of the results of work that was conducted independently, is in itself a significant argument in favour of this theory."

Most probably, neither Dr. Israr Ahmad nor the worthy translator knew this fact; otherwise, they would not have missed mentioning it.

[198] *Commenting on the use of 'eternal' for God we have shown that it is reminiscent of un-Qur'anic ontology borrowed from Greeks, but is prevalent amongst Muslim theologians and commentators since centuries.*

[199] *Ibid, 7.*

[200] *Ibid, 9.*

[201] *Richard Swinburne, The Coherence of Theism Oxford, Clarendon Press, 1977, 217.*

[202] *Conf. ibid, 9-10.*

[203] *Conf., Ibid*

[204] *Dr. Israr Ahmad, ibid, 12.*

[205] *Ibid., 12.*

[206] Fāzli, "The Qur'an: Creation or Command" International Journal of Humanities and Religion [IJHR], 2(10) December 2012: 75 -83, India. Ash'ari discusses this problem in his book *Al- Ibanah an Usul Ad-Diyanah*, Eng. tr. *The Elucidation of Islam's Foundation* by Walter C. Klein. at 66, 67, 76.

[207] *'Speech' includes among the seven sifat-i-wujudiyyah, which they also called sifat-i-'aqliyyah or rational attributes. M.M. Sharif, 316.*

[208] *Dr. Israr Ahmad, ibid, 11.*

[209] *Ibid.*

[210] *Hazrat Nūh's son did not believe in his father, he did not belong to Hazrat Nūh (pbuh). Similarly, Hazrat Lut's wife and Hazrat Ibrahim's father did not believe in them, so they did not belong to them.*

[211] *cf. Review article by Muzaffar Iqbal on Leif Stenberg, The Islamization of Science: Four Muslim Positions, Developing an Islamic Modernity, Coronet Books: New York, 1996.*

212 *Leif Stenberg, The Islamization of Science : Four Muslim Positions, Developing an Islamic Modernity, Coronet Books: New York, 1996, 240.*

[213] *ibid*

[214] *Cf. Seyyed Hossein Nasr, Ideal and Realities of Islam, 15-16.*

[215] *Ibid, 270.*

[216] *Ibid, 273.*

[217] *Review article by Muzaffar Iqbal on Leif Stenberg, Ibid,*

[218] *Not everyone is qualified for the demarcation of limits for the relationship between truth and untruth. 'Those who know and those who do not know are not equal.' Az-Zumar, 39:09) 'Only those who are endowed with understanding grasp the Message.' (... Wa Mā Yadhdhakkaru 'Illā 'Ūlū Al-'Albābi. Āl-i-Imrān, 03:07).*

[219] *Al-Qur'an, 3:7.*

[220] *Also in line with the Divine decree: la talbisul Ḥaqqa bil baṭili ... (Do not mix up falsehood with truth.) Q. 02:42.*

[221] *We are making use of western system of medicine, methods of physical and psychological treatment, all kinds of technology, economic, financial, commercial, educational, administrative and social institutions*

but with a feeling of doubt or a sense of guilt. Why not make use of these products of modernity with an open heart based on religious sanction of innovation (bid'at) reconstructing them according to our Qur'anic paradigm.

[222] When Allah spoke to the angels about the appointment of Adam as vicegerent on the earth, He told them that everything on the earth was meant for the use of humankind. The angels saw that the true purpose of vicegerency was to use resources of the world with great efficacy. They also saw that it would not be possible for humankind to live like angels. Having no social life they have nothing to share with each other. The inhabitants of the earth will fight and shed blood on the use of things needed for the fulfilment of their desires. There is an apparent possibility of mischief and bloodshed when man has a vast capability of using things and these are to be shared by him with others. To make it clear to the angels that there will be no mischief and bloodshed if the knowledge of using things is God-given because then everything is kept at its proper place, Allah taught Adam the names of all the objects he had to use in his life. The name of a thing does not mean just a spoken sound by which it is identified, it also denotes its proper use, right measure, place of use, benefits and remedy in case it harms. The aggregate of all this information constitutes knowledge of things. In the Qur'anic perspective 'to evolve this knowledge of using things, which nullifies any chance of mischief and bloodshed is the purpose of all research.' (cf. Q. 2:30-33)

[223] Robert Reilly presents Dr. Fazalur Rahman's comment to support his suggestion.

[224] The part of kalām dealing with questions of 'natural philosophy' was called daqīq al-kalām, while the other larger part, dealing with questions of the divine attributes, punishment and reward, and the Day of Resurrection, was called jalīl al-kalām. Basil Altaie, God, Nature, and the Cause: essays in Islam and science,(KR&M, 2016), x.

[ccxxv] Hafeez Fāzli, Free Will and The Appointed Term (Ajl-E Mussamma), The Qur'anic Theology ......, 207-224.

CPSIA information can be obtained
at www.ICGtesting.com
Printed in the USA
BVHW020607290623
666442BV00022B/449